SURVIVORS OF A FUTURE

that never happened

A Cultural Review:
1974 – 1994

Robert Coe

MONTREAL PUBLISHING COMPANY

Montreal Publishing Company

ISBN: 978-1-7386548-2-6

SURVIVORS of a Future that never happened
A Cultural Review: 1974 – 1994—1st edition.

Cover: Nelligan Design
Editor: Christian Fennell
Copyeditor: Nathalie Guilbeault
Publisher: Montreal Publishing Company
November 15, 2022

ACCLAIM FOR SURVIVORS of a Future That Never Happened
A Cultural Review: 1974 – 1994

"Robert Coe's *SURVIVORS OF A FUTURE THAT NEVER HAPPENED* doesn't bother trying to create a smooth, coherent narrative. For one thing, that would betray both his subject – two decades (1974-1994) of dense cultural transformation – and his own temperament as a passionately curious participant-observer. Compiled from published and unpublished writings, this volume reflects Coe's extraordinary ability to craft smart journalistic profiles of epochal theater and dance artists with the Olympian sweep of an academic researcher and more than a streak of gonzo memoirist. Instead of encyclopedic, he goes fractal, juxtaposing renowned cultural creators like Robert Wilson and Twyla Tharp with gay Buddhist poet John Giorno, ground-breaking female bodybuilder Lisa Lyon, a punky self-educated Freud expert, and a posse of die-hard skydivers. Equally aimed at seasoned spectators and savvy students, this unpredictable mashup of subjects and styles makes for a fun and compellingly personal playlist-in-print."

- Don Shewey, Critic and Writer

SURVIVORS is more than a glorious book; it is the life's work of a great writer. It is not only insightful in the most brainy way, but it is also delightfully funny. The writing has a warmth to it that is constantly inviting - most remarkable, given the sometimes-icy waters. At times Coe watches silently from a web in the corner of the room as a peripheral participant, but very often, he is a vital player in the articles and essays that span a pair of decades in American culture. He manages to hopscotch over a great range of topics from Robert Wilson and the Wooster Group to Skydiving in Elsinore, California to Barbecue Restaurants in New York City. There are times when one is reminded of the Gonzos. There's a bit of Norman Mailer with a splash of Joan Didion, but all in all, the book has an eclectic style all its own. It's postmodernism with a smirk and a twinkle. If you were there, you'll be glad to go back again. If you weren't there, you're going to feel as if you were. It wants not just to be consumed, but devoured.

- Des McAnuff, Playwright, Songwriter, and Director

"People usually have no idea of how significant some present events are until they are seen in hindsight. When the importance of these fixed moments in time is chronicled by a gifted storyteller such as Coe, the result is a treasure. The author's book consists of a compelling series of first-person reflections by an artistic spirit frantically capturing the sights and sounds of an entire generation's potential. These are broken up into thoughts, snapshots, and moments, each being viewed by the main character, struggling to define, and empower, and emerging atmosphere of the day. There is a transient quality to the characters, a vivid Greek chorus that seems to jump in and out of frame every few pages. SoHo of the 1960s shines, and the communal energy of these various characters and memories seems to linger with the reader long after they have been traded in for different events and concepts. Each one brims with youthful mania and liberation, the author's wistfulness turning them into shadows as the book progresses. This interesting and engaging book does an outstanding job of grasping the historical ideals and changing convictions of the age that serves as its backdrop. It also manages to catalog all the different aspects of this unusual era. The author has written a truly personal opus and one that captivates as well as inspires. It is brimming with imagery and rich pathos that never seem over-indulgent or forced. It's merely a personal journey and experience, yet the author's narrative is filled with nostalgic reflections that transport the reader. Told in a thoughtful and masterful manner, Coe's book is certain to delight anyone who picks it up."

- Robert Buccellato, the US Review

"From his front-row seat on the sofa in the artist's loft, Robert Coe's *SURVIVORS OF A FUTURE THAT NEVER HAPPENED* swirls up an astonishing blend of cultural history, multi-arts criticism, and memoir, moving with dazzling fluency across the hybrid worlds of visual and performance art, dance and music-theater, and experimental just-about-everything. Coe celebrates the mad pioneers of America's most surreal cultural era in a gorgeous, insightful prose that matches their marvels. Whether practicing yoga in an electrified treehouse in Big Sur, parachuting from planes in the desert, writing early illuminations of the Wooster Group and Cornerstone Theater Company, or surveying bodies of work by Twyla Tharp, Peter Sellars, and Robert Wilson or the work of bodies like muscle woman Lisa Lyon and photographer Robert Mapplethorpe, he astonishes with a "You Are There—Can You Believe You Are There?!?" sense of wonder, mapping a cultural renaissance that seemed to dissolve even as it first appeared."

- Todd London, This Is Not My Memoir (with Andre Gregory)

"From yoga in Big Sur to New York City rib restaurants to the works of Peter Sellars and Robert Mapplethorpe, Robert Coe serves up a delicious bacchanal of Americana in *SURVIVORS OF A FUTURE THAT NEVER HAPPENED.* Now, it has..."

– Mark Seal, Staff Reporter, Vanity Fair; author of Take the Gun, Leave the Cannoli: The Epic Story of the Making of The Godfather

CONTENTS

SURVIVORS OF A FUTURE

that never happened

A Cultural Review
1974 – 1994

Robert Coe

INTRODUCTION

I graduated from Stanford University a left-leaning, draft-card burning counter-culturalist with a Z-Z Top beard and a Vietcong armband. After working the cash register at a natural food store for a year, I volunteered for Peace Corps Ghana, to help coach that country's national track team. Turned out the program I was to join didn't even exist. I ended up coaching future high school P.E. teachers how to jump, put the shot, and throw the javelin four mornings a week. I was a spear-throwing instructor in Africa on the payroll of Uncle Sam. I took an honorable discharge after three months and returned to Palo Alto, where I became founding manager of a new natural food store.

After another post-collegiate year, I decided to go to graduate school and read more American literature, which I hadn't read much of in college. I applied to Ph.D. programs in English, got in a few places back East, and decided to make up my mind where to go when I got there.

My days of freedom were numbered. I had to figure out what to do with myself over the summer ahead. I decided I would move to a garret on the Left Bank, in Paris, to read and write and work on my intermediate French. I was so taken by this highly-unoriginal notion that I talked about it to everybody, including the guy who was taking over my position as manager of Country Sun Natural Foods.

Upon learning of my plan, Abe stared at me for a few seconds, then shook his head, as if he couldn't believe how thick I was.

"Don't go to Paris, Robert. *Fuck* Paris! Fuck fuck *fuck* Paris!"

"Okay Abe, got it!"

"You'll just sit around in cafés all day spending your money!"

"You know something? You've got a point there."

"Save your money for school! You need to go to Big Sur," he told me, arching a dark eyebrow, slowly stroking his long black curls and studying me with a Mephistophelean scrutiny. "Yes," he said at last, as if convinced of my destiny now. "Big Sur is *right* for you, Robert."

Big Sur: ninety miles of Pacific coastline, equidistant between San Francisco and L.A., with literary advertisements by the likes of Jack London, Henry Miller, Robinson Jeffers, John Steinbeck, and Jack Kerouac. Big Sur: home to Esalen Institute, the leading think tank of the global human potential and consciousness revolutions, which carried some weight with me in those days. My occasional characterization of Big Sur as "designer wilderness" aside, it remained a place where Native Californians had gone for millennia to purge themselves of their pasts and mind-meld with Nature at her most awesome and ravishing. So, I packed my gutless '64 Chevy Impala station wagon with books, clothes, household items, and a mattress, bade farewell to my friends at Country Sun, then drove west over the Santa Cruz Mountains to the Pacific, where I swerved south down U.S. One into the heart of Big Sur, anticipating a final summer of adventure before settling on the East Coast for the next chapter of my life.

Stuck in Buffalo long enough to pass an oral exam for a doctorate, I moved to Downtown New York to study dance and work as a journalist for the *SoHo Weekly News* and the *Village Voice.*

I danced with some very good choreographers, wrote plays for some important theaters, and collaborated as a dramaturg and songwriter.

My journalism was eventually published by *The New York Times Sunday Magazine, Op-Ed* and *Arts & Leisure* section, *Rolling Stone, Vanity Fair, Esquire, New York, California, American Theater,* and *Tricycle: The Buddhist Review.* I look back with tremendous fondness on these pre-internet days, when magazines were "the white-hot center of media," as Condé Nast Editorial Director James Truman recalled in a later century. I worked on books, too, but it was as a freelance journalist that I squeezed out a living expressing my interests not in the mid-range of contemporary life, but in extremes of human nature, consciousness, and action.

The writing collected here is a fraction of what I published, plus seven instances that never saw the light of day *(Prelude: Big Sur, Summer, 1974; South of Houston, North of Canal; The Theater of Images; Subversive Pleasures; Off Earth;* and *The Living Theatre: The '80s Movie.)* The journey from Big Sur journal-keeper to cultural historian may seem jarring at first, but so was my life at the time. Two articles I'm re-publishing – *A Revolutionary Movement* and *Making Two Lives and a Trilogy* – I have faithfully re-written, because in my fondness for both, I saw ways to make them better than I could manage as a cub reporter. Otherwise, I've trimmed and tightened and improved here and there, dressed up a few things in better clothes, but the thrust of the chapters remains as written at the time.

These chapters produce different tones and different rhetoric – different ways of looking at things. Some are popular journalism; some art criticism; some are cultural history. The majority of the chapters are profiles – life histories, career sagas, odysseys reflecting my interests in the journeys people take, especially the ones artists live by and through. I always loved going in places, meeting people, and figuring out what made things tick. Impermanence is a constant theme, as it inevitably is: many of the things I wrote about have either disappeared or been drastically altered with the passage of time. Another constant would be the complex, constantly-evolving relationship between innovation and tradition.

I have an affinity for the brilliant, the outlandish, the contested, and the ignored. Many chapters comment on what I call "the madness and surreality of the American Age." These chapters can be read as a kind of cultural review, touching mostly on the live and visual arts, but also art neighborhoods, skydiving, poetry, ceramics, barbecue restaurants, cultural theory, Freudian psychology, women's body-building, Buddhism, and the politics of race and revolution. I write about people who survived the cultural revolution of the '60s and went on to fashion some of the most extraordinary creative endeavors of the twenty years in scope.

The future didn't exist back then. It had to be invented.

This is a collection, not a narrative. Why didn't I settle on a single voice to tell this story? Perhaps one day I will, but not this time out.

If you want to jump around here and there, I'm okay with that, unless you want to read it from beginning to end, in which case be my guest. Revisiting these writings from my younger times and places has been thrilling for me, and I hope you can find even a fraction of the pleasure I took re-reading them as I did in reporting them at the time.

BIG SUR, SUMMER, 1974

Note: *A previously-unpublished memoir about the last summer I spent in my home state of California before heading "Back East" for good. Go East, Young Man.*

SWEET NEPENTHE

Abe told me where to watch for a sign on Route 1, but I missed it on the first drive by. I had to tick back a tenth of a mile on my odometer from another marker, as alternatively instructed, and even then, had to get out of my station wagon to search through a dense, low-lying wall of green redwood branches before discovering the gap that Abe had told me was there. The gap opened on to a steep one-and-a-half lane red dirt road down a long still canyon past towering redwoods for two miles, dead-ending at the foot of a driveway so steep I doubted my timid Impala could make the grade. After several failed attempts, I gritted my teeth, floored it, and just managed to hold the curve at the top before skidding to a halt, screw-shy in the middle of a muddy clearing in a redwood forest primeval.

Just ahead of me rose a ramshackle twenty-five-foot-high A-frame house that looked as if it had been erected by an army of stoned hippie carpenters. (I later learned it was.) A small garden with a few sad tomato plants on sticks and strings and a scraggly lemon tree were visible at the side of the house, tucked up close to an enormous redwood-covered mountainside so steep that it looked like it might come crashing down in the next earthquake or a hard rain.

I killed my engine as a woman emerged through Dutch doors and slowly approached. The owner of this queer chalet, whom Abe considered his soul sister, was Hannah, who Abe thought might be willing to become my landlady for the summer, if the vibes were right.

The story of Hannah (not her real name) was a '60s Romantic-Tragic Fantasia up there in Edie Sedgwick territory. The sheltered daughter of a wealthy conservative San Francisco Catholic family, Hannah grew up a convent girl and debutante before heading East to attend Finch College in New York, where one of her classmates was Tricia Nixon. But Hannah was a free spirit who would not be finished by any East Coast schooling. She ended up dropping out of Finch and falling into the arms of Peter Revson: "Revvie," the Fitzgeraldian scion of the Revlon cosmetics fortune and a Formula One race car driver who blazed across the society pages and the tabloids with a host of dazzling women, including a former Miss World. When Hannah's relationship with Revvie inevitably fell apart, Hannah did, too, experiencing a full-blown nervous breakdown, according to Abe's gospel, which I was never able to verify, but never doubted from the moment I met her. Family flew Back East to bring her home, but Hannah defied them again by enrolling at the San Francisco Art Institute and becoming a painter, traveling extensively in South America, and immersing herself in a series of love affairs with Black jazz musicians that resulted in three gorgeous children, each from a different father – again, all of this according to Abe. I never would get the full low-down on the dads, or anything much about Revvie, because Hannah found it unbearable to speak of him. Peter Revson, one of the most legendary Playboys of the '60s, had been killed in a fiery Formula One crash at the South African Grand Prix just this past March 22nd, only a few months after I arrived at Hannah's doorstep, looking for a place to crash myself.

As we spoke, Hannah's kids wandered from the house in various states of melancholic reverie, eyeing me with guarded curiosity; the youngest, a poised, handsome, inward-looking seven-year-old with the presence of a dark prince, looked like the watchman of the place. Hannah had reconciled with her family in exchange for enough money to construct this homestead in the redwoods, where she could raise her dark-skinned brood, out of her Bay Area family's sight and presumably far from its thoughts. Hannah was as Abe described her: a sensitive, high-strung woman in her early thirties, a distracted but devoted mother, with an infectious smile and soft, delicate features. I liked her right away.

Abe had already told Hannah that he didn't think it was safe for her to be living alone in the bottom of a canyon with three young kids, so after ten minutes she came out and invited me to spend the summer on her property, in exchange for occasional baby-sitting and weeding in her vegetable-and-flower garden. Her house was cozy, funky, and definitely not to code, and I liked it, too. The question was where would I sleep.

I spent my first night on my mattress in the back of my station wagon, surrounded by the crushing silence of the redwoods. Stretching in the clearing in the morning, I noticed a large heap of discarded building materials – two-by-fours, even store-bought doors and windows – piled in a heap near the house. I asked permission, and Hannah said yes.

The treehouse I built for myself in Hannah's eight-hundred-year-old redwood forest took shape over several days. First, I built a six-by-ten-foot platform on a steep hillside, extending out between three medium-size redwood trees. My treehouse was not a modest affair as treehouses go. It had thick floorboards and eight-foot walls, a wide flat roof, a store-bought paned window, a built-in platform bed, a built-in desk, two bookshelves, and electricity from a seventy-five-foot-long power-line I strung from the house for lights and a hotplate. That I was able to pull this off was remarkable, because my carpentry skills were minimal. A saw, a hammer, the right nails and a fluid level measure got me through.

My most inspired design element was a void: you came into my treehouse up a three-step staircase through a pre-fabricated front door and faced a missing wall, blocked by a banister. I had an unobstructed view into the redwood forest, baleful pillars of bark, some towering one hundred and fifty feet overhead. When it rained, which it did a lot that summer, I could tug a large plastic tarp off the flat roof to cover the gap. Otherwise, my tree house was open to the air, to the elements – to Nature.

"The squirrel got in again today," I noted in my green-paged journal, "but at least he remembered to wipe its feet." This frisky varmint, who had furry testicles the size of garbanzo beans, had left his muddy tracks across my green page. On the old journal open beside me, remembering this summer long ago, I see his footprints still.

While I labored on my forest aerie, another practical concern was finding a paying job. Abe had taken care of that, too, arranging an interview at Nepenthe, a Big Sur institution since 1947, situated off Route 1 in a stunning redwood, glass, and adobe building designed by a Frank Lloyd Wright student, who was killed in a construction accident when Nepenthe was being built. Perched a thousand feet above the ocean, Nepenthe offered an unmatched view of sixty miles of plunging Pacific headlands. On my interview day – the dictionary defines *nepenthe* as "anything inducing a pleasurable sensation of forgetfulness," though "no worries" was how people translated it around here – I was led into the private quarters of Nepenthe co-founder Lolly Fasset, who along with her husband Bill had purchased the property from Orson Welles and Rita Hayworth, who kept a love nest here.

Like her niece Hannah, Aunt Lolly was a refugee from their conservative San Francisco Catholic family. Aunt Lolly cut an impressive figure with her glittering Southwest Indian turquoise jewelry, her long white hair held in place by Spanish combs, a fresh hyacinth tucked behind one ear. She was fantastically stout and perpetually shrouded in fringed shawls and a tent-like kaftan, radiating a Buddha-like calm that probably masked depression. I would have taken any gig she offered, so I was stunned when she gave me one of the plum assignments of the entire summer operation: running the one-person juice-and-sandwich-bar, a few steps below the main dining area, facing on an enormous circular outdoor deck that offered one of the most breath-taking views in all of Big Sur: sixty miles of coastline visible across the juice-bar countertop.

I would be my own boss there, run the whole show, in charge of everything from supply ordering to food prep to handling the money.

This had to be more than beginner's luck. Lolly was bumping me up the local hierarchy because I was helping Hannah.

And so my summer was made: I would be living in an electrified tree house in a near-millennial redwood forest, occasionally watering Hannah's tomato plants and baby-sitting her fantasy-laden children, when not pulping carrots, squeezing oranges, and perfecting a killer guacamole dip six days a week in my own juice bar-cum-love shack, open to rolling fog, brazen sun, squawking blue jays, dipping hawks, and a sixty-mile view of the Pacific coastline – all for $2.75 an hour plus tips.

"WE MUST GATHER IN SMALL GROUPS"

I showed up at ten a.m. on my first day, as I would every day except Mondays all summer. A T'ai Ch'i class was in progress on the circular deck that faced my juice-bar shed. Thirty people gliding through their forms. A brilliant sky shone overhead, while thick billowy white clouds hugged the ocean below. The view was like looking out of the window of a 747. It was a sight that never failed to give me a catch.

I unlocked and raised the window flaps to my two-sided shed and unlocked the juice bar's battered door, the only entrance to the place, other than vaulting the countertop. Someone from the restaurant upstairs had cleaned overnight, so all I had to do was take in the day's supplies by the door and reacquaint myself to procedures from a three-page handout, listing duties and recipes.

My earliest customers were the T'ai Ch'i practitioners, joined by refugees from the "human potential" workshops underway at nearby Ventana Campground down U.S. 1. Sleepy men and women in earth colors, requesting breakfast cappuccinos and baked eggs with tamari, which I whipped up in a countertop oven. Mornings were generally slow, as I had been warned, but business picked up considerably for the hours around lunchtime, when the first drive-through customers arrived, requesting Coke, Pepsi, any soft drink (which we didn't carry), sequestering themselves at the outdoor tables to yell at the kids, grok the views, inhale my pita sandwiches, carrot juice, tuna melts and protein smoothies, then pile back into their cars to drive on to the next tourist destination. Some of these Middle Americans looked so embalmed in polyester that they looked like they were stepping out of a George Segal installation – as if Life was imitating Art, and not vice versa.

Running a juice bar in Big Sur, I naturally met hundreds of countercultural hipsters cruising through – spiritual seekers from both coasts, eager to Make the Scene, soak up the vibes and vistas, and talk about whatever was on their minds as a matter of course. There were honest pilgrims among them, but with my eye for aspirants on the make I watched actors perform, naturally, unnaturally, invariably from L.A.; San Francisco painters and poets, sharing their wet, malleable impressions of the world; and spiritual vagabonds who just rambled on. Maybe it was a function of my service job, but whenever I wasn't actually taking orders or preparing food or spending time alone, reading or writing or just sitting there waiting for customers, I was almost always gabbing with somebody. I can't say I minded this window on the Human Comedy, Big Sur style.

After the lunch rush, things quieted down again, and I had more time to read or write in my journal. By six o'clock – time noted on a wind-up alarm clock hidden away on a high shelf – I typically had around $250 in the till and fifteen bucks in my tip jar. I would balance the register, lock up the window flaps, hide the empty register drawer under the counter, and head up to the restaurant with the day's take and my food order for tomorrow.

Then I would drive back to the cold, lonely stillness of my forest aerie, where I would continue to read or write before an early bed.

Those first mornings before work and after my tree house was habitable, I explored the redwoods at the end of the road in Sycamore Canyon, as this place was weirdly named. There must have been a sycamore grove somewhere, but I never found it. A soundless hum of phenomenal solitude dominated that forest, like all of Big Sur. Henry Miller wrote about Big Sur as "a region where one is always conscious of an eloquent silence... The face of the earth as the creator intended it to look."

I re-read Jack Kerouac's thin paperback *Big Sur*, his 1961 account of his final collapse of body, mind, and spirit in a cabin near the base of Bixby Canyon, miles north. I knew where to go look for it, but I never did.

Call me superstitious, but Jack's friends said that after his time in Big Sur, he was never the same man, or the same writer, again.

Hannah's neighbors were few and far between down at the end of the road. Our closest was just across the road, one of the founding members of the Beach Boys, Al Jardine, who I never saw and never visited – not after seeing the skull-and-crossbones "Trespassers Will Be Prosecuted" signs he had posted along his gate, beneath jagged rows of barbed wire. I hated those signs, and that fucking barbed wire. My occasional jape about "designer wilderness" aside, a part of me wanted to embrace the Esalen-inspired notion that Big Sur was the Brook Farm of late twentieth century communitarianism. People like Jardine, who had no truck with any countercultural circling of the wagons, pissed me off.

A friendlier note was sounded at a party Hannah threw during my second week on the property. Loud jazz played on Hannah's excellent sound system as her friends lounged around on low pillows, surrounded by Hannah's collection of South Asian erotic statuary and murky abstract-expressionist canvases—all of us stoned out of our fucking gourds from a hash-tobacco blend, smoked in a chillum. A chillum is a commonly-employed North African smoking pipe that resembles a tuba mouthpiece and requires a tricky two-handed grip and some practice to pull off, but once mastered, provides monster hits from glowing bowls.

When someone said something about Watergate, the scandal in its endgame in Washington D.C., someone else murmured, "We must gather in small groups." The rest of us were like yeah, man, right on. This guy was toast, and so were we, but that didn't mean he was wrong, or that we were, either. America was slouching towards the end of the long national nightmare of Watergate and a seemingly-unending war in Southeast Asia, but nobody in Big Sur was watching it play out on TV, because nobody I knew owned a set. And I doubt the reception was any good anyway. In fact, there probably wasn't any reception at all.

The better I got to know Big Sur, the more I saw this place as being about close circles of friends: anarchistic coteries of weavers, jewelry makers, ceramicists, potheads, pot dealers, meditators – free-form cultural associations scrambling to escape the crush of the collapsing '60s and carry out the people & things & ideas they most wanted to carry forward into whatever history coughed up next. Gathering in small groups was what people needed to do in these latter days.

If that was true, where was my group? Hannah quickly grew comfortable enough with me to work topless in her garden and share her private bathroom with its Rube Goldbergesque assemblage of plastic pipes and hoses for the delivery of well water. But Hannah's friends were her friends, not mine. Where were *my* locals – or would I have to settle for juice bar regulars? My impression was that the truly hard-core Big Sur types were quasi-hermits squirreled away in the forests and canyons, avoiding outsiders, especially the summer ones – purposefully eluding the "energy vampires" (one reveler at Hannah's called them that) who roll up from L.A. or down from San Francisco in search of sex, drugs, and whatever other cheap thrill they can drum up in the redwoods.

But was I not one of these people? Just another outsider come looking for a buzz? I had hung out in some fabulous high hippie scenes, as I vainly reminded myself, from Ibiza to Amsterdam, London to Berlin, but had never seen anything quite as cliquish, cultish, and entrepreneurially New Age-y as Big Sur in 1974 – especially around Nepenthe, where I would see total strangers kiss each other on the lips to say hi. This struck me as not only presumptuous, but suspiciously phony.

So what *was* I doing in Big Sur? What was I *really* doing here? I was two years out of college, and except for a three-month Peace Corps stint in West Africa, teaching high school P.E. teachers how to throw the javelin (a story for another time), I hadn't done anything worth speaking of, or writing about, since graduation, except for opening the Palo Alto natural food store Country Sun (a going concern more than a half-century later.) This was part of why I thought I deserved a summer in paradise before "Real Life" set in – a "Real Life" in which I was about to become the first member of my family to reverse the general drift of the American migration West – reversing the progress of my father, a working-class Connecticut Yankee who had never traveled west of Yankee Stadium before arriving at Stanford to pursue a doctorate in Chemistry, and meet the Judge's daughter from L.A.

I decided I was in Big Sur for its half-wild ameliorative effect on the spirit, more than a clarification of any future direction. Yet I continued to think I had made a mistake coming here at all, as I noted in my journal: "I didn't bargain on this feeling of isolation, this disinterestedness in preoccupations which from a distance seemed so inviting – camping, lying on a beach, etc." But being a disciplined sort, I made a commitment to waiting it out, because I knew things would change, because they always seemed to do at that time in my life.

My feelings of separateness evaporated at Nepenthe's first Zodiac birthday celebration of the summer – a communal dance event held on the last Wednesday of every astrological sign. Nepenthe's Zodiac parties attracted hermits from ravines and mountaintops all up and down the coast. The presiding figure at this year's Cancer party was Aunt Lolly, who only danced at her birth sign event, launching her fantastic girth across the upper terrace with an Oliver Hardy-like grace.

I knew almost no one there, other than two or three restaurant staffers, but I went ahead and danced alone, under the influence of several Dirty Mothers (tequila & milk) and a couple of hits from a bowl of Afghani hash publicly offered by two strangers in a corner – prancing and twirling in the billowy brown velvet pants I had picked up at a costume shop in Bath, England four years earlier; also knee-high boots, a long pleated nightshirt, and not a care in the world – sweating, grooving, preening, sanctified – when out of nowhere these two gorgeous women approached me and smiling nakedly into my eyes, wrapped their swan-like arms around my neck, glued their crotches to my thighs, and took turns giving me big wet sloppy tongue kisses to the music of Otis Redding, without hearing any protest from me whatsoever.

Their names, they told me at a break, were Siri and Jory.

"We're from New York!" the more androgynous one cried in my ear. Jory was a Midwestern-born New York City fashion model and the former girlfriend of the mayor of Madison, Wisconsin. "We live in this very cool loft in an artist neighborhood called SoHo!" The term "Loft" meant nothing to me, but I did recognize "SoHo" from London's west-end. "We're taking a forty-day 'Arica' training at Ventana Campground!" Jory told me. Dancing with Siri and Jory for three hours, gazing into their eyes and souls enraptured, I freed my ass and as foretold, the rest followed along.

"Do you know who you are when you dance like this?" I asked Siri. I swear this did not sound dumb at the time.

Siri shouted back in her posh accent: "No, I don't! Do you?"

"Should we?" Jory asked. All three of us laughed together. Our eyes full of yes, our bodies locked again, tongues on tongues, none of it promising anything more than what was happening at that very moment.

And that was how it turned out: at three a.m. I crawled into my tree house bed, thoroughly drunk, stoned, enchanted, and alone.

I was afraid this might be the last I would see of these magical creatures, these visions of human liberation, and wondered how I could have played my cards differently when they turned up at my juice bar the very next afternoon, dressed in patent leather platform heels, plastic miniskirts, and bright pastel fuzzy sweaters, as if they were heading out to a nightclub later, and not some waterfall deep in the forest primeval.

Siri, a graphic designer by trade, was from London originally, a sex-exuding Brit with a Marilyn body and a lived-in face. Jory was gamine, boyishly athletic, bright-eyed, confident, and smart. She was SoHo's version of Audrey Hepburn. It didn't seem possible to be as incredible as both these women were, and yet as down-to-earth at the same time. They were miles over my head, I knew that, but it was my good fortune that while the kissing thing never happened again, they did become juice bar regulars over the next few weeks. "We like that you have a mind," Jory told me, talking at length about SoHo and about the "Arica" workshop they were attending at nearby Ventana Campground.

The New Age was dawning. The '70s was tossing up all sorts of spiritual schools and higher consciousness trainings. Arica was one of the first, assembled a few years earlier by a mysterious man of indistinct origin named Oscar Ichazo, working with a group of fellow seekers in the Andean village of Arica, Chile. "The 9 Ways of Zhikr," Siri and Jory's workshop, involved different styles of meditation, with special emphasis on the body and exercise. Arica incorporated elements of Zen, Western humanist psychology, and the teachings of another mysterious Central Asian sage, G.I. Gurdjieff, all packaged into what Dolphin intelligence expert John Lilly called "the boot camp of spirituality."

I knew about Arica because my last girlfriend left me six months ago for the Living Love Center in Berkeley, but had recently taken up with an Arica trainer in Florida. I was planning to visit in Gainesville on my drive Back East. The Living Love Center didn't interest me at all, but Arica did. Arica was sophisticated. It was smart. It was worth taking seriously. I thought about Arica a lot that summer, and not just because Jory and Siri were its messengers. I had fooled my way around Europe, but at the age of twenty-four I was still getting over the Palo Alto townie who had left me for Living Love.

Vetted and verified by the likes of Siri and Jory, I was allowed to crash Arica's nighttime circle dances on an outdoor platform in Ventana Campground, just down U.S. 1 from Nepenthe. During quiet times at the juice bar, I dabbled in Arica's psycho-calisthenics. I did exercises on my side of the counter. I drank Arican teas and high-energy protein mixes and dipped into Jory's copy of the "Opening the Rainbow Eye" – a 120-page, step-by-step meditation kit, which included a tabletop, a tablecloth, candles, incense, bell, cup, and beads – that in the end virtually guaranteed Satori – Enlightenment – to the diligent practitioner.

"Take the 'Me' out of America, you get 'Arica,'" Jory told me one morning, then licked off a carrot juice mustache with her long tongue.

"Then why do you still have to pay so much money for it? Six hundred bucks is a king's ransom for a guy like me, works in a juice bar."

"You pay that much because they're expanding the organization, and they want you to give value for value." This was practically the only time Jory ever disappointed me.

"The ideas are simple, really," said Siri in her plummy voice, checking off bullet points on red fingernails. "'We have only our bodies.' 'Our bodies are the expression of divine consciousness.' 'All dualities are illusionary.' Why? Because humanity is one!" And lastly" – flashing her gorgeous, fully-realized smile – "'Life begins with total realization!'"

"Hopefully before then," I muttered. I was thrilled this made them laugh. I adored these women, especially Jory, but a part of me continued to be skeptical about any group selling shortcuts to Satori. I knew that they were far more involved in Arica than I could ever be.

THE PHOENIX MUSES

I cultivated my regulars, but still had time on my hands, so when I wasn't reading or writing, I people-watched. On some days, especially foggy ones, this was as boring as daytime television. Big Sur householder and movie star Ryan O'Neal came by one early afternoon, drunk, or at least with a buzz on. Seedy rocker Johnny Rivers ("Seventh Son," "Secret Agent Man") wandered on to my deck, stoned and mumbling unintelligibly. Henry Miller's daughter Val, who lived in a cabin visible at the top of the ridge, dropped in once for a protein smoothie. A chatty fellow claimed to be the personal attorney of motorcycle stunt jumper Evel Knievel, and told me all about Evel's plans to jump across Idaho's Snake River Canyon a few months from now. One afternoon news reached the lower deck that Julie Christie was on the upper deck with two handsome young hunks, all dressed in white. I abandoned my post and trotted up the steps. When I saw her, she was looking at me, which caused her to violently start and look away, as if someone had jabbed her with a cattle prod. That was my Julie Christie moment.

But Big Sur wasn't all celebrity sightings and great conversations under blue skies or starry dynamos of night. Periods of sun would be followed by days and nights of impenetrable rain and fog – foul and gloomy days when nothing seemed to be happening anywhere on earth, but there you were left holding the bag. As the new boredom gathered momentum, so did my sense of wonder, not only about what I was doing and not doing in Big Sur, but what I was doing and not doing with my life.

Neil Young had nailed it with a demi-quaver from his Fortress of Solitude in the Santa Cruz Mountains, not far away: "The Dream is Over." My problem, the problem of almost everybody I knew, was that the Revolution of the '60s had ended, and almost nothing had changed. John Lennon, from the other side of the planet: "You say you wanna revolution, well you know, we all wanna change the world..." The Revolution we wanted hadn't happened – not that I or anybody I knew had seriously thought it would. And it certainly hadn't been televised. The Watergate Investigation was hoisting Nixon by his own petard, not ours. The progressive wing of the Democratic Party lay in ruins, the war in Southeast Asia continued to rage, and the countercultural opposition – rock music, the whole hippie love *thang* – had been assimilated, defanged, turned into commercial product and the boilerplate of pop history and popular culture, too. "The Big Picture" – the thing that kept us all mesmerized and engaged throughout the decade when *"The Whole World is Watching, The Whole World is Watching"* – the living in Headlines, the Acid Trips, the police riots – had dissolved into one big fat blob in the middle of a TV screen. There was nothing left to do on this scorched earth, except to talk and write one's way out of it, because the only way out of it, was *through.*

But aside from lengthy letters to friends and long journal entries that I posted nearly every day, I wasn't writing a thing.

I felt tremendous guilt about this lack of activity. It was why I had applied to graduate school: to gin up my writing game. Meanwhile I studied a nondescript fellow who dropped by for a croissant and coffee every single morning when it wasn't raining, sun or fog, and never said more than three words to me – "it's a novel" "it's coming along" – before planting himself at a picnic table and filling page after page after page of a yellow legal pad with writing, as fast as his little pencil could carry him.

"An inspiration," I noted in my journal.

More and more locals came to hang out. Chattiness was more the rule than the exception in a place where winters are long and summers brief. Once you got people talking in Big Sur, it was hard to get them to stop. I can't tell you how many "how I ended up here" stories I heard that summer, but off the top of my head I recall (along with Hannah's) the tale of a hugely-rich Wall Street broker who gave it all up to sit and watch flaming sunsets over the Pacific; two former L.A. sit-com actors who had made enough money to build a cabin, come out of the Closet, and bow out of the Game; a successful gestalt psychiatrist who had been thrown out of Stanford Med School for experimenting with L.S.D. years before Tim Leary and Richard Alpert were kicked out of Harvard; a cardiac-arrest survivor who founded a hugely-successful local produce co-op; and a half-dozen retired soft drug dealers, all living here & now in paradise and not doing much with themselves worth mentioning from any exterior point of view.

A local hill carpenter and Rasputin look-alike showed up at my juice bar one afternoon, barefoot, wearing nothing but a pair of can't-bust-'em overalls and tripping on three tabs of acid, or so he said. He sat silently on a stool across from me at my counter, watching as I brewed his herbal tea. It was one of those brilliant sunny days, with butterflies and the scent of mountain flowers, when you couldn't imagine a more glorious place on earth. I asked him his name, which he declined to share, but remained perfectly friendly.

"The way to a perfect life isn't to make karma, it's to burn it," he said after five minutes of silence, creasing his skull into a smile, his eyes vanishing behind narrow slits between cheeks and brow.

"Say more about that, brother!"

"We all need to escape the Great Wheel and become something other than what we are, and who we seem to be! Check it out, man! It's like Rennie Davis of the Chicago Seven said: 'We're survivors of a future that never happened!' Ex-citizens of a country that lost a war it never should have fought, you dig?"

"Right on," I told him. He pulled a fat roach from his breast pocket, and after a hit, passed it across the countertop to me. I was working, but nobody on the Nepenthe staff minded a little weed.

"It's time we shed our skins," he went on, his eyes blackening as he cradled his teacup. "It's time we let it all fall away…"

"I hear you," I said. I later learned that this man was a much-decorated Vietnam War Vet, in addition to being a sweetheart. I would see him every week or so and always enjoyed his visits.

My best friends were the basement staff of the Phoenix, Nepenthe's luxury crafts shop, tucked away from the main restaurant and a short walk from my juice bar deck. The upper level of the Phoenix was devoted to local craft items and high-end Southwest Indian jewelry, much of it from Native American pawn shops – Navajo, Hopi and Sunni stuff as good as anything you'll find anywhere outside of a backroom on the Res. The lower level, which sold mostly clothing and fabrics, employed a trio of local weavers/sales people who marketed their own rugs and clothing alongside original items by other Big Sur artisans.

These three women, taken together, individually, or anyway you wanted to take them, were so nice, so natural, so beautiful inside and out, that you will probably think I'm making them up out of whole cloth.

Christina I met first, because Christina could not be missed: Christina, an in-your-face, world-liberating, mushroom-devouring, long-frizzy-haired Amazonian Hippie Love Goddess, was as wild and untamable as a sunbeam – radiantly healthy, sexually rampant, and always the soul of industry, always working on a half-dozen projects at once: scribbling lyrics on paper napkins, weaving on her loom, dispensing astrological advice – always one hundred percent present and seemingly one of the most straight-up people you could ever hope to meet.

Kathy, I met on Day Two – Kathy of the jet-black ringlets, dimpled smile, twinkling eyes, and the biggest, perkiest breasts on Route 1, supported by posture so erect I assumed she was a dancer until she told me that seven of her vertebrae had been fused mid-spine; an iron rod ran through it. Kathy was fun-loving and curious. She also struck me as the most level-headed of the Muses, although when I told her this, she laughed hysterically for thirty seconds and told me I was completely insane.

Sharon, I met last, the willowiest, the demurest, and in some ways the most intimidating of the Phoenix Muses: a Grace Kelly look-alike with platinum blonde hair, translucent skin, and robin's-egg-blue eyes that rendered even the most confident men tongue-tied—either that, or left them standing in a pool of butter. I saw this happen a lot as the weeks progressed, though her manner was always dependably warm and mindful.

Sex was in the air that summer, current and currency, entangled with everything human about the place: personal growth, hedonism, spirituality, sacrament, *ekstasis*. Sex in Big Sur was mostly conservative, with monogamy more the rule than the exception, which meant that infidelity, practiced often, came with hell-to-pay intensity.

Both Sharon and Kathy had boyfriends, although neither of them ever came around. Still, I respected their situations. This left me with Christina.

My June 22nd journal entry, written just after the Cancer party, notes my attempt to "go out alone" with the Hippie Love Goddess, who took in my invitation with both hands on her hips, gazing forthrightly into my eyes, indicating that when she replied, she would mean every word she said.

"I am a total Scorpio woman, Robert. Going out with me means one thing – *fucking* – and believe me, I am too much for you. Way way *wayyy* too much for you! And not because you're not a great guy – " she said, unexpectedly flinging herself across the space between us, flattening her palms against my chest to gaze up into my eyes, inches from her own rapturous baby blues. "It's just that love & sex are chemistry & souls, and you keep saying all you want is a good time – "

"I never said any such thing, Christina!"

"But you know yourself well," she said, scowling at me now. "You? You'd get all heavy on my ass in a heartbeat." She shuddered as if her blood had just run cold. "You Aries men are all alike – "

"But casual sex doesn't have to be trivial sex," I pretended to whine. This stopped her for a second. Then she laughed from her belly and pushed me away.

"You're a total idiot, but no dice, baby. I am definitely not the one for you."

I thought about this exchange a lot. Would I get all heavy on her ass in a heartbeat? Probably. But in time, I came to agree that she was probably not the one for me—although this didn't mean I didn't want to hang out. I think Christina knew that, because the next time she came down to the juice bar she greeted me with a big sloppy French kiss, distracting me from her fingers sneaking down my butt crack to tweak the hairs around my ass.

Now if that's not intimacy, you tell me what is. I would be fending off Christina's fingers for the rest of the summer.

The family vibe in the basement – the candid conversations we had with no subjects barred – inspired a field trip one night. I picked the Muses up in my station wagon and we drove fifteen miles south, down U.S. One to Esalen Institute, where Big Sur residents were welcome to use the hot springs free of charge after eleven p.m. We spent the night together naked, all four of us soaking in low-lying concrete tubs by candlelight and moonlight, the Pacific surf crashing on the rocks thirty feet below, then hopping on to leather-topped tables and trading deep muscle massages. Losing my erection was a full-time job and I didn't always manage.

Our most memorable conversations were with a Nepenthe waiter soaking with us. Arnie was openly gay at a time when not many people around me were. Arnie had taught Lord Byron's poetry and the man at Columbia University on New York's Upper West Side, where I was accepted to graduate school in English and American literature. (I didn't go.) Arnie had been an avid player in the bathhouse scene in Greenwich Village and along the Hudson waterfront. He told us about glory holes where members were inserted for fellatio from eager mouths.

Arnie proselytized that night for the most radical promiscuity possible.

"Without our bodies, what are we?" he asked. "A puddle! A breeze! A pile of earth! A flame! So why not have as many sexual partners as possible? We are not living under the spell of a patriarchal God!"

Sharon, Christina, Kathy, and I studied one another across the dark water, then chimed in simultaneously – "Yeah! Sure! Why not? Sounds cool!" Then we shared a long, warm laugh about everything.

I felt so close to them that night, and the effects of that night's body makeover for the next two weeks.

I would come back to Esalen often that summer, either to soak after midnight or to hang out with the young bucks on the Esalen custodial staff – the hippie gardeners and cooks and caretakers who lined up to check out the incoming human potential traffic off the bus from L.A. like so many Club Med instructors. Their stories about the B-List Hollywood celebrities they banged were hilarious. I soaked it all in, and as I did, felt the tensions of the Bay Area exiting my body at last. I told myself to stop worrying, because everything was going to be copasetic. I noted in my journal on June 25th, "enjoying Big Sur more and more."

"THROUGH NATURE TO HEAVEN"

I was encountering more of the humanity of the place, but also wanted to taste more of Big Sur's natural wonders, and to that end planned a weekend trek "through Nature to Heaven," as I noted in my journal: an overnight hike into Big Sur backcountry. This wilderness trek would be a reunion with my good friend Decker Underwood, a former track & field college teammate, who drove over the mountains from Palo Alto to join me on the hike. Our destination was the Tassajara Zen Center, the first Zen Buddhist monastery outside of Asia, a few days before the Forest Service closed the canyons for the summer, due to the fire hazard.

I recorded the events of our first day by moonlight in my sleeping bag, surrounded by the blessings of a wet spring, near enough that the meadows we had crossed were green and exploding with wildflowers.

"Twenty miles on first day, last two miles straight up, two or three thousand feet climb. Had long hard pull high into Big Sur River Canyon. Writing this at Pine Ridge Camp. Made wrong turn for extra two miles. Warm day. Late start. Decker climbing into his bag just now, saying 'How nice! How nice!' Passed long-haired naked man on the trail who said, 'Hey! Howdy!' Fields of yellow, purple, white flowers. Twisting trail, helicopter passing, clattering overhead. Three fat girls on their first hike. Made good time. Sykes Campground has warm baths and good swimming holes, clean rushing water over stone-dappled bottom. Light filtering through bright green trees, big redwoods, lunch... Into drier country. Century plants in bloom, long stalks with thousands of yellow petals. Rocky trail. Dine at top of Redwood Creek Campground, where mosquitoes dine on us. Then the long climb up to Pine Ridge. Only nine miles left for tomorrow, most of it flat or downhill... Decker and I talk for hours, abstract dharma raps sweetening the day..."

The flat reportorial shorthand was out of Kerouac, or somebody's version of it, but also resembled my grandfather's diary entries, which he had kept his whole life. I used to kid Grandad that he kept records of records. All that day hiking, he was in my thoughts. It would have been his seventy-seventh birthday that day, but he had gone away in February. My late grandfather, the L.A. Superior Court Judge who paid my way through his alma mater, would never get to see how I turned out.

"Next day now, stiff drudgery in early morning, but light is fine and views magnificent. Stopped by Indian grottoes at Church Ranch, saw handprints on cave walls – nice place to live if you're into gathering acorns... Four more miles to Tassajara, went on high road up up up, caught a ride the rest of the way. Sat zazen for two hours, back hurt. Rejuvenated in baths, met a dancer with the Joffrey Ballet. Walked downstream to diving pools and leapt naked from white cliffs. Spent night in meadow devoured by skeeters, then hitchhiked to breakfast at the Mad Hatter with a guy from the Monterey Jazz Festival. Then Kathy [the Phoenix muse] drives by and picks us up! Went to Molera Beach and fought sandflies. Kathy wants to have a 'primal experience,' and asks me to give her one – Right. [I was pretty sure she wasn't hitting on me, but otherwise I didn't know what to do with her request.] Then on to Palo Colorado to see her peaceful little place and her boyfriend Lorenzo's drawings. I nap in a hammock, then back to the trailhead for the car, and home."

Leaving the Santa Lucia Mountain watershed, I felt fully in my body and in my senses for the first time, six weeks into my Big Sur adventure.

The next morning, walking down the short trail to my juice bar job on a terraced path lined with flowering bougainvillea, honeysuckle and jasmine that perfumed the air, I knew I was shedding skin, firing on all cylinders, enjoying my newly-acquired sense of liberation and detachment from need. I was in a state of grace, fulfilling a cultural entitlement by living on holiday – an easy feeling to welcome when you're white and twenty-four years old and are sure you have all the time in the world.

Abe had been spot-on: Big Sur *was* right for me.

In this pleasurable state of forgetfulness, with wonderful new friends and loneliness abated, I started thinking: why do I need to go to graduate school? Quaff, oh quaff this kind Nepenthe! – stay in Big Sur! Who needs a larger purpose in life? My family had almost given up on me ever choosing to do anything with myself – they still wanted me to go to law school – but who needed to resolve these ancient conflicts between the generations? Who needed Western civilization? Who needed a Van Gogh painting in a Woolworth Frame? (An image I had in a recent dream.) Abe was right: Fuck Paris! Fuck fuck *fuck* Paris! And while I was fucking Paris, who had time for something as slow-footed and high maintenance as a personal identity? Not my selves. Not when I could soak all night in a hot tub with beautiful women and shout across a wilderness canyon on a mountain trail at dawn!

I dropped by the Phoenix to discover Kathy and Sharon in hysterics: apparently Christina had been having a pee in the closet lavatory when Michel walked in on her and the next thing you know she had fellated him, as she subsequently announced to everyone in the Phoenix basement.

Michel was the fourth member of the Phoenix sales team, a piece of work and a work of art: a pansexual hippie and his own art object, with multiple tattoos and piercings, sideburns like scimitars, billowy pants tied at the ankles, day-glow puff-sleeve pirate shirts, all accessorized with fantastic Salvador Dali-goes-Navajo turquoise jewelry that he designed and made himself. He looked like Aladdin's Genie.

Michel and I were friendly, but never friends; he had too many secrets. He was said to be the lifetime beneficiary of a psychological disability check from the U.S. government. Victim of failed drug experimentation? A witness relocation program? Vietnam basket case? Only Christina knew the truth, it was said, and Christina wasn't saying.

"I let her do it as a favor," Michel insisted. He seemed embarrassed that I was there for this. "She said she wanted to keep in practice!"

"Oh, give it up, Michel," Christina said, waving him off with a crooked smile as she wiped the corners of her mouth with her fingertips. "It was just a blowjob."

Christina's libertine innocence was a trip sometimes.

She and I did eventually hang out alone, mostly at night at her place, a tiny trailer hidden in the park behind the restaurant kitchen. I had taken to calling her Cookie, which suited her, and at the same time didn't suit her at all, and the contradiction was what made "Cookie" feel like what I wanted to call her. One night she casually mentioned that I could sleep over if I wanted to. Literally sleep. I didn't make a practice of spending the night with beautiful libidinous women unless sex was involved, but for Christina I could make an exception.

I was disappointed to learn that she slept with her radio on – maybe she wasn't as comfortable in her own skin as I thought she was. But lying against her warm body in the womb-like silence of the Nepenthe trailer park, I felt as if I had penetrated the sanctum sanctorum of Big Sur at last.

On one of my days off, Sharon invited me up to her spectacular home on Partington Ridge, literally the highest point in Big Sur that still had an ocean view. She had a plan in mind that involved me.

"I want you to talk to Gabriel" – her boyfriend – "and see if you can coax him out of his shell." Her boyfriend was spending nearly all of his time in an abandoned cylindrical water tower on the property, which he had converted into his study. He rarely saw another human besides Sharon.

Gabriel (not his real name) had one of the greatest '60s odysseys I have ever come across. A 4.0 Philosophy major at Berkeley, he was working on his Honors Thesis "On the Multidimensionality of Time" when he decided one semester before graduation that he knew nothing whatsoever about the multidimensionality of time. To remedy this, he set out on a journey across southern Europe, overland to India. Somewhere along the way he lost the only copy of his thesis, which he took as a sign that he needed to venture further and discover something new—either that, or the wisdom of the ancients. In India he met a wandering Sadhu and vowed to this beggar that he would take a hit of hash every hour on the hour, 24/7, for the next five years. Gabriel set out to accomplish this truly monumental task, and quite predictably entirely lost his mind. Within months he had sold his sleeping bag for money to buy hash to smoke and was living in a loincloth, begging for food on the streets. After some months, he connected with an Indian con artist and traveled with him to remote villages in the south, pretending to be a Western doctor so that his partner could sell the peasants worthless medicines. Gabriel managed to pull himself out of this hellish vortex by contacting his sister, who sent him money to return to California. Once stateside, he set up a lucrative hash-trafficking business and during an interlude as a preschool teacher in San Diego met the Grace Kelly lookalike and retired with her and his smuggling fortune to Big Sur, buying this jaw-dropping property on Partington Ridge, and converting a former water tower into his study, where he was attempting to reconstruct his undergraduate thesis on the Multidimensionality of Time.

Sharon told me this story as we sat in their glass-walled living room, near the massive loom where she wove her beautiful rugs and tapestries.

"I'm not sure I can help you," I told her – "even if Gabriel did want to meet me!" He had to know I was there, because she had told him I was coming, and he must have heard the car. But so far, he hadn't left the tower.

Sharon eventually went up and practically dragged him down to stand in his own kitchen. He wore a beard that covered his chest and hair half-covering his face, so tongue-tied, so lost in his head, that he couldn't speak. When Gabriel left, Sharon gave me a long, warm, hug in her kitchen. She understood that I knew how bad the situation was. She sadly walked me to my station wagon and sent me on my way.

NOTES FROM A WOODSHED

"Be complete in woods," I scribbled in my journal. Over time I furnished my Zen-Thoreauvian detachment with a one-burner electric range, thrift store pots and pans, a small mirror, and an old-fashioned pitcher and bowl to wash my face in the morning. Every morning in my tree house, rain or shine, I would be awakened at dawn by the family peacock, a creature of violence I came to loathe with a passion. Every morning this fucking bird from hell would flap up on to my flat rooftop, stick his head between his legs through the gap in the wall, and scream at me at the top of his lungs. Mission accomplished – I would be jolted awake – he would flap away, leaving me under my ocean of quilts and sleeping bag, gazing into the forest primeval and more days than not its wispy fingers of fog. More than once that summer, I fantasized about the sadness I would feign when Hannah and the kids came home to find the family peacock throttled on the driveway, in a nest of feathered eyes.

I would typically spend my first few minutes in bed jotting down my dreams, which I remembered in extravagant detail, before rising for a long pee over the banister. Then, after a minute or two of stretching, I would sit on my red-and-yellow Zen cushion on top of my mattress and loosely engage my out-breath for a half-hour or so, half-gazing through the open wall, sensing the towering redwoods and the smell of moist earth, far from the civilized buzz. Afterwards, if there was time before work started at ten, I might climb back under the covers and grab a few more winks, or maybe jam some twelve-bar blues (badly, but improving) on my Brazilian rosewood Takamine guitar.

But most often during the heart of my morning, I would turn on the space heater, sit cross-legged on my bed, and read.

My journals record scads of books – a hodge-podge of the topical, the recommended, and the long postponed. In the latter category I inhaled the *Alexandria Quartet*, Lawrence Durrell's four-part anatomization of the delusionary nature of romantic love. Like other people in these woodshed days, I read for power, and thought hard about what I was reading. One journal entry in my handwriting quotes from Alan Watt's "Beat Zen, Square Zen, and Zen": "'The Westerner who is attracted by Zen and who would understand it deeply must have one indispensable qualification: he must understand his own culture so thoroughly that he is no longer swayed by its premises unconsciously... He must be free of the itch to justify himself. Lacking this, his Zen will be either 'beat' or 'square,' either a revolt from the culture and social order or a new form of stuffiness and respectability.'" "But how," I wrote in commentary, "can the premises of one's own culture not sway one – especially unconsciously! Through what skillful means or application of discipline is one not to be swayed by everything?"

Seeking an answer to these and other spiritual questions, I drank the blood of mystics: Saint John of the Cross, Brother Antoninas (who wrote beautifully about Big Sur), the *Bhagavad-Gita, Zen Mind Beginner's Mind: Informal Talks on Zen Meditation and Practice* by Shunryu Suzuki, and *The Divided Self,* R.D. Laing's short meditation on madness, a book that argued for the eradication of "mental illness" as a category of thought. "The very existence of psychopathology," wrote Laing, "perpetuates the dualism that psychopathologists wish to avoid and that is clearly false…"

None of my reading that summer, Beat or Square, offered me anywhere to stand, until I found my life raft.

How could it have taken me so long to discover Ralph Waldo Emerson! I breathed Emerson that summer, less for his aphoristic Yankee wisdom than for the dazzling rhythms of a mind transposed into prose. How I wished I could steal the Promethean fire of that magisterial voice! I would have sacrificed a tooth to write with Emerson's power and acuity about my own time! Words from Emerson's "Self-Reliance" gave me the conviction to re-inhabit my private woodshed, despite my floundering: "In this pleasing contrite wood-life, which God allows me, let me record day by day my honest thought without prospect or retrospect, and I cannot doubt, it will be found symmetrical, although I mean it not and see it not."

Recording day by day one's honest thought was a pandemic in Big Sur. Everyone I spoke to about it said they kept a journal that summer. My journals were tomes of therapeutic self-inquiry – places to wander, record, comment, work things out. We only have our bodies? We have our records! We have our Legends! When the juice bar was slow, my people-watching segued into a "yoga of observation:" scribbled reams of overheard dialogue, flat-footed reportage, and quick-sketch portraiture: of Tom, the restaurant manager: "The Company Man as Taoist… a confection of friendliness, a Mormon missionary… the straightest gay man I've ever met;" Barbara, the hippie baker in Nepenthe's kitchen, "face dusted with flour, naked baby on one hip, shoving bread into the Nepenthe ovens while happily discussing the Russian Novel." This was the same Barbara who would make a massive success with her "Barbara's Bakery" products. And Barry, the Dulcimer Maker, "shrouded in werewolf hair and a preternatural calm, squatting outside the kitchen by the compost heap, carving walnut wood with a knife and smiling up at me."

Never had my journal seemed more transparent to my thoughts. My journal was the voice of my alienation, the scent of my disquiet, the residual goo of my private education – pages of gassy, sophomoric speculation about the Nature of Everything – really classic hippie juvenilia – along with an amazingly-detailed record of my hyperactive dream life. Immersed in the New Age soap opera of a white man's paradise, I felt free to wonder, "Does the external world exist at all?" Woolgathering, to call a spade a spade, curried my thoughts in those woodshed days, although every so often a good question emerged.

"Big Sur is where people end up who think they want some version of 'living day-to-day,'" I noted, a moment before denouncing this statement as cant. "But how do you live well day-to-day without a past or future, a history or a place to go? What, indeed, is the present without the past and the future?"

People in Big Sur could sit around speculating about such things for hours, not the least bit shy about venturing bold opinions on everything under the sun. A riff I encountered more than once involved the wholesale denunciation of the Western World, which I suspect informed a dream I had during my first week in the redwoods: "I am wandering a college campus, unable to find the humanities building... A sepulchral voice is intoning the great names of culture – 'Goethe... Schiller... Wagner... Mann...' and I weep madly, because they are no more..."

I woke up sobbing into my pillow. The cultural coarsening of the '60s and early '70s had a mourner: a juice bar worker, living in a tree house in a redwood grove in Big Sur, weeping over the death of Goethe.

A fundamental re-consideration on an almost daily basis was my intention to return to Academia. Along with Emerson, R.D. Laing had provided me with a vocabulary for revisiting the all-too-familiar sensation of "waiting to become myself... rather than living in the present ('a' present?)." Why was I failing to surrender entirely to Big Sur, for instance? Was it because I knew I was leaving Paradise to winter in Siberia? (Buffalo?) But how could I reconcile obtaining a Ph.D. in English with the on-going collapse of Western Civilization? Or was this supposed cultural collapse really just an elaborate cover story for the loss of a certain gentility, which I had traded in for tree house living? What was to become of the once-promising young man who still wanted and needed, in a very un-Zen-like fashion, to justify his ways to Society and Family, Man and God, if there was one, which there wasn't, was there? I braced myself with the knowledge that I had a talent for survival within this precarious amalgam of identities known as Me. I was suited to this incipient Age of *Me,* struggling to become *Us.*

One morning in my tree house aerie, my new guru Ralph Waldo served up a compelling vision of a possible future: "Editor, backwoodsman, musician, congressman, spending a few years on each..."

What inflation of my soul was moved by Emerson's vision of Me, Me, Me, moving, shaking, doing it all? I was as-yet unaware of the many Downtown New York artists who were making videos, creating sculptures, exploring performance art while engaging in political activism, writing art reviews, waiting on tables, and presumably going through existential crises not dissimilar to mine.

I weighed this option carefully. I did not come from bohemian stock. I was not raised by wolves. I came from a family of White-Anglo-Saxon Protestant swans and worker bees. The Coes and Condees: we were not the kind of people who believed in having something to fall back on. We went out and worked for what we wanted. But did I truly have an alternative calling? Was I really one to follow my heart, my own instincts and inclinations into unknown worlds? Was I really willing to risk becoming some weird babbling flotsam, drifting inexorably towards the rocks? Or was Emerson's vision of self-reliance through shape-shifting identities really just the ür-image of the "well-roundedness" I had often ridiculed in the Stanford student body?

Or worse, unadulterated narcissistic grandiosity, a virtual prescription for dilettantism?

Or to stand this thought on its head: was my interest in playing multiple roles an expression of a deeper yearning, as I wrote my dear friend Kitty, who was living with her boyfriend in a forest in Cape Cod near the Woods Hole Oceanographic Institute, "to move beyond any single gloss of 'reality,' to assume any role you need to and leaving it behind at will, always to have energy *there?*" This was more than a brief for a Dilettante. This was a schematic for a Chameleon. But at the moment, this future Congressman, editor, musician, etc., was making protein smoothies at a Big Sur juice bar for $2.75 an hour, plus voluntary gratuities.

I decided to embrace my summer. I would love Big Sur for its trippiness, its physical freedoms, and the reckless abandon it bred in my soul. In the Song of Nature, the Body hears its own Humanity. Big Sur and Nepenthe were remedies for grief, a place to ply the spirit, hide and mend – to rise from the ashes of oneself and build a new life, like Hannah and dozens if not hundreds of others had done before me.

The sculpture on Nepenthe's upper deck was of a Phoenix Bird.

My problem was that I wanted more than a rebirth. I wanted more than access to who I was. I wanted to be part of the world. I wanted to be part of more than what made my senses tingle. I wanted worldly cares. I wanted to feel the slings and arrows of outrageous fortune. I wanted to get all heavy on someone's ass in a heartbeat. I wanted the Faustian glory of getting really, really heavy about *everything*.

"'Mellowness' is all well and good," I wrote Kitty, "but brooding and sober reflection are virtual no-no's here – especially during the summer, when everyone seems to be looking for some spark to immolate themselves. 'Nepenthe' indeed! What about the truth of suffering?" I went on in my Young Werther voice. Goethe again. "Not that I want to suffer, exactly. But I need to get out of California – to leave this formlessness behind! O for the organization of life behind something other than maintenance or intoxication! To be moved by purpose! Compelled by some believable destiny!" Seeking that destiny had cast more than one pilgrim on the shores of civilization, which was where I was heading.

Who gets to wear a lot of hats in a redwood forest?

ON THE ROAD: WATERGATE

"A feeling of great sadness," I noted in my journal as my departure date approached. "Am I going to regret my decision, experience a change of heart at the last minute, and stay after all?" My time in Big Sur had lasted barely three months. Still not fully believing I was turning my back on Paradise, but knowing I had to, I made a final trip over the mountains to say goodbye to friends in Palo Alto. I learned from an employee at Country Sun that my Big Sur sponsor Abe had been skimming the cash register for $500 a week.

What a clever move, to get the previous manager out of town, and simultaneously leave him eternally in your debt!

I returned to the redwoods behind the wheel of a fire-engine red '71 Datsun pickup truck with 5,000 miles on the odometer. I had traded in my Chevrolet Impala and paid fifteen hundred for a small Japanese pickup truck: Datsun. I had a month left before school started, plenty of time to visit family in L.A. and Texas, the Living Love/Arica ex-girlfriend in Gainesville, and Kitty in the woods outside Woods Hole, Mass.

Kitty had been sending me enticements, addressed with my name on them to the restaurant, and only partly tongue-in-cheek: "Our house is utterly integral, very peaceful and stimulating. For life is full of sumptuous, arcane secrets waiting to reveal themselves to adventuresome explorers of heart and psyche..." Or maybe she wasn't tongue in cheek at all. I would need to go to Woods Hole to find out.

As a thank-you to Hannah, I made her and the kids a farewell brunch served *al fresco* on the brick terrace near the sad garden, with its pitiful tomato plants and one scrawny lemon tree. I felt guilty that I had only baby-sat for this single mom a half-dozen times, if that, and never did get around to weeding her garden. Hannah spent the meal obsessing about her new boyfriend, a sitarist she met at a private concert on Partington Ridge. She was already thinking about packing up her kids and following him to Bangladesh, where a reign of terror had left a million East Bengalis murdered by their own government three years earlier.

"Watching Hannah fall in love," I noted in my journal, "is like watching someone go over Niagara Falls without a barrel."

I treated her to a full-body massage that last night on her living room floor and left her there, naked, crashed, and lightly snoring, to creep back to my cozy tree house for another dream-filled sleep, but not until dropping a blanket over her first.

Nepenthe's severance gift was the riotous Leo party, which at the end of the night found me on top of a naked woman in Michel's bed in the trailer park. She was down from L.A. with her fourteen-year-old hash-head son, who was in their cabin at Ventana when we did the deed. With furtive, kohled eyes, she bore a faint resemblance to Gloria Swanson's paranoid younger sister but was more than happy to share her creaturely comfort along with the excellent hash she had hidden in secret compartments of the boat-like Citroën she berthed in the parking lot, which was where we smoked it. The following morning, after sharing breakfast at her campsite at Ventana, she and her already stoned fourteen-year-old son drove on to Carmel, leaving me with phone numbers of two of her middle-aged girlfriends I should definitely look up when I got to Manhattan.

I reflected on my Midnight Cowboy/Boy Toy turn in my journal, a little startled that I had ended up behaving like one of the Esalen custodians, banging the trade from L.A. I dared to venture Emerson's opinion of one-night stands: "'While the world will be whole and refuses to be disparted, we seek to act partially, to sunder, to appropriate, for example – to gratify the senses we sever the pleasure of the senses from the needs of the character…' I don't want to be a thief," my journal continued. "I want to be a 'good upstanding man.' Durrell posed my question in *Clea*" – the fourth volume of *The Alexandria Quartet*: "'How to harness time in the cultivation of a style of heart?'"

At that moment in my life, I didn't think I could harness time in Big Sur. Literature and the infernal cities were calling. Siri and Jory had already decamped to their Greene Street loft in SoHo, leaving me with their phone number and an invitation to visit.

My most difficult goodbyes were with the Phoenix Muses.

In the basement a few days before I left, Sharon studied me for a long moment, then asked: "What would it take to get you to stay in Big Sur? Let's open a craft shop together. We'll go fifty-fifty on it. I know a roadside property we can rent for a really decent price, on my dime and your sweat equity." A future flashed before my eyes: boyfriend Gabriel would vanish into the Multidimensionality of Time, and I would end up with this very classy, totally down-to-earth Grace Kelly look-alike and Berkeley grad, the co-owner-operator of a really cool New Age crafts shop in Big Sur. It touched and warmed me. It was something I would think back on later in life. But at the time, I took a flier.

My Phoenix friends weren't through playing with my head.

"Are you a good fuck?" Kathy asked me one afternoon, then giggled and covered her mouth like a geisha. Sharon giggled, too. This wasn't a come-on. It was a sweet invitation to stay in Big Sur and see what might happen.

"I'm a fantastic fuck, what do you think?"

"That's not what Christina says," Sharon laughed, and Kathy laughed, too. I wasn't surprised they knew that Christina and I spent Platonic nights together. I would have been surprised if they didn't.

My goodbye to Christina was at the juice bar, where she showed up on my last day for her usual sixteen-once carrot juice, wearing nothing but torn blue jeans and a see-through blouse with no bra underneath.

"I'm tripping on mushrooms," she announced, after giving me her usual sloppy French-kiss hello while I intercepted her fingers.

"Wait a moment," she said, and snatched my pen from my hand to jot down something on a napkin. She had thought of a lyric. "This is music week," she explained. "Last week was fabric week."

I did my best Jack Nicholson impression: "Maybe it'll be sex week before I leave." I had heard about Cookie's Sex Week from a number of people, since it left a swath of pissed-off women the length and breadth of the Nepenthe trailer park.

Cookie laughed, and reaching across the counter, slapped my cheek with a stroke as light as a butterfly's wing.

"Sex Week was before you got here," she whispered.

I adored Christina, but as I got to know her better, I realized there was something untouchable about her – something not transparent at all. It had taken me most of the summer to figure it out, but one day it hit me: Christina was madly in love with Michel, but was unable to admit it even to herself, because Michel was either a registered commitment-phobe, or gay as a parade.

After chug-a-lugging the sixteen-once carrot juice I made for her, Christina slammed the paper cup down on the countertop, grabbed her own skull and jerked it, once, hard, to the right; reversing her grip, she jerked it the other way, too. Her cervical vertebrae crackled like a marimba band.

"Cookie! Do that to me!"

She walked behind the counter and after massaging my shoulders roughly for a minute or two – she had strong hands – she grabbed my head and chin and jerked it one way, then changed the grip to do it the other way.

My neck crackled like a box of Rice Krispies in a quart of milk.

"God! Cookie! That felt like a million dollars!"

Life stretched before me like a golden road.

My going-away present to myself was a beautiful turquoise Navajo ring from the Phoenix gift shop, which I hardly ever wear, because I don't like it on my index finger, which is the only digit it fits.

I left Sycamore Canyon behind the wheel of my Datsun pick-up with a camper purchased second-hand from a couple in Carmel and newly installed by me. It even had an electric light that worked. I stopped at the juice bar for a final smoothie, then continued south on Route 1 for my swing across the southern U.S. I had a photograph that Siri and Jory had given me of Swami Muktananda, a Hindu guru identified in India by Baba Ram Das, née Richard Alpert, the defrocked Harvard psychology professor who wrote about Muktananda in his countercultural bestseller *Be Here Now*. Muktananda was living on New York's Upper West Side now, reportedly enlightening people with a single swat of his peacock feather.

I meditated on Muktananda's face as I drove, singing at the top of my lungs a little Sanskrit ditty I had picked up at one of the Arican training sessions in Ventana: a hymn to Gopala, the heavenly one, the cowherd boy: *Gopala Gopala Devaki Nandana Gopala....* At dusk on day two, with thunderheads looming in three directions, I drove forty miles out of my way to visit the grave of Billy the Kid in Fort Sumner, New Mexico. I had to scale a fence in a raging thunderstorm to read the tombstone by bolts of lightning — *"William H. Bonney Alias Billy the Kid Died July 18"* — the rest of the inscription was eroded.

Drenched to the skin but thrilled to the root, I climbed back into my truck and continued driving for the rest of the night, supported by the occasional toke on a roach someone left behind in my ashtray, into a pink and hazy dawn, a long morning, then the afternoon across the miserable flatness of Tex-ass, arriving just before dark in Pedernales River country, sleep deprived, stoned, and actively imagining the corpse of Lyndon Baines Johnson, the thirty-sixth President of the United States and a prime mover of so many of the '60s' dreams and nightmares, resting in his nearby grave, but surely finding astral means to tune in to see Dick Nixon resign the Thirty-Seventh Presidency at seven p.m. Eastern. The dirt-floor Texas roadhouse where I watched had an old rabbit-eared black & white TV on top of a battered beer cooler. In the company of working men and redneck pool players who barely glanced up from their game except to spit on the floor and mutter, *"Fuckin' a-hole," "Piece o' shit,"* and *"Kiss my ass, your break,"* I leaned back in my folding chair, nipped on a cold LSD – Lone Star Draft – and thought Holy smokes goddamn and all ye falling candles of heaven smash, Tricky Dick is finally going down. I finished my beer, climbed back into my truck, and continued east, still boyish, equivocal, Emersonian, half-formed, but freshly-resolved to end my family's perception of me as a bohemian n'er do well, and perhaps become a writer on the way.

SOUTH OF HOUSTON, NORTH OF CANAL (TO '75)

Note *This chapter is from* POST-SHOCK: The Emergence of the American Avant-Garde, *an unpublished manuscript, about how SoHo became SoHo. In some ways it's cultural history (but un-footnoted) of what I learned about what happened during the years before I arrived. I first visited SoHo in the fall of '74, a month removed from my Big Sur treehouse. Despite the warnings that the financial center of the world was a "berserk colossus"* (Life magazine) *in the middle of its worst economic meltdown since the '30, I loved Downtown New York from almost the moment I arrived, and was eager to learn everything I could about its visual and performing worlds.* Wilderness=SoHo *is about that neighborhood.* The 'De-Materialization' of Art *is about a range of art world movements and events;* The "Death" of Painting / Conceptual Art, *about that.* Post-Minimalist Environments: Earth and Lofts *is about Environmental Art, mostly.* Public Lives, Private Selves *concerns Video and Performance Art, leading innovations in the performing arts of the '70s. I was a dancer in those days, having started modern dance classes in my last quarter in college, and came to learn about* Nature, Movement, and the Body, *which tells part of the story of the Lower Manhattan dance world. I moved into a dancer's loft in SoHo in January '76, and except for nine months back in Buffalo to finish my Master's degree, I was Downtown to stay.*

WILDERNESS = SOHO

In 1962, a civic improvement group calling itself the City Club of New York described an under-utilized manufacturing and warehouse district between the skyscrapers of Midtown and the downtown Wall Street area as an unredeemable slum, worthy only of complete destruction and renewal. The 43-square-block area, which was bordered on the north by Houston Street, on the west by Sixth Avenue, on the south by Canal Street, and on the east by Lafayette, had a long history of urban transformation and neglect. Originally built on the site of a fever-infested swamp, and later the growing city's garbage dump, this twenty-acre neighborhood had been transformed by mid-nineteenth century urban development into a fashionable shopping and entertainment center, and later a notorious red-light district. Between 1860 and 1890, the area was rebuilt again with multi-story factory sweatshops and warehouses. Light industry prospered into the early twentieth century, exploiting the cheap labor on the immigrant Lower East Side. SoHo, not called that yet, was a factory hub. What became the South Houston Industrial District, only later known by the abbreviation "SoHo," was home to the world's largest collection of cast-iron buildings, along with numerous other architecturally-distinguished structures. But the decades between the world wars had claimed at least half of Manhattan's factory jobs, and the neighborhood had declined into a semi-abandoned no-man's land where subcontractors handled seasonal work and midtown businesses moved their overflow – a way-station for truckers, import-export businesses, dress manufacturers, fabric houses, rag balers, and waste paper processors. Most of the hundreds of medium-size high-rises in the district were half-to-two-thirds unoccupied. Streets noisy in the day were empty and unlit at night, littered with trash from the local pulp industries.

The opinion of the City Club of New York was not much different than that of most American urban planning groups in those days: no consideration at all was given to an industrial district's conversion to residential status. Yet landlords had been only too happy to provide illegal leases to artists who needed workspace and were willing to declare war on the rats and install plumbing and interior walls, which could be passed along to the next tenant for a "fixture fee," usually a few thousand dollars or less. In the early '60s, lofts in SoHo could be rented for a song: as little as $100 a month or less for five thousand square feet was commonplace. SoHo's early living and work lofts were Spartan affairs, with cold water sinks and toilets; most were heated, if at all, only during the day, and never on weekends. As late as 1974, I had friends on an upper floor on Greene Street who had an elevator that you worked by pulling on a rope. The '50s' pioneers, which included composer Lou Harrison and the dancer and filmmaker Elaine Summers – lived in constant fear of eviction, despite bribes passed under the table to corrupt city inspectors. Inhabitants would hang curtains over windows to hide interior lights at night. Visitors had to shout up from the sidewalk, catch a set of thrown keys on a parachute or rolled up in a sock, then scramble over a loading dock into darkened lobbies or stairs.

Compared to slum apartments, the interiors were huge – typically at least 2,500 square feet, most with high ceilings, columns, and double strength hardwood floors that could be sanded for the bare feet of modern dancers. Sculptural objects could go as large as loft windows or freight elevators could handle. The resident population of artists in the '50s and early '60s remained small, so building owners who couldn't or wouldn't rent illegally sometimes resorted to arson to get their money out. SoHo became the site of so many suspicious fires that firefighters dubbed it "Hell's Hundred Acres." In 1960, when a firefighter fell to his death down an unmarked elevator shaft, the city took action: in August 1961, an Artist-in-Resident (A.I.R) program became the first move in what would become a long battle for legal residency.

The Artist-in-Resident program permitted artists to live in certain buildings under strict codes and supervision, which ended up restricting rather than protecting artists' rights, as many loft-dwellers who registered for the program soon found themselves in court. But AIR signs continued to crop up on the sides of buildings in SoHo, with painters (including the 24-year-old Princeton grad Frank Stella), photographers, sculptors, dancers, musicians, writers, and filmmakers providing the South Houston Industrial District with an acronym of its legal district, redolent of London's West End and the call to the hounds: "So-*Ho!*" "Art is the avant-garde of real estate," the American-Romanian poet Andre Codrescu claimed, but if SoHo hadn't already existed, it would have had to be invented.

Postwar creativity needed a place to live and work and grow.

Pioneer loft dwellers were not averse to picking up a hammer and saw, but most did not enjoy acting as real estate developers, so that role fell to George Macuinas, the founder of a loosely-knit affiliation of far-fetched experimentalists known as Fluxus. Macuinas was the driving force behind the city's first major co-op movement for artists: the first "Fluxhouse" co-operative opened at 16 Grand Street in 1967, but soon went under. The oldest surviving Fluxhouse is at 64-70 Grand – three former sweatshops and a factory building divided into residential loft spaces and a parking garage. Macuinas, the "real" (estate) father of SoHo, continued to purchase buildings and turn them over to artists for $2,000 to $5,000 per loft – roughly a dollar a square foot. By June of 1968, seventeen Fluxhouses on Prince, Broome and West Broadway. SoHo was home to over a thousand artists, living and working in six hundred lofts. Pioneers of urban self-sufficiency, SoHo loft-dwellers paralleled the counterculture's back-to-the-land ethos with a back-to-the-loft survivalism of their own. That same year, 1968, art exhibition began in SoHo: ten artists formed a collective known as "10 Downtown" to host exhibitions at various open studios. Other SoHo artists established a restaurant and day-care centers, and in a few more years occupied a nearby abandoned West Village school, P.S. 3, forcing the city to reopen it for the public education of SoHo's school-age children. Inevitably, established dealers entered the vortex: in 1968 Park Avenue dealer Richard Feigen opened a warehouse in SoHo to service his Uptown showroom. Also in '68, Paula Cooper opened SoHo's first public art gallery at 98-100 Prince Street, on the third floor of two adjoining lofts, showing work that emphasized a pared-down minimalist abstraction.

The run-down condition of Prince and other SoHo streets in those days did little to ensure the attention of well-heeled art collectors. SoHo's streets tended to feel alternately violent and empty. Cooper later recalled how "the only place to get a drink was Fanelli's," referring to a local working-class saloon that closed at 8 p.m. But the advantages were five thousand square feet of "beautiful, funky and raw" space, which Cooper confessed gave her "a mystical feeling," as well as proximity to a Downtown way of making – and unmaking – art. Responding to budding neighborhood alliances between the visual and performing arts, Cooper pioneered the presentation of poetry, music, dance, performance art and film in SoHo galleries. On Christmas Day 1969, Holly and Horace Solomon used the money that they ordinarily would have spent collecting art to support younger artists in their earliest endeavors: 98 Prince Street opened as a combined exhibition and performance loft. Earlier that year, Ivan Karp, the long-time uptown adjutant of Leo Castelli, the world's most famous contemporary art dealer, broke with Castelli over his acceptance of trendy but unprofitable minimalist sculptors and moved to SoHo, taking over a 7,000-square-foot former warehouse on Broadway: the clearest signal yet that art world momentum was shifting away from West 57th Street, Madison Avenue and the Upper East Side.

The drive for legalization was led not by gallery owners or generous collectors, but by artists themselves. Filmmaker, curator, and Fluxus associate Jonas Mekas was leading a campaign to obtain a legal permit to open a Cinematheque at 80 Wooster, where he, Yoko Ono, and dancer Trisha Brown had lofts. This campaign resulted in the formation of a new community group in the spring of 1968 – a few months after the Tet Offensive in Vietnam – to fight for legal status. This struggle was promptly dwarfed by a much more serious threat: New York State3 master builder Robert Moses had his long-dreaded Lower Manhattan Expressway cleared for construction. Faced with the prospect of a ten-lane superhighway slashing across SoHo at Broome Street, the SoHo Artists Association rallied opposition, spread information, negotiated with the city, and performed various public relations feats that contributed to the defeat of Moses and the bulldozers in 1969.

Community activists chose to turn up the heat for legal residency with a new tactic: to throw in their lot – rhetorically, at least – with corporate capitalism. The construction of the Chase Manhattan Bank in 1960 – the first new Downtown skyscraper in more than two decades – became the catalyst for a Lower Manhattan building boom that would add forty million square feet of office space to an area that had previously changed little since the late nineteenth century. The Port Authority's World Trade Towers opened in 1973, the two tallest, largest buildings in the world, providing office space for forty thousand workers. A SoHo Artists Association White Paper argued that a Downtown arts enclave "contributes to making New York an attractive place to be" and enhances the city's reputation as an international business center.

This was "a game the artists decided to play to keep their lofts," one historian of SoHo would note, "but in time it would become a self-fulfilling prophesy."

Media responded to this glossier image: *Life* published a five-page spread about SoHo in May 1970, describing artists surviving against the odds, humanizing a once-forbidding warehouse district. The First SoHo Arts Festival that summer offered hundreds of events in streets and lofts, attracting German, Japanese and local film and television crews. So much attention was lavished on SoHo that by January 1971, when the City Planning Commission finally voted to re-zone South Houston and legalize the residential use of lofts by artists in all forty-three square blocks, a New York arts neighborhood was already a *fait accompli* – a creative act of urban necessity for which city planners took full credit.

With full legalization, growing numbers of established Uptown galleries began to relocate, following the lead of Leo Castelli, who had already moved in 1969 into 420 West Broadway – the "Grand Palais" of SoHo art – along with his ex-wife Ileana Sonnabend, Andre Emmerich, and John Weber, thereby ensuring SoHo's future as a major international art center. SoHo's cast-iron construction was ideal for plate-glass window display, making SoHo a wonderful neighborhood for a weekend stroll or window shopping. Uptown openings were typically stuffy affairs, but SoHo galleries went after new buyers, younger professionals or upper-management types looking to take up art collecting as an expression of their new-found status. These same young lawyers and brokers and bankers compared their cramped co-ops on the Upper East and West Side to the roomy artists' lofts and began to move illegally and in increasing numbers into a neighborhood supposedly reserved for artists.

SoHo's communal lunchroom was Food, founded in 1969 by Gordon Matta-Clark, Tina Girouard, Suzanne Harris, Rachel Lew, and others from the Anarchitecture Group, using dancer-photographer Caroline Gooden's modest family inheritance to transform an old Puerto Rican luncheonette into a community kitchen and dining room. Planning the space as an art event, Matta-Clark designed everything from the tables and counters to the cooking utensils, which proved too costly to build; instead, he and his friends used what they had and simply "built it, tore down the old restaurant, in total joy, filthy and feeling good about it," Gooden later recalled. Opening two weeks after the Castelli Gallery opened at 420 Broadway, Food was a bright, no-frills room with huge windows that faced Prince Street. Tina Girouard estimates that as many as forty artists worked there weekly, with hours tailored to individual schedules. Actors with the experimental theater troupe Mabou Mines, Ruth Maleczech and JoAnne Akalaitis worked in the kitchen, the company's director and writer Lee Breuer scrubbed floors, and company newcomer Terry O'Reilly washed dishes after Philip Glass, also in Mabou Mines, finished installing plumbing and heat. Workers included performance artist Julia Heyward and the Grand Union's Nancy Lewis, wife of the Glass Ensemble's Richard Peck, a native Louisiana jazz and R&B saxophonist. Sunday's ten-dollar special had "guest artists" contributing conceptual fare: Eads Hill, a theater group from Memphis, supplied Southern food; Matta-Clark, live brine shrimp in boiled eggs and a meal of sculptural bones. Visiting dance companies, theater troupes, communal families, and the art world public came by for (on occasion) Indian, Greek, and Middle Eastern food. "From the beginning, Food was a combination of play, idealism, high creativity, and common sense," according to chef Akalaitis, who helped pioneer all-natural ingredients and open food preparation – cooking-as-performance – a decade before every nouveau restaurant in L.A. did the same.

More upscale bars and restaurants were on their way to SoHo, and the first retailers and boutiques appeared. Kenn's Broome Street Bar, an artists' hang-out on West Broadway, fought pitched battles with drug dealers from the nearby Italian neighborhood, but kept its doors open. At least two galleries, two boutiques, and one major restaurant I knew about were founded on hash and marijuana smuggling fortunes – a major source of Soho investment capital from the beginning. Similar processes in urban restoration were in progress in inner cities around the world – in Newark, Boston, Los Angeles, San Francisco, Rome, Paris, and Tokyo's Rapongi district – wherever artist-bohemians moved into former industrial neighborhoods to revitalize decaying inner-city real estate, and succeed in convincing local governments to promote cultural activities to reverse the decline of inner cities – at Baltimore's City Fair, New York's South Street Seaport, San Francisco's Fisherman's Wharf, and San Antonio's Riverwalk. But SoHo remained the late twentieth-century's pre-eminent and quintessential example of innovation in inner city redevelopment – the largest and most vital international model for a new urban lifestyle.

By 1973, twenty-six SoHo blocks were set aside as a National Historic District, permanently protecting 120 cast-iron facades and at least forty other buildings from destruction or alteration, and city officials, the City Club notwithstanding, began asserting that "the mixed combination of art and industry found in SoHo points the way for the core of an old city to be given new life." The revival of Hell's Hundred Acres was the verve, initiative and sweat equity of artists themselves.

THE "DE-MATERIALIZATION" OF ART

SoHo from its founding was a post-revolutionary urban oasis where artists could "escape art" and live simpler, less expensive, more communitarian lives. SoHo was an ideal neighborhood to survive what the German filmmaker Rainer Werner Fassbinder termed "that strange post-revolutionary period" between the '60s and '70s." Minimalism, a major Downtown art movement of the '60s, had become academicized almost as quickly as Pop Art had. Minimalist sculpture had become a corporate collectible – "plaza plop," in the words of erstwhile sculptor Gordon Matta-Clark – with public art works such as Tony Rosenthal's "Alamo" (1967), a 3,000-pound revolving black cube at Astor Place and Lafayette Street, gateway between the West and East Villages, shedding whatever radicalism they might have once implied. Pluralism was the buzzword of the post-revolutionary consensus, describing a condition in which no single movement had the authority to dominate any other – producing an artistic balkanization that would spell disaster for the aggressive, moralizing thrust of the avant-garde, but would sustain the traditional vanguard defiance of elitism, commercialism, and "High Culture," an opposition that much if not most of SoHo represented.

The pluralist condition was fuel for a third wave of postwar cultural rebellion. Michael Murphy, co-founder of Esalen in Big Sur, described the first wave as the New Bohemians and Beats, who opposed mass consumption; then the Hippies, also separate from the straight world, but avid consumers of popular culture; and now the Sadhaks, the "heavy meditators" – still countercultural, but also contemplative, analytical, preoccupied with minds and bodies, and transforming every institution they touched through their intense insistence on art's personal and social dimensions. Advanced art had been "normalized as a professional activity within society," as Harold Rosenberg had noted in 1966, but SoHo's "revolution in consciousness" was partly a retreat into private worlds—a time of cults and spiritual sects, gurus, shamans, prophets, and mystics. The encircling art world may have been pluralistic – no single artist or group of artists bestrode it – but artists in SoHo were choosing to challenge the "iron triangle" of museums, galleries, and media by emphasizing alternative organizations and new relations between creative processes and lived experience. The English art critic, novelist, painter and poet John Berger: "None of the reasons for being an artist exist anymore. New reasons have to be found, or art should be abandoned."

Yet many SoHo artists thought less about "Art" and more about "Work" – about actually making things, concentrating on issues of production and reception, exploring all manner of minimalist and post-minimalist anti-dance, anti-theater, and anti-form. Donald Judd assembled anonymous stacks of colored metal boxes, imagining he was escaping the hierarchical and "anti-democratic" compositional relationships of the European past. Minimalism could provide a certain intellectual glory: Sol LeWitt's gallery-filling "46 Variations on 3 Different Kinds of Cubes" reminded the young Black artist and Harvard Philosophy Ph.D. Adrian Piper of the plays of Samuel Beckett and the geometry of a Bach fugue. But many SoHo sculptors reacted against the manufactured, calibrated, systemic, and commodifiable aspects of minimalist sculpture, preferring to create works that were "almost uncollectable," as sculptor Keith Sonnier put it – employing cast-off substances and casual debris that rhymed with their unfinished lofts and previous industrial usage. *Artforum's* editors labeled this trend "Anti-Form" in April 1968; others called it "process" art, noting its emphasis on impermanence, roughness, and hand-made order.

Sonnier made free-standing assemblages and wall pieces from neon, cheesecloth, dangling electric lights, and synthetic fiber mesh; Barry Le Va worked with strips of felt; Robert Morris, temporary heaps of earth, felt and metals. Lynda Benglis made works out of foam rubber; Richard Serra, rubber, neon, crumpled lead, and heavy metal plates of Cor-Ten steel, which he leaned against one another or a wall, or assembled as outdoor "site-specific" works, rusting in subtle gradations, like a Rothko canvas. Post-Minimal Downtown art could also be extravagantly messy. Early in 1969, an "Anti-Form" show at the Castelli warehouse in SoHo, curated by artist Robert Morris, together with the Whitney's "Anti-Illusion: Procedures/Materials," revealed a new generation combining Constructivism and Dada, forcing the public to once again ask, "Is this sculpture, or *what?*" Anti-art indeed remained "art," as the German-American political theorist Herbert Marcuse had predicted, but in the words of the critic and curator Robert Pincus-Witten, "formalist dysfunction" was driving SoHo's emerging identity. Pincus-Witten coined the term "post-minimalist" for a host of tendencies and a range of forms and materials, independent of frames and pedestals.

1968 was "the crucial year," as *Voice* critic Kim Levin noted a decade later, such that by the early 70s, "Formalism" was roundly and routinely condemned as guilty, insane, dying, or dead already, exposed for its complicity with the marketplace. SoHo artists were generating Concepts, Actions, and Voids, dethroning the Object, removing the pedestal, and dislodging the proscenium, or at least questioning the authority of tradition and any of its ongoing power.

By the early '70s, "The Death of Painting" in SoHo was a neighborhood cliché, confirmed by its receding glamor. With Nixon in the White House and napalmed babies in Vietnam, what was left to paint? Photorealism emerged as a school in the late '60s, often dealing with Pop-like imagery, but working away from Pop Art's iconic quality. Robert Bechtle and Richard Estes copied ordinary color photographs of cars, trailers, storefronts, parking lots, motorcycle engines and reflective surfaces on their large-scale canvases, often painted with the aid of slide projectors. Photorealism was "the triumph of mediocrity," in the view of the journalist and (non-)art critic Tom Wolfe, but many artists felt the need to cleanse their work of obvious meaning. The replication of unadorned "reality" re-asserted the power of artists to project their own meanings, which in pluralism tend to proliferate, waffle, break down, lose potency, and place all art under duress. "The Uneasy Object," in Rosenberg's phrase, symptomatized an art world in which any "subversive" form could briefly appear and disappear from view. An accompanying need kept artists constantly on the lookout for some new and timely approach to art-making, stimulating what L.A. artist John Baldesarri called an "escalation of fantasy" that cast in-house reputations in high relief.

Theory mattered at Raoul's, a restaurant on Spring Street, at Fanelli's on Prince, and at Max's Kansas City a mile or so north, where the conceptual heirs of the abstract-expressionists engaged in their "fastest-guns-in-the-west art conversations, you know, real pricks, real killers," recalls Joseph Kosuth, a conceptual artist who would join Robert Smithson, Serra, and Carl Andre on the international circuit and the trend-setting, cutting-edge pages of *Artforum*. Important cultural battles tend to be refought periodically; the politics of anti-form—which began in America with Jackson Pollock, who asked of his own work, *"Is it even a painting?"*—continued to provide the surest ground for post-'60s artists to wage war on institutional standards. Robert Hughes blamed the collapse of formalism (in his lexicon, good taste) on SoHo's "constructivist nostalgia for social effects," which in a way was true: the neighborhood's emphasis on "information" and "process" related to the theatrical character of the postwar protest. "Politicizing the aesthetic" was SoHo's most compelling form of resistance to art-world formalism, inspired by a belief that the forms of art can both reflect and construct change in people's lives. Neo-feminists urged a re-evaluation of concepts, resources, and lived experience, but also a liberation of desire. SoHo became a site for women and others to restore the art object to fetishism and ritual, a late modernist return to feelings, and to hand-touch sensibility, personal iconography and ritual, after a decade of machine-made Pop and Minimalism. The '60s-'70s transition became an escapist interlude that saw constructivist, "temporary" art empower artists of both genders to revive older myths of instinctual creation.

Women of the SoHo generation led the way in deconstructing what the American-Argentinian art critic Sylvia Kolbowski termed "the white, moneyed, heterosexual, masculine spectator assumed by pop, minimalism and some but not all conceptual art." Lynda Benglis, Eva Hesse (dead at 34 in 1970), Dorothea Rockburne, Nancy Graves, and Ree Morton were among the many who passed through the blast furnace of minimalism's "what-you-see-is-what-you-see" aesthetic to re-introduce Dada-esque mockery, references to the body and nature, and a tone of personal and spiritual discovery. "Surely never before in modern art," wrote Pincus-Witten (whose criticism had taken a diaristic turn), "had this kind of elaborately eccentric, magically endowed, autobiographically transmuted, talismanic art appeared."

"At all costs," wrote Ree Morton in 1971, six years before her death in a car accident in Chicago, "the deities must be made to laugh."

Conceptual art emerged in the context of theory and the disavowal of the marketplace. Whether as idea, process, raw material, or environment, a lot of art of the late '60s in SoHo was "de-materialized," as Lucy Lippard suggested in a celebrated essay of 1968, largely in protest against any art world consensus and the continuing exploitation of art as a market resource. Foreshadowed by Robert Rauschenberg's "Erased de Kooning" drawing in 1953 (in which he did just that), conceptual art in SoHo challenged or at least questioned art's status as something to be bought and sold – an attitude that arose effortlessly among post-minimalists who emerged from the supermarket atmosphere of American universities, with access to intellectual resources so vast as to defy the ability of art historians to describe discrete movements.

Like the earlier post-revolutionary generation of the '40s, the post-revolutionary brain trust of SoHo turned to French intellectuals: in this case, Michel Foucault, Roland Barthes, Jacques Derrida, and Jacques Lacan, who proposed new techniques for "deconstructing" objects and events. Meaning was no longer a matter or function of metaphysical truth, but of the relationship between representations. Human consciousness becomes a structure or a picture of all the "texts" in the world. The formalist criticism of Clement Greenberg, the dominant critic of the postwar years, was replaced by French theory and the primacy it placed on language and the symbolic, particularly the study of sign systems – semiotics – which was having a wide influence on literary criticism and anthropology as well. Post-structuralist theory sought to demystify a world that lacked stable meanings and references – a world-congerie of "signs," adrift in a pluralistic world of "texts" – proposing "an archaeology of modernism in exhaustion," as Columbia University professor Andreas Huyssens later suggested.

Paul Goodman, anarchist author of *Growing Up Absurd*, a countercultural ür-text published in 1960, wrote about speaking with certain radicals in 1972, shortly before his death, and realizing "that they did not really believe there was a nature to things. Somehow all functions could be reduced to interpersonal relations and power... There was no knowledge, but only the sociology of knowledge... To be required to learn something was a trap by which the young were put down and co-opted. Then I knew that I could not get through to them." The *Times'* neo-conservative critic Hilton Kramer believed that the '60s had "discredited" the intellectual profession, when nothing could have been further from the truth. It was closer to the case that the '60s saw "the student movement... flushed off the streets and driven underground into discourse," as the British public intellectual Terry Eagleton suggested a decade later. "In one sense, Theory has been the continuation of radical politics by other means – carrying the revolution into signs and sexuality, discourse and discos, into all of those vital areas of everyday culture which a high male rationalism had traditionally shut out."

When the walls of the city shake, the intellectual music changes: in the '50s, the object, *le geste*, and French existentialism; in the '70s, the anti-object, *la pensée*, and French post-structuralism, channeling the introspection and despair that accompanied the '60s-'70s transition. Theoretical issues prevailed at the July 1970 "Information" show at MoMA, which for some observers marked the definitive end of the '60s. "'Information' has become the shibboleth of the '70s," grumbled Hughes, "a vogue word, as 'flatness' was in the '60s and 'gesture' was in the '50s." The avant-garde's traditional enemies – Puritanism, Capitalism, the Class System – remained under attack, but the "Information" show seemed far more preoccupied with esoteric issues of knowledge and perception, mounting its theses on walls like big game trophies.

Much Conceptual Art stemmed from an implicit assumption that art observes only its own development. The conceptual artist Lawrence Weiner provided instructions for an artwork that "need not be built." Daniel Buren painted a thin red line around a gallery wall, accompanied by reams of exegesis about how "the Museum/Gallery instantly promotes to 'Art' status whatever it exhibits with conviction." Joseph Kosuth cribbed the central theses of French semiotics for a wall piece that served as a blunt lesson in post-structural representation: "One Chair and Three Chairs" (1969) showed a dictionary definition of the word "chair," a photo of a chair, and an actual chair mounted on the wall. Fluxus flyweights proposed all manner of antic projects, gamey descriptions of future and often undoable deeds. Neo-Dadaist Jean Toche threatened by mail to kidnap the director of the Museum of Modern Art, inspiring Alfred Barr's successor William Rubin to forward the offending art-missal to the F.B.I. The conceptual art umbrella was broad enough to cover virtually every genre and medium. Choreographer Remy Charlip made conceptual "Airmail Dances" – stick figures drawn on postcards – that were sent around the world for dancers to interpret and perform. In 1968 *Kulchur* magazine "published" a ream of blank paper.

John Cage had made boredom permissible through his use of chance operations in music and poetry; Andy Warhol had made boredom fashionable through the sheer banality of the imagery he employed. Now some conceptual artists were institutionalizing boredom, perpetuating the loss of sensual reality characteristic of a televised era of "medium cool" – withdrawing into arcana at least partially in reaction against the contemporary glut of visual imagery, but also in a spirit of criticism and transcendence. SoHo conceptual art only rarely required space, just a crazy quilt of thought. Some conceptual artists couched their work in the language of scientific treatises on quarks. "To me," wrote Pincus-Witten in 1971, "what is vital in current art is not a function of object but a function of idea. It's never 'inherent beauty' – whatever that is – that induces a sense of wonder but only the argument into which the object – and here I am regarding conceptual art as a kind of object – can be fitted."

One could argue that the inability to experience "whatever that is" is a good definition of philistinism, but conceptual artists' refusal to be seduced by shopworn notions of "beauty" did help some to undertake new ideas in an art world all-too-recently deafened by Pop Art and silenced by the muteness of Minimalism. Insisting on the powers of art as language, information, and idea, Conceptual Art addressed a need for communication and meaning, however exclusive, at a time when most artists and critics felt these things slipping away. Conceptual art sometimes demonstrated how art could be engaged, and sometimes even engaging, without pandering to pop philistinism or the marketplace. Some conceptualists were tapping into social issues: Hans Haacke's Guggenheim installation in 1971 involved maps, photographs, and other documentation to discuss racism, classism, and the disenfranchisement of the poor in Harlem and the Lower East Side, as well as the art world's complicity with the war in Southeast Asia. (Museum director Thomas Messer canceled the show as "inappropriate," and fired the curator who dared to defend the artist's freedom of expression.) Many in the visual art establishment hoped and believed that the conceptual art fad would fade – some observers felt this had to be the whole purpose of MoMA's "Information" show, to tie a bow on it – but conceptual art's recovery of alternatives to corrupted usages and institutions, its insistence on insight and understanding as goals, continued largely as a Downtown and European phenomenon. "The withdrawal of art into itself may be its saving grace," wrote critic Ursula Meyer. "In the sense that science is for scientists and philosophy is for philosophers, art is for artists."

POST-MINIMALIST ENVIRONMENTS: EARTH AND LOFT

Some artists in the '70s sought to slip the confines of art entirely, creating work in places that neither collectors nor the art world could meaningfully possess, or in most cases ever experience first-hand.

Christo, a Romanian-born artist who had lived in SoHo since 1964, "wrapped" the Museum of Modern Art with fabric and rope in 1968, and also traveled to Australia to conceal a million square feet of coastline under polypropylene fabric, and all his neighbors in SoHo ever saw of the work were photographs. Some "Earth artists" viewed commercial enterprise as inherently elitist, but still required patrons with deep pockets. Michael Heizer's "Double Negative" (1971) displaced a quarter of a million tons of dirt, creating two huge gaps mirroring one another across an arroyo somewhere outside Las Vegas. The artist assigned ownership of these gaps to the Dwan Gallery in Manhattan. Walter de Maria forbade photographs of his early environmental work, which did little to further his reputation, but most earth art was exhaustively-documented, stimulating the emergence of photography as one of the major art forms of the '70s. MoMA's "New Documents" show back in March 1967 had sped the advance of documentary photography and its confrontation with the "real" world.

Robert Smithson investigated the documentary potential of earth art more thoroughly than anyone. One of the great art works of the '70s, Smithson's

"Spiral Jetty" (1972) was a 1,500-foot-long rock pile curling into Utah's Great Salt Lake, exhaustively reproduced on film and in a museum installation of photographs and objects from the site. "A lot of the so-called conceptual art is nothing but atrophy," Smithson told *The New Yorker's* Calvin Tomkins. "I think we're just discovering the multiplicity of nature's ways." Smithson's mystical *frisson* eventually sank beneath the lake's rising waters, only to resurface periodically, while the artist himself died at the age of thirty-five in a 1973 Texas plane crash, during an aerial viewing of his site-specific creation, "Amarillo Ramp."

Renewed attention to nature and the environment paralleled artists' moves into decaying urban spaces.

"To convert a place into a state of mind" was the intention of Gordon Matta-Clark, an information nexus and compulsive pothead, the older twin son of Roberto Matta, the Basque Surrealist whose friendship with the painter Arshile Gorky had ended disastrously in 1948, when Matta took up with Gorky's wife, and Gorky hung himself. Abashed by his father's reputation, Matta-Clark had studied architecture at Cornell, but upon arriving in Manhattan became a catalyst in the early SoHo arts community, converting the raw space at 98 Greene into a performance gallery for collector-sponsors Horace and Holly Solomon. When not constructing lofts, Matta-Clark was carving huge slices from derelict buildings Downtown and in New Jersey after 1971, evading police and dealing with the vivid architectural dangers created by the cuts themselves – exposing new geometries and perspectives that commented on existing structures, both psychologically and formally.

Older post-minimalists were also challenging institutional structures, but unestablished baby boomers remained more concerned with developing ideas and friendships in their own communities. Matta-Clark's notions of "undoing" and "destructuring" evolved in discussion with the Anarchitecture Group, a group of like-minded sculptors, dancers, painters, performance artists and critics interested in issues of space, anarchy and architecture. "Informalists," as Pincus-Witten suggested such people call themselves, pursued art as an anti-traditional social work across multiple disciplines. Post-minimalist concerns with spaces – conceptual, physical, rural, and urban – dominated the arts of SoHo in a host of ways, across disciplines. In the spring of 1970, visual artist Jeffrey Lew invited former Cunningham dancer Steve Paxton to perform a piece recently censored at NYU – it had involved nudity – in Lew's loft at 112 Greene. Other friends expressed interest in working in a similarly casual environment, and so after a rag-salvaging business vacated the ground floor and basement, Lew opened SoHo's first artist-run co-op, known as 112 Workshop. Sculptor Jene Highstein remembered it as "the funkiest place in the world – so beautiful and impossible at the same time." Tina Girouard described the tumult of gathering and curating shows. "Trucks would pull up from everywhere and there'd be ten shows laid out on the floor and Jeffrey would try to convince us – you know the dialogue that goes on – 'Throw that out, Jeffrey... yes, that's good, leave it...' So there'd be this grand edit which was the show and it was exciting..."

Uptown collectors and Europeans, especially Germans, frequented SoHo's commercial galleries, but only insiders knew about 112, where the front door was always unlocked and works were stolen as often as works were sold. No one was sure where operating funds even came from, although for a time Rauschenberg was secretly providing money. Matta-Clark grew mushrooms in the basement and later dug a deep well after the suicide of his twin brother, Sebastian. Philip Glass recorded music in 112's basement. Deborah Hay performed her early Sufi-inspired circle dances at 112, created after her move from Downtown to Vermont in 1971. William Wegman, the future photographer of the famous costumed Weimaraners, showed some of his earliest images. The painter and conceptual artist Mel Bochner had his first show at 112 in 1971. There was a video series, a performance series, and on-going rehearsals by dance and theater groups, all conducted in an atmosphere of casual co-existence. Painter Susan Rothenberg recalls feeling somewhat ill-at-ease at a place where "the women were all dancers; the men were all sculptors." But Alice Aycock showed sculptural work at 112, too, and Marjorie Strider sent brightly-colored plastic foam oozing out the windows of the upper floors. "Showing at 112 was license to do anything at all," claims Lew, who's twenty-four-hour "Madness Workshops" encouraged information-sharing and work across genders and genres. Sculptors danced, critics made video art, and made "performance art," defined (by me) as any live event happening over time in the context of the art world's interests and concerns.

PUBLIC LIVES / PRIVATE SELVES

With object-making corrupted in the eyes of many, and with Art de-materializing, Performance became a vanguard medium. Performance Art occurred in every nook and cranny of the South Houston Industrial District. During an outdoor SoHo performance, *Love America or Live* (1970), Turkish performance artist Tosun Bayrak had a group of men appear to rape a female bystander, then had pig blood sprayed on spectators from the roof of a nearby building. Another piece by this largely-forgotten shock artist involved littering a street in SoHo with slaughtered animals, then releasing hundreds of rats to devour the corpses – infuriating a community that had a vermin problem already.

Post-'60s performance in Europe had turned outrageous and shocking, prefiguring Punk. Viennese neo-expressionist Hermann Nitsch brought his "Orgies-Mysteries Theater" to a storefront south of SoHo, pouring thick blood, warm lymph, and egg yolks over the genitals of young boys, and violently-disemboweled dead animals. The ultimate art-pornography of 1969 was performed abroad by a 29-year-old Austrian, Rudolf Schwarzkogler, who amputated his own penis segment by segment and recorded the fatal deed on-camera. These grueling photographs were reportedly exhibited at the 1972 Kassel Documenta. "[T]he artist, deprived of his capacity to protest, or sensing the inadequacy of protest, turns against himself," noted Barbara Rose.

Shock was a vanguard tactic throughout the developed world, but performance in SoHo's conceptual hothouse was typically more intimate, as artists probed the era's collapsing forms and dissolving systems through more ephemeral encounters. Christos Gianakos tossed flour in the shape of an X at the busy intersection of West Broadway and Broome in 1971 and photographed the traffic as it destroyed his creation. Then he disappeared. I never heard of him again. Typical of High SoHo Days were Performance Art pieces that set up terms for an unusually boring event, nevertheless seen through to its conclusion. Sculptor Dennis Oppenheim stretched his body between two walls, and that's all, folks. On another occasion he sunburned his chest while sunbathing with an open book laid on it. These and other pieces were not "simple egocentrism," as Whitney curator Marcia Tucker assured a bemused public, "but rather [used] the body to transform intimate subjectivity into objective demonstration." Post-minimalist processes acquired flesh in *Mirror Check* (1970) when Joan Jonas, a visual artist and veteran of the dance scene at the Judson Church on Washington Square, stood naked in her Mercer Street loft twenty feet from her audience, inspecting every inch of her body she could reach with a hand mirror.

Intimate inquiry got a serious leg up with the arrival of the first portable Sony Video recorders. Sony's relatively-inexpensive $1,200 Port-a-Pak system enabled SoHo artists to investigate "icebox thoughts" and ludicrous private behavior. Video art could become a public revelation of private experience. The seminal video show, "TV as a Creative Medium" at the Howard Wise Gallery in 1969, showed the work of twelve artists who shared a more-or-less Utopian view of television as a possible interface with the social realm. Video art's American broadcast premiere in 1969 on WGBH-TV in Boston featured works by Nam June Paik, Allan Kaprow, the latter the father of the '60s' "Happenings," and several others. Video art was on the art world map, attracting other artists to take up the medium. Within a year of the arrival of the Sony Port-a-Pak, Video Art had its first museum survey at the Rose Art Museum at Brandeis University in Waltham, north of Boston. SoHo's pioneering video artists – including Vito Acconci, Benglis, Jonas, Levine, Serra, Sonnier, Wegman, and others – tended to be process oriented, re-situating post-minimalist ideas in an electronic venue. Some video artists concentrated on the formal vistas of the TV rectangle, the fluttering horizons of the horizontal bar, and the use of quick cuts and primitive image-processing to re-approach private and public life.

Nam June Paik, often called the father of video art, believed it was "like doing your own anthropology, because through video you learn about life." The privacy afforded by portable video cameras allowed for a psychic and physical stripping-bare – a blurring of public self and secret life. Bruce Nauman jiggled his testicles on camera (not for PBS), painted them black, contorted his face, sprayed water through his lips, and clapped his hands together in a series of turn-of-the-decade videotapes. Closed circuits of artist and videotape exemplified the early '70s' "umbilical gaze." Rosalind Krauss' influential essay "The Aesthetics of Narcissism," published in a new journal, *October*, in 1976, described video art as "consciousness doubling back upon itself."

Of the many SoHo artists working in video and live performance, Vito Acconci was the most conceptually violent and driven. His wide-ranging explorations of identity, privacy, and obsession were "showing myself to myself" and "turning in on myself." An intellectually-garrulous man with a spider-like body and long stringy hair, Acconci once sat at a table at Max's, the art world restaurant of the hour, and rubbed a spot on his left forearm until a sore developed. He titled this piece, which only he attended, *Rubbing Piece* (1969). Later that year, he trailed strangers on the street until he could follow them no further; this was *Following Piece*. Acconci bit himself, ran in place for two and a half hours, crushed live cockroaches in his pubic hair, and dressed his penis up in doll's clothes, all for the benefit of the video camera. In 1971 he blindfolded himself in the stairwell of a SoHo gallery with a heavy metal bar and threatened to assault anyone who dared approach. That year he also waited at the end of Pier 17 just west of SoHo each night at one a.m., volunteering to share a secret he had never revealed to anyone with anyone who showed up. Acconci's most notorious work, *Seedbed*, also in 1971, involved the construction of a ramp at the Sonnabend Gallery, under which the artist engaged in "a private sexual activity" for several hours each afternoon, his miked groans and live free-associative monologues broadcast over loudspeakers. This barely seemed scandalous within the conceptual hothouse of SoHo. Acconci's illustrations and fantasies had a comprehensible goal: "I used to think that art was not about therapy," he told an interviewer. "Now I think it is."

The therapeutic impulse – this merger of art and therapeutic values – was alive and well in SoHo. A search for psychic health and meaning had been a cornerstone of twentieth-century modernism denounced or ignored by formalist criticism, and specifically targeted by Clement Greenberg as literally the enemy of Art. Therapy & Art intertwined in SoHo like the Bramble and the Rose, providing a highlight of the broad-based recovery of art for artists' sake. It's fair in this context to call Feminism therapy, certainly much more than therapy, but essentially the voice of women's personal liberation. Performance artist and painter Carolee Schneeman was a feminist avatar. News from the industrial wastelands of downtown Los Angeles spoke of Suzanne Lacy, Rachel Rosenthal, and others creating feminist performance art, emphasizing conscious actions within life. Eleanor Antin recorded daily nude shots of a thirty-day diet; Linda Montano and Tom Marioni handcuffed themselves together for three days in San Francisco, and documented the experience. Living in "Berzerkly," Howard Fried framed most of the events of his daily life as performance art. Much of these early '70s' performance fell somewhere between self-help and therapeutic exorcism.

The best-known and the least laid-back performance artist of the era was Californian Chris Burden, who undertook a lunatic series of self-inflicted art-punishments, using shock and boredom to test American perceptions of violence and pain. Burden's bizarre acts of public masochism included having himself crucified with nails on the roof of a Volkswagen, and sealed inside a high school locker for six days. He once crawled fifty feet over broken glass with his hands tied behind his back, and hid under a canvas in the middle of a busy thoroughfare in L.A. – a performance piece that resulted in his arrest as a public nuisance. All of this had happened in the name and spirit and community of "Art." In his most famous art action, Burden had a friend shoot him in the arm with a .22 caliber rifle at a Venice art gallery in 1972, producing a wound larger than the one he had anticipated. (Laurie Anderson wrote a song for Burden: "It's Not the Bullet that Kills You, It's the Hole.") As Burden himself later explained in an influential new Lower Manhattan art journal, *Avalanche,* "How can you know what it feels like to be shot, if you don't get shot?" (Seriously?) Early in 1974, Burden came to SoHo to lie face-up in the freight elevator at 112 Workshop, while an audience volunteer stuck four pins into his bare torso, observed via closed circuit from the gallery floor.

"Whenever you do life consciously, life becomes pretty strange," acknowledged Kaprow, newly-installed as art professor at U. C. San Diego. This was a decent summation of the Art-in-Life spirit of a post-revolutionary time. Performance and video artists risked their own seriousness to explore possibilities that resisted treatment in any other way, reflecting a community desire to de-commodify art and bring it closer to life, freed from the constraints of galleries and museums. New York's commercial galleries continued to serve "as school, forum, and news transmitter," as the city cultural commissioner Henry Geldzahler noted in 1969, but the most communal, therapeutic aspects of '70s' post-minimalist, conceptual, video, and performance art initiated a process that confirmed the non-profit alternative space, where much of this action took place, as a hallmark of the decade.

NATURE, MOVEMENT, AND THE BODY

SoHo's dancers in the '60s in the main were *naturvolker* adhering to the pioneer hardiness of the loft movement, emphasizing interpersonal communication and the spirit, stripping bodies of urban stress and re-conditioning them as more sensitive, humane instruments in time and space. Exploring Art and Life, Culture and Nature, inner vision and "just the facts, ma'am," dance in SoHo became a countercultural flashpoint asking a fundamental question: how would a natural body move?

Simone Forti – born in Italy from parents who fled antisemitic persecution – grew up in L.A. and after Reed College in Oregon and time in San Francisco, performed for the first time in SoHo in 1960. She avoided the emerging scene at Judson Church, staying largely in the Happening and performance art worlds. Her experience at the Woodstock Festival in '69 inspired her to sell her Downtown loft (for $4,000) and move to a commune in the countryside, to be herself, and move there.

"Most of the serious hippies ended up in the country," Simone's friend Trisha Brown would remark years later, and Simone made good use of her time, returning to the city a few years later to continue exploring elemental human activities – crawling, walking, and circling – along with what she termed "animal empathy," human equivalents to the movements of mammals, birds, and reptiles. Forti could swoop from a brisk bipedal walk into a brisk four-pointed crawl, then become upright again, without any apparent transition or loss of momentum – a feat of virtuosity (just try it) that seemed to recapitulate the phylogenetic evolution of the whole human race. For Forte, dancing had become a holistic quest for a "state of enchantment" that she likened to the physical response of infants, or to Carlos Castaneda's idea of the "warrior" – "a state the warrior can be into where his powers are awakened," and conducted parallel explorations of meditation, t'ai ch'i, and visual imagery to generate movement. She also undertook a formal study of vertebrate anatomy, kinesiology, and relaxation techniques.

Simone and Trisha Brown used to climb a fire escape and slip through an open window to improvise on a good hardwood floor they discovered in an abandoned building just northeast of SoHo. Brown had a classically-proportioned, supple body and a vulnerable fearlessness. Trisha was a "wild, out-there animal" in her early Judson days, according to her good friend Bob Rauschenberg. In *Yellowbelly* ("which means 'coward' in my hometown of Aberdeen, Washington"), Trisha invited viewers to shout out the title if they wanted her to keep moving.

Brown was interested in the links between improvisation and community, but she had an infant son to raise and was unable to dance as much as she liked. Early residence in a top floor loft at 80 Wooster Street required frequent trips to the basement for buckets of water, and on one occasion, concealment, while a city fireman pounded on her door, shouting, *"Who's in dere?"* When she did find time to dance, her improvisations focused on private issues of body, spirit, space, and illusion, leading to her signature blend of antic seriousness and kinesthetic glory.

Her "equipment pieces" included *Man Walking Down the Side of Building* (1970), which was precipitously that: a block-and-tackled stroll down the back of 80 Wooster, seven flights to the ground below. *Walking on the Walls of the Whitney Museum* (1971) put her on the dance map horizontally – an illusion undercut by the visible ropes and pulleys (funded by Rauschenberg) that made her defiance of gravity possible.

"I have in the past felt sorry for the ceilings and walls," said Brown, deadpan. "It's perfectly good space, why doesn't anyone use it?"

Rooftops were usable spaces, too: that year, she stationed dancers on top of buildings above a twelve-block area of SoHo, relaying semaphoric flag signals from body to body, downtown for fifteen minutes, then uptown the same.

The post-minimalist notion of dance as "information" eventually took Brown far from improvisation to the creation of dances whose structures were "visible and bare bones simple." For *Accumulation* (1971), performed to the Grateful Dead's "Uncle John's Band" – a song about learning to lean together in frightening times – Brown began with a gentle, rotating twist of the fist, followed by a repetition of the same gesture with an added turn of the left thumb, then repeated both movements followed by a brushing foot, and so on, accumulating an A, A-B, A-B-C, A-B-C-D accumulations down to the lower reaches of the alphabet. Fatigued one afternoon, she lay down on her studio floor and made *Primary Accumulation* (1972) – an eighteen-minute "supine solo" analogous to a Carl Andre aggregation of bricks or the poured lead sculptures of Richard Serra. This relentless logic culminated with *Group Primary Accumulation* (1973), a company piece performed in Battery Park, then outside a Midtown office building, and finally on a series of rafts in Loring Lagoon in Minneapolis.

Brown's increasingly-sophisticated image of the body as both the subject and object of inquiry projected an amused intelligence and improvisatory naturalness that furthered her conception of the dancer as an ordinary person with extraordinary sensitivity and skills – an attitude indissolubly linked to the concerns of SoHo post-minimalism.

Another Judson Dance Theater participant was inspired by the work of SoHo minimal and post-minimal visual artists, in particular their fascinations with the Grid, a of the modernist preoccupation with form and style, said the art critic Rosalind Kraus. Lucinda Child was herself all angles and classical curves who had not flourished in the McLuhanite '60s. Her unhappy experience in the 1966 Bell Laboratory's "Experiments in Art and Technology" at the 69th Regiment Armory on the Upper East Side triggered an opposing urge "to reconnect myself with *movement* – however simple, however stark." Pursuing studies in ballet, gymnastics, and tai chi, writing dance criticism on the side and teaching on occasion, Childs worked privately in her Downtown loft with fellow dancer Judy Padow, exploring a catalog of slowly-permuting walks, runs, jumps and rolls, executed with obsessive concentration on the steps themselves.

"What gave me the courage to continue was the lack of 'pure' geometry in Frank Stella, in Larry Poons," said Childs, who was living in Poons' building near Canal Street. "Or a single line in Barnett Newman. He didn't paint the thing with a ruler, he did it *by hand.*"

In her early works – *Calico Mingling* (1973) and *Congeries on Edges for 20 Obliques* (1975) – Childs' post-dancerly abstraction rang all sorts of changes on the simplest themes and patterns: tracing curves, grids and diagonal patterns with a minimum variety of steps, subtly magnifying and framing aspects of dance that usually escape notice. *Untitled Solo* (1968), her last work until a group version surfaced at the Whitney five years later, looked like an exercise in reductive repetition, but Childs' structures, which were executed without music or sound other than the feet and breath, would eventually later yield a solution to a problem that did not yet vex post-Judson dance in SoHo, but would eventually: how to organize movement with enough breadth, velocity and momentum to fill an opera house stage. This was of no concern to Yvonne Rainer, who many considered the central Judson Church choreographer. Rainer was making "dances" in the art world context of anti-art, and even anti-dance.

"No to spectacle, No to virtuosity, No to transformations and magic and make-believe," she urged in her influential post-minimalist manifesto of 1965. "No to the glamour and transcendency of the star image. No to the heroic. No to the anti-heroic. No to trash imagery. No to involvement of performer or spectator. No to style. No to camp. No to seduction of spectator by the wiles of the performer. No to eccentricity. No to moving or being moved." With all these no's on the table, Rainer was one of four choreographers who appeared in the spring of 1968 for a week of experimental dance at the Billy Rose Theater on Broadway. Rainer's casual use of a blue movie prompted the *Times'* dance critic Clive Barnes to blast the Ford Foundation for funding the event. *The New Yorker's* Arlene Croce took a tougher stance, declaring that Rainer's work was "no more interesting than an ant farm... or six-year-olds in some inordinately supervised sandbox." Among Rainer's concerns was her increasing ambivalence about "choreographing" the behavior of others. The formalism of her seminal *Trio A* (1966), which involved no music, only a seamless flow of everyday movements – toe tapping, walking, kneeling and the like – suddenly seemed "tenuous and remote" from the social crisis. For *Continuous Project – Altered Daily* (1969-70), Rainer went behind the scenes to make a dance about making a dance from rehearsal to performance, while at the same time leaving room for what she hoped would be the "spontaneous behavior" of performers.

Continuous Project – Altered Daily – its title and concept stolen from an arrangement of earth and discarded metal that Robert Morris was exhibiting and altering daily in Leo Castelli's Downtown warehouse – premiered at the Whitney Museum uptown, where it met with considerable acclaim. At a subsequent performance in Kansas City, the improvisations of Steve Paxton, David Gordon, and two former Cunningham dancers, Barbara Dilley and Douglas Dunn, literally took over the show – an effect which Rainer found painful, but also exhilarating. "I got glimpses of human behavior that my dreams for a better life are based on," she wrote to Dilley – "real, complex, constantly in flux, rich, concrete, funny, focused, immediate, specific, intense, serious at times to the point of religiosity, light, diaphanous, silly, and many leveled at any particular point." Out of many discussions and explorations, an improvisational dance company calling itself the Grand Union – named in part after SoHo's nearest supermarket – brought together some of the neighborhood's star dance-conceptualists for no higher purpose than their communal self-invention in a pluralistic age.

Grand Union appearances were grand re-unions of larger Downtown communities—a chance for dancers, performance and theater artists, sculptors, painters, poets, to see what SoHo's hot-house in-house improv ensemble had dreamed up next.

Performances might begin when company members entered the arena – a gym, a loft, or a church – dressed in workout clothes, carrying a few props and a record player, and sometimes nothing at all. At times they seemed like they were just goofing off, but on innumerable occasions the Grand Union was breath-taking, even profound – courting high-wire disaster with dance virtuosity and commonplace pedestrianism, TV schtick and backstage horseplay, raw character-building and vintage character-breaking. "The medium is people," said Paxton, echoing Andy Warhol, "and what they are doing to and with each other."

Always willing to laugh at itself, the group gradually developed an even more presentational style, beginning at a February 1972 performance at 112 Greene, when Rainer started hysterically demanding to know who stole her eyeshadow. An unexpected battle with cancer forced Rainer to leave the group in 1973, at which point Paxton, Dilley, Gordon and Dunn were joined by Trisha Brown and Nancy Lewis. The revitalized Union dipped into a seemingly bottomless bag of routines and schticks, B-movie parodies, athletic events, pop tunes, and free-associational patter. "Everything was fair game except fair game," says Brown. Personas coalesced: Trisha, the flyaway wit; Dilley, the mystic princess of her own fantasia; Dunn, the elegant urban loner; Gordon, the showbiz conceptualist; Lewis, the wily Petrouchka; Paxton, the can-do-anything Athlete of the Spirit. By 1974, *Artforum* was complaining that the group had fallen into "a crowd-pleasing trip," but such things were relative.

"You could sit through endless hours of boring shit to catch two minutes of Douglas and Steve dancing together, and suddenly the whole thing was worth it," JoAnne Akalaitis would recall years later. Despite legendary status, the Grand Union was experiencing strains from within the group. *The SoHo News* reported its approaching breakup, for reasons a lot of groups were breaking up in those days: weariness over money struggles, disagreements on aesthetic matters, personal rivalries, and a desire to focus on individual careers. But folks stayed in touch, so when George Macuinas located an 1868 cast-iron building for sale at 541 Broadway and told Trisha about it, Trisha called Lucinda, Douglas, and Gordon & Valda. Each took a floor in a magnificent building that extended a city block to Mercer Street, where more floors were taken by performance artist Joan Jonas and the museum painter Jasper Johns.

541 Broadway was hosting a cadre of post-Judson choreographers who would help determine, as *Voice* critic Jill Johnston had prophesied, "the major directions in the dance of the next decade or two."

A REVOLUTIONARY MOVEMENT:
Spinning in Contemporary Theater and Dance,
Village Voice, June 1978

Note: *Writing for the* SoHo Weekly News *and the* Village Voice *about dance, theater, and performance (also about a political boycott and boxing and some other stuff), I found myself thinking about the phenomenology of Spinning—turning in one place. I would start similar essays about Walking and Jumping for* Sports Illustrated, *which I have somewhere, but this was the only one that was published. I am not sure that I succeeded in discovering the fate of the universe in the turning dance of the Malevi, the "Whirling Dervishes," but I did my best.*

A common view of the universe has everything spinning around something else: the earth around its axis, the moon around the earth, the earth and planets around the sun, and the sun around the distant center of the Milky Way – a sister black hole, the sky's symmetrical negation, an invisible companion ten times closer than the nearest star.

Sitting at my breakfast table, I add milk, stir once, and lift the spoon away. Café au lait swirls around the center of a perimeter of china. The fate of the universe is less clear than the behavior of our local stars and morning coffee. If the universe exploded from a mighty block of matter eons ago, then the site of this primordial bang is center and source, with everything hurtling away in birth, humanity making culture on an infinitesimal spec of the shattered egg, bright in the hope that space bends, as Einstein predicted, that curves and returns are fated – that the universe itself is an enclosure, like the Dervish in the whirling dance. More recent evidence has suggested that if there is a center to the universe, the center does not hold, and no longer can; the universe exploded too rapidly, and lacks the gravity to re-convene itself, dooming the centrifugal universe to bleed into infinite space and dissipate – a cosmic death without rebirth. In this view, cosmology is permanently altered. We're looking at something that will happen only once, and won't be happening again.

This conflict in modern science suggests the difficulties of thinking about the startling emergence of Spinning as a statement and practice in American theater and dance. Laura Dean, Andy de Groat, the Iowa Theater Lab, Kenneth King, Robert Wilson and many others have employed spinning/whirling/turning as a central metaphor or major element of their presentation. The spinner spins in contemplation of an inner gyroscope, but the spinner has also become a performer in a public space, part of wider conversations. The first thought is that this is some kind of Gnostic revival: the Dervishes have come West. "What is the whirling dance," asked Rumi, 13th century founder of the Whirling Dervishes, a Sufi branch of Islam, in a recent translation by W.S. Merwin.

> "a greeting
> from the center of the heart
> their messages arrive
> and the whole universe is renewed"

The spinner is at the center, the still point of the turning world. The spinner forms a Mandala of Self. "Philosophy is finished. Now is the time for love," said Sheik Muzaffer of the Malevi, the Whirling Dervishes. But spinners in contemporary performance aren't necessarily trying to hold the world together, renew the universe, or recuperate some religious truth. Spinning requires a physical center or you fall on your bum, but the center doesn't have to be anything more than a physical axis. It doesn't need to be a mystical heart.

"It doesn't seem to me there's much to it," says Kit Cation, who has spun in works of Robert Wilson and Andy de Groat. "You just do it." Spinning can have a spiritual purpose outside the context of a Sufi order: the "Arica" human potential training developed by Oscar Ichazo and a team of devotees in the village of Arica, Chile, employs spinning for long periods of time. [*I had practiced spinning at an Arica training in Big Sur two years earlier.*] Spinning can be simply a way of moving, anatomic and kinetic, a matter of velocity and weight. In its simplicity, spinning is part of the postmodern project to re-sensitize dancers and dance audiences to more fundamental human motion.

Spinners in the lofts of lower Manhattan know this isn't Konya, Turkey, where the Malevi make their home. Knowing where you are is important for everybody, including the ecstatic Dervishes. Andy de Groat's heroic turners who filled the Metropolitan Opera House stage in Act III, Scene II of Robert Wilson and Philip Glass's *Einstein on the Beach*, like the dancers in Laura Dean's contemporary rituals, challenge ordinary notions of time, boredom, and repetition in performance, discovering new life within what Susanne Langer, an American philosopher known for her theories on art on the mind, called the Magic Circle: the source of dance, rhythm, energy, and impulse.

Spinning gives us time to think, and is humanizing if only for that. Its "playful physics," as Marcel Duchamp might have said, is nerve-racking for the impatient, boring for the inattentive, and a head-trip for head-trippers. "The more minimal the art, the more maximum the explanation," Hilton Kramer has sneered, though one could just as easily argue the opposite – that spinning's literalness creates a kind of aesthetic silence. Spinning can be a chance to observe oneself being nervous, bored, or abstracted. At its best, spinning and watching other people spin can create a loss of an adamant sense of performer / spectator. The separation of Life and Art evaporates in a grace of change, a meditation on the wind, the patterns of feet and arms, the moment's catch and the gap, the recollection of thoughts, and the stereoscopic world. "Spinning is the attempt to take in all the horizon at once," said the mid-twentieth-century modern dance master José Limon. Frances Alenikoff of SoHo's Eden's Expressway, a dance space on Broadway, spins, too: "It's nice to have the world turning around you finally."

For some of you, Spinning is also a quick way to lose your lunch. Laura Dean worked with a dancer who vomited at every rehearsal. Dean teaches spinning by asking people to put their hands together and look at their thumbs, then start stepping around themselves. If you keep reversing directions, you don't get as dizzy. It's harder to go slow than fast, De Groat will tell me. "People are either natural turners or they can't turn at all." Spinning is what meets the eye, and a great deal more at the same time. "The more perfect the dance," Susanne Langer wrote, "the less we see its actualities." From that perspective, Spinning is perfection.

Downtown's Edwin Denby, arguably the greatest living dance critic, understood something: "The idea that you can understand something only if you can verbalize it is what I don't think is true or useful." Is spinning something we can even talk about? Or is it pure evacuation? Humans have been spinning in dance for a long time. The Western classical ballet dancer pirouettes in toe shoes or on the balls of feet. An old Black comedian from the Chitlin' Circuit and *The Red Foxx Show* turned on his knees, crawling around himself like a speeding armadillo. The famed Circus aerialist Alfredo Cardona, the first man to do a triple somersault in performance, spun at 75 miles per hour attempting his quadruple, which he never stuck. Professional ice skaters commonly spin at forty to fifty mph, but Bobby Crockett of *Holiday on Ice* spins even faster. He becomes completely featureless in his spin, a technical realization of the Sufi dream of non-substantiation.

Christopher Knowles, a mentally-different 18-year-old who has co-authored and performed in some of Robert Wilson's most extraordinary work, has a particularly vivid spinning style: wild, but somehow under control, obedient to a center that is almost unobservable. "Chris spins to charge his batteries or when he gets really excited," says de Groat, who says that learning to spin is simply learning to walk with no front or back. "Christopher is antigravitational. He seems to levitate sometimes." I was at a Lower East Side dance party when I watched Chris watching a "Crazy Eddie" commercial on TV. His face was three inches above and three inches away from the screen. His body was trembling with excitement. At the end of the sixty seconds, and the world-famous sign off—"Crazy Eddie's prices are... *insane!*" Chris leapt up with lightning quickness on to a nearby bed and began to spin – galloping around himself on the whirled sheets and blankets, looking over his shoulder as if in high-speed pursuit of his own left arm, and also seemingly in danger of entangling himself in the bedding and seriously injuring himself, but somehow never coming close to falling. Watching with me was Simone Forti, a postmodern dance legend, who after several minutes turned to me and said, "You know, I've always felt very close to Christopher."

Forti and Terry O'Reilly moved around while Peter Van Ripe spun with his saxophone in the sanctuary at St. Marks Church, the sound distorting as he turned and played. Repetitive turning has a long history in traditional modern dance, from pioneers Mary Wigman and Ted Shawn (in *The Mevlevi Dervish,* Shawn was reputed to be the greatest turner of them all) to José Limon and Ann Halprin, the latter in *The Prophetess*, a dance from 1955. Both Dean and de Groat told me that Barbara Dilley, who danced with Merce Cunningham and The Grand Union, the great improvisatory troupe of the late '60s and early '70s, was the most exquisite turner of all. Back in the early '70s, Dilley performed *Dancing Before the Beloved* in a loft on Crosby Street in SoHo, spinning utterly naked, bedecked with garlands of white flowers. "My Hindu phase," she told me when we spoke about it at Naropa, a Buddhist institute in Boulder, Colorado. And Dilley is spinning still: *Field,* a dance to a Philip Glass score with a superimposed free-form bass line and environmental sounds of a corn field (flies buzzing), performed in Colorado, Vancouver, and Seattle just last year. *Field* ended with three minutes of Dilley turning in place.

A spinning body as the site of its own mechanics: what was the muscle in the front of my calf that bothered me when I first learned to spin? Around and around and around we go, where we stop, nobody knows.

Kenneth King suggested that if I really wanted to write about spinning, I should write about my own experience, because he didn't want to talk about his. "It's something you do," he told me, and something he's been doing since the late '60s. In King's most recent work, *Dance S(p)ell,* performed at BAM in March, Kathy Ray and Charles Dennis seemed to be spinning backwards around themselves, looking over their shoulders as if falling through the air, then walking to another spot in the performing arena to turn again, slower this time, like they were falling beyond words into a place where time had vanished.

"Ah swear to me again," wrote the German Romantic Novalis, "that you will be mine forever. Love is endless repetition." Spinning in front of people, you don't necessarily feel separate or apart; you first have a sense that something is being done. In her program notes for *Spiral,* performed at BAM last fall, Laura Dean wrote that spinning is done in the dances of the Dervishes, in South American Candomblé, and in South Indian, African, and European folk dances. But "my favorite image of spinning is the five-year-old who spins until he or she falls in a dizzy, laughing heap." Dean's work has been likened to folk dancing, but she sees spinning as movement that "clears my head." In its simplicity, it's a correlative to motionlessness. Spinning can create a space where concepts and associations fall away, and as the dervishes claim, the intellect is lifted out of the turning body. "Stop acting so small," Rumi told his disciples. "You are the universe in ecstatic motion."

Julia Busto and de Groat spun for three hours on a four-by-four-foot platform raised on stilts in an orchestra pit between the stage and the audience in Wilson's 1974 work on Broadway, *A Letter for Queen Victoria.* "A visual drone," Douglas Dunn called it. They turned slowly for the most part, uniting performers and viewers in their net of seeing.

"Spinning is like being there," Busto tells me.

"'Like being where?" I ask her. "What does that mean?"

"It's a way of discovering your center, if you think you have one."

Busto now lives in India as a Tibetan nun. Because of her Buddhist practices, de Groat found her the perfect person to spin with. Tibetans place the dream eye at the base of the throat, near the brain's motor center: movement and dream touching.

"The interesting thing about spinning at first wasn't to perform it," Ritty Burchfield told me. "It was a personal yoga."

Burchfield took Busto's place for a week on *Letter* when Busto fell ill, and has worked with Wilson and de Groat ever since. The first time she ever spun, during one of de Groat's early workshops in Paris, she did it for an hour and a half. She never gets the least bit sick or dizzy.

She claims she once spun for six hours in her living room and came out of it feeling refreshed, as if she'd just gone for a long, invigorating walking.

"Learning spinning bent over or spotting the ceiling is hard, but the rest of it isn't that bad," she claims. With her special gift, she has spun all over the world – "it's all I do," she tells me facetiously. Some stood to applaud her solo turning in *Einstein*. Watching Ritty Burchfield spin, there is nothing to spinning, except *spinning*. Kenneth King told me, "Ritty and Kathy Ray [another Wilson/de Groat dancer] are the purest experience of spinning in America."

The Dervishes of Konya (from *darwish:* at the door) require students to complete three months of training on a three-foot-wide platform with their first and second toes lodged around a heavy nail. Only after mastering the no-doubt bloody nail can a student enter the Sema, or Dance. The Whirling Dervishes have come to New York only once, in 1972, and according to their current leader will never return. Andy de Groat was in Konya when they were in New York, where Laura Dean saw them, and remembers. "It's slower than I like to do; it's a sort of crossover step with an up-and-down wave, very beautiful and meditative."

"It's not possible to repeat movement," Dean claims. All of her dances are concerned with repetition, patterns of geometry, and evidence, though her dances also have added licks of what look like African dancing, clog step dancing, and the Supremes on busman's holiday. Watching her spinners in *Spiral* turning in tight concentric circles amidst one another reminded me of the deaf-mute tango dancers in Thomas Pynchon's *The Crying of Lot 49*, whose protagonist Oedipus Maas speculates about how long "could it go on before collisions become a serious hindrance. There would have to be collisions. The only alternative was some unthinkable order of music, many rhythms, all keys at once, a choreography in which each couple meshed easy, predestined. Something they all heard with an extra sense atrophied in herself." Dean says:

"We're not hoping we don't hit. We know where we are. Most of the time." As with de Groat's work, spinning in tight formations makes the viewer aware of how people organize and cooperate physically, and how important it is to gather inside oneself to be in relationship with others.

In October 1970, Dean gave two workshops at the Byrd Hoffman School, Robert Wilson's loft on Spring Street in SoHo, asking her class to walk in figure eights carrying candles. Participants also spun. Curiously, De Groat was in Iowa at the time, working with Wilson on *Deafman Glance*. Listening to Sibelius one evening, he simply stood up and turned. "I had a feeling like I'd been taken," he says. He had no sense of time passing, but knows he danced to the whole side of the record.

There is an innateness to de Groat's turning. He has beautiful comportment, but little formal training, which seems to have contributed to his quiet directness and his lack of preciousness about moving. Burchfield tells me, "Andy doesn't turn, he whirls. In spinning, you make your own space, but Andy is the only person I spin with who makes me feel I am in the same space he is." As he whirled to Philip Glass's manic organ music in an eight-foot clearing in St. Mark's Church on January 1st, 1976, encircled by spectators, including me, all of us cross-legged style on the floor, I never worried about him losing his balance and falling into our laps. As Wilson's choreographer and companion, De Groat introduced spinning in Wilson's *Life and Times of Joseph Stalin* in 1973, after working out a lot of his ideas in Paris the previous year. (Wilson himself spins with a center that is off balance, bouncing on the tips of his toes, arms chopping the air like scissors. "It's very bizarre," says de Groat.)

"At first my spinning was very isolated, soloistic, kind of virtuosic. At the next stage, people began to watch me and think about what it was. Then I moved into spinning to connect people spatially, and developed things like spotting and the gestures. The beginning of all that was worked out in Paris." Of Wilson's early works, de Groat prefers *A Letter to Queen Victoria*, which had a brief Broadway run. "The piece was about listening, and there we were, listening to the audience. We helped unite it; visually, too. All of Bob's work has been about that — bridging the gap, not separating performance from just being there and doing it. Bob asked me to do two dances in his new piece

[*Death, Destruction and Detroit,* which premiered in Berlin in 1979], but I turned it down. Those big production pieces are just too crazy."

De Groat has been doing solo spinning performances for years now, but *Angie's Waltz,* only the second large group piece he has done apart from Wilson, had one short spinning sequence. Composer Alan Lloyd's "Perpetua Mobile" made spinning's romantic associations clearer than Philip Glass's more austere repetitions. I asked de Groat if his latest work in progress, *Get Wreck,* would also include spinning.

"I don't know yet. I shut my eyes and listen to the music and I see spinning, but I don't know." In the end it did include spinning, which was used to transition between phrases, gathering movements to bundle sections, and to my eyes and feelings, it did just that.

Imagine, if you will, that your attention has slipped. Then empathize with people who think watching spinning is a perfect waste of time. *The New Yorker's* Arlene Croce finds spinning "a bore. It's like waiting for someone to get off the phone and back into conversation." She feels that anything done in performance more than forty times in succession loses its dynamics as dance – the number forty presumably getting her over the classic thirty-two *fouetté* turns in *Swan Lake.* But watching people spinning challenges the very idea of boredom, in terms similar to what Renata Adler described in her novella *Speedboat:* "It is not at all self-evident what boredom is. It implies, for instance, an idea of duration. It would be crazy to say, for three seconds there, I was bored. It implies indifference but, at the same time, requires a degree of attention. One cannot properly be bored by anything one hasn't noticed."

To think of spinning as boring is to pay insufficient respect to the intelligence of your own attention. Boredom is a play of indifference and attention. Spinning in performance isn't entertainment so much as a potential mutual involvement of performer and spectator – an intersubjective meditation. There's something fascinating, at least I think there is, about watching a body presenting itself in such a simple, wholly visible way. Spinning can do more than that, too. Spinning also provokes specific thoughts and feelings, and almost inevitably does. In Wilson and Knowles' *$ Value of Man* (1975), the spinners seem self-enclosed – victims, perhaps, of Capitalism; in *Einstein,* the spinners are triumphant, human, heroic, and at the same time electronic, playing out a sketch in their floor patterns of the physicist's great discoveries. Amy Greenfield's video piece *Dervish* seemed to relate spinning with sexual ecstasy: she cries out and stumbles through her last turns, and finally collapses, panting in a heap. Spinning doesn't homogenize people. Frank Conversano, the shiny-bearded dancing bear who has worked with Wilson, de Groat, and David Woodberry, spins differently than Grethe Holby, a slender M.I.T.-educated dancer who has had a lot of dance training.

Robyn Brentano spins herself and has filmed Busto and de Groat turning with ropes in *Syracuse Sequence:* "Spinning is a way to cut through this idea of representation," Brentano claims. "Watching it or doing it can create gaps in [the perception of performers and audiences that create a sense of spaciousness that isn't either 'descriptive' or conceptual, particularly." Wilson has spoken in a similar vein about how repetition and boredom cause people to give up identifying with what they see.

But Spinning can represent everything from confusion to exaltation, self-enclosure to self-exposure, and a host of things in-between. The improvisation-based, non-verbal Iowa Theater Lab performed *Catskill Dervish* at the Entermedia Theater in November 1977. Most of the Lab's performers seemed to have never related to their bodies before the house lights went down. Warped by personal histories, lacking the standardization brought about by formal training, they were overweight and underfed, with hunched shoulders, collapsed chests, and flat feet, and running in a tight circle with ritual grunts and chanting for long minutes. They left the stage with the audience still sitting in a circle around a now-empty space—confronted with the presence of an absence as we listened to the chanting that continued off stage. When the performers return, their arms interlocked, one of them is naked.

A man slips the circle of dancers and spins madly on his own. Another man trips him as he spins, but the man rises and continues to spin. A Christ figure now, he is spat upon by everyone. Then his turning slows and a woman approaches to kiss him hard on the mouth. A man arrives and does the same. I am struck by the Iowa Theater Lab's commitment to these activities. The Lab is primitive in its lack of polish, but it's not a nostalgic: their energy is grounded in a community of shared purpose. Rick Zank, director of the Iowa Theater

Lab, has taught spinning to differently-abled kids in Baltimore, and reports that it brought many out of their shyness.

Spinning with other people suggests the possibility of a collective as well as an individual selfhood. Autocrats and totalitarians don't like people's personal lives very much. The father of modern Turkey, Kemal Ataturk, so disapproved of the Dervishes' supposedly "primitive" religious practice that he banned it in 1925. The God-intoxicated could not spin legally in Turkey until 1953. Even today, Dervishes are permitted to spin for only two weeks a year, around the time of Rumi's birthday in December, although reports of illegal spinning in Istanbul are most likely true. Spinning in Turkey is a political statement, because it is an affirmation of a private space. I enjoy watching spinning because I enjoy watching a simple movement performed from a physical center. It centers me, or empties me of a center, I have no way of knowing which. And I don't mind not knowing, watching a good spinner spin.

Are we orphans on a spinning planet, our planet an orphan in space, or are we revolving in the mechanics of the curve? The muscle in the front of my calf is the *Peroneus Longus*, a Latin name in an extinct language. Also in Latin: *Haec decies repetita placebit:* things that are repeated are pleasing. On the other hand, everything may be happening only once, which means the best response might just be to pay mindful attention.

"THE THEATER OF IMAGES:"
Monk, Wilson, Foreman, The Performance Group, And Mabou Mines

The Theater of Images was the name given to "the great Elizabethan flowering" of Downtown experimental theater in the '60s and '70s. More than any other art form with the exception of dance, I harnessed myself to a Golden Age of Downtown theater—an idyll (or so it seemed from my perspective at the time) that seemed to end only a few years after I arrived. This chapter concludes with remarks on the Downtown close of the strange post-revolutionary period between the '60s and '70s.

The surge of theatricality in the postwar avant-garde opened tremendous reservoirs of collective feeling across the performing arts of Lower Manhattan. An "Elizabethan era," as Richard Schechner framed it, was climaxing in the visionary theater collectives of SoHo, the capstone of one of the great eras in twentieth-century American theater history – an era of formal precision, ritual enchantment, therapeutic play, and public participation, reflecting powerful communal urges in a world that seemed to many to be on the verge of some cataclysmic upheaval. Performing artists continued the boundary-busting, genre-bending spirit of the '60s whenever they investigated time and space in musical and imagistic ways. SoHo's earliest non-linear, site-specific "operas" were also linked to "the sonic, possibilities, ranges and gut meanings of Asian and 'primitive' theaters, where there is no hard division between music, dance and drama," as Schechner, leader of the Performance Group on Wooster Street, had written. "Music-Theater," a term newly-coined by composer Eric Salzman, was meant as "a catch-phrase encompassing the great range of work falling in the gap between traditional opera and musical comedy." Downtown theater also had roots in art world Happenings, the political work of the Bread & Puppet Theater, and the Living Theatre in the '60s. But one younger composer, singer, and dancer went off on a search for what she called "the wholeness of the human being," reviving tribal emotions and long-lost worlds of childhood memory and play.

"MEREDITH MONK was born in Lima Peru" ran the playful playbill bio at the ill-starred Billy Rose Theater Broadway event in 1968: "grew up in the West riding horses/is Inca Jewish/lived in a red house.../started dancing lessons at the age of three because she could not skip/did Hippie love dance at Barney's Roaring 20's in California/has brown hair." Equal parts countercultural fantasist, wild child, and visionary saint, Monk at age twenty-five was an American original. Her vision was rooted in the Voice. Her mother had been the original Chiquita Banana ("And I'm Here to Say...") and a grandfather a violinist to the Russian Czar before founding a music conservatory in turn-of-the-century Harlem. Monk says that she was singing before she could talk. Her later vocalizations were likewise pre-verbal: nonsense syllables, repeated consonants and vowels, whining shrieks, microtonal yelps, and monkey chatters

– a medley of soul-sounds capable of surprising expressivity, purity, and range, with a fully-developed contralto vibrato shining behind the weirdest howls and folk-inflected syllables, lodging in the mind as ineffable states of being.

Monk studied dance, theater, composition, and voice in high school and at Sarah Lawrence College up the Hudson, leading even before graduation to her thinking about "the next thing," as she put it: "putting all these things together." Performing Downtown while still an undergraduate and living in a garret in the West Village after graduation, Monk plunged into the Happening and Off-Off Broadway scenes. Judson Dance Theater was inspirational, but as a member of its second generation, Monk felt more attracted to other things, including the notion of magic in an alchemical as much as a theatrical sense.

"Minimalism: I just couldn't squeeze my head into a cube," Monk would recall years later. "Yvonne Rainer thought I was a romantic, but I think instinctively I've always gone for the heart."

"John Cage says there's enough order," she once remarked. "I say there's enough chance." Monk resisted impersonal composition. Her influences were her contemporaries, including Kenneth King, an Oberlin grad in philosophy whose multi-channel theater events related to Cunningham and intermedia Happenings. Monk and King's collaboration at Judson, *Duet with Cat's Scream and Locomotive* (1966), yielded whacky results, but her Judson solo *Sixteen Millimeter Earrings* in November 1966 signaled the arrival of a major music-theater artist.

Red ribbons fluttered up from a white steamer trunk, where Monk dabbed her face with white paint, tore hair from her tattered wig, and lowered a white drum over her face as a surface for film projection. Then she rose completely naked from the trunk to hum a few bars of "Greensleeves." Scattered, outrageous, weirdly beautiful, *Earrings* "has the wit of its means and an emotion like that of a Jacobean drama," observed Arlene Croce, not usually a friend of Downtown performance. Monk moved on to a series of group works in her loft on Great Jones Street in "NoHo" – North of Houston Street – collaborating with six long-haired intimates, "found" personalities known collectively as The House.

Investigating architectural and non-theatrical settings, *Overload* and *Blueprint* were performed in various locations around Lower Manhattan, with maps informing audiences where to proceed to observe simultaneous events. Monk returned briefly to the proscenium as one of the four choreographers at the Billy Rose in '68, which included Monk on an otherwise empty stage, be-wigged, be-powdered, and be-gowned like a latter-day Marie Antoinette, accompanied by a recording of Ethel Merman belting out "There's No Business Like Show Business." Dime-store surrealism – but Monk claims to have been fortified by the debacle.

"It was complete liberation after that," she said twenty years later, "because I'd seen what I *didn't* want to do."

Wondering aloud "whether conditions in the world will make it possible to produce art because the survival factor will be so heavy," Monk went on to create a series of site-specific music-theater works for unusual environments, augmenting her utopian House with additional performers for each new event. The first installment of *Juice: A Musical Cantata in Three Installments* (1969) was a spectacle performed in the interior of the Guggenheim Museum on Fifth Avenue. Seventy-five white-clad "angels" chanted and hummed as they spiraled up the museum ramp, exploring the resonant acoustics of Frank Lloyd Wright's six-stories-high domed space. A quartet of combat-booted refugees in red clothes and red make-up trudged belly-to-back up the spiraling ramp, and the audience followed, moving past thirteen "living tableaux" in front of Pop canvases by Roy Lichtenstein. Then Monk – a petite, long-haired, slightly cross-eyed woman – appeared below, playing droning chords on an electric organ and singing a mewling song, like a muezzin's call.

Later that year, *Tour: Dedicated to Dinosaurs* was performed in the Dinosaur and Whale Rooms of the Smithsonian Institute in Washington D.C., and *Tour 2: Barbershop* was created for a museum in Chicago. Environmental music-theater was nothing new – Julian Beck and Judith Malina of the Living Theatre, the founding company of the postwar experimental theater, had attended an opera under the Manhattan Bridge in 1950 – but Monk's events were unique in part due to their minimal musical vocabulary, modeled on the ostinato patterns of folk music. Monk's music was shifting tapestries for the voice "to run on, fly over, slide down, cling to, weave through," she once wrote – evoking imaginary folk cultures or the Hebraic chanting of a midnight choir.

Vessel (1971), Monk's "opera-epic" about Joan of Arc, opened with an overture in Monk's new loft below West Broadway. Viewers observed a group of shadowy figures performing small, incongruous movements at a distant end of the space. Monk embodied the voices of St. Joan; performers also spoke lines from George Bernard Shaw. A King scattered coins and a woman picked them up; another woman unrolled her long hair; two soldiers dueled with rakes. The audience traveled next to the Performing Garage on Wooster Street in SoHo, where Monk had draped the set of another production with white muslin, creating a snowy mountain where Joan/Meredith, painted silver now, was tried before a court presided over by a King and Queen. *Vessel's* final section occurred a block south, in an empty parking lot (next to Soho's only gourmet grocery store), which had been transformed into an ancient battlefield and campsite across the street from an old Dominican church, the site of Joan's ultimate immolation and martyrdom, represented by thick sparks. (The church was ultimately demolished to build the SoHo Grand Hotel.)

A multi-form epic involving over a hundred volunteer performers, *Vessel* was the richest, most thematically-unified work that Monk and The House had yet produced, as well as a magical summation of the arts community that SoHo had become. "The Wagner of the Happening," as critic Adrian Henry called her, Monk had discovered a style of musical theater that bridged conscious and unconscious life, marking her one of the truest beginnings of what Michel Guy, director of the Avignon Festival in France, had termed (in 1971) "The Theater of Images," which along with performance art would become the most important movement in the performing arts of the decade of the '70s.

Monk's music-theater was romantic and Asian-influenced; the early "silent operas" of Robert Wilson were more classically Wagnerian, conveying spectators into what Wagner called a "spiritualized state of clairvoyance." A gifted therapist, painter, architect, stage designer, and a performer in some of Meredith Monk's early work, Wilson would bring a host of influences to bear on his theatrical evolution. But most importantly, it was his experience as a therapist that launched his earliest work—that, and his extraordinary insight (as critic Stefan Brecht observed) into "the nightmare and wonder of individuals who lack a social language."

Robert "Bob" Wilson was born and raised in Waco, Texas, the son of a middle-class lawyer who became City Manager, basically Waco's Mayor, and a housewife who he says never touched him until the day he left for college. Wilson grew up "knowing the drama of those who fight to conquer a language" (as an Italian critic would write), as he likely had a learning disability, and sometimes reads with awkward slowness. At seventeen he was relieved of an annoying stutter by a local ballet teacher, Mrs. Byrd Hoffman, who taught him how to take his time. Given to strange dramatic gestures in high school – he once recited an original poem, "Birdie, Birdie, Why Do You Bond So?" at school assembly – he was nevertheless a charismatic, popular figure, a fact attested to by warm tributes from classmates that fill his yearbooks.

Wilson began his performance career in children's theater at the University of Texas. His vision would never depart far from the perspective of childhood, including its dispensation from the rigors of adulthood. A business major and frat member at the University of Texas in Austin, Wilson returned to Waco during summers to run another children's theater, where on one occasion he wrapped a group of naked boys in saran wrap, something that his father considered "not only sick but abnormal." Leaving U.T. without a degree, Wilson moved to Paris to study painting, then came back to enroll in an architecture program at Pratt Institute in Brooklyn, where he continued to work with young people as a physical therapist. Eventually he moved on to work with brain-damaged and hyperactive children, the aged, and the terminally ill. Wilson proved to be an extraordinarily-gifted therapist, helping patients to perform simple, repetitive actions to stimulate mental activity and increase their confidence and self-awareness. Institutional authorities typically wanted their wards to become acceptable within the normal horizons of human life, but Wilson "encouraged them to do what they wanted to do," he says today, "instead of trying to correct or teach." Autistic children – those feral children of the psyche – seemed to him to possess a special innocence, an almost mystical insight into human experience. Fascinated by aberrant perception, Wilson intuitively suspected that some degree of abnormality is something everyone shares.

He became part of the Lower Manhattan arts community while still at Pratt, making short films, earth art, happenings, midnight theater events, as well as the masks for the Open Theater's Off-Broadway hit *America Hurrah*. He also performed in works by Kenneth King and Monk, who says he introduced himself by saying, "You're a star! You're a star!" ("That's Bob," Meredith told me.) Monk's *Blueprint* had performers seated motionless for an hour. Wilson drew further inspiration from the films of Andy Warhol, the writings of Isadora Duncan, and John Cage's seminal book, *Silence*. All influenced Wilson's sense of theatrical time, but the crucial figure in Wilson's eventual direction was Jack Smith, the transgressive gay filmmaker whose plotless *Flaming Creatures* (1963), inspired by the melodrama and excesses of Hollywood B-movies and burlesque, was a seminal influence across the performing arts of SoHo.

Additional influences included Merce Cunningham and George Balanchine. "I wondered if the theater could do the same things as dance, and just be an architectural arrangement in time and space."

Taking over the Open Theater's former Spring Street loft in 1967, Wilson continued to make performances, but within a year, discouraged by his failures as a painter, he flew back to Waco, took a cab forty miles outside of town, checked into a motel, and swallowed an overdose of sleeping pills. He survived, and was committed to a mental institution, where he dressed in a long robe, let his hair grow long, and barked like a dog at his parents. After an extended incarceration, he feigned normality sufficiently well to gain his release and return to New York, where he committed himself to visions larger than the painted rectangle.

SoHo's complex weave of anti-art and self-help merged in Wilson's "madness workshop," depoliticized from the heights of the Living Theatre's *Paradise Now* (1968), and recast as therapy. Through a series of workshops and performances, Wilson became the leader of a group of amateur disciples – "ordinary people, borderline psychotics," wrote Brecht – whose free-spirited behavior proved crucial to the development of Wilson's theater. The newly-named Byrd Hoffman School for Birds (Wilson sometimes called himself Byrd Hoffman) became a forum for improvisational frenzies, ritualistic slow-motion, and the mechanical repetition of meaningless tasks, often performed under the influence of psychoactive drugs, and sometimes not. Wilson came to think of theater as organized insanity, and a higher sanity, too. His work progressed without interpretation or psychological and symbolic implications. Wilson hated emotiveness, but the Laingian notion of "letting madness speak" fascinated him, believing as he did that people in "normal" reality are by definition unaware of what they're actually feeling.

Like many SoHo performing artists, Wilson had no problem working with "found" personalities – volunteers, friends and acquaintances, who had little in common except that Wilson saw something in them. Stefan Brecht later claimed that "it would be hard to find another group of people so into performing who are so ungifted for it," but a dozen or so of them were living together in a loft that Wilson paid for on Canal Street – living "on rice and moonbeams," as participant Ann Wilson remembers. "Nobody had jobs. Not when you got up at five in the morning and didn't go to bed until three in the morning. We were at the Spring Street loft working eighteen hours a day. Oh, it was crazy."

Wilson's most notable departure from nearly all of his Downtown contemporaries was his embrace of the proscenium arch. His latest work took place in framed environments where objects could float in space and animals appear in drawing rooms, on a time-scale fundamentally different from the rhythms of life – "time to think," said Wilson, an observation that Calvin Tomkins used as the title of his 1974 *New Yorker* profile. Wilson's psychologically inscrutable theater proceeded with the leisureliness of dreams – dark fantasies of psychosexual disaster paraded with an architect's sense of scale and a child's whimsy. For *The King of Spain* (1969), Wilson built twenty-foot-high cat's legs that could stride across a Victorian drawing room – a room that split in two, revealing a sunny "exterior" inspired by Gordon Matta-Clark's sliced-up architecture. Wilson moved both towards and away from some imagined unity, evoking both a Peaceable Kingdom and the Terrors of Childhood. *The Life and Times of Sigmund Freud* (1970) was a "silent opera" of apocalypse and redemption, involving a murderous woman and an innocent child.

Wilson's themes of impairment and of compassion for a helpless boy found their muse in 1968, when he rescued a ten-year-old Black orphan and deafmute from a beating at the hands of police. Institutional authorities considered Raymond Andrews to be incorrigible, but Wilson discovered Raymond's extraordinary capacity for remembering movement, as well as his ability to "hear" sounds and communicate with a voice that had never heard a spoken word. Arranging for Andrews to move into his Spring Street loft, Wilson adapted the boy's drawings as stage designs for another "silent opera" based on Raymond's contributions and Wilson's imaginings about his mind and perceptions. In a new series of workshops, the Byrds imitated Raymond's sounds and movements, as Wilson shaped dance, mime, and dream imagery into a three-and-one-half-hour mystery play that seemed to exist independently of analysis. *Deafman Glance* premiered in Paris in 1971 as a vision of extraordinary integrity and beauty. *Le Monde* hailed it as "a revolution in the plastic arts that occurs once or twice in a generation."

"After the howling and confusion, here is the rehabilitation of silence," wrote Jack Lang, head of the great performance festival in Avignon; "after the theater of gesticulation here is *the theater of images*" – the first use of a term later used as a book title by New York theater writer Bonnie Marranca. The English stage and film director Peter Brook, Max Ernst, Madame Pompidou, and French actor, director and mime artist Jean-Louis Barrault all praised *Deafman*. The "Absurdist" playwright Eugene Ionesco called the twenty-nine-year-old Texan the theater's greatest innovator (besides himself and Beckett) since William Shakespeare. The aging surrealist Louis Aragon, who had damned the rebels of '68, praised Wilson's "extraordinary freedom machine" in the form of a letter to his long-estranged friend, the father of the Surrealist Movement, Andre Breton, who had died five years earlier. "The miracle came about long after I stopped believing in them... The world of a deaf child opened up to us like a wordless mouth... I never saw anything more beautiful in the world since I was born."

"All of Paris read that review," Wilson would tell me later, "and in the morning I was famous."

Hailed as a genius in Europe, the 30-year-old director rejoined a burgeoning tribe of SoHo artists and performers moving into the '70s, contemplating work within the dimensions of natural phenomena, like dawn and dusk. Dressed in the plain dark sports jacket and horn-rimmed glasses of an insurance account executive, the six-foot-four-inch Texan with the whooping, shrieking laugh parlayed his new fame and fashionability into support well beyond traditional theater circles, attracting commitments from wealthy patrons in society, fashion, and the visual arts. Riding a wave of cultural chic, the Byrd Hoffman School was very much alive and thriving through the mid- '70s, with open movement workshops and an extended community of volunteers and workers that for a time contemplated forming a commune in British Columbia.

Wilson's Uptown contacts proved helpful: he collaborated with Broadway legend and New York City Ballet choreographer Jerome Robbins on the creation of a downtown experimental performance space, American Theater Laboratory, in 1965, and later inspired Robbins' *Watermill* (1971) for City Ballet. But the scale of Wilson's iconographic imagery and his exuberant personality had triggered the kind of high-culture worship that attracts growing numbers of wealthy patrons to his Spring Street loft: all sorts of "bigshots" (as one Byrd groundling called them) came Downtown to stoop under the Hoffman School's four-foot-high door and ogle Thursday nights' open movement workshops.

One patron was Paul Lepercq, whose family name would grace the upstairs space at BAM after 1974; the Grinsteins of Brentwood, Stanley and Elyse, who would sponsor a 1974 simulcast between their west coast residence and 112 Workshop; and Christophe de Menil, granddaughter of the founder of Schlumberger, the world's largest manufacturer of tools for oil discovery and drilling, and a scion of one of the nation's great art collecting families, which had also provided major financial support for the civil rights movement and Martin Luther King. The Empress of Iran (the Sufi wife of the evil Shah) parted with personal jewelry to finance Wilson's appearance at the Shiraz Festival, which had attracted Downtown artists since 1967, despite Iran's status as a country with one of the poorest human rights records in the Western bloc.

Attempting to promote the Shah's name for "civilization" and culture, the Shiraz Festival had become one of the few places in the world for advanced experimental artists to work with full financial security, as well as one of the few breaches in Iranian censorship, allowing at least some Iranians contact with the West. Joe Chaikin of the Open Theater refused to support the Shah and declined an invitation, but the 1972 festival included Merce Cunningham, John Cage, Karlheinz Stockhausen, and "The Persepolis Event," a *son et lumière* spectacle with decor by Andy Warhol. Wilson seized his opportunity "to make a piece that would leave no separation between art and life," he later wrote. *KA MOUNTAIN AND GUARDenia TERRACE* (1972), which Wilson subtitled "a story of a family and some people changing," involved five hundred performers in a 168-hour-long performance on an Iranian mountaintop, near the graves of seven illustrious Sufi poets. They were in rehearsal when Wilson was arrested for possession of hashish at an airport in Crete, and jailed there for several weeks. Rehearsals in Shiraz were taken over by Cyndi Lubar, a Byrd who had gone clinically mad (in the opinion of Stefan Brecht) and turned the play into her own ritual of purification and release. Freed from jail (with the help of Robbins' lawyer), Wilson arrived in Shiraz in a terrible mood, declaring that he had rethought the entire piece in prison. At one point he kept a lion and a camel exposed to a pounding midday sun for so long that collaborators had him arrested so they could save the animals' lives.

Shiraz was the culmination of Wilson's countercultural phase and the end of any imagined fluidity between his Art and his Life.

The Byrds' earliest proscenium masterpiece opened at BAM in December 1973: *The Life and Times of Joseph Stalin*, a twelve-hour retrospective of Wilson's earlier work, which included dancing fish, flamingos, frogs, and an "ostrich ballet." A huge turtle took an hour to cross the stage. A ragged chorus line of forty Black "mammies" waltzed to the strains of "The Blue Danube Waltz." (Seriously.) Budgeted at $120,000 for four performances only, *Stalin* had a cast of hundred and forty-four, ranging from a seven-month-old infant to Wilson's 87-year-old grandmother from Waco. Only five or six hundred spectators made the seven o'clock evening curtain in the 2,104-seat Opera House, and just three hundred or so stayed until dawn, but the subway ride from Manhattan was as much a part of the show as what happened on stage. Uptown labeled *Stalin* the Emperor's New Clothes – John Simon termed it an event "for escapees from thought, feeling, and confrontations with reality." But Wilson's Grand Opera for the Post-Revolution secured his reputation as SoHo's most visible theatrical vanguardist at a singular time, evoking the disconnection, the spacious wonder and terror that seemed to hover over all of Downtown at the close of the Nixon years.

This climactic moment of postwar theatricality in the '60s was accompanied by, and indeed required, the destruction of all confining visions of drama, which writer-director Richard Foreman understood as "a hypnotic act which has power over fools (which we all are except at moments), based on inertia, entropy, deadness as conflict works out to resolution and meaning." By 1968 Foreman had come to believe that "the theater became hopeless." But what theater could still do was prod audiences into an awareness of the disaster of the world.

Richard Foreman, born in 1937, was the only child of an upper-middle-class Scarsdale couple who he thought were his natural parents; he only learned as an adult that he had been adopted. He grew up an excruciatingly-shy, bookish youth who didn't like crowds. His discovery of theater at age nine provided him with means for contacting other people and ways to interact "with an authority not otherwise mine in my kid-life." His discovery of Bertolt Brecht at fifteen established his "lust" for a political theater, even as he continued to see all the boulevard shows on Broadway. He studied creative writing at Brown, then took a Master's in Drama at Yale, and hated that, too. He arrived in Lower Manhattan in time to see the Living Theatre productions of *The Connection* and *The Brig,* which impressed him enormously. So did underground film, which transformed most of his ideas about what art was and could be.

"Most of the interesting insights of the '60s came from drugs," Foreman would later contend, "and we are living off a lot of artists who destroyed themselves in the process." As a volunteer at Jonas Mekas' Film-Makers Co-op, Foreman witnessed Jack Smith's seminal *Rehearsal for the Destruction of Atlantis* in 1965, which demonstrated to Foreman's satisfaction that being "mentally 'non-handleable'" was the proper activity of art. The notion of exploiting one's own awkwardness led him to the works of Gertrude Stein, which also evoked a "continuous present" in a non-empathic, irrational world where the best response was mental clarity. "That's what I'm interested in," Foreman decided: Waking Up.

Overseeing the reconstruction and legalization of 80 Wooster Street as the home of the Filmmakers Cinematheque, he also visited SoHo art galleries, where the works of minimalist and post-minimalist sculptors was "tremendous therapy for me," he later claimed. "It enabled me to say, 'Look, I don't have to inherit Arthur Miller or even Brecht, I can just start from the beginning.'" His raw, unedited playscripts seemed unproducible on the page, but in the spring of 1968, after the city refused to allow 80 Wooster to open as a cinema, Mekas offered the space to Foreman as a theater, which police were willing to ignore. Foreman had no ambition to direct, but no one else knew how to stage his plays, so he mounted his own *Angelface*, and a year later, *Ida-Eyed*, transforming the tiny 80 Wooster space into a kind of Joseph Cornell box for the quirky mechanisms of his own thoughts.

A Foreman production was a bizarre world of disassociated epiphanies, buzzers, bells and fractured speech, revealing the off-balance rhythms of a mind ceaselessly at work – excluding nothing, not his ripest erotic fantasies or his stupidest, most maladroit *pensées*. Performers appeared in two-dimensional tableaux, moving in mechanical repetition or popping up from behind distorted doors and mirrors; naked women, as faceless and impersonal as figures in a de Chirico painting, blankly addressed audiences. Like Monk, Foreman worked with "found" friends and acquaintances, including many who had no thirst or talent for performing; he would suppress even the slightest expressiveness or collaborative input, personally conducting proceedings from a sound-and-light board in full view of the audience – a powerful image of authorial preordination and control. Foreman's hysterical acceleration of Brecht's "alienation effects" attempted to combat emotional manipulation by replacing it with entertaining or surprising jolts, some involving physical discomfort, bright lights, rock-hard seats, ear-splitting buzzers, thuds, gaps, and sudden movement, while otherwise offering only the barest hints of narrative, theme, or psychology.

"Art must keep man rooted in imbalance," Foreman announced in his first "Ontological-Hysteric" Manifesto – a term he coined to evoke "the danger that arises when one chooses to climb a mountain and halfway up one wishes one hadn't." "Ontological-Hysteric Theater," Foreman wrote on another occasion, "is a form of 'concrete theater' in which the moment-to-moment resistance and impenetrability of the materials worked onstage are framed and re-framed so that the spectator's attention is redistributed and exhilaration slowly invades his consciousness as a result of the continuous presentation and re-presentation of the atomic units of each experienced moment." This adaptation of Stein's "continuous present," Cagean silence, and post-minimalist aesthetics was largely ignored by the press, including the progressive *Village Voice,* but for the director, a great deal more was at stake than success or failure. Ontological Hysteria represented Foreman's personal confrontation with all of Western epistemology – his therapeutic collision with everything he knew and felt about the world.

"Basically, art is therapeutic, and I think in the twentieth-century that's the only thing art can be," Foreman told me once. He was fascinated with nineteenth-century French melodrama, and its elaborate love triangles, which he said "are basically hysterical at their roots, in terms of classical psychiatry, the hysterical syndrome. And I'm trying to redeem them, and open up holes by which more – well, it sounds pretentious – more *cosmic* conceptual concerns bleed through, that are really ontological concerns in the Heideggerian sense."

Aggressively-brainy, sensually-hostile, Foreman's plays were nearly unapproachable in conventional terms until the arrival of Kate Mannheim, a 26-year-old French-born library worker and actor, who joined the cast of *Hotel China* in 1971 – a play composed entirely of false starts. A curvy woman of considerable intelligence, Mannheim was soon sharing Foreman's Wooster Street loft and helping to reorient his work towards what the director acknowledged was "a new razzamatazz" – more absurdist schtick and recognizable characters and settings, however short-lived. By *SOPHIA= WISDOM Part 3: THE CLIFFS*, in December 1972, Mannheim's character Rhoda – "real womanhood" in Foreman's fantasy – was centerstage, spending half the evening with lady bush and ample breasts exposed, enduring all manner of abuse under the whip of her boyfriend, the *Auteur,* and personally addressing the world in an annoying nasal whine with an almost hallucinatory awareness of her hapless victimization. Foreman's plays increasingly became the Perils of Rhoda – her illuminations and nightmares, her witty questioning of reality, and her ontological-hysteric tumble down the rabbit hole.

"Look," drawled Ben, Foreman's *manque,* in *Hotel China.* "She's smart when she's in a position which isn't natural."

Foreman's career took another turn in July 1972, when a music-theater piece he wrote with composer Stanley Silverman, *Dr. Selavy's Magic Theater: The Cure,* became a surprise hit of the 1972-73 Off-Broadway season – "one of the funniest madhouses I've ever encountered," wrote the *Times'* Clive Barnes. Produced by the year-old Music-Theater Group at the Mercer Art Center, based in a former hotel on Broadway just north of SoHo (which would shortly collapse due to structural deficiencies into a pile of rubble), *Dr. Selavy* exposed a line of work that began with Foreman and Silverman's *Elephant Steps,* a music-theater piece created in the summer of '68. Named after Marcel Duchamp's famous alter ego, *Dr. Selavy* employed all of the tricks and devices of Ontological Hysteria: slides and billboards, ludicrous sexual imagery, animated and miniaturized props and objects, bare lightbulbs, forced perspective, and surveyor's strings to "diagram" the stage.

Foreman's theater had evolved into a signature style of overwrought melodrama, comic hysteria, and paranoiac control, while paradoxically creating one of SoHo's earliest moves towards wider audiences. But Foreman was uninterested in following up "success."

"I tend to lead a certain kind of lethargic existence, like an animal dozing," he wrote several years later, "who can yet awaken at the slightest 'signal' of the appropriate sort."

That signal came in 1973, when the city permitted Jonas Mekas to re-open 80 Wooster for his Anthology Film Archives, displacing Foreman, who took over a new fourth-floor loft on Broadway, where the Ontological-Hysteric Theater would continue to be difficult, cultish, conceptually-unresolved, skeptical of collective affinities, and declining to name any easy fix for the human shipwreck. The most uncompromising theater artist of his generation, and along with Monk the most original, Foreman wanted "to give courage to ourself and others to be alive from moment to moment which means to accept both flux... and the perceptual constituting and reconstituting of the self."

The theater that went furthest of all the post-revolutionary SoHo collectives in defining the collective liberation of performers and audiences as material for the stage was The Performance Group. Its principal intellectual force, founder Richard Schechner, was a thirty-something NYU theater professor whose stewardship of *The Drama Review* in New Orleans represented his early attempt "to restore virginity to the theater, and purpose to theater workers," in part by introducing the achievements of European high modernism to American theater artists. When *The Drama Review* relocated from Tulane to N.Y.U. on Washington Square in Greenwich Village, Schechner arranged for the first

American workshops of the legendary Polish experimental director Jerzy Grotowski, in 1966. He also participated in a 1967 "piss-in" at the Pentagon, and got naked at BAM for the Living Theatre's *Paradise Now*. That same year he created his own theatrical hybrid, hoping to use Grotowski's core message – "that emotions and physicality are the same thing," as Schechner later stated – to set himself up as leader of a company of ten N.Y.U. acting students to work on an adaptation of *The Bacchae*. University productions across the country were exploring or had already explored Euripides' twenty-three-hundred-year-old tragic bacchanal and tragedy for its parallels with the '60s' counterculture, identifying with the play's God-besotted celebrants, rather than voicing fears about the dangers of such intoxication.

Schechner leased a former commercial garage on Wooster Street in SoHo and worked closely with designer Jerry Rojo, creating a flexible 150-seat "environmental" performance space, capable of adaptation for a given production. What Schechner envisioned was a Grotowskian "poor" theater (for philosophical reasons, and because he had no money) with the immediacy of a ritual, a rock concert, a street fair, or a sporting event. To this end, his company of N.Y.U. students "de-constructed" Euripides' text into something leaner, preserving just six hundred lines of the original, and leaving room for interactions with audience members and the space itself. Acting at The Garage was being re-conceived as a libidinal awakening and a commitment to self-exposure, with a conscious understanding of the uses of cross-cultural ceremony and encounter. Confession, intimate encounter, and self-display – meaning nudity, touching, trance and mirroring exercises – sometimes led to mini-psychodramas, intended to "blow" an actor's image and expose him or her in an uncomfortable light, so he/she would get off his/her shit. Rehearsals for *The Bacchae* conjured up angry, violent energies, particularly around the murder of Pentheus, king of Thebes and Dionysus' cousin. Pentheus was a preserver of law and order, a military man, and a stern patriarch. Schechner claimed he wanted to address his murder head-on.

Audiences arrived for the first performances in June of '68 with the Bacchantes already moving along a maze-like system of towers, catwalks and platforms ringing the playing space. An actor, clothed during the first few months of performance and naked after December, strode into the arena to announce that he, William Finley, was actually the God Dionysus, and that he has come "to establish my rites and rituals... and to be born, if you'll excuse me." What followed was "the birth of a God," an activity that Schechner, a cultural anthropologist as well as a drama theorist, lifted from an Eskimo ritual. Naked women stood with their legs spread, pressing their groins against buttocks, writhing and groaning while Dionysus squirmed between their legs across the bare backs of a row of prone men. Once "born," Dionysus invited viewers to celebrate his nativity by "having a groovy time tonight" – which was all the prompting some audience members needed to remove their clothes, too, and join in an ecstatic dance to flutes, drums and cymbals.

Equal parts group therapy, sacred ceremony, and hippie freak show, *Dionysus in '69* (even the title was a come-on) was a hippie-dippy Euripidean orgy that instantly put The Performance Group on the national theater map, scandalizing local authorities as well as classical Greek scholars on its subsequent national tour, producing what actor Patrick McDermott termed "a pan-sexual, flesh-vibrating, universal eroticism." Four people, Schechner among them, would be arrested for indecent exposure in Ann Arbor, after performing in the nude on the university campus. Performer Ronny Davis thought Schechner's "cooptation of Grotowski's jargon" was a fashionable trick, but Schechner had Americanized Grotowski in terms of contemporary therapy, but he considered that one of theater's obligations. "I believe that healthy people are more able to create full, rich, and suggestive art than are wounded fragmented persons," Schechner wrote. "We may never be able to heal ourselves, but at least we do not cherish our wounds."

Some critics guffawed at undergrads playing Greek gods – the *Voice's* Jay Novick called it "the funniest Greek tragedy I ever saw" – but Schechner insisted they had found "a way of performing an arcane ritual in the catacombs of Wooster Street. We all assumed a religion even if we had none." Behind closed doors, these celebrants of a New Age Mass were a collective in turmoil. Shortly before *Dionysus* went nude and a year into the group's existence, McDermott stopped a rehearsal to demand that they "'stop sweeping shit under the rug and start dealing with one another,'" as Schechner later wrote. Collective creation by its nature requires an examination and deconstruction of authority, but Schechner was unwilling to relinquish all of his. A man of fierce intellectual energies bound to his insecurities, Schechner acknowledged his preference for highly-structured, emotionally-raw situations that he could easily dominate. "I want to know my colleagues," he once wrote, "not only by the sound of their voices but by the smells of their skin and the tastes of their flesh" – a chilling image of parental cannibalism. As the Kronos of the Garage, Schechner excused himself from these personal encounters and intimate acting-outs, such that professional gestalt therapists had to be brought in to mediate direct, often brutal confrontations, usually focused around the director.

With therapy, the situation improved, but by the time the show closed in July 1969, much of the audience participation that Schechner had wanted in the piece was either modified or dropped.

As one actress put it in a note to the director, "I didn't join the group to fuck some old man under the tower."

A new environmental work went into rehearsal, an adaptation of Shakespeare's *Makbeth,* which Schechner described as "an angry play of blood, power struggles, betrayals, fleeting contacts, brief flashes of quiet punctuated by screams," consciously reflecting events within the group. *Makbeth's* unpopularity with actors, audiences, and critics deepened the crisis of authority, which led Schechner to re-assert his power, interiorizing the role of old King Duncan, fated for assassination. When he used a bulletin board to dock his actors' salaries after a vote was taken to cancel an unattended performance: that was the last straw. "My destiny is my own," one actor wrote Schechner – "and not to be changed by a fucking memo from anybody." When *Makbeth* closed in January 1970, the original group disbanded in recrimination and dislike.

The original group had not survived its '60s' *ekstasis.* Schechner was probably correct in his later claim that the problems had come as much from the streets as from within the company itself. The Performance Group reconstituted itself in Year One – March 1970 – with key figures on-hand: company stalwart Joan MacIntosh (at some point Schechner's wife), Stephen Borst, and Spalding Gray, who had arrived late in the *Makbeth* rehearsals. During a TPG residency at Swarthmore College, Gray had met New Jersey-born visual artist Elizabeth LeCompte, who became Schechner's assistant director. With this new, tightly-knit company – "a collective, artistic, participatory democracy," as Gray later recalled – work began on a dark rebirth: *Commune* (1971), "a play about Middle America, by the children of Middle America – no copouts, no kidding," as Schechner wrote in *The New York Times*. Congealing around fantasies of violence – most vividly, the My Lai massacre and the Tate-LoBianco murders by the Manson family – *Commune* evolved in part over a seamless round of summer workshops, parties, mountain picnics, skinny dips in lakes, and acid trips in the woods outside upstate New Paltz. "The changes, man," said one character; "the changes are what it's all about." Touring in Poland, *Commune* set off a riot when a pack of hippies bent back the bars of a backstage bathroom window and invaded the theater.

Back on Wooster Street, company members were cooking, showering and sleeping in the theater, as director Tom O'Horgan had wanted to do during the musical *Hair's* Broadway run. TPG's all-night dance parties were drugged and drunk bacchanales; Schechner was accused of exploiting participants during one all-night trance dance.

"The charges struck home," he later wrote. "Was the ecstasy dance just an ornate structure sheltering simple erotic impulses? But at the same time I wondered what was wrong with that?" LeCompte was not alone in thinking that Schechner's sense of his position in the company was taking precedence over the work itself. Years later, LeCompte told me that Schechner ate his own shit at a Garage event. In October 1971, Schechner and MacIntosh left for a seven-month-long pilgrimage to Asia and the Pacific. Visiting the Aurobindo Ashram in Pondicherry, Schechner lay his head on the lap of an ancient woman known as the Mother, submitting himself to a master greater than himself. On his return in April 1972, he discovered that LeCompte had revised *Commune*, among other things empowering actors to express their unhappiness with the original production, and to create a new one.

Collective imperatives pointed towards democratic reforms: TPG reconstituted itself as a not-for-profit entity, with all members legally part of its decision-making processes. Schechner's dreams of presenting performers as themselves, within the contexts of their own lives, had liberated their voices, but at the same time caused him to lose control of them – marking a shift in experimentation that launched The Performance Group into what would become its greatest period of work, post-1974.

Unique among the collectives of the SoHo era – Meredith Monk's House, Richard Foreman's Ontological-Hysteric Theater, Robert Wilson's Byrds, and Richard Schechner's Performance Group – Mabou Mines never surrendered to utopian fantasies, never identified with therapeutic goals, and never entirely abandoned the traditional resources of the trained actor. Responding to the era's crises of authority, Mabou Mines dispensed with the role of artistic director altogether, sanctioning all participants – directors, actors, composers, technicians, and visual artists – to function as equal partners in the creation of theater worlds. Emerging in part through the Downtown visual and musical arts community, the company touched every major *ism* of the '70s, from Minimalism and Post-Minimalism to Buddhism and Feminism, fusing the visually-oriented theater of Wilson and Foreman with the actor-centered theater of Joseph Chaikin and Jerzy Grotowski – merging images and words when not many theater companies were employing language as a form of enchantment or song. Mabou Mines gave proof to the interconnectedness of the arts of Downtown New York, in part through an association with the birth of Minimal Music, through an original member of Mabou Mines company, composer Philip Glass.

Mabou Mines' distant origins were on the West Coast, beginning when Ruth Maleczech and Lee Breuer met as undergraduates at U.C.L.A. in 1957. A nineteen-year-old theater student, born and raised in Arizona, Maleczech was already a gifted actor; her personal loyalty, intellectual skepticism, and fierce insistence on artistic integrity would make her the soul of the future company. Philadelphia-born, Breuer had grown up since the age of nine in the San Fernando Valley and gone on to become a prize-winning college playwright, an English major, and a frat boy living like a beatnik on the Sunset Strip, idolizing Albert Camus.

After graduation the couple gravitated to San Francisco – she to the Actor's Workshop and Breuer to wait on tables in North Beach and toil over a novel. His Bay Area directorial debut, Brecht's *Caucasian Chalk Circle*, caught the eye of Alan Schneider, the first American director of Beckett, Pinter and Albee, who facilitated Breuer's acceptance as an Actor's Workshop director-in-residence. Focusing on the classical avant-garde of the '50s – Brecht, Beckett, Genet – Breuer and Maleczech formulated some of their earliest ideas about what it meant to act and write for the theater. Influences came from outside the Workshop when Maleczech became a founding member of the San Francisco Mime Troupe in 1960, and a performer in *The Eleventh Hour Mime Show*, part of a series of late-night happenings at the Encore Theater, in which Breuer participated as a co-conceptualist. A third focus of the San Francisco performance underground was the San Francisco Tape Music Center, the city's major crossover of art, music and theater worlds, where young Steve Reich, a Cornell and Juilliard grad, had begun his early experiments in phase-shifting and tape collage, which became another source of the musical minimalism to come. Breuer formed a short-lived collective with Ronnie Davis, Anna Halprin, and Ken Dewey, developing some early refinements of the "Happening" aesthetic. His *Composition for Actors* (1962) – an early anticipation of Mabou Mines – was a wordless piece that required its trio of performers to move through five acting "beats," shifting without transition from fright to laughter to sorrow and so on.

Among these actors was a recent from a Stanford doctoral program in Philosophy who had left graduate school and moved to San Francisco to "explore the emotional side of existence" as an actor. Born into a working-class Lithuanian Catholic family in Cicero, Illinois, JoAnne Akalaitis had escaped the ghetto through the University of Chicago, where she earned a B.A. in Philosophy. An avid student of Greek and Catholic philosophy, she hung out with Students for a Democratic Society (SDS) and headed to Stanford on an academic scholarship, where she was around Ken Kesey's scene long enough for Kesey himself to dose her with L.S.D. (her first trip), without informing her ahead of time. Her first paper at Stanford was titled "The Question of Suicide in the Novels of Albert Camus." It was returned to her by a professor who said "that's not the kind of philosophy we do around here." Disgusted, she returned to her childhood interest in theater, playing Beatrice in a student production of *All's Well That End's Well* directed by Alan Schneider, who was working on campus; he also cast her as Widow Begbick in Brecht's *Man Is Man*. Schneider encouraged her theater aspirations. Eventually she dropped out and moved to the City to hang out around the Actor's Workshop, where she befriended Maleczech and Breuer. Ruth impressed her as a substantial actor already. She found Lee "refreshing, free from cant, and a formidable intellect." But the politics of casting at Actor's Workshop were daunting, so Akalaitis shuttled back and forth between the City's various performing worlds.

This early coming-together of what became the core of Mabou Mines broke apart in the aftermath of the Kennedy assassination and the thickening drug scene in North Beach. Breuer had a *succès d'estime* with Frank Wedekind's *Lulu,* but decided against forming a company in San Francisco, and instead headed to New York with Maleczech. In January 1965, they caught a tramp freighter to Greece. "All in all, the early success was a disaster," Breuer later claimed. "I went to Europe and said, 'I'm not a director, and I've got to get something down on the page!'"

Akalaitis, meanwhile, took an apartment on Bleecker Street in Greenwich Village in order to pursue a more-or-less conventional acting career. She spent a summer in North Carolina summer stock, where a local critic praised her as "a whirlwind of versatility." Back in Manhattan, she renewed her relationship with a composer she had met in San Francisco several years earlier, whose musical career would both parallel and advance Mabou Mines, and launch a major world music career.

Philip Glass, born in 1937, was raised in East Baltimore, the grandson of orthodox Jewish immigrants from a Lithuania ghetto. He began his formal studies on the violin at six, and flute at eight. By twelve he was working at his father's record store, and at fifteen enrolling in the Great Books program at the University of Chicago, where he started piano (late) and where he composed his first piece: a string trio in the twelve-tone mode. After graduating from Chicago at nineteen with degrees in philosophy and math, the prodigy took a job at a Baltimore steel mill to raise money to enroll at the Juilliard School, where he would continue to imitate the academic music of his time.

Glass was part of the same classically-trained generation as LaMonte Young, Terry Riley, and Steve Reich, each faced with "the choice of writing in a dead language or an artificial one," as critic Michael Sahl articulated their dilemma a decade later. "The dead language was the language of the 18th and 19th centuries and the artificial language was the language of modern serious music," then dominated by twelve-tone composition, which required ordering all twelve notes of an octave, each with more or less equal importance, so as to avoid being part of a key. (I probably am not describing it correctly, but you get my point.) All seventy-five of Glass' student compositions were performed; he won prizes and fellowships, and spent a summer in Aspen, Colorado, studying with Darius Milhaud. Long nights at New York City jazz clubs listening to Ornette Coleman, Miles Davis, and John Coltrane did not inspire him to try his hand as a jazz composer. Juilliard composers were discouraged from performing, and Glass was no virtuoso anyway. Instead, he entered the visual art world through his friend Larry Poons, taking a Front Street loft above the sculptor Mark di Suvero, and fraternizing with artists and critics at the West End Bar near Columbia.

"Temperamentally the art world suits me better," Glass remarked decades later. This was something John Cage and Charles Ives had discovered, too: Glass found "it's more interesting being innovative."

Musical innovation was hard to come by in the early '60s. On a Ford Foundation grant to work in public schools in Pittsburgh for two years, Glass published some twenty compositions vaguely in the style of Aaron Copland, without recognizing himself in the music at all. At twenty-seven, Glass realized he needed a big change, so he applied for and received a Fulbright Scholarship to study in France with the seventy-seven-year-old nemesis of academic twelve-tone composition, the former teacher of Copland and Igor Stravinsky: Nadia Boulanger.

Crossing the Atlantic on the Queen Elizabeth with other Fulbright recipients – among them sculptor Richard Serra and painter Nancy Graves, who became lifelong friends – Glass arrived in Paris and moved into the former atelier of the painter Hans Hofmann, a Left Bank carriage house on the Rue Sauvageot, not far from La Coupole, the brasserie of the '20s "Lost Generation." Akalaitis would join him in October. Both lived lives of classic Left Bank bohemian-student poverty: while Akalaitis studied French and spent time around the theater at the American Center, Glass toiled with Boulanger, who took him back to basics in counterpoint, and later in harmony and score analysis. Her only compliment during two years of study concerned a single measure in an early composition. "Mademoiselle" Boulanger – JoAnne would joke that "she called herself that so people would know she had never had sex"

– made Glass feel like he had never studied music before. "I was finally learning the skills that make music go."

Paris, not San Francisco or Manhattan, brought the founding members of Mabou Mines together. Vacationing in Greece in a battered car, Glass and Akalaitis re-connected with Breuer and Maleczech, who had been living in a horse stable on Rhodes but were out of money and contemplating hitchhiking to Germany for factory work. All four drove to Venice, and on the way visited Ruth's mother's native town in Yugoslavia. Back on the Rue Sauvageot, the foursome shared the tiny unheated atelier (JoAnne later joked about burning stale baguettes in a wood-fired heater to keep warm – "Throw another baguette on the fire!") and struggled to break into the English-language theater scene in Paris. In a workshop at the American Center, Akalaitis met a sartorially-elegant Englishman of Irish extraction and an up-and-coming editor at *Realites'* English-language edition named David Warrilow. Maleczech and Breuer met Fred Neumann, the American expatriate "King" of the English-language film dubbing scene in Paris – the English language voice of Jean-Paul Belmondo and Marcello Mastroianni. Neumann helped everyone secure lucrative dubbing work. Maleczech achieved a particular mastery of the microphone.

With the first real money of their lives, she and Breuer traveled across Europe and North Africa on holiday, while Akalaitis and Glass hitchhiked to the south of France to attend the world premiere of The Living Theatre's *Frankenstein* (1965), a seven-hour-long performance.

Frankenstein dazzled Glass with its great scale and sense of time. He would later compare it to the Kathakali theater of India and the work of Robert Wilson, citing it as the first "Theater of Images."

Akalaitis was impressed enough to want to join the company, and Glass would have as well. They followed the Living Theatre to their next stop in Berlin, where they sat down with the Becks, but Judith didn't warm to the idea, so a destiny was averted.

Returning to Paris, Akalaitis and Glass resumed their previous lives filled with great theater and film, but left them feeling like outsiders. The only musical action was a classical series organized by Pierre Boulez, basically regurgitating the mid-century ideas of Arnold Schoenberg, Carl Webern, and Alban Berg.

"Unconsciously," Akalaitis would say years later, "Phil was looking for a new direction."

He found it, working on director Conrad Rooks' film *Chappaqua,* which Glass later described as "an early psychedelic fantasy, involving such heavies from the New York literary underground as Allen Ginsberg, Peter Orlovsky and William Burroughs." *Chappaqua's* composer was the Indian sitarist Ravi Shankar, not yet known by many Americans, as this was before his appearance at the Monterey Pop Festival in 1967.

"Ravi, not drugs, were my acid trip," Glass later told *Newsweek.* A yoga student since 1962, Glass had somehow never properly listened to Indian music before. But as Shankar sang nine instrumental parts over the course of several months and Glass transcribed the notes (Phil's perfect pitch helped), he had no problem doing the transcriptions, but he did have a problem in figuring out where to put the measures.

"Out of sheer desperation, I just eliminated the bar lines altogether," Glass later wrote – "which revealed that Indians don't divide music the way Western theory says it must be done." Instead, Glass decided, Indian composers *add.* Musical experts would later disagree with him, pointing out that Indian music is not additive—it's cyclical—but Glass's "mistake" was of the kind that often stimulates fresh approaches in art. Music based on time-lengths rather than measures and harmony had been employed by Western composers since Erik Satie and Jelly Roll Morton, but Glass' investigation would lead him to his own reconsideration of rhythm apart from the Western musical tradition.

"That was as close as I'll ever get," he later remarked, "to a moment when the creative light suddenly kicks on."

A theatrical direction opened up, too. Breuer, Maleczech and Akalaitis were rehearsing a somewhat recent one-act play by Samuel Beckett, postwar theater's greatest minimalist, titled *Play* (1964). *Play* was three characters reflecting from the grave on their love triangle in a previous life. David Warrilow joined JoAnne and Ruth for four months of rehearsals in the tiny atelier on the Rue Sauvageot, concluding with a production at Paris's Studio Theater at the American Center in 1966. The show also featured Glass's first minimalist composition: ten twenty-second-long solo phrases for saxophone – two lines of two notes in alternating, pulsing intervals. Glass at this point knew of the music of LaMonte Young and his exploration of sustained tones. Akalaitis recalls Glass listening to Terry Riley's seminal "In C" (1965) at some early point and loving it. Steve Reich was pursuing his early experiments, unbeknownst to anyone in Paris.

But Glass's score for *Play* represented his personal discovery of an *objective* music that "resisted the efforts of my normal instincts to experience it as a confusion between myself and it," he later explained. "When we listen to Mendelssohn or Beethoven, what we hear is the drama of the violin. We get confused. We think we're the violin. Now I'm sitting in Paris wondering what the hell is going on."

Play was a big success inside their circle of friends, inspiring the group to plan to work together again at the first opportunity.

But once again the group split, in part because Akalaitis wanted to resume an acting career in Manhattan at some point. Glass considered spending a third year with Boulanger, but perhaps understood that his technique had already been remade. He and Akalaitis had hitchhiked often in Spain, and on one trip got married in Gibraltar and spent a one-day honeymoon in Tangiers. This time – it was the summer of 1966 – they left Paris with plans to journey all the way to the Asian subcontinent, where Glass would find his future creative and spiritual direction.

Many SoHo artists in the '60s and early '70s made the passage to India, among them Yvonne Rainer, LaMonte Young, Joan Jonas, Joel Shapiro, Keith Sonnier, Richard Schechner, and Joan McIntosh, to name only a few. Now Glass and Akalaitis journeyed to the south of Spain, then Barcelona, Italy, Greece, and Turkey by train. Buses carried them across Iran and Afghanistan, over the Khyber Pass and into the Punjab in the fall. Glass had been invited to study with Swami Satchyananda, a famous yoga teacher from Sri Lanka. But in New Delhi, Glass learned that the Swami had been detained in New York, so he and JoAnne pressed on to Rishikesh, the yogic center of northern India, where Maharishi Mahesh Yogi was in residence, a year before his August 1967 visit from John, Paul, George, and Ringo. In Darjeeling, the entryway to the Himalayas and the way to Tibet, Glass met Domo Geshe Rinpoche, recently exiled after a long imprisonment by the Chinese in his home country.

(Rinpoche means "precious one," a term similar to Reverend.) Glass accepted Domo Geishe as his teacher, and would later assist in his re-settlement in upstate New York.

Buddhism had thrived in the Downtown art world for decades. It wasn't much of a stretch to imagine minimalist sculpture and a lot of conceptual art as not exactly Buddhist, but close enough for horseshoes and hand grenades. John Cage, a professed Buddhist though not part of any lineage, viewed the world as theater, which was close enough to a Buddhist idea to be worth thinking about. Buddhism wasn't Robert Wilson slowing down time, or Richard Foreman asking us to wake up and not grasp at what we can't understand; it wasn't an all-white or an all-black canvas, otherwise featureless. But the experience of these and other art works felt closer to a Buddhist worldview than a Western, Aristotelian one. The '60s had broken with certain Western traditions to instill a spirit of innovation and discovery, drawn from the power and immediacy of lived experience. This seemed thoroughly Buddhist to me. If the '70s was "the Do-It-Yourself Decade," as one *Voice* art critic claimed, Buddhism was a good way to Do-It-Yourself. Explaining his silence for many years on this aspect of his life, Glass much later remarked: "[M]y music is so very odd already that I see no reason to make myself sound any odder."

Glass and Akalaitis finally returned to New York City after thirty months away, sailing from Bombay through the Suez Canal on a regional liner and their last stretch on the Queen Mary, from Southampton to the city, where they settled in a two-floor apartment over a ghost-haunted 23rd Street deli to enter the "politics, factions, stratagems and worlds within worlds that make up the New York art scene," as Robert Pincus-Witten observed.

"It was really our isolation from everyone else that threw us together," Glass recalled in a 1978 interview he conducted with Steve Reich, who had moved from San Francisco and given his first New York concert at Paula Cooper's Park Place Gallery in 1966. Third World music inspired a variety of musical scenes and genres across Lower Manhattan in the late '60s, eluding the presumed exhaustion of modern music. La Monte Young and Terry Riley were studying with the Indian vocalist Pandit Pran Nath; Glass became a student of Tabla master Alla Rahka. He was abandoning the pursuit of a conventional music career to support himself and his household as a plumber, a furniture mover, a carpenter, a cabbie, and assistant to Richard Serra, at a time when SoHo galleries were laying out the new post-minimalist trends. Jonas Mekas met Glass at a party and invited him to perform at the Film-Maker's Cinematheque at 80 Wooster. What Phil made was "Strung Out," a solo piece for amplified violin, involving a fifteen-foot-long paper score mounted around the corner of a wall, so that the violinist needed to move around the room in order to perform it. In line with the Cagean vanguard, others in the Downtown music scene were making works with performance elements. Steve Reich's "Pendulum Music" of 1968 involved swinging microphones over amplifiers, producing random feedback.

Glass's November concert at the Cinematheque featured an ensemble that Reich and reed player Jon Gibson had formed in 1967 that was actively playing in galleries and lofts across Downtown. Reich and Glass began sharing this ensemble in repertory.

Along with the jazz lofts of Soho, Balinese gamelan music, African drumming, and the ragas of Northern India, Rock was part of the Downtown mix. Akalaitis recalls Steve Reich dropping by their apartment one evening in 1969 with the Beatles' new *White Album*, which they listened to long into the night. The Who had already recognized minimal music as a cousin under the skin with "Baba O'Riley" of 1971, a trebly synthesizer anthem named after the composer of Terry Riley's seminal minimalist composition "In C." Glass' occasional visits to the Fillmore East on Second Avenue made him aware of the power of amplified music. Rehearsing a new work for three organs and two woodwinds, he realized the instruments needed to amplified and mixed live if they were to be heard properly, so he built his own speakers and obtained the rest of a sound system with financial help from Richard Serra, Nancy Graves, Sol LeWitt, and the Jasper Johns Foundation.

The newly-electrified ensemble premiered at the Guggenheim Museum in January 1969 with the drive of a rock band: fast, loud, and maddeningly supercharged, while involving only the simple addition, repetition, and removal of rhythmic units, and just a handful of notes. The ensemble he still shared with Reich defied most people's expectations of a music concert, and consequently didn't do that well outside art and music circles. Downtown performances were mostly "Rug Concerts" in private lofts, named to distinguish the seating arrangements. The ensemble performed in SoHo galleries, too – Leo Castelli, Paula Cooper, 112 Greene Street, John Weber – with audiences attending mostly by word of mouth. Chuck Close's well-known photorealist portrait – "Phil" (1969), long on view in the permanent collection of the Whitney Museum – dates from this period.

"I sometimes thought," Glass later wrote, "that we were in the business of entertaining this small community."

Seventy minutes into Glass's ninety-minute "Music with Changing Parts" (1970), Glass introduced a harmonic shift, which was Reich's last straw. At a lunchtime concert at the Fifth Avenue Presbyterian Church, Reich stormed away (according to one ensemble member), declaring that Glass's music had gone to the dogs and that this was the end of the minimalist movement. "In 1970, we went to Europe," Reich later recalled, "and that got a bit tense – one ensemble and two composers – so the group basically split." Glass got the group, while Reich went to Ghana for a further study of rhythm. He would soon compose a minimalist masterpiece, "Drumming," which premiered at MoMA in December 1971 – a percussion work of such dazzling virtuosity and feeling that many hailed it as one of the greatest achievements of the SoHo generation. Later performances at Town Hall and at BAM met with thunderous standing ovations, something unheard-of at minimalist concerts. Reich had a major role to play in the creation of the first popular White "art music" to emerge in more than thirty years.

In the spring of '69, Richard Serra had needed Phil to come along with him to Europe to assist in the creation of his poured lead sculptures in gallery spaces. To entice his participation, Serra arranged a series of solo organ concerts in Holland and Switzerland, during a time of rising anti-American and anti-war sentiment across Europe. At a program of minimalist art at an Amsterdam contemporary art museum, an audience of several hundred people pounded their feet in protest during a Glass solo concert. An audience member leapt on stage to pound on Glass's keyboard, and the composer – who competed as a fifteen-year-old lightweight wrestler at the University of Chicago – punched the intruder while barely missing a note with the other hand. The screening of

Michael Snow's forty-minute film *Wave Length* — a slow-motion zoom in deteriorating light across a long room—was greeted by so much heckling that Serra and a Fulbright painter, Bob Fiore (who co-directed a *Dionysus in '69* film with Brian de Palma), began physically ejecting the rowdiest customers. Some of them waited afterwards to "discuss."

"Fuck you, I'm not talking to you guys," Glass said. Serra's poured lead sculptures were subsequently stolen from the museum.

One witness of this concert-melee was Lee Breuer, who had traveled to Amsterdam from Paris to find Glass's new music and Serra's latest work revelatory. "I saw the work of Keith Sonnier, Bruce Nauman," Breuer later told me. "I began to feel I was missing some exciting developments by staying in Europe." Not that Europe wasn't providing excitement, too: Breuer and Maleczech had traveled to East Berlin in December 1967 to observe Brecht's old company, the Berliner Ensemble, still one of the world's great resident theaters. A month later the couple embarked on their own ensemble production of *Mother Courage,* done "the way Brecht would have liked it," Breuer claims.

After living through the revolutionary events of May '68 in Paris, Breuer staged an adaptation of Brecht's *Messingkauf Dialogues,* which enjoyed critical success at the Edinburgh Festival that fall. But money was a constant problem, as it always seemed to be around Breuer. A film foundered in 1969 due to a lack of funds. At this juncture in Paris, they received a letter from JoAnne, who described Manhattan as "violent and frightening," but noting many stimulating developments in art and dance. She was attending workshops with The Performance Group, Yvonne Rainer, Deborah Hay, Joyce Aaron (Sam Shepard's first New York girlfriend) and with the Open Theater. But when a play JoAnne was cast in at La Mama, flagship of the Downtown theater movement on East 3rd Street, failed to open, she contemplated leaving the theater altogether. Then Maleczech wrote, suggesting that they attend a workshop in the south of France with Jerzy Grotowski and his leading actor, Ryszard Ciezlak, shortly before their first scheduled visit to America. That April, Akalaitis and Maleczech undertook a three-week ordeal with the theater guru of the moment, which provided another crucial element to the group that would become Mabou Mines.

Grotowski viewed acting less as an acquisition of skills than an eradication of blocks. Ruth and JoAnne considered Grotowski's approach brutal and sexist, even by the standards of the day. Workshop rules forced Maleczech to conceal her three-month pregnancy, and Akalaitis had to hide her six-month-old nursing infant Juliet at their hotel with a local nanny. She escaped the workshops to nurse by climbing through a bathroom window, then crawled back in through the window after the break was over. But the dazzling presence of Ciezlak, the Lab's leading actor, somehow proved Grotowski's methodology, demonstrating how an actor "could be a creative, rather than just an interpretive artist," as Maleczech later explained. "It was a strange idea to us at the time, this idea of not playing parts. But Grotowski had a method for that." Numerous Grotowskian techniques would reappear in the later work of Mabou Mines, including the idea of acting as the internalization of a sequence of tasks, and the notion of a "partner in security" – an imagined, non-judgmental observer for whom the actor performs. "Or the simple idea of conquering physical fear," Akalaitis later told me. "Grotowski was very smart to figure out that by doing that you could conquer all kinds of other things. He didn't depend on the psychology of character. Acting became an encounter between an actor's personal history and the world of the text. There are no ideal parts. You are simply you and always you." The most important part of Grotowski's work for JoAnne was his "river of memory," which many considered an advance of Stanislavski's motivational techniques. (Working with the memories living in your body was something I have yet to understand.)

When the workshop ended, JoAnne and infant Juliet returned to Manhattan, while Maleczech and Breuer traveled on to the Polish Theater Lab headquarters in Cracow, Poland, where they were joined by Warrilow, who had been pursuing a traditional acting career in London. Plans for an English-based company had faded around the time Akalaitis wrote again from Manhattan, suggesting they all come and live together in the two floors above the 23rd Street deli. Phil had assembled a studio there, and JoAnne had a studio, too, where she was teaching Grotowskian exercises to Spalding Gray of The Performing Group and her former San Francisco roommate Karen Grasle, the future Pioneer Mother on TV's long-running *Little House on the Prairie*.

Just before Christmas 1969, Lee Breuer, Ruth Maleczech and their infant daughter, Clove 333 Galilee, arrived from Europe, followed by Warrilow a week later. With the West Coast, Europe, and India as preludes, a new five-member New York City theater collective was born: five adults and two very young children, sharing that $75-a-month apartment above that ghost-haunted deli on West 23rd. Moondog, a gifted older American musician, composer and inventor, blind since the age of sixteen, lived with them for a year, until JoAnne got pregnant again and asked him to leave. Moondog could otherwise regularly be found on Sixth Avenue between 52nd and 55th Streets, wearing his trademark Viking helmet and cape, sometimes busking, and sometimes just standing around. The household's theater work was supported by Phil with his un-licensed plumbing during the SoHo loft boom. Zack's parents were so broke, they had to have their second son Zack delivered at a free clinic instead of at a hospital.

While Akalaitis and Maleczech taught Grotowskian exercises to David and Lee in their workspace, Breuer struggled with a "performance poem" about the coming-to-consciousness of a horse.

The Red Horse Animation evolved as a shifting tapestry of puns, aphorisms and wordplay, intermingling events imagined from the Red Horse's fictional life with Breuer's paradoxical reflections on art, selfhood, and theater. Akalaitis, Maleczech and Warrilow did not so much perform roles as embody aspects of a single consciousness.

Lee stepped outside to direct. Phil taught the actors wrestling moves. Barbara Dilley of Grand Union dropped by to contribute movement ideas. Blending a physical style with literary content as both evolved through the rehearsal process, *The Red Horse* reflected "process" art; it also suggested the lines and circles of SoHo dance, and paid homage to the animated cartoon, anticipating the Pop performance of the coming decade. As a fifth collaborator, Glass contributed a "hoofbeat" composition, "One Plus One," employing a technique of adding and subtracting beats. Performers would tap the score with their fingers on a hollow stage, miked for use as a drum.

The Red Horse Animation was shown as a work-in-progress at the Paula Cooper Gallery in the early summer of 1970. It attracted the attention of Ellen Stewart of La Mama, who had an enormous three-year grant from the Ford

Foundation, enabling her to offer the group production dates and individual salaries of fifty dollars a week—the first time any of them had ever been paid for theater work in the city.

With the promise of early winter performances at La Mama, the group traveled a thousand miles northeast to a fifty-acre property on the eastern shore of Cape Breton Island, Nova Scotia, which Glass and a close friend, the novelist, screenwriter, and fellow Buddhist Rudy Wurlitzer, had recently purchased, after Phil inherited $10,000 from the sale of one-sixth of a Baltimore parking lot. This former campground, built by a member of the Rockefeller clan, had cliffside meadows overlooking sandy beaches, the warm waters of the Gulf of St. Lawrence, and Margaree Island two miles off-shore. The main lodge was a looming A-frame overlooking the Gulf. The thickly-forested land concealed six small A-frame cabins for the privacy of guests.

The founding members of what became Mabou Mines spent three months in Cape Breton that summer, rehearsing *The Red Horse Animation*. Phil and visiting painter Power Boothe built the hollow sounding board in an old boathouse on the property. There were softball games on the meadow and barbeques on a beach, where Joan Jonas did a performance that people watched from the high cliff. As many as seventeen people, most of them Americans, showed up for dinner.

At this point the company needed a name. Lee suggested Margaree Forks, a nearby town, but then JoAnne thought of Mabou Mines, a former coal-mining village a half-hour south from the Glass-Wurlitzer property, where only a few dilapidated buildings remained, including the year-round home of photographer Robert Frank, author of *The Americans,* a collection of black & white images that gave the Beat Generation its visual style. The company's Cape Breton summer lasted until early October, when the group finally returned to the city, vowing never to put themselves under the strain of living together again.

Mabou Mines premiered *Red Horse* at the Guggenheim in November. Clive Barnes, the first-string critic at the *Times,* suggested they all go back to the mines. This review upset delicate relations with La Mama and cost them bookings and rehearsal time. Even the *Voice* found the company "lost in formalities, in gentility, in its celebrations." Maleczech believed these reviews set the company back five years.

Mabou Mines' critical wipe-out ended when Breuer took another shot at Beckett's *Play*. Three performers encased in funeral urns (designed by sculptor Gene Highstein), their heads poking out the top, their faces visible through voice-activated spotlights as they remember their former life, *Play* premiered on a double bill with *Red Horse* at La Mama in April, 1971. "The beautiful performances, spoken in quick pulses, in awful, clipped, rushed meters, suggest that death is like a perpetually running orgasm which has ceased to give any joy," the *Voice's* Arthur Sainer wrote. Continuing to liberate Beckett one-acts from '50s' production styles, Mabou Mines premiered *Come and Go* at the Brooklyn Bridge Festival in June, with Akalaitis, Maleczech, and Dawn Gray, a friend from San Francisco, whispering into body mikes in a soft, dove-like coo. Mabou Mines' realizations of Beckett's one-acts would eventually be recognized across the United States and Western Europe, but for now, many theater people still dismissed the company as "too closeted with self," as Sainer noted in 1972. The art world remained supportive, so that was where Mabou Mines worked through most of the early '70s, showing works-in-progress at La Mama and also gallery and performance spaces.

Mabou Mines slowly worked its way into an emerging national performance network. The running joke was that Mabou Mines would rehearse for eight months to open a show at an art gallery in Duluth, but now a visit to the Walker Art Center in Minneapolis continued to San Francisco, Portland, and Bellingham. Breuer developed a relationship with Southwestern College in Memphis, inspiring the creation of Eads Hill, a local experimental theater company that Ellen Stewart would fund, on Breuer's recommendation. A year later, he returned to Memphis with *The B. Beaver Animation*, a work-in-progress based on a bleak, amphetamine-driven short story he had written in Paris in '68. *B. Beaver* employed Fred Neumann, the voice-over artist from Paris who stuttered like a sufferer, and architectural elements by sculptor Tina Girouard, the wife of Phil's Cajun saxophonist Dickie Landry. But Breuer's time-consuming work methods were causing problems at La Mama, whose Ford money had run out, forcing Ellen Stewart to ask the company to conform to a schedule. (How Breuer stole Stewart's truck was a matter I never got to the bottom of, because I don't know if anyone did.)

Mabou Mines left its frail harbor at La Mama and cast itself on the sea of public fund-raising. The company applied for its first N.E.A grants, and rehearsed in the Idea Warehouse, a loft space south of SoHo. Breuer's "Animations" went to the Theater for the New City, then to The Performing Garage, and finally to the Byrd Hoffman School on Spring Street, where Benedicte Pesle saw it—she was the New York director of a pioneer arts management organization recently founded in Paris by Wilson's European agent. Jane Yockel's Performing Artservices was already handling fund-raising, booking, and public relations for Robert Wilson, John Cage, Merce Cunningham, Joe Chaikin, and Richard Foreman; now they offered to manage Mabou Mines' miniscule $14,000 annual budget. This meant that for the first time, money would have to dictate some aesthetic procedures.

"We lost control of our schedule and have never gotten it back," Maleczech lamented a half-dozen years later. Mabou Mines received a *Voice* Obie Award for General Excellence in 1974, but company meetings were growing increasingly rancorous, degenerating into business wrangles. Breuer and Warrilow decided to dream up the cheapest Beckett production they could think of. *The Lost Ones* was a monologue adapted from a Beckett short story about a race of people trapped in a purgatorial cylinder. Audience members observed with binoculars as Warrilow manipulated tiny toy figures along a circular wall and a platform two feet in diameter, described as a place "fifty meters round and eighteen high."

A brilliant production idea and David's unforgettable performance intertwined. "Mabou Mines Performs Samuel Beckett" opened in the spring of 1975 at the Theater for the New City on Jane Street in the West Village: *Play*, *Come and Go* (with Akalaitis, Maleczech and newcomer Ellen McElduff), and Warrilow's *Lost Ones*. Hailed by Mel Gussow in the *Times*, Jack Kroll in *Newsweek*, and Barbara Rose in *Vogue*, the Beckett Trilogy marked the company's shift into a larger theater world. Such recognition "never happens to us," Breuer told journalist Linda Winer, who reported him "part amused, part delighted, and part concerned about keeping his audiences small enough for intimacy without sounding elitist." After more than a decade of struggle, Mabou Mines was on the American theater map.

The success of the South Houston Industrial District suggests that complexity is more stable over time than simplicity, something that is also true of Nature. SoHo had become an interdisciplinary launching pad and a homestead where the post-'60s' "long loneliness" no longer applied.

"You could walk from West Broadway to Broadway and it was only people you knew," said Larry Bennett, a painter who tended bar at Fanelli's. Nixon's war was in its "Vietnamization" phase and George McGovern had gone down in flames, but SoHo remained its own neighborhood, a village within a global city, with its own newspaper since 1973 – the *SoHo Weekly News*, founded by one of the Woodstock promoters. SoHo had its own Sufi Mosque and its own Zen center. Pearl Paints, probably the world's best arts supply store, was on Canal Street. Dave's Corner on Broadway and Canal served the "world's best" egg-creams. With its half-finished lofts, exposed plumbing and poorly-lit stairwells, SoHo promoted the casual intermingling of private worlds.

SoHo was not paradisiacal: relations between the sexes were explosive, as years of second-class citizenship were addressed. Few marriages survived. "Reputations preceded intimacy," said the Hungarian-born critic Edit deAk. "People had very definite opinions, and everyone was terrifically competitive," recalls painter Jennifer Bartlett. "I imagine there were very few people doing abstract work who were acceptable to [abstract painter] Brice Marden and very few people doing sculpture who were acceptable to Richard Serra." Dancemaker David Gordon had gloomier memories: "Writing about someone's life in relationship to their work leaves out the days, the weeks when nothing was happening, or when nothing good was happening. Or the times when one doubted. Or the times when one doubted everyone else. The lows seem not to have existed and the great highs seem somehow flatter than they were." Yet nostalgia for the recent past was moving apace: "Broome Street was like Montmartre," Dutchman Walter Germans, who opened SoHo's first arts shipping business, told me in 1978. "It was like the painters in the '20s looking over the roof of Paris – that twinge of foreignness to watching the trucks rumbling down Broome Street."

Casual coteries like the Anarchitecture Group and 112 Workshop continued to work among themselves, participants crossing over into different scenes. Richard Foreman and Kate Mannheim held open houses on Sundays that brought together the theater and arts communities armed for intellectual big game. Sculptor Gordon Matta-Clark, painter Susan Rothenberg, actor Spalding Gray, performance artist Joan Jonas, and dancers Douglas Dunn and Kenneth King all participated in Robert Wilson's Thursday night open movement workshops at one time or another, where you might find Bob Telson of the Glass Ensemble improvising on an old upright piano. The Experimental Intermedia Foundation, in Phill Niblock's loft on Centre Street south of SoHo after December 1973, served the needs of innovative production and presentation. A New Year's Day 1974 reading from Gertrude Stein's 925-page *Making of Americans* attracted dozens of artists from across disciplines to the Paula Cooper Gallery for a fifty-hour marathon that became an annual event.

SoHo's self-involvement acquired an architectural motif in 1974, when The Kitchen – a video-and-performance space founded in the kitchen of the old Mercer Hotel before it collapsed—moved to an 1890 building on Broome Street that had an elaborate façade, including a medieval motif of a dragon devouring its own tail. This was an alchemical symbol of the world's primordial unity to some, to others an image of SoHo's insular self-involvement. SoHo was mostly Caucasian, there could be no denying that bit of visual evidence, but a loft jazz scene was attracting increasing numbers of African-Americans and Latinos to Greene Street. SoHo didn't have a rock club, so when the Polish Theater Lab visited in 1969, Mabou Mines had to take them to the Fillmore East over on Second Avenue to hear Jefferson Airplane.

But something new had come into existence: a large-scale artists' community in downtown New York.

Plumber Philip Glass had noticed gentrification arriving as early as 1972, when he started installing pipes not just for sculptors and painters, but for psychologists and architects. One day he was putting in a dishwasher for *Time* art critic Robert Hughes, who recognized him and refused to allow an "artist" finish the job – instead of saying thank you so much and paying him double. "The avant-garde has finally run out of steam," Hughes would note that December, perhaps composing his thoughts at Food, where he frequently dined;

"...faced with the choice between amateur therapy and finicky, arid footnotes to Duchamp, the mind recoils." But perhaps it is more accurate to say that the '70s included a lot of art "that was not for the consumer sensibility," as Paula Cooper recalled a decade later. "Conceptual art (which effected the present boom in photography), performance art, video art, and land art are too elusive for the American practical ethos." Ultimately, however, it was clear to the art writer Lucy Lippard in 1978 that SoHo's "temporary, cheap, invisible, or reproducible art has made little difference in the way art and artist are economically and ideologically exploited."

Contemporary works only occasionally reached auction houses in those days, but the October 1973 sale of the Robert C. Scull Collection at Sotheby Parke-Bernet on Madison Avenue sold fifty estimable works, most of them acquired at relatively little cost, raising an astounding $2.2 million. The auction market would sag through the 1972-74 recession, but art sold from the South Houston Industrial District continued to surge. By March 1974, SoHo was home to an astonishing sixty-four art galleries, compared to seventy-four on Madison Avenue. Leaving behind its collective idyll, SoHo also slipped its ghettodom: what Hilton Kramer described disapprovingly (in 1973) as "the Age of the Avant-Garde" had made contemporary art a focus of interest among a growing public, not only in New York, but across America, Europe, and Asia. An interdisciplinary arts community without parallel since Paris in the '20s prepared to leave its "closets of self" and direct its energies towards experimental culture around the world.

THE DROP ZONE:
The Village Voice, September 1978

I enjoyed writing about adventure, especially when it carried me into colorful scenes and arenas that weren't necessarily in the art world. Skyworld, a dirt airstrip in the high desert of Southern California, provoked a different voice: slower, keyed through the sky to the great outdoors.

Lake Elsinore, California, a resort town of jerry-built homes and trailer parks by a natural lake seventy-three miles southeast of L.A., is a place where the sun bakes the empty streets and keeps the low-riders toned down. Except for eating tacos, playing water sports, or gambling at a hi-lo poker casino with the retired folks, there's not a whole lot to do around here except drive around. But at the far end of the lake is one of the most famous sport-parachuting drop zones in the world, where locals Billy Man, Smooth Fred, Art the Geek, and Goofball are warming themselves like lizards at the long packing tables in front of the main hangar.

It's 8 a.m., the night cool has already burned off, and the motionless air is already hotter than a three-dollar pistol.

"Good day for jumping," says Smooth Fred. The largest natural freshwater body in Southern California, Lake Elsinore shimmers across acres of dry fields where jumpers splatter when they miss the nearer drop zone. A brushfire is burning out of control over hundreds of acres between here and Corona fifteen miles away, sending up tongues of flames on the far ridges and a thunderhead of smoke six hundred feet into the sky.

A yellow Cessna buzzes overhead with an enormous haunch hanging out the side door. Billy Man, a master jumper and eight-year Marine Corps veteran, takes the opportunity to remark, "If that Fat Sucker goes in, it'll rattle the whole valley." Going In, also known as Bouncing, or Frapping, is what follows shortly after a chute fails to open when it's supposed to. Statistically there's not much chance of that happening to the Fat Sucker, which is why Billy Man can joke without totally creeping the flesh of any loved ones who remain behind. Black humor is corollary to the satanic pride of dropping out of airplanes, for the real, trembling beauty of skydiving, aside from the sentimental romanticism that has people flying through the air, is that it's great not to die. Jokes can feel like a little pinch.

Nobody plans to, but locals will tell you that three people have frapped here in the last six months, all just off student status, learning to free fall and getting tangled in their lines. The most outrageous piece of jump apocrypha has it that one of their names was Mr. Frapp, and the airport closed for a day in his memory. On a high-speed malfunction, you have several seconds to deploy an emergency chute, depending on your altitude. If you fail to do that, or if *that* chute doesn't open (two failed chutes, an almost unheard-of statistical anomaly that would suggest foul play), you impact at 120 mph and bounce a few feet into the air before settling back into the hole you just made, guts exploded and a dribble of blood coming from your nose and mouth.

People into the excessive style of reality-mongering known as "blackdeathing" find it wise to pick their company.

Two chain-saw gliders zip past overhead, ratchety as dragonflies. The windsock picks up a little as clumps of sleepy men and women struggle toward the hanger coffee stand from the ramshackle collection of gardenless thirty-year-old trailers and nouveau-plastique mobile homes known as the Ghetto – a community, according to Smooth Fred, of assorted winos, geeks, ex-servicemen, drop-outs, "retards," and antiques waiting to die, and who on average don't do much besides jump out of airplanes, service the business in some fashion, and hang out at the airport.

Fists around glazed donuts and Styrofoam cups, a few early risers have entered the hangar offices to open up the jump school and the Manifest, while legions of the Saturday unemployed venture from the hangar across the territory of the red ants to the small crew scattered near last night's empty beer cans on the packing tables. Talk is of the TV movie NBC is shooting at the nearby Perris Airport.

Conversation breaks off to watch the Fat Sucker climb out the door and on to the wing at 3,000 feet. The Cessna dips slightly. Smooth Fred pounds his crutch into the dirt and laughs, using the corners of his long blond Fu Manchu to dab the tears from his eyes and cheeks. The Fat Sucker is out for a hop and pop – hop out and pop the chute, also known as a Clear and Pull.

Art the Geek drones like a Conehead: "UFO, UFO..."

"He's bigger than the chute!" screams Goofball after the canopy opens. "Looks like an equipment drop," Billy Man comments a couple of minutes later as 280 pounds rip into the earth in a mushroom cloud of dust just outside the soft, plowed up drop zone beyond the packing tables.

When the Fat Sucker stands up, somebody cheers. Carrying so much weight, the Fat Sucker wrecks an ankle or a knee every third jump and lies on the ground "like a dead fish," says Billy Man. This is the 65th jump of the Fat Sucker's life and his first in nearly three weeks, because of a knee he shouldn't be jumping on at all. But he's got one for the logbook. Full-grown men and women have been known to give up productive careers to hang out here, kibitzing jumps, waiting for planes. Ex-Nurses, Social Workers, Stock Brokers, College Students, Idle Kids: they're all living for free fall. All they want to do is skydive.

Billy Man, who has done 970 jumps since 1965, says that skydivers are the smartest of all athletes. "You have to be smart to think fast. It said so in *Psychology Today.*" Billy Man's plenty smart. With his modest beer belly over his hand-tooled monogrammed black belt and buckle, he looked like what he is: an ex-Marine who's left off sit-ups, but could still probably take you out with one hand tied to his codpiece. At the moment he's holding somebody's little boy over his head and suggesting they put a dress on him and pack him for a pilot chute. The kid's eating it up – another budding altitude freak.

The loiterers shift their critical eye to a vanload of Japanese just arrived in the parking lot from a nearby sporting lodge.

"Break out the used equipment," mutters Art the Geek, but they brought their own. Like all jumpers into relative work, the ultimate art of skydiving – unison configurations in dead plummet – they're wearing extra-large canvas jumpsuits for wind resistance and a slower trip down, the longer the better. The eight-man Japanese team could probably fit sixty basketballs into their sky clothes. Art the Geek doesn't really mind people he calls "Orientals;" he's just testy ever since being grounded for pulling too low. You're supposed to pull the ripcord at around 2,500 feet, but the Geek pulled at 800, which would have left him no time to handle a 'function' if he'd had one. "Geeking" is doing anything for attention, which Art doesn't do – he just gets into it, forgets, and ends up in trouble. He could still geek out at Perris, but feels more at home at Elsinore, with friends like Goofball, a member of the notorious skydiving team known as "Grim Business," disqualified at the recent national championships in Indiana this summer for pulling at *700* feet. Like Hamlet, the Elsinore team waited too long and got too dramatic, but unlike the Prince of Denmark, they survived the play.

The Japanese team has set up lawn chairs and are doing pull-ups on the packing-table roof supports. These athletes have come to America because air-right legalities in Japan prohibit skydiving from over 4,500 feet, meaning you can't free fall for more than twenty seconds or so in the Land of the Rising Sun. Here they can do several jumps a day from 10,000 feet, which allows for sixty seconds of free fall at speeds in excess of 100 mph. The world speed record for a human being bombing out of an airplane in the Cannarozza position – head straight down – is 185 mph, which is the fastest any human being has ever gone without the aid of a mechanical device.

The airport is backing up with jumpers now: sun-bleached Geeks from the Orange County Heartland in their Rabbits, Land Rovers, BMWs, one with a license-plate reading U FIRST; some Chicano ex-paratroopers down for the day from El Monte; a half-dozen nervous college students following up on a dare. Nobody moves much in the heat, only enough to get to the Coke machine. Some up-and-coming young attorneys, insurance salesmen, dentists: they're Weekend Geeks. But anyone willing to fall out of the sky from an airplane is okay to the people who live around here. The only visitors they don't like are the assholes in Bermuda shorts and nylon socks who come around with binoculars around their necks, hoping to see somebody frap.

In the relative luxury of the air-conditioned Manifest office, seasoned teenage Racquel adjusts her bikini top with her left hand and seizes the microphone in her right to announce over the airport loudspeakers: "We've got a DC-3 going up in about an hour and a half. People who want Jump Instruction should report to the Equipment Room." The pilot is late for work again, and nobody knows where he is, but fortunately the DC-3 has been pulled out front and is being serviced.

Through the Manifest window, Racquel sees Billy Man holding forth at the packing tables. "And Billy Man, your Momma is on the phone. She wants to talk to you." Billy ten toes it to the office on a bald ruse: Racquel wants to go dancing in Riverside tonight, and doesn't have a ride yet. Billy Man talks to her through the Manifest window and finally tosses himself halfway through on top of her desk, where he wiggles and thrashes for a moment before squeezing his butt through the window – all for the benefit of the packing-table crew, who split their guts laughing.

They miss the Japanese team moving Indian-file on to the dirt runway to board the Blue Norseman, an ancient single-engine Canadian bush plane designed to take off and land on unimproved surfaces, like the lumpy runway at Skyworld.

The packing table crew turn their attention next to Lars, a Swede and a Skyworld employee, wheeling a battered white truck through the parking lot and skidding to a halt in the dust outside the hangar office. Lars lost one of his arms to an airplane prop. They watch the Fat Sucker climb down from the back, sweating profusely, clutching a dead chute and a sugarless Tab he must have had with him on the jump. He calls out to Goofball, pointing at the eleven people they've packed into the Norseman. Its engine is turning over now in a flood of black smoke.

When the smoke clears, the plane does appear to have a few extra bodies on board. "I hope they brought a deck of cards," says Goofball. "That thing will be lucky to climb 200 feet a minute."

A lot of horseplay, but nobody is "going in" because of somebody else's mistake. The chute packers work silently in the back rooms of the hanger, where safety precautions cut through the worst hangovers and subtlest preoccupations.

Addressing first-time jumpers in the second-floor classroom, Tracy, today's instructor, broaches the psychological: "Why do you want to jump out of an airplane? The answers vary from "I dunno" to "I thought it'd be fun." She talks about the eight-person star she was part of a couple of weeks ago, eight bare naked ladies holding hands in freefall – a world's record for keepers of such things. One jumper landed in a tree in some old lady's backyard. After hearing the basics of skydiving safety as many times as we need, about eight, students essay mock jumps out of a dead Cessna frame and practice leaps from a small wooden tower to simulate the feet-together roll. Tracy explains the emotional problems of counting to six in the moment's hysteria after leaving the plane, when you look over your head for a chute, if you don't feel it already. She tells us what to do in case of a low-speed 'function, when the chute inflates improperly (cradle the front emergency parachute in your lap, pull the ripcord, reach into the pack, and throw out the canopy), or a high-speed 'function, when you have no chute at all (pull the ripcord and punch the pack.) The first-time jumper doesn't have to sweat opening the main chute. It will be popped open by a static line attached to the plane.

Tracy has 670 jumps under her belt, a "Skydiver" patch on the crotch of her short shorts, and one high-speed malfunction to talk about, with an emergency chute packed by her dear husband, Goofball.

"On a high-speed malfunction you'll have twelve seconds to do something about it or in seventeen seconds, you're dog meat." The class is sobered. She tells us that if we get blown toward some power lines, don't try to make yourself skinny and drop between the lines, as most instructors recommend. "You'd hang there and swing back and forth and get fried. I would rather break both arms and legs then fry in a power line. If you tell anybody I said that, I'll deny it."

The pedagogy of a little blackdeathing and a lot of repetition impresses the demands of the sport on student cortexes, and nail-biters like me may begin to feel submitted to an ordeal. Tracy says not to worry, there's been only one malfunction on a first jump at Skyworld, and the student handled it. We sign waivers and documents releasing the airport from any liability and are fitted in white jumpsuits, heavy boots, old crash helmets, and parachute rigs cinched in so tight it's hard to stand up straight. With any luck, we'll be taken up in the battered Cessna immediately, because waiting around gives you too much time to think about what a crazy thing this is – really, how unnecessary, isn't it? Once you board the plane, it feels good for a moment. You protect the ripcord on the emergency chute, having been warned that if the pack pops and the handkerchief-sized pilot chute, which deploys the main canopy, opens accidentally, you will be torn through the fuselage of the plane and take everybody else along with you.

For many reasons, you can hardly wait to get out of this airplane.

At 2,500 feet, Tracy checks out the window for the drop zone, allows for the slight wind, and at the right moment motions you forward.

The air turns to nitrous oxide as you hunker up to the doorless opening. She attaches the static line, which will open your chute, to a hook by the door. She makes you focus your eyes on hers to see if you have any wits about you. Then she plants a kiss on your lips, signals to the pilot to cut the prop, and you climb onto the wing as you were taught: right foot to the six-inch-wide platform, right hand to the wing strut, left foot and head following after.

Then you're squatting on the wing of an airplane in a 90-knot breeze, staring ahead with the high desert landscape flowing beneath your feet. You hear shouting and remember you're supposed to be looking back at Tracy, who immediately nods you off backward into the sky. You do it, and you're falling, flying, trying to count and arch through a blind adrenalin-fed panic, the sky, the plane, and the earth all tumbled together, no up or down. Then the main chute opens from the tug of the static line. The fall has taken about three seconds, and there you are, dangling by your crotch from a harness 2,000 feet in the air, in an unreachable kingdom where you are the Absolute Monarch and Sole Survivor. You feel like screaming blue murder, so you do. The idea that not a soul on earth can touch you for the next two minutes you find utterly exhilarating. You survey the territory. You play with your toggles and change the direction of your view. The brushfire is magnificent from this elevation. Even with the smoke and smog that creeps down from the L.A. basin, you can see for thirty miles. You look up at the most beautiful parachute you've ever seen in your life. You have maybe one hundred and twenty seconds of this before you're three telephone poles off the ground and steering your ass in the same direction as the tip of the airport windsock, so your forward speed will neutralize the slight wind. Keep your eyes on the horizon and your ankles together. A jumper's adage: the last half-inch is the hardest. Some people land like brick shithouses, others like they're jumping off an ottoman. You hit the ground, do an approximation of the roll you were taught, and leap up to chase after your billowing parachute before it drags you away.

You're unscathed, and in all likelihood utterly seduced by a cheap but glorious Victory over Father Death.

The wind is blowing up dust demons, baby tornados. Carmela Luciano is smoking Marlboros and not relaxing. She comes to Elsinore every weekend from her job as a receptionist with a small Hollywood production company. A desire to see Elvis brought her to California from Pennsylvania in '67. She only discovered skydiving last year. With twenty-three jumps to her credit, she's still a novice, but packing her own hogback – a rig with the main and emergency in the same backpack – and doing five-second delays this weekend. Five seconds of free fall, and she pulls her own chute. "Don't you think what I'm doing is dangerous?" she asks her new friends, who tell her yes but stop sweating it. She remembers that the three who had died recently were all in her stage of training. Though only one out of every thousand jumps has a 'function, Carmela is under the mistaken impression that six out of seven of these accidents are fatal. She's still trying to figure out if she's a neurotic death tripper or a sportswoman. She only knows that skydiving turns her on. So does Disco. She thinks she's lucky: on her twelfth jump she hopped and popped and got no chute. She thought: I'm having a high-speed malfunction. She did a hand deploy of her emergency chute and it worked, but she landed funny, not knowing she could have controlled her descent without the main canopy toggles by reaching around the front risers, the lines attached to her canopy. She lay in the dirt, thinking about blacking out, but not doing it until the truck arrived.

She had compressed a disc in her spine and couldn't jump for three months. But it was worth it. She has the divine knowledge that she can handle a high speed 'function. She bought her emergency chute packer at Elsinore a case of beer.

Carmela is at Skyworld with her best friend Suzie. They're an unusual couple because Suzie broke her back in a jump a while ago, and hasn't jumped for months, though she's dying to get back to it and comes every weekend to watch. Some skydivers can go years without a serious accident, but most hardcore have hurt themselves at least once.

"I've had my 'function,' I know I can handle it," Carmela is saying again as she punches out her cigarette. "I know I'm good for a couple hundred more jumps."

But today Carmela went up in the Norseman, got in the door, and froze. She had forgotten how to step out on to the invisible launch platform curving under the belly of the plane, even though she'd practiced it countless times. She signaled the Jump Master No Jump, and slunk back to her seat. She would not have had this an option in the Cessna: if a jumper gets cold feet on the wing, some Jump Masters feel obliged to shove him or her off with a foot, rather than risk the student climbing back in and accidentally opening the chute. Carmela is freaked at herself, but nobody is calling her psycho, or even thinking that way.

Nearly everyone in the Ghetto believes than when the vibes are wrong, Fuck Not with the Forces of the Universe. Just don't do that.

The Norseman's second run with the Japanese is the last plane of the morning. When the wind is over 10 mph, no students are permitted, and much more than that makes the landings too rough for anybody. Lars, still the Catcher in the Truck, picks up the fallen Japanese in the drop zone and drives them in. They had dropped through the sky in an octagonal ring and pulled low. One of the sleeves had been slow to slip and open the canopy, producing a few seconds of anxiety and maybe even fear among the Geeks on the ground.

Back at the lawn area by the tables, the Japanese team are repacking their chutes and fetching metal basins from the vans to do their laundry. They're jumping parafoils, known as Squares, the small, maneuverable parachutes that look like a ribbed biplane wing. Originally developed for air force pilots to have more mobility to evade ground fire, the square dominates the world of sport skydiving. They're tricky to use, but give the skydiver the agility of a kite.

With the airport closed until late afternoon, some of the locals decide to grab lunch or go water skiing on the lake or trout fishing in the mountains. Out-of-towners who can't face the lunch stand burgers leave to find a better place to eat.

Two Dutchmen camping out by the lavatories play chess.

"It's time to kickback around here," says Billy Man. Smooth Fred, on Valiums for a broken first metatarsal, crutches into the equipment room for a nap, where he dreams, he tells me later, about a water jump into the Colorado River. Billy entertains a group of young women with tales of the guy who jumped off the Eiffel Tower wearing nothing but a pair of bat wings. Everybody else just goes home, or to the Skyworld parking lot to drink Buds and smoke dope.

Steve shows up, ostensibly to sell humorous jump T-shirts from his two-story van. Steve is a local legend who once went in with a third of a chute. People saw him frap at fifty-five miles per hour and bounce into the air. The white truck didn't even hurry to pick him up, but when it did, Steve was lying in the hole he'd made, blinking at the world. They gave him the cigarette he asked for, then sent for an ambulance, in the meantime taking a few photographs of him lying there, smoking. Steve had broken his back, all his ribs, an arm, and a leg, and got the second full body cast of his life. He got the first being when he was blown out of a helicopter five klicks from the DMZ, and fell 60 feet with nothing to balloon him but his G.I. Khakis.

Carmela rates Steve 98 percent pure. He's got a Willie Nelson face and beard and a rebel flag tattooed on his arm. He's a keen storyteller, chin music in a genteel Mississippi accent. He's a long way into the tale of a guy who caught his trousers on the outside of a plane at 10,000 feet when the airport manager shows up – a late-thirtyish fellow who I was told once told a good palmist to get away from his hand, because he didn't want to know "a goddamn thing" about his future. After a lot of skydives, some people begin to feel their future getting a little too close. The absent owner of the airport no longer jumps at all.

"I don't want to have to tell you guys again," the manager shouts, not angrily though. "All the drinking in the parking lot has got to stop. The state and the federales are looking for a way to lock our doors and we can't give them any excuses. You don't see them here, and we don't see them leave, but they tell us about the drinking and the sunset loads and the condition of the planes, those three things. So drink in your vans, I don't care, but not outside."

The boys are apologetic and hustle their beers into the cars.

Sunset loads involve taking off with the last of the sun and landing the planes in the dark, which is hairy at Skyworld, because there are no runway lights on the dirt strip at Elsinore. Yet tonight, management is organizing the first night jump in some time, so the boys discuss the moonrise. Some say before nine, others after ten. Nobody bothers to check the newspaper, but there are no newspapers here anyway. The manager says he'll put out smudge pots to light the runway, but we'll see. Conversation drifts to dope smuggling by airplane from Mexico, the evils of PCP, and the responsibilities of family life.

"You know what'll calm you down sooner than anything?" says Steve. "Financial problems."

At about five the wind has settled enough for the DC-3 to get back off the ground. The waiting around, the hanging out at the nap-time airport is over. Suzie helps Carmela strap into her rig. Billy Man's been telling Carmela not to worry, and Carmela confides to Suzie that Billy is good with girls. Around thirty jumpers are going up in this sortie; an average weekend can get off anywhere from 200 to 300 jumps a day – there were 37,000 here last year. The Japanese waiting by the plane rehearse their relative work, standing in an octagon and grunting in unison as they turn around themselves. They're shooting for five formations this trip.

The World War Two-vintage DC-3 wheels into view from behind the bay of the hangar garage. She's got 149,000 air hours on her, this noble craft, millions of miles, stripped clean years ago of everything from ashtrays to toilet. Patches of ceiling insulation hang in long shreds. It's not an inspiring machine, but it's gotten thousands of people into the air.

The fat, bald, shirtless pilot, whose name I never caught, carries a plastic toy pistol under his sun visor, he says, "to deter hijackers."

Rushing down the runway ahead of a thirty-foot rooster tail of dust, it's the slowest big plane in the world.

Jumpers sit on the half-painted plywood flooring in three lines between each other's legs, like tobogganing. Few talk. The plane spirals slowly, almost lazily up the valley, gaining altitude. They cut the engine at 3,000 feet to dump Carmela and a few others. The Jump Master says go and she goes, rocketing away from the plane like a stone dropped down a well. Five seconds later, when she pulls her chute, she's three hundred yards from the plane and invisible to us. Climbing to 10,500 feet, the pilot cuts the engine again and eight local skydivers shoehorn into the doorway. At least three of them are completely outside the plane, clinging by their fingernails to the opening, each other, a rivet. They want to be as close as possible to start their relative work quickly. It's a rehearsal for the world-record 72-man star contemplated for later in the summer.

Some of the men and women seconds away from free fall look panicked, others casual or grinning like madmen as the icy air plasters their face and clothes. Their eyes meet, the time is right, and they're out the plane, all eight together, a few in lazy barrel rolls quickly stabilized by hitting the arch position and flying belly downward toward the earth with arms and legs extended, backs bent like bows, locked into the gravity of the situation: the total responsibility for their own lives and the call of the earth. Nobody cried Geronimo, as far as I heard.

On the next pass the entire Japanese team bails out together, all eight quickly measuring velocity, flipping and repositioning with practiced skill as they run their routine. None of this gets seen from the plane, as jumpers are lost in fifteen or twenty seconds against the checkerboard landscape.

The final pass on the run has four jumpers ready, including Lars, who strapped on an artificial arm for the occasion. With him is an arm brother, this one with a nasty-looking hook, mirrored sunglasses, a giant mustache, and a circa World War I leather aviator's cap. He looks like Thor with a Prosthesis. The fourth member of the team has a Nikon camera screwed on his cap like a beanie propeller.

They bounce in place and shout the count: "One two three – Go!"—and they're out of the plane and falling like Satan, with nothing to count on but their own mental alertness and a mechanical device as nearly fail safe and exquisite as Leonardo could have imagined when he invented the first. They fall like they were blown out of a cannon, up and down irrelevant. Thor gets a little outside the grouping and will have to fly over. Invisible from the plane, Thor changes his stable arch position to a medium delta, sweeping his wings behind him like the Concorde's wings, causing him to move diagonally through the air fast enough to catch up with his friends, who were probably wondering where he was. Thor clips his hook on to Lar's jumpsuit and they've got their four-man star. Screaming into each other's faces, they break apart and pull. A fantastic feeling to fuel the night from the last jump of the day!

In the cool of the evening, many weekend jumpers go back home to Santa Ana or Pomona, while the locals gather at the Ghetto to rest and do a few lines in a 1949 Sleepeezee Trailer, barbeque, drink beer, and magpie about the day's jumps. Other folks have kids to feed and put to bed. Many people oppose mixing dope and skydiving, but a few of the Ghetto rats have their own idea of how to have a good time, which involves getting wasted on Quaaludes and dropped out of an airplane. No muscular control in freefall may be a rush, but also sounds vaguely suicidal, and nobody in his or her right mind advocated it. But apparently, in some quarters, it was a secret pleasure.

This evening all talk is about the night jump, wondering when the moon is coming up. You leap into a black void. You can't tell where the ground is. The only way to know how high you are is from the altimeter on your wrist or on your jumpsuit. It's scary as shit. Some people mention the dangers, such as colliding with another free faller in the darkness, but it doesn't seem to deter anyone, as people in Elsinore have made up their minds to be or not to be already. Only experienced jumpers are permitted, so Carmela, who has connections with the Ghetto people, a friendly bunch, lies back on a built-in bed in a twelve-foot trailer, stoned with six other people and listening to an L.A. rock station. She came back big today on that last jump, and in a mood to celebrate.

The night jumpers, friends, families, and voyeurs gather under the bare electric light bulbs at the packing tables.

"Don't drink too much beer," Racquel warns over the P.A. tongue in check, because three cases are in circulation. She's still hoping to score a ride to Riverside. It's 9:30 p.m. and neither the pilot nor the moon has made an appearance. The manager hasn't put out the smudge pots, either. He tells me, "The FAA is asleep by this hour."

The night's jumpers are taping battery-powered lights and green glow bars to their helmets and altimeters. "It makes it easier to find the bodies in the dark," someone jokes. People are nervous and chatty. Word passes that somebody threw a rock through a hangar window for some reason. A well-known local bounced a big check in the shop, and puns proliferate. Goofball had Chinese for dinner and got a fortune cookie that read, "You're taking your life for granted." All of "Grim Business" has shown up, as well as some of the "Skygods," the other half of the eight-man Elsinore team. The Skygods fancy themselves the Princes of the Air. On Monday night they're jumping into Anaheim Stadium as part of a Rolling Stones concert. Steve doesn't like them, says they're cliquish. A lot of men and women agree that somebody ought to take a flamethrower to the old bat with the orange eyebrows who's been cashier for the past three weeks and acts like she owns the place.

A lot of the old-timers are showing up for this one. Dirty Hal has come. Dirty Hal has done over three thousand skydives. This means he has spent about a day and a half of his life in free fall, and that's not counting when he's sleeping. Dirty Hal looks tired tonight. He spent the day topping trees. He tells somebody, "Sit down on the ground and let me kick sand in your face, you turd," but they say he's actually a nice guy when you look past the verbiage.

Everybody is looking for body warmth. Grouper, a local real estate agent, arrives with a blinking red motorcycle light on his leather hat. He sees Old Tom with the peroxided beard, who's been away at Nationals. Old Tom says to Grouper, "I just snorted two grams of coke. *I'm* not scared of my first night jump!" He starts shouting and hopping up and down. "Get Scared! *Get* Scared!"

Several beer pop-tops go off at once. Grouper grabs Old Tom in a bear hug and two of them pogo around.

"We hate night jumps, we hate night jumps," Racquel chants over the loudspeakers. The pilot arrives when the nearly-full moon is one hand over the horizon. In the Milky Way, a strange plane cuts its engines and lights for a few seconds, as if to say hello. The rival airport at Perris has heard about the night jump, and is flying over to check things out.

"Scramble, Scramble!" shouts the airport manager at everyone. "Get that DC-3 up there and get those boys!" The crew runs out to the warm up and prepare the plane. Racquel calls muster over the loudspeakers.

"Mouse, Debby the Polack, Benny Quaalude, Wog, Godflicker, Warm Walter, Cleareye… all you guys, report!" A ragged line forms outside the hangar. "Good luck on your last jump!"

It's well past midnight. A dozen cars have parked in a circle with headlights turned on the drop zone, like the Chickie Run in *Rebel Without a Cause,* or some pagan circle of light. Also a good target from the air. Despite the big moon and 2,000 stars, outside the circle of light the night is pitch dark. Carmela is in a Dodge pickup with Suzie and some guys, doing blow and listening to a Stones tape. The DC-3 that lumbered off the ground is circling overhead, gaining altitude on the way to 12 grand five. That's a long senseless fearfall in black if you've got the nerve to keep your fingers off the handle. Most jumpers will probably pull early.

At quarter to one, almost directly over the drop zone, the DC-3 cuts its engines and turns off the lights. It's as if it was swallowed by the Bermuda Triangle. A few ground viewers think they see tiny lights coming from the hole where the plane had been. That would be the skydivers bailing out, instantly enveloped by the black night.

There's nothing to do on the ground but watch the fire dance on the ridges at the other end of the valley. The word is out that it's arson.

Then we hear sounds that are hard to hear during the day: the sounds of chutes popping open, like pods spewing seeds.

A blinking redlight streaks across the northwest sky. That has to be Grouper with his motorcycle helmet. A moment later the air explodes in peacock screams, rebel hoots, cowboy yodels, barn owl screeches: the skydivers are coming in. People on the ground respond: *"Geek geek geek geek geek!"* The parafoils swoop out of the night from all directions, a few tearing across the face of the moon, men and women dangling by faint lines from arching bat wings. Jumpers brake hard and crash into the drop zone from every angle.

Tracy the Jump Instructor comes in on her feet ten yards from where Carmela stands. She's shaken up and won't say much.

"It was terrifying. That's the last time I ever do that. I think I just missed hitting somebody." Everybody's alive, though one group landed halfway to the lake. Nobody wants to go to bed. The night is young for the Voluptuaries of the Sky.

"Let's go Boogie in Riverside," someone cries. "Buncha Geeks."

MAKING TWO LIVES AND A TRILOGY:
The Village Voice, November 1978

Note: *This was the first article "the Countercultural Paper of Record" ever published about the Wooster Group, which would go on to become arguably the most brilliant and controversial Downtown theater of the late '70s and '80s — a highlight of what The Performance Group's Richard Schechner called "the great Elizabethan flowering" of theater in Lower Manhattan.*

Theater is possible because of the imagined intimacy between the invented and the actual, the unreal and the real, the contrived and the natural, the character and the actor — between theater and life. Spalding Gray and Elizabeth LeCompte, primary composers of the Performance Group's trilogy *Three Places in Rhode Island,* have developed a style of theater that blends abstract movement, visual design, music, film, "acting," and personal documentary to challenge and at times transcend their exhilarating and often painful contradictions.

For LeCompte and Gray, the stakes are high. They're attempting to re-assemble their lives as Art. When it's not a dizzying aspiration, it can be a barren one. Gray and LeCompte use extremes of self-reflection to make theater with whatever comes to hand and mind.

Sakonnet Point (1975), *Rumstick Road* (1977), and *Nayatt School* (1978), in rep at the Performing Garage on Wooster Street through January 14th, offer a "style" of theater, in the sense given the word by Roland Barthes: style is "the decorative voice of hidden, secret flesh, rising from myth-laden depths," unfolding in an arena just beyond conscious control. Gray is the *Trilogy's* central performer and anima, the source of much of the intensely subjective imagery; the director LeCompte assembles materials in an impersonal order, placing emphasis on the visual – they've been thinking of trying to get away with calling the trilogy a triptych. In place of clear analysis and linear narrative, *Three Place in Rhode Island* presents viewers with an imagistic theater of thorough-going intimacy, mystery, and dispassionate beauty.

LeCompte and Gray share a loft down Wooster Street from the Garage. They rehearse in both places. The days I visited were serious and gray – a Rhode Island sky. "Life is very insular for us here," LeCompte told me, although they're just back from Amsterdam. Both are in their mid-thirties, and have lived together for eleven years. Gray states with gentle solemnity that there is no part of himself that he consciously conceals from her. Even in conversation, both are tirelessly self-revealing, and yet just as compulsively ironical about their insights and opinions. Their theater shapes their private need for constant revelation, followed by nuanced qualifiers – a need to put their cards on the table, then casually grab them up and reshuffle for the next game. "The ironist is the man who remakes the world," wrote the German idealist Johann Gottlieb Fichte. This distanced vulnerability suggests a pregnant sense of loss, a tender sadness lingers inside the trilogy – as if nothing is ever quite "real" enough to last.

Sakonnet Point was named after the summer beach where Gray spent his summer vacations as a child. Audiences listen to delicate children's music and the obtrusive ratcheting of a wound clock; watch a leering man in a green bathing suit crack a whip while a woman on a beach towel serenely downs a glass of milk. Each image, set against the others in a stirring and fathomless counterpoint. In *Rumstick Road,* actual tapes and slides of Gray's family expose the tragedy of Spalding's mother's madness and subsequent suicide, mingling it with the emotional exhaustion of life in small-town Rhode Island. And yet in context, this material is transformed into a hauntingly beautiful evocation of a vanished childhood.

Emotions with no psychological ground are consistently parodied, qualified, or distanced. In *Nayatt School,* Ron Vawter applies glycerin to his eyes in order to weep as the audience listens to a recording from T.S. Eliot's *The Cocktail Party.* The audience sees him administer the glycerin, but can't help being affected by the sight of his tears. Despite this apparently unmoored, uncommitted emotional life, *Three Places in Rhode Island* is ruthlessly courageous in approaching his private subject matter.

"I took a walk in Central Park today," Gray tells me in his unmodulated voice and gentle Rhode Island accent. "I could only approach it aesthetically. There was no other way to make sense of it." For Gray, the overwhelming gravity of the world urges facts into a single frame. At this point he has no other interests besides performing. He wishes he did, because a lot has been left behind.

Spalding has a gentle Yankee face and a Thoreauvian disposition, nurtured in lonely musings and a bleak Rhode Island landscape. Rumstick Road was the street he grew up on in Barrington, Rhode Island; Nayatt School, where he attended grades one through four. He is obsessed with his past, his childhood, and what he left behind, although at the same time he knows he never really felt part of it. He has that distinctly American quality of being inside and outside his experience at once, making him part of an American tradition extending from Nathaniel Hawthorne to Jerry Brown. It's led to a style of performing in which he can be both active and reflective, assertive and passive, at one with and at a distance from what he's doing on stage.

"I've never had the experience of being inside anything," he tells me. "I gave up yearning for it and decided to go the other way." Then he adds in the next breath, "I would always feel cheated when I was doing scenes about something. It's great to finally do the thing in itself."

"Spalding is so self-involved," LeCompte explains, "he gives of himself completely."

In the Performance Group's 1973 production of Sam Shepard's *Tooth of Crime*, Gray played the central character of Hoss. "I was doing scenes with Joan MacIntosh where we had it down so cold that it was like pushing buttons. I became distanced from it, ready to fight somebody. It would take five or six beers just to come down." Just before starting work on the Rhode Island Trilogy, Gray became involved in improvisational movement with choreographer Kenneth King and at Robert Wilson's Byrd Hoffman School – he had always thought it would be interesting to become a dancer. In a recent issue of *Performing Arts Journal*, Gray wrote about discovering for himself the liberating power of what he calls "abstract-personal" improvisation – the room it leaves for internal reflection and the "energy field" it generates between performers. He wanted to bring this energy to The Performance Group.

After nearly a year of talking about it, rehearsals began in February 1975 on an exploration of what for Gray and LeCompte would be a new style of collaboration: a libidinal commitment to self-exposure. This was a departure from the Performance Group's more structured approach, in which Spalding says "one always had to know what a feeling was." The five actors began with no conscious objectives, no ideas, and no subject matter. They were simply going to make a "piece." Gray would arrive at rehearsals with random props – a doll's house, trees, toy soldiers, a small airplane – along with music and a few ideas for specific actions, and the group would improvise and free-associate around them. Their subsequent actions and repetitions would press people into their own subjective responses or personal memories, prompting still more images and actions. The presence of eleven-year-old Erik Moskowitz, the son of New York painters, led them toward what came to seem like an evocation of childhood. "We were just trying to make scenes out of who we were in the room," says LeCompte.

Very early on, Gray asked her to step outside and direct. Gray characterizes her as the "classicist" in their collaboration. LeCompte would curb Gray's natural tendency toward romantic movement, and dismantle legible narrative as soon as it appeared. Strong-jawed, strong-willed, and energetic, Liz selected all the images during *Sakonnet's* two-month rehearsal period – "almost to a one," she tells me. "I don't know what that means in our relationship," she informs me, un-coaxed. "I don't care. It makes me paranoid to think about it. I've set up this character 'Spalding,' and I have this paranoia of disappearing behind him." Using her instincts and training as a visual artist (and sometimes her anger, according to one associate), LeCompte selected images that interested her and held her eye – "almost as if the action was taking place on a TV screen," says Gray. "It became a mother-child thing. We would all play in front of Liz, and she would choose."

Sakonnet Point premiered at the Garage in April 1975 – a wordless play syncretizing dance, theater, music and the plastic arts, meeting Nietzsche's definition of Apollonian art by radiating "the full delight, wisdom, and beauty of illusion." *Sakonnet's* cool, surreal, dreamlike quality and occasional Dadaesque strokes were nevertheless permeated with a sadness that Gray and LeCompte's friends attributed to a fact of Spalding's biography: his mother Margaret Horton Gray had committed suicide while Spalding, said to be her favorite son, was away on vacation in Mexico. "I went catatonic," he told me. "It got so where I was sleeping twenty hours a day. If I'd drink two or three cups of coffee, I'd cry."

Predisposed to valorize extremity, and something of an anti-materialist like his Christian Science mother, Gray didn't realize right away that he was hypoglycemic. In his baldly frank way, he continues: "I had a very strong Oedipal tie with my mother. When I would come home from college, she would be my date. I was in Mexico when she killed herself. My father picked me up at the airport and told me about it on the ride home. My immediate reaction was that she'd died of a broken heart. He had her ashes in the bedroom by his bed. I never had a proper mourning for her. I wasn't even there when he scattered her ashes in Narragansett Bay." *Rumstick Road* would become Gray's metaphysical solace for the loss of his mother – a kind of displaced mourning. In *Performing Arts Journal*, LeCompte would write that the trilogy is in part "about Spalding's love for the image of his mother, and his attempt to repossess her through his art."

Theater predisposes audiences to the pathos of selfhood. When Gray discusses the "confessional energy" of *Rumstick*, the notion of art as an impersonal aesthetic ordering would seem to be replaced by the idea of art as self-help. *Rumstick Road* is as loose and freely associative as *Sakonnet*, but if it's considered as a psychiatrist's couch, it's important to note that there's no psychiatrist: no authority to appeal to for healing. It's less therapeutic than purgative. "The only way I can get myself on an airplane is to act out my fear of flying," Gray tells me. As usual, he approached the work from the outside. "I had a terrific distance on my mother's suicide by the time we started *Rumstick*. I was thinking of Ginsberg's *Kaddish* and [Eugene O'Neill's] *Long Day's Journey Into Night*. My mother's suicide was material for me." *Rumstick* would become what art critic and historian Erwin Panofsky might have called a "prospective ritual": an act to help the dead rest and leave the living alone.

Sakonnet Point had evolved with relative ease; the making of *Rumstick Road* was an agonizing process that began in September 1976, not to conclude after almost daily rehearsals until April of the following year. "We had to come at it from a lot of different places," says LeCompte. The action in *Rumstick* occurs in an ingenious environment designed by LeCompte and company designer Jim Clayburgh. The audience sits in triangular rows of benches, their apex jutting towards the bifocal stage, which represents the house on Rumstick Road, with the two areas separated by a sound and light booth commanded by a plainly-visible Bruce Porter, the show's technical director.

Like *Sakonnet*, *Rumstick* uses lots of majestic music and obscure, repetitive movement. Libby Howes flails her hair like a whip for long minutes; a fight for a gun looks almost like a tango; a slapstick chase scene continues interminably. But *Rumstick* adds spoken words: Spalding, or Spud – a literal character now – talks to the audience for the first time, surrounded by crucial props and images that are Spalding's actual family memorabilia, which includes slide images as well as letters and tapes of Gray's family talking. *Rumstick Road* is a dreamed archeology of Margaret Horton Gray's suicide, her visions of Christ and her beatitude, her involvement with Christian Science, all revealed through the sights and sounds of her surviving family and favorite son.

"Spalding was good enough to give us his life to play with," says performer Ron Vawter. But *Rumstick* isn't precisely autobiographical; perhaps autobiological would be more accurate, the company working through improvisations and free association – "arguing, shifting parts, working with and without texts," according to actor Libby Howes. Howes, Vawter, and LeCompte all felt that they were working on their own personal histories, not just Spalding's. But watching the slides of his family and home and listening to a tape of his grandmother commenting on them, Gray the performer has time to reflect. "It's a personal ritual of reuniting with my grandmother… I look at the slides and I try to imagine the places that are just outside the picture frame."

Gray and Ron Vawter lip-sync a taped conversation between Spalding and his father. Gray made the tape with the idea of using it in the piece. In it he has his first real talk with his father about the facts of his wife's suicide. Gray's father refused to credit his wife's visions of Christ and her out-of-body experiences, and in general downplayed her mental instability, as well as his son's memories of her. It's painful listening, especially with the knowledge that it's a "real" situation in the life of the actor sitting calmly in front of us, performing an occasional abstract gesture while his lips follow the words.

"I'm paranoid about my father's reactions to using it," Gray admits. "I've had hallucinations of the audience leaving, for instance."

Gray also performs "live" his half of a taped phone conversation with the psychiatrist who treated his mother through her breakdown. The psychiatrist unfeelingly discusses shock treatment, and ends by telling Spalding not to worry about the fact that mental instability is usually inherited. Although a pseudonym is used for the psychiatrist on the *Rumstick* playbill, the taped voice is that of the actual shrink; most people assumed it's an actor. The conversation was bugged without the "beeper" required by law, prompting some members of the *Voice* Obie panel to argue that *Rumstick* should be withdrawn from their deliberations when they discovered this violation of a physician's right to privacy.

"I thought there would be repercussions," Gray tells me. "We were warned by our lawyer not to do it. We had no justification." But Gray doesn't believe there's a moral question involved. "I felt the psychiatrist was a 'catch.' It was a caprice to call him; we had the tape equipment around, so it happened." Gray's self-exposure was ruthless. It uncovered others in the process. He isn't particularly interested in abstractions he doesn't find useful, like the right to privacy of someone who will probably never learn that his privacy was violated. Transforming intensely private material for his own purposes symbolizes the largest movement in Gray's life: the choice of art over the past, his family, and bourgeois life in general.

"My bridges are burned," Spalding tells me. "I can't go back to commercial theater. The chances of Liz and I ever having a family are slim." Hence the fascination with children in the Trilogy? "I realized that when I moved to New York just after my mother's death, I opted for art over the family. I changed. I dropped my WASP background and became something else… In *Rumstick*, I'm a fictive character in my own world and I'm myself in the performance." Lee Breuer of Mabou Mines has written about how *Rumstick Road* declares, "I'm my own material on all fronts – visually, psychologically, intellectually, and emotionally. I am myself and I create myself before you… This is as big and important a current in the art of acting as was the development of motivational technique and the notion of the Brechtian or 'epic' performance. In other words, this is the third new idea about acting in this century." At a more immediate level, *Rumstick Road* reconstituted a meaning for Spalding's life by transforming his personal history into what T.S. Eliot would have called "a series of timeless moments." Richard Schechner, founder and artistic director of The Performance Group, which Liz and Spalding are still part of, claims that *Rumstick* is as "removed from the precipitating situation as El Greco is from the crucifixion."

Gray has moved from the Freudian myth of Oedipus to the performative myth of Orpheus, who Dionysus tore to pieces as an infidel, although his severed head continued to sing.

The encompassing themes of the third work in the Trilogy are the loss of innocence, the end of limits, and the death of the censor. Gray and LeCompte were prepared to trust their methods to a point of manic hysteria, which the work depicts with astonishingly pointed brilliance. *Nayatt School* carries characters or character tendencies from the earlier pieces, and some familiar props, too – the red tent, another view of the home on Rumstick Road, the family recordings, and the white sheets prominent in *Sakonnet*. Only here Spalding performs as a teacher giving an absurdly laconic lecture about his personal history in the theater, and also commenting on a reading of Act II of Eliot's *The Cocktail Party*, a play that sets up options Gray felt in his own life: the characters Alex and Lavinia choose a sterile but comfortable bourgeois existence, while Celia (who Gray identifies as his mother or, alternately, himself) chooses sainthood and martyrdom as a missionary among the Savages.

"For a while, *The Cocktail Party* was my Bible, my way to live," Gray tells me. LeCompte tells a different version of the story: "We used it because it reminded Spalding of his mother and because we heard it on the radio and thought it was interesting." She believes that what they are staging was the definitive production of *The Cocktail Party*, the one "Eliot would have wanted if he was smart enough to recognize it… We make the play make sense" – even though they skip over most of it and play the third act with a group of wildly misbehaving children dressed in floppy adult clothes; Eliot did call it a comedy. The kids' nervous energy and joy inspire more than Eliot's sterile imagination of the "Real" and the "Unreal." *Nayatt School* explores a multiplicity of role-playing that becomes so confusing as to pull the plug on the notion of identity itself.

"In *Nayatt,* we wanted to work with something irrevocable," says LeCompte. She had included the Kennedy assassination as an event that shifted her life into another modality. Bruce Porter was able to get his hands on copies of the Zapruder and Nix films of the motorcade, which were projected on paper, and a frame frozen so the performers could sketch a gunman on the grass knoll or hiding behind a limo tire. The idea ended up scrapped. Along with the genesis of the artist, as encapsulated by *The Cocktail Party*, Cancer – the uncontrolled division of abnormal cells in the body – became the central metaphor of *Nayatt School* instead. Gray had found a British record album on how to conduct a breast self-exam and it "interested" him – that empty/full word again. Physical examination had been part of *Rumstick*, too, and here in *Nayatt School* one of Libby Howes' breasts is exposed and checked out in a magnificently comic scene inside the house on Rumstick Road, which has a Plexiglass roof enabling viewing by the audience from precarious seats above and to the side of the performance space. Spalding's lecture is delivered from a long table just in front of the audience, at the edge of a precipitous drop to the stage below. "I enjoy transposing junk images," says LeCompte, and many appear here: an old vaudeville skit about a visit to the dentist's office, a cocktail party drowning in a proliferation of plastic cocktail glasses, a melodramatic murder, the red tent becoming the chicken heart that grew – a Bill Cosby rip-off, unacknowledged. The energy swells maniacally; the piece has become cancerous, and finally self-destructs.

Not surprisingly from people so concerned with precision, *Nayatt School* had another difficult birth: three to five hours a day, five or six days a week, for seven months. "Three or four months into rehearsals," Gray relates, "Liz just stopped and started crying. 'It's pure shit.'" The work disturbed some early supporters of the trilogy, including at least one former company member. But the powerful final image seemed to capture all the dangers of what they were attempting: Gray, Vawter, and Howes squat or stretch on top of on three turning record players on the long table in front of the audience, all naked or nearly so, gnashing their teeth, contorting their faces, flaccidly masturbating as they run the record needles over the records: an image of "the records" – the Past – being destroyed by a spate of tormented, solipsistic madness.

If *Sakonnet Point* is pastoral and *Rumstick Road* historical, then *Nayatt School* is apocalyptical. Where to from here? What next on Wooster Street? The heat comes and goes in LeCompte and Gray's loft, and as usual the Performing Garage is out of money and threatened with closing. Gray contemplates another visit home to Rhode Island, though it always confuses him to see the remnants of his family. He hopes to find inspiration for an afterthought/postscript, *Point Judith*, about his father, thinking of it as a kind of wake for the Trilogy. Gray has in mind a "configuration" of three men and a boy sitting around playing cards and telling dirty jokes. He would like to direct it [although in the end Liz will.] "I have the feeling that my work would be very different from Liz's... I feel the need for more responsibility. I either have to find a way to make money or start an even more radical theater." He entertains thoughts of retiring and becoming a "conceptualist," or maybe he'll try writing "seven autobiographies, one a year for seven years." LeCompte and Howes have an idea, off the top of their heads, to do a Passion Play. LeCompte has also become interested in pornography. "I'd like to make the consummate porn film at the Garage," she tells me.

But Spalding Gray and Elizabeth LeCompte have no adamant schedule or agendas. They have instead a style of performance that they now believe constitutes their lives – one that works at suspending judgments, attenuating meaning, at once exposing and covering up pain and confusion – merging the ominously quiet madness of the past with the timeless beauty of the present.

Still, the question remains: where to next on Wooster Street?

POSTSCRIPT: *Word reached me that Richard Schechner was disgruntled that this article gave him little-to-no credit for giving the Gray-LeCompte faction of The Performance Group their "wings," as Spalding himself conceded; in hindsight I think Schechner had a case. Spalding told me he liked it, except he was curious what I meant when I said he "valorizes extremity." "You consider your most extreme states of mind to be your most valuable ones," I tell him, which is probably not what Spalding valorized about depression. I also heard through friends that LeCompte thought I made her and Spalding sound like "the Lunt & Fontanne of Downtown theater," which was no longer the case, if it ever had been: she and Spalding had ended their eleven-year relationship between galleys and publication. Liz would no longer be "given authority by Spalding," was how she described the change to me. When Schechner's next two productions were less than completely successful, the Performance Group dissolved and a new entity, the Wooster Group, rose from the ashes to continue their savage deconstructions of the White American Middle Class. As Liz told me on an earlier occasion: "From the moment I walked into the Garage, I wanted it."*

Spalding would go on to international fame as a monologist and storyteller, while Liz turned the Wooster Group into the most uncompromising, consistently extraordinary experimental theater in America. And she would eventually direct that porn film, working with Libby Howes and her own future husband, the father of her son Jack, actor Willem Dafoe, in the sex film collage that closes Route 1 & 9. *(It was heavily edited, so you didn't see much.) The astonishing thing to me was that my piece never mentioned, in the context of* Rumstick Road, *that I had lost my own mother when I was three years and eight months old, and she was twenty-seven.*

THE ART OF IMPERFECTION:
Peter Voulkos and the American Ceramics Revolution, *The Village Voice,* September 1979

An editor asked me to write this piece during the months I was sitting in front of an Olivetti in a cubicle at the Voice *on University Ave.*

Peter Voulkos hulks by the wet bar on the top floor of the Contemporary Crafts Museum in Midtown, nursing uncharacteristic diffidence with a stiff drink and wondering how the hell he's going to get back to the hotel to change his clothes. Hundreds of folks, all dressed up to see him and thirty years of the dirty work that made the Clay Revolution, as they call it – though at least a few of the slashed, pitted, patched-up plates on these walls were pulled out of a hot kiln in Berkeley less than two weeks ago. Voulkos likes to look at his stuff when it's recent, but at the moment he's got a slew of Upper Eastside arts-and-crafts people to meet and a bow-tied museum director doing the introductions. Chain smoking, Voulkos gives up and decides that anywhere is exactly where he is right now. "Information," he calls it, then goes on to tell a friendly-looking older lady about his bursitis. "The only way to get rid of it is to get rid of it. Work it out." He rolls his hunched shoulders like an organ grinder. The matronly smile attenuates.

"You've got a long evening ahead of you," a friend murmurs after this exchange, and Voulkos concurs, gazing heavenward. That's the mug the poet Charles Olsen took for a Native American's when Voulkos visited Black Mountain College during the fructive summer of 1953, on the trip back east from L.A. that would change the history of American ceramics. Voulkos didn't let on right away that he was as Greek as the urn man, though Montana born and raised; when Olsen found out, he switched to calling Voulkos' drawling, rangy self an "archetypal Westerner." Voulkos attended his first poetry reading at Black Mountain, and also watched Merce Cunningham rehearse. "I couldn't believe what you could do with your body," Voulkos tells me. Late in that summer he drove north in a battered car with potter/writer M.C. Richards and composer David Tudor to spend three weeks in New York, where he got to know Kline and deKooning and hung out at the Cedar Tavern.

"I was young at the time [29] and I felt like a big blotter. All I'd seen was in Montana in the art books and a little L.A. Socialist Realism and Ashcan stuff from the '30s and '40s. I saw the new painting and I really flipped out. My pottery changed. I started painting myself. I started to confuse the two, run them together."

Already a ceramicist of international repute, Voulkos returned to L.A. to begin a legendary outpouring of work that would propel ceramics from the realm of craft into the fine arts – a distinction Voulkos has never related to at all. In all-night sessions of drink and work, Voulkos shaped idiosyncratic pots, plates, cups, vases, and abstract sculptures, covering them with strokes and splashes of color, seemingly-primitive glazes he developed himself. Voulkos made an art of imperfection: his pieces would be warped and asymmetrical, gashed or scratched at, patched with strips of left-over clay, or left with holes gaping "to let the dark out." He would even epoxy purposely broken pieces back together, something no self-respecting potter had ever done before him. Clay proved to be an ideal medium for the energy and physicality of abstract-expressionism. "Clay is just a big blob that moves," says Voulkos, "and you're got to respond to it. It's almost like thick paint… you touch a piece of clay and it changes." Ceramics had always involved a certain functional and/or religious piety; Voulkos's work revealed instead the potter's intimate involvement with the plasticity of his material, the spontaneity of hands and an entire body at work on the clay.

Gradually the humble potter moved in the direction of a heroic monumentality. "I got going on things and they just kept getting bigger and bigger." Learning to throw fifty pounds of clay on a wheel, Voulkos assembled cubist-inspired sculptures that stood up to eight feet tall, mind-boggling technical feats that he could complete in a single firing – though more than a few blew up in the kiln. Voulkos also became a master brass worker, after moving from L.A. to Berkeley in the early '60s. In a single night at L.A.'s Primus-Stuart Gallery in 1961, Voulkos and a team of welders assembled a huge brass sculpture designed on the spot "out of spare parts" and finished in time for the morning opening. Voulkos tells me there's still an oil stain on the floor from his forklift.

Today Voulkos is a professor at U.C. Berkeley and paterfamilias to a burgeoning tribe of East Bay potters. For the past five years he's been working on a series of plates "for people who don't like soup… trying to get it down to pure gesture, like a drawing." He's also moving into a new 40,000-square-foot abandoned food plant near the Oakland train station, where sixteen artists will build living spaces under a thirty-foot ceiling. He has a painting studio and a hot tub there, and would like to be back finishing the plumbing. Instead, he's in the town of his inspired youth, attending his thirty-year retrospective, warming up a bit to greet friends and ex-students who've shown up from all over the Northeast. He's glad for the show (which will run until December 31st); some of the stuff he hasn't seen since he did it – didn't even know where it was. Still, a midtown museum opening isn't the best place for a man with what he calls a "hand sensibility."

'This show that's hip here has taken a lot of energy out of me," he tells me when he gets a minute. "They wanted it ten years ago and I kept putting it off. I tell ya, I'll be glad when it's over so I can forget about it." Voulkos has worked his way down to the ground floor. Out of curiosity, I ask if he eats off his own plates. "I eat off some old, white, surplus plates. I can eat a hamburger off an ashtray. I never paid much attention to the idea of utility. It can be a psychological thing, too… I had a whole kiln of plates come out perfectly a while ago. I tried to duplicate the conditions, but I couldn't get it." Which plates are these? "They're not here, I left them home. I didn't want them to get broken. Most people couldn't tell the difference anyway… Every so often I go back to the little teacups. I've made only one or two teacups in my life that were pretty. I look at the Japanese cups that've come down through the centuries…" The Father of Modern American Ceramics shakes his head in amazement.

The museum director bustles over to inform Voulkos that his family has returned from the observation tower of the Empire State Building and are back at the hotel. Which reminds Voulkos that the opening is halfway over, he still hasn't changed his clothes, and it's looking more and more like he won't get around to it that night.

HERE'S LOOKING AT YOU, RIB:
The Village Voice, October 1978

Note: *The only restaurant review I ever wrote was the result of eavesdropping on a Sex Therapist at a brunch in a restaurant on Thompson Street in SoHo, and introducing myself. He had such good info, I pitched it to the* Voice.

My friend the Sex Therapist is into ribs. He's eaten short ribs, baby back ribs, spare ribs, and Chinese pork ribs uptown and down in at least forty restaurants in New York City, without ever satisfying his lust. He says "You can't get a good rib in New York." He's been known to fly to Florida for the weekend to eat ribs at Fat Boy's in Key Largo. Flynn's in Perrin, Florida, sends him a case of their special sauce every couple of months for his private gourmandizing. Friends in the city got him a Marzipan rib for his birthday cake. But what he really craves are the ribs in the Everglades, where folks slaughter their own stock, bonfire the whole hog smothered in Seminole sauce, and make necklaces out of the gnawed bones. This is my friend the Sex Therapist's idea of an orgy, and I've got to admit, my nostrils flare at the thought.

My brothers, sisters, and I grew up on Sunday ribs, chucking the stripped bones onto a plate in the middle of a plastic tablecloth. As far as I'm concerned, eating ribs involves heavy breathing and not much conversation. Just you and the rib, a napkin tucked under your collar and your elbows on the plate. Pig out until you can't stand the sight of it, and don't even think about dessert.

When my friend the Sex Therapist told me he'd reveal the three best ribs restaurants in New York, I bit at the opportunity.

J.G. Melon's (Amsterdam Avenue and 76th Street), a male saloon with dark wood, brass rails, and pictures of melons on the wall, didn't even inspire me to remove my jacket: a fair price ($6.50), but small portions and the spare ribs were dry. The Sex Therapist claimed it was an off night and just wait. Rusty's (73rd and Third Avenue), owned by ex-Met Rusty Staub, features hard-to-find Canadian baby back ribs for $8.50. Regular spare ribs lie under the breast and bacon of the pork, but baby-backs lie under the pork chop; they're shorter and sweeter and virtually without fat, and at Rusty's they melt in your mouth like a good rib should. The waiter told me that when Staub was traded from the Houston Astros to the Montreal Expos, he found a terrific source in town; shipped through Michigan, they still taste fresh. (If you buy ribs to fix at home, be sure they're light pink. Streaks of blood mean they're young and good.)

The best came last: Horn of Plenty (Charles Street at Bleecker) offers "Food from the Soulful South," and the taste of their short ribs ($9.50) ran through my blood like a Mayan sacrifice. Short ribs are from the middle of a beef rib – neither the Sex Therapist nor the Lobel Brothers, the famous Upper East Side butcher shop, know another place to buy or dine on beef spare ribs in New York City. The portions at Horn of Plenty are huge and the cornbread is delicious, too. The cooks marinate the whole side of ribs, beef or pork, in their special sauce, bake it, cut it into individual strips, broil it with still more sauce, then sauce it again for the table. The most famous ribs joint in New York used to be Jerry's in East Harlem, but it's gone out of business; the *cuchifritos* ("fried stuff") dives on 115th Street offer decent ribs from hogs slaughtered in the local *mercados,* then boiled prior to broiling. Downey's, on Eighth Avenue, is well-known for huge racks of ribs, but they serve the sauce on the side and the grease gets to you in the end.

Presently the absolute best ribs joints in New York hands down, according to the Sex Therapist, is Ellan's, and Ellan's mother's place. My friend won't divulge their addresses and hasn't offered to take me yet, but these women dangle the ribs from the inside of the stove on a paper clip to cut down on the grease, which is how ribs are prepared in the Caribbean. Constant marination is also key. Each generation makes a different sauce, and won't tell the other the recipe. The sex therapist is constantly besieged to choose between the ribs of the mother and the ribs of the daughter, but he categorically refuses.

"Apples and oranges," he tells them.

BECOMING BUDDHA:
The Life and Times of Poet John Giorno - *Tricycle: The Buddhist Review*, Fall Issue, 1994

Note: *My personal interest in Buddhism dates from the early '70s, and I became a relatively-serious practitioner in 1975. I stopped my practice a few years later, but continued to write in a Buddhist context for* Tricycle: the Buddhist Review. *John Giorno was fascinating personally because of how courageously and outrageously he bridged the spiritual and the social, and for his wonderfully coherent thoughts about the future of Dharma in the West.*

Located in the heart of Lower Manhattan's restaurant supply district, 222 Bowery is an unlikely dharma fortress. Constructed as a YMCA in 1884, this solid-looking brick hulk has become the home and studio space of a number of well-known New York artists and writers, among them the poet and Buddhist practitioner John Giorno, who has resided in the Y's former library since 1966. Greeting me on the building's wide interior staircase, his handsome, somewhat smashed face lighting up with an infectious smile, Giorno beckons me into a large square room, then pads barefoot over a carpeted floor to make us coffee. His hair is short and faintly hennaed; his voice, flaring, reedy, and excitable. He has a youthful affect and enthusiasm belying his fifty-seven years.

I had visited 222 Bowery's large mezzanine floor loft a few evenings earlier, and watched Giorno sitting in full lotus, listening along with eighty others to a talk by Tibetan Lama Kyentse Jigme Rinpoche, an old friend who was visiting Giorno from France. Several years ago, Giorno converted his space into an elaborate shrine room for use by Tibetans from the Nyingmapa, Kagyupa, and Sakyapa schools – all the extended lineages of Padma Sambhava, known as Guru Rinpoche, who brought Buddhism to Tibet from India in the eighth century. Important lamas who have used 222 as their Manhattan center and dormitory include Khempo Padden Sherab, Khempo Tswewang, and His Holiness Sakya Trizin, head of the Sakyapa lineage. H.H. Khempo Jigme Phuntsok and

Dodrup Chen Rinpoche have also given teachings here, thanks to Giorno's generosity. The shrine-room has three massive porcelain urinals in the lavatory; it was once a YMCA locker-room and for six years the "Bunker" of Beat legend William S. Burroughs, who reportedly enjoyed the heavy psychic traces of countless naked boys.

Life on the world's most famous skid row sometimes tumbles over the edge: Giorno arrived home one winter night a few years ago to find a frozen corpse on his front steps. CBGBs, the original petri dish of punk music, is a few blocks north; Giorno performed there occasionally in the '80s, fronting a four-chord rock band. Further north is St. Mark's Church-in-the-Bowery, where Giorno the poet has appeared innumerable times since the '60s, ranting about romantic humiliation and sexual exaltation, drugs and tantric sex – fist-fucking, water sports, and poppers. In his 1970-72 poem "Guru Rinpoche," Giorno mixed pop imagery with sacred sutras, portraying gay eroticism as a form of spiritual devotion:

<table>
<tr><td></td><td>He carries</td></tr>
<tr><td>He carries</td><td>He carries</td></tr>
<tr><td>The Vajra</td><td>in his right</td></tr>
<tr><td>in his right</td><td>hand</td></tr>
<tr><td>hand</td><td>the Vajra in his right hand</td></tr>
<tr><td>the Vajra in his right hand</td><td>with palm</td></tr>
<tr><td>with palm</td><td>upwards</td></tr>
<tr><td>upwards</td><td>with palm upwards</td></tr>
<tr><td>with palm upwards</td><td>against</td></tr>
<tr><td>against</td><td>the chest</td></tr>
<tr><td>the chest</td><td>against the chest</td></tr>
<tr><td>against the chest</td><td></td></tr>
<tr><td></td><td>feeling</td></tr>
<tr><td>feeling</td><td>his cock</td></tr>
<tr><td>his cock</td><td>feeling his cock</td></tr>
<tr><td>feeling his cock</td><td>swelling</td></tr>
<tr><td>swelling</td><td>even more</td></tr>
<tr><td>even more</td><td>swelling even more</td></tr>
<tr><td>swelling even more</td><td>inside</td></tr>
<tr><td>inside</td><td>the man</td></tr>
<tr><td>the man</td><td>inside the man</td></tr>
</table>

Asked what his Tibetan friends think of his work, Giorno laughs. "I don't think they understand my poetry because they're not readers. But when they come to live performances, they see the energy. They see the intentions aren't bad, so they usually don't have any judgments at all."

A pioneer of performance poetry – one of the leading creative trends of the '90s – Giorno has fashioned a signature style of intense, highly-amplified, repetitive verse, with subtle shifts of phrasing, volume, and pitch to alter time and sense. Giorno has also been crucial in the expansion of avant-garde poetry and music via new technologies: his record company, Giorno Poetry Systems, has released twenty-eight albums since 1967, producing experimental rock groups New Order, Sonic Youth, Live Skull, Husker Dü, and Cabaret Voltaire, as well as Tom Waits, Patti Smith, Debbie Harry, and Diamanda Galas, and selling upwards of 20,000 CDs, LPs, and tape cassettes of each release, along with Video Paks. Many of Giorno's albums have wonderfully mordant titles: *Big Ego; Sugar, Alcohol and Meat; Smack My Crack;* and *Better an Old Demon Than a New God.* His compilation album *A Diamond Hidden in the Mouth of a Corpse* (1985) included Burroughs' scatological recital of *Mr. President,* which led to Giorno Poetry Systems' abrupt de-funding by the Reagan-era National Endowment for the Arts.

Sixties Renaissance man, '70s media maven, and '80s art-provocateur, Giorno has also been a devoted Buddhist practitioner for almost twenty-five years, exemplifying the cultural phenomenon of the activist-as-yogi. His Poets & Artists with AIDS Fund gave away $88,000 last year, providing gifts to the sick and needy, along with help for the Tibetan Medicine AIDS program of Dr. Trogawa Rinpoche, and funding for the Gregory Kolovakas Award for AIDS writing. "It's one of those blessed things that we always have just enough money to give to every request," Giorno says. Little known outside avant-garde poetry and music circles, having long ago rejected intellectual chic, he has opted for following his heart, and leading a more or less compassionate life.

Born in Manhattan in 1936, the grandson of Italian immigrants who came to the United States in the early 1880s, John Giorno was raised in upper-middle-class Roslyn Heights, on the north shore of Long Island, where his father commuted to Wall Street. "I was part of a generation of privilege who believed we could do anything," Giorno recalls. He became a poet at fourteen, when a school assignment gave him "a blissful feeling of recognition." At sixteen he also realized he was gay, and he never backed down from that identity, either. Devouring modern literature in high school and majoring in comparative literature at Columbia University from 1954 to 1958, he studied with the resident greats – Mark Van Doren, Lionel Trilling, Eric Bentley – and idolized the T.S. Eliot of *The Waste Land*. He even edited an issue of *The Columbia Review*. After attending three of Dylan Thomas' famous 92nd Street YMHA readings (the first was early in 1951), Giorno nearly wore out his LP of *Under Milk Wood* – the distant origin of his own performance poetry. Then one night during Easter break, someone gave Giorno three joints and a copy of Allen Ginsberg's *Howl,* which sent him running through Morningside Heights to Riverside Park, screaming with joy.

"In 1956, to read Allen's words was like liberation," he says. "Before that, there was just nothing but the dismal, depressing '50s, you know?" Attending the Iowa Writer's Workshop after graduation, he lasted in the Midwest six months before returning to New York, where a broken love affair spurred a suicide attempt in 1959, prompting his parents to withdraw financial support. He took a job on Wall Street – "which at the close of the Eisenhower years was a place you wandered in at 10:00 or 11:00, and the place closed shortly after 3:00," Giorno recalls.

After work, he usually went home for a long nap in preparation for a night of partying with a group of thirty or forty downtown visual artists, dancers, and musicians who tended to show up at the same openings and performances. Giorno was widely known as "the poet who works as a stockbroker." Giorno met Andy Warhol late in 1961 and became his Platonic date and occasional lover through the early years of the Pop explosion, as well as a footnote in cinema history, as Warhol's first "Superstar." The aspiring filmmaker used to watch Giorno slumbering in bed for hours at a time, and eventually made him the subject of *Sleep,* which showed the poet in various positions over the course of a very uneventful six hours. Saving a little money, he went back on his parents' dole and left Wall Street to focus on poetry, although it still seemed "totally out to lunch" to him in those early years.

Pop Art influenced him. Giorno's "found poems" of the early '60s utilized images taken from "everyday life, coming into my sense inputs from newspapers, magazines, radio, TV, or books," as he wrote a decade later. Giorno's first book, *The American Book of the Dead*, published in 1964, bore unmistakable parallels to Warhol's contemporary "suicide" silkscreens of car crashes and electric chairs. They were with one another in November 1963, weeping in front of a TV set at the Kennedy assassination. But shortly after the opening of Warhol's West 47th Street Factory in November 1964, Giorno chose to leave that scene behind, and in short order meet Brion Gysin, a white magician, world-class storyteller, and champion of the literary "cut-up."

Gysin had introduced this technique to his friend William Burroughs, who at age forty was the recent notorious author of *Naked Lunch* (1962), a novel *Newsweek* had hailed as "a brutal, priapic, terrifying, paranoiac, and savagely funny book that swings giddily through uncontrolled hallucination and fierce, exact satire." Giorno kept running into Burroughs and Gysin at parties and readings, and by March 1965, he and Gysin were lovers. The older man was very much the mentor, and Giorno the devoted adept – a recurring theme through the poet's middle years. The two men took 34 L.S.D. trips together in Room 703 at the Chelsea Hotel. "Brion was not a meditator in any formal way," Giorno recalls of this period, "but he did sit in lotus position and follow his mind – not watching it to see its nature, but just following it, the opposite of meditation... But I gradually discovered that if I didn't hold on to a thought and just let it go, my mind rested, and that this was very powerful. And then, if one was lucky, one had a degree of bliss or a shot of white light that lasted for as long as one didn't grasp after a thought. A fleeting glimpse of the relative that only mirrors the absolute... Brion and L.S.D. changed my life."

Technology did, too. Gysin was an early pioneer in the use of special effects in recorded poetry, and collaborated with Giorno on some of his earliest sound tapes, collage verses backed with ambient sound. After Gysin and Burroughs departed for Europe that August, Giorno followed, sharing his lover's apartment in Tangier next door to the writer Jane Bowles and just below her husband Paul, the American expatriate composer, author, and translator. In the ancient city of Fez, Giorno dropped L.S.D. to visit the ruined tomb of the Merinides kings. Traveling further south to Jajouka, he and Gysin smoked keef with Bedouin tribesmen and heard the "Pipes of Pan," not long before all the old masters died and their culture and music vanished entirely.

By September 1966, Giorno was back in New York, alone and befuddled. "It was like all those things: the '60s sound heroic now, but the other side was that that was one of the most unhappy periods of my whole life. Everyone was always grasping at anything and miserably unhappy. There were suicides and fights, somebody was always breaking up with their lover – it was really sort of hellish."

The expanding counterculture had improved the climate for public art. Two weeks after returning from Morocco, Giorno moved into 222 Bowery and took a job as Robert Rauschenberg's video camera operator for Experiments in Art & Technology (EAT), a historic collaboration with Bell Lab Sciences at the East 26th Street Armory. Rauschenberg and Giorno became lovers, too, their work together advancing another motif in Giorno's career (besides accomplished lovers): a belief in grassroots dissemination. His second small press book, *Poems by John Giorno* (Mother Press, 1967), was lauded by art critic John Perreault as "a literary event, a paradoxical indictment, and a perverse indictment of raw-ad-mass language." His *Consumer Product Poetry* (1968-1974), consisting solely of words and phrases printed on matchbooks, T-shirts, flags and chocolate bars, was commissioned by a German gallery.

Eventually Giorno followed Rauschenberg into environmental performance, taking all five senses into account. His first "Electronic Sensory Poetry Environment," *Raspberry* was a March 1967 "Happening" at New York University, which had five hundred people smoking pot and wandering around under a black light in what looked like a tank of ultraviolet water, listening to the poet's recorded verse over loudspeakers.

Although Giorno had not yet fully embraced the Dharma, he was firmly on a path of transformation and self-exploration, pushing himself into some of the most radical art experiments of his day. His most notorious art & technology endeavor of the '60s was inspired by the National Weather Service. The original "Dial-a-Poem" began at the Architectural League of New York on West 64th Street in December 1967, featuring two-and-one-half minute recorded phone poems by Giorno, Burroughs, Allen Ginsberg, John Cage, Diane di Prima, LeRoi Jones, Frank O'Hara, Abbie Hoffman, Black Panther Bobby Seale, and

East Village teenager Jim Carroll. After *The New York Times* and *The Today Show* ran favorable pieces, the phone lines were deluged with tens of thousands of calls an hour. *Junior Scholastic* published an article, while suburban kids dialed in to hear Burroughs' homo-erotic scamper *The Wild Boys* and Carroll's drugs-and-sex-soaked *Basketball Diaries*. This prompted a parent's complaint, which led to the phone service being temporarily suspended. The New York State Council on the Arts helped restore the lines, which stayed open until June 1968, logging well over a million calls in all. Giorno had also become a gossip columnist for *Culture Hero*, a short-lived, *Interview*-like quarterly founded in 1968 by artist Les Levine. His column infuriated the art world with accounts of extramarital affairs, former lovers' penis sizes and sexual proclivities. Gysin in Europe reportedly referred to Giorno as "the Pepys of the pariah set."

Were Giorno's "Vitamin G" columns attacks on the self-serving images and growing commercialization of the New York art world, or a boorish response to not having his ex-lovers' wealth and fame?

"Maybe underneath it all there was some malice, but that certainly wasn't the intention," Giorno says today. "I thought I was just mirroring their own maliciousness." Dharma friends characterize Giorno as "a trickster," wanting to expose people, blow their covers. Whatever his motivation, Giorno would continue his tendency to burn bridges. In a 1974 interview in *Gay Sunshine*, he branded Allen Ginsberg "a pushy Jew... a founding father of the bullshit liberals," and "more or less a bad poet" who hadn't written anything worth reading since the '50s – a possible explanation for why Giorno would remain uninvited for thirteen years to the poetry school Ginsberg would help to create at Naropa Institute, a Buddhist center in Boulder, Colorado.

Giorno was angry at the art world for its apparent lack of concern with the political crisis and the war in Vietnam. By the fall of 1969, he was actively involved with the co-founders of the Yippies, Abbie Hoffman and Jerry Rubin. Determined to make poetry "a razor blade... cutting through the ego of American karma," Giorno was the central organizer of a thirty-hour-long New Year's Eve 1969 benefit at St. Mark's Church for White Panther "political prisoner" John Sinclair, who had recently been busted for selling joints to an undercover agent. In March 1970, Giorno participated in a press conference that kicked off "free radio" WPAX, and eventually assembled ten ninety-minute recordings of rock music, gay and women's shows, and anti-war news for Radio Hanoi, which was aired in both the north and south of Vietnam. After the broadcasts, Vice President Spiro Agnew denounced Giorno and Abbie Hoffman as traitors, "would-be Hanoi Hannahs," and called for their arrest. No one had been convicted of treasonable speech since Aaron Burr, and Giorno's lawyers assured him this could only occur during a declared war, which Vietnam was not.

Antiwar work continued at the "Information" show at New York's Museum of Modern Art in June, where Giorno installed twelve Dial-a-Poem tapes, including political messages from Bobby Seale and Abby Hoffman. Diane di Prima's "How to Make a Molotov Cocktail" was on line the day a large bomb exploded in the city's IBM building, raising the possibility that the Rockefellers' favorite museum may have provided information to terrorists. Panicky trustees allowed the Dial-a-Poem program to continue for three more months, in order to avoid the appearance of censorship, while free publicity pushed callers to 60,000 a week.

The fusion of mass poetry, technology, and politics that characterized Giorno's turn-of-the-decade activism proved an uneasy one: his third book, *Balling Buddha* (Kulchur Press, 1970), written before he took formal vows of refuge, suggested the poet's longtime casual sense of himself as Buddhist and a growing desire to "make it" to some higher spiritual ground. *Balling Buddha's* surrealistic evocations of war, brutality, joy, and explicit sex introduced the formal device of double columns running down each page, which Giorno has employed ever since. "After doubling the line, tripling it, I found musical rhythms developing in the flow of the words, like chanting," he later wrote.

Otherwise, the poet felt on the verge of a nervous collapse.

"His power consisted of whispering potent phrases from newspapers," he wrote in one poem, echoing both the era's minimalism and his own mounting despair. "Everything failed," Giorno later claimed. "Drugs failed – they gave you an indication of the nature of mind, but you ended up crashing and being totally depressed."

Visiting upstate in Cherry Valley at Allen Ginsberg's summer place and tripping on L.S.D. every three or four days in fact, Giorno kept asking so many annoying questions on spiritual matters that Ginsberg finally bellowed, *"Ahh!!*

Stop asking me so many questions! Why don't you go to India and find out for yourself?"

"I went through shock, then anger, then feeling – 'What a great idea!'" Giorno recalls. By March 1971 he was in New Delhi and on his way to Almora, a hill station near India's western border with Nepal, in the company of his friends Wynn and Sally Chamberlain, who were Hindus. In Almora they rendezvoused with their friends Nena Thurman, whom they knew through her ex-husband, acid guru Timothy Leary, and Nena's current husband, Robert Thurman, the future chairman of Indo-Tibetan studies at Columbia University and the first Westerner ordained as a Tibetan Buddhist Monk since the Chinese takeover in 1959, although he had recently renounced his Gelugpa vows. Thurman invited Giorno to accompany his family across northern India to **Dharamshala,** where they would spend two weeks as houseguests of the Dalai Lama.

Giorno sat silently for hours listening to Thurman and His Holiness converse in Tibetan.

Returning to Almora, he met a Nyingmapa teacher, Nyichang Rinpoche, and went with him to Sarnath, site of the Buddha's first teachings after Enlightenment. Giorno spent July and August there, studying the Tibetan language and religion.

His spiritual wandering was soon to end. An American friend, Dhammadipo (John Mills), went with him overnight by train to Darjeeling, where he met his friend's teacher, His Holiness Dudjom Rinpoche. Giorno stayed with Dudjom for the next two months, during which Rinpoche accepted Giorno's vow of refuge.

"One takes refuge in one's own Buddha-nature, which is no different from that of the historical Shakyamuni Buddha," Giorno says today. "But in reality, as a practitioner you take refuge in your teacher, since he is an example of that Buddha-nature which is beyond concepts, beyond subject-object relations. You take refuge in him as a lover, in the best sense – or you should, at least – and with great devotion. That's the preliminary. And then over years of practice, one takes refuge in one's own wisdom-mind, one's own enlightenment, and there is no longer any difference between the teacher's mind and the disciple's mind. And that's the source of all refuge, and it manifests beautifully at various levels."

In his classic '60s-to-'70s conversion, Giorno had not only embraced the Buddhist notion of enlightened mind; he had also become the unlikely favorite American student of the leader of one of the four principal schools of Tibetan Buddhism. Nyingma means "old school" or "ancient ones," and traces its origins to Padma Sambhava, the Indian sage (and non-monk) who along with the monk Shantirakshita introduced Buddhist teachings to the Land of Snows. The pinnacle of Nyingmapa teachings is an approach to meditation called Dzongchen, or Great Perfection. The Nyingma grant special importance to the notion of *tertons,* treasure finders – twenty-five reincarnated disciples of Padma Sambhava, whose scriptural discoveries and visionary revelations maintain the freshness and vitality of the teachings. Dudjom was one of the treasure finders, widely venerated as a scholar and a great meditator.

Studying with him and living in a Tibetan-run guest house in the shadow of Dudjom's residence, Giorno felt entirely blessed. Returning to New York in September 1971, he resumed serious Buddhist practice and studies at 222 Bowery, in private classes with a Western scholar, Arthur Mandelbaum. In December, he visited Chögyam Trungpa Rinpoche's year-old Vermont retreat center, Tail of the Tiger (later renamed Karma Triyana Dharmachakra, or KTD), doing Nyingmapa practices with Trungpa Rinpoche, who, Giorno believes, helped him immeasurably.

But repercussions of past events continued to affect the present. During the trip across northern India, Giorno had suffered an accidental blow to his left testicle, and the injury never healed. By November 1972, during yet another acid-drenched "Happening" at St. Mark's Church, he was approached by Nunau, a Japanese Zen poet-monk, who told him he looked sick and urged him to see a doctor.

Examining physicians at Bellevue wanted to operate immediately, but Giorno talked them out of it. He eventually went to Memorial Hospital, where doctors relieved him of a testicle that had swollen rock hard and was the size of a lemon. A biopsy revealed four kinds of cancer, three of them extremely lethal. Five surgeons went to work, displacing Giorno's small intestines through a twelve-inch incision, removing fifty lymph nodes along his spine, replacing his intestines, and sewing him up.

Ten days later, he was home; three days after that, at a ski lodge in the Grand Tetons, attending a seminar on the eight aspects of Padma Sambhava, conducted by Trungpa Rinpoche.

Meditation, hot saunas, and rolls in the snow brought Giorno back to life. *Cancer in My Left Ball* (Something Else Press, 1973) registers the shock and recovery, although most of the poems were written prior to surgery. Finishing his 100,000 prostrations, the required preliminary practice, Giorno was eager to see Dudjom again and to meet other lamas.

By Labor Day 1973 he was back in India, accompanied by fiction writer Michael Brownstein and the poet Anne Waldman. "John had a real plan," Waldman told me. "Surrendering ego, giving up reference points, leaving behind personal history – the trip was a powerful way to enter the mandala."

Landing in Delhi, the trio traveled directly to Darjeeling, where a number of great Nyingmapa lamas lived within a quarter-mile of one another: Kangyur Rinpoche, a legendary holder of the Dharma library (who would be dead within a year); Chatral Rinpoche (who became Waldman's root Lama); and Dilgo Khyentse, Dodrup Chen, and other major Nyingmapa Rinpoches in Darjeeling, which lay on the historic trade route from India to Tibet. Giorno spent three months in Dudjom's household, living as a virtual family member.

"Dudjom Rinpoche was a very elegant, gentle man, and the whole family adored John," recalls Vivian Kurz, another of his longtime student. "The lamas love eccentrics, personalities. They like people who are themselves. They look for an interest in transformation – a spark, an openness to develop the mind and develop compassion."

Giorno's homosexuality, which he never concealed, was never remotely an issue with the Tibetans, in part due to what the poet considers the Nyingmapa tradition of loving tolerance.

"All the monasteries in all of the traditions are very, very gay," Giorno claims. "When I was visiting the dormitories at Sarnath, I'd see these really young men – they may have been nineteen but emotionally they were fourteen – sleeping in each other's arms. They may not have called it gay, but they were lovers – they made a heart contact, they loved each other the way you love a person… I've had wonderful relationships – I've had many Tibetans completely in love with me… To have that emotional connection was enough. It was without problems – never jealousies, none of it." But strictly speaking, wasn't homosexuality frowned upon? Giorno responds: "I'm not sure about the various traditions, but at least among the lamas I've spoken to, they're very aware that a man's mind and a woman's mind is the same mind – we're all made up of male and female energies – and that some people have a need for more of one or another, more masculine energy or female energy."

After a five-week retreat at Kangyur Rinpoche's monastery, Giorno returned to New York in late January 1974, confident that his spiritual "retreat" was not an evasion. He may have lost much of his faith in Western art, but he felt increasingly intent on expanding and disseminating alternative cultures. A two-record set based on the Dial-a-Poem series, *Disconnected* (1974) was followed by a William Burroughs album, a Frank O'Hara album, a record of his own poetry, and another of Waldman's. By late spring 1975, Giorno was traveling to Kathmandu, where Dudjom had relocated, with plans to invite his teacher to start a center in New York. Raising money from a number of wealthy American practitioners, Giorno welcomed Dudjom in April 1976 to a permanent dharma center opened on West 16th Street as a place "to lure the lamas back," says Kurz, who joined Giorno, Les Levine, and screenwriter-novelist Rudy Wurlitzer on its board of directors.

Giorno enjoyed a spiritual double life through the late '70s and early '80s. He split time between His Holiness Dudjom Rinpoche and William S. Burroughs, who moved into the 222 Bowery Bunker in November 1975.

"I'd be coming down the stairs and William would wave me in for a joint and a vodka and tonic," Giorno recalls with a laugh. "Then I'd go to 16th Street and the Tibetans would laugh at me. I told them I did it for my work." Whenever Dudjom returned to the city, Giorno essentially moved in, becoming especially close to Dudjom's wife and two daughters – Nyingmapa teachings emphasize the presence of consorts and female energies. Giorno had also drifted into the East Village Punk and New Wave music scene, in much the same way that many other artists did – partially in reaction to the boredom and corruption of the art and poetry worlds. Giorno's book *Shit, Piss, Blood, Pus and Brains*

(Painted Bride Press, 1977) made connections with Punk, but his new fascination with "street rock" also represented an integration of what he had always been: a cutting-edge extremist and a popular communicator.

Giorno played the central role in the creation of the Nova Convention, a historic high point of Punk/New Wave that brought together academics, art world figures, and entertainment stars for a three-day-long "gathering of the tribes" in early December 1978, celebrating Burroughs' growing eminence across genres and generations. The Nova Convention capped the decade of the '70s, attracting extensive media coverage and standing-room-only crowds, but Burroughs was entering his seventies then, and slowing down. In 1981 he left the Bunker for Lawrence, Kansas – the same year that Dudjom Rinpoche's health began to decline, prompting his retirement from teaching at Yeshe Nyingpo, as the 16th Street center was called. With His Holiness rarely on the scene, internal politics and money squabbles grew increasingly acrimonious, and Giorno chose to withdraw from active participation in the center, glad to leave behind a competent director, Jon Pfaudler. Friends suspect that Giorno's mixed experience at Yeshe Nyingpo was the major factor influencing his current, more casual, nonsectarian center at 222 Bowery.

No longer the devoted adept following the lead of a magician-mentor, Giorno at forty-five was on his own, increasingly in demand, nationally and internationally, as a performance poet. The worldwide ascendance of Punk and New Wave music had opened a wealth of musical possibilities for poets, inspiring Giorno to assemble a consortium of art-rock heavyweights to record an album, "I'm Rock Hard," in the spring of 1982, then to front his own touring group to clubs in Toronto, Montreal, Miami, Houston, Oklahoma City, and Detroit over the next five or six years. Keeping the John Giorno Band alive proved difficult financially, however, and it folded in 1988. At the same time a new cultural threat had emerged, in part an aftershock of the previous promiscuous decade – "the first in human history in which people did more or less everything they wanted to do sexually," as the novelist Edmund White would note.

"In the late '70s and up until about 1980, I was virtually the King of promiscuity, and there is no way I did not come into contact with the AIDS virus," says Giorno, who practiced unsafe sex as late as the summer of 1982, in one instance with graffiti artist Keith Haring in the men's room at the Prince Street subway station, when Haring already knew he was HIV-positive. "But for whatever reason, it's never manifested," Giorno claims. "That's my karma, my luck – and that's rare these days." With his fellow practitioner and longtime companion, the classical pianist Paul Alberts, Giorno founded his AIDS Treatment Project in 1984, a year before he himself was tested and found negative.

"My intention is to treat a complete stranger as a lover or close friend," John says today. "My way is to give money personally and directly, with strong emotional support – by bringing it to the hospital or to the person's apartment, or by the person coming to my home. Indiscriminate compassion, not making distinctions between people – not 'I'll help this one, but not that one, because I didn't know him.'"

By mid-1994, Giorno's one-man operation, administered out of his own pocket, had given away $460,732, including a $50,000 grant to the University of Miami Medical School to fund a research chair in neurological AIDS. He has also provided spiritual support through ten-day *phowa* – "the practice of conscious dying" – retreats in the Bunker.

Giorno explains: *"Phowa* is a specialty of Ayang Rinpoche, who travels around the world giving teachings and retreats on what happens in the moment of death, and how you can eject your consciousness from your heart center through the crown of your head into a Buddha field. It's a little similar to gymnastics. If you practice this and perfect it in your life, then at the moment of death it will be like a habit, and you'll do it. Dudjom Rinpoche said that if you're not a perfected Dzongchen master who can dissolve your mind at the moment of death, and you're not a perfected Vajrayana master who can dissolve your consciousness to primordial wisdom at the moment of death, then you essentially better get your ass going and perfect *phowa,* because if you don't, at the moment of death you are really in trouble, because your mind will be at the mercy of your own terror."

Giorno devotes seven days a week to his AIDS project, but tries to limit administrative work sessions to an hour or two a day. Poetry is his greatest passion – even if he tends to dismiss his writing as not worth talking about, preferring his live performances. Not everyone agrees: his publisher Lita Hornick described *Grasping at Emptiness* (Kulchur Press, 1985) as "a unified commentary on both our civilization and man's fate," while William Burroughs calls Giorno's newest book, *you got to burn to shine* (High Risk, 1994), "litanies from the underworld of the mind that reverberate in your head and ventriloquize your own thoughts."

Giorno is terrific company – a funny impressionist, a lover of gossip, and reportedly an excellent chef – but above all a Buddhist, devoted to the pursuit of enlightenment. In contrast to Giorno the avant-garde, over-the-edge, gay radical poet, Giorno the Buddhist embraces an orthodoxy rare among American converts. He puts unquestioning faith in his guru, in the empowerment of his lineage, and, more than anything else, in the supreme efficacy of devotion and practice.

"His lifeblood is really Buddhism," says Kurz, who arranged the Bunker talk by Kyentse Jigme Rinpoche, Giorno's old friend from France. Quietly but fiercely Nyingmapa, Giorno has welcomed other orders to his shrine room, but Gelugpa monks have yet to request the space. Giorno alludes to their "problems" with women, marriage, and sexuality, as well as their belief that non-monks cannot be enlightened – although he understands that the Dalai Lama, who heads the Gelugpa order, is more broad-minded about this. Giorno's current activities exemplify the Dalai Lama's recent re-emphasis on the true purpose of religion: "to bring about inner transformation by helping others."

RC: *Have you experienced homophobia among the Tibetans?*

Giorno: Not personally, no. They're very funny that way. Because they have to be traditional Buddhists – the Vinaya, or monk's vows, and the Lower Vehicles are very much against homosexual activity. His Holiness Druk Chen, head of the Drugpa Kagyus, who's a good friend of mine – he was five years old when I met him in Darjeeling in 1971 and he now comes and stays in the Bunker when he's here – His Holiness said to me (and this was a very personal thought of his) that when the Buddha gave teachings 2,500 years ago, he didn't do it in a vacuum and he didn't do it to an enlightened audience. He gave teachings in a very primitive culture in which homosexuality was a taboo. So the Buddha reflected that in the teachings. This early Vedic culture 2,500 years ago was also very patriarchal and demeaning to women. And the Buddha reflected that view of women, just so that he would be taken seriously. You don't start out teaching by alienating everyone in the room. And so these views of sex and gender became the basis for the first level, the Vinaya: to include the morality of the day. As the Buddha worked up in the higher vehicles, these concepts fell away.

RC: *Are the Nyingma perhaps more tolerant of sexuality generally, given the fact that marriage is permitted?*

Giorno: The Nyingmas have a great veneration for women, and their way of dealing with this is marriage – or having a girlfriend, and doing heterosexual practice that way. The monastic traditions in the Nyingma are no different than other traditions, they're very strict, but inside everyone there are all these emotions… I remember one of Dudjom Rinpoche's disciples talking about how, if you're going to do this sexual practice, *tab lam,* you do that practice with a woman. In most countries, these yogic practices are done with a woman. Then I said, "Why not with a man? That's being homophobic and discriminatory against women!" And I said, "I have one wish, and that is that Padma Sambhava will bring forth a *terma* [a hidden teaching] – because presumably it's always there – a practice enabling gay men and lesbian women to have some kind of practice to reach enlightenment. I didn't want it in my lifetime, and I didn't ask for my own personal gain, but for the benefit of all gay men and lesbian women who have suffered for all these many millennia!" I told this to a disciple of Dudjom Rinpoche, and he actually shook his head, as if he was displeased with my attachment to being gay. I saw that, and so I went through it one more time, just so he would hear all these things that we've been talking about here in America, starting with civil rights and going into women's rights and feminism and then into gay rights. It isn't about being attached to gay sexuality – it's the idea that one should use sexuality as a means to become enlightened. In the Vajrayana you use everything to become enlightened – you only become enlightened by your own phenomena! And if you're a gay man, or a lesbian, you should be able to use that, and not be conditioned by the Tibetan culture, or small-minded traditions going back to Vedic times. Gay and lesbian Buddhists have been victims of discrimination for millennia, and I want to change that.

RC: *Have you encountered people in the sangha who feel that somehow your poetry and your gayness are too extreme?*

Giorno: No one has ever said that to me.

RC: *But do you sense a growing cultural conservatism among American Buddhists?*

Giorno: Yes, and I'm appalled by it. To be a practitioner and a householder is probably what's best for most of the world, but when it's put forward as a view or moral code that cannot be violated, and other alternatives are seen somehow as not acceptable – that's a problem. There are certain elements within the various Buddhist traditions, Tibetan and Zen and otherwise, which are by their nature – and this is my personal view now – puritanical. The recent conference in Dharamsala about Buddhist morality and the morality of Buddhist teachers, over which the Dalai Lama presided, became a kind of – and I'm exaggerating now – a great fundamentalist movement arising inside of Buddhism. I don't think that it arose because Tibetan lamas in India decided that they needed to purify the Western teachings. I think it arose here, among Westerners who have these ideas, perhaps politically motivated, and made what I think is a rather unpleasant situation. I'll give them the benefit of the doubt, they're unaware of what they're doing, but in some of these people, a lot of it arose out of anger! And that's a nightmare. You can't tell a teacher what to do. You're talking about what some teachers may do personally with their disciples, especially sexually – and you cannot tell a teacher, a guru, a buddha, that he shouldn't do something – or anything! It just doesn't work at the Vajrayana or tantric level. And that's a big problem!

RC: *Some years ago you said, "Drugs let me see the nature of mind." What are your feelings about that now?*

Giorno: I was explaining what happened in the '60s when a lot of us took L.S.D. trips. What I meant is that drugs allow us to see not the nature of mind, but the display of mind. Drugs and alcohol numb the central nervous system and allow the naturality of the mind to flow free – that blissful state that is always inside all phenomena. I don't take drugs anymore, but drugs are sacred substances, and I think it's disrespectful to discriminate against them. In the '70s, L.S.D. and the rest became sexual drugs: you took drugs and made it with one or more people for endless hours, although inside a drug experience one never stopped watching the nature of one's mind. But what happens with all drugs – and I'm not talking now about heroin or cocaine or speed, but about drugs that are not physically addictive, like marijuana and L.S.D. – is that once you have a successful experience, you don't get that kind of experience again outside of drugs, unless you're a completely realized being. So you go back to the drugs because you're not going to get these experiences again by just being your normal self. If your intentions are to get those kinds of experiences in meditation, drugs aren't such a great thing to take. They can block all progress.

RC: *So drugs are not something recommended for practitioners who want to embark on a Buddhist path.*

Giorno: No, obviously not. It's not the way you create a foundation for your practice to come to completion. But among the many people out there who are between the ages of sixteen and twenty-one, there's a new resurgence of taking L.S.D. And I always think of them, those people suffering at the mercy of their minds, as people like myself, who will hopefully see an indication of the nature of his or her mind, which will start them on the path to complete enlightenment.

RC: *I'm quoting now from* Literary Outlaw, *Ted Morgan's biography of William Burroughs: "As a Buddhist, Giorno had a theory that in the use of those sex drugs they had transgressed certain other realms, whose attendants had become angry, with a lethal anger from the spirit world."*

Giorno: That was just one of my dumb concepts. In the mid-'80s I had this idea that back when we took all those great drugs, one indeed entered into other realms. There are a hundred million heavens, and as many *naga* or spirit realms. And when protectors of the god realms become angry, they're very powerful. That was my thought. Whether it's true or not, I've no idea. But it's a possibility. That's how bad things sometimes happen. In the canon of all religions, there are curses from deities who become angry: pestilence, epidemics, this or that. This was one possible subtle cause for the AIDS epidemic, along with the possibility that it's a man-made virus, but they've completely covered their tracks, and we'll never know. Dudjom Rinpoche prophesied that in the age of the Kali-Yuga [the degenerate age], which we're at the beginning of now, there will be eighty-two new diseases that have been heard of before, for which there will be no cure. He thought AIDS was one of those diseases.

RC: *You have described your work as what arises in your mind: "My poisons transformed or not transformed." What do you mean by this?*

Giorno: I write about the five poisons – desire, anger, ignorance, jealousy, and pride – and their luminous empty nature. Whatever it is, anger or desire or whatever, at the moment that thought or emotion arises it is very pure. It becomes a poison one instant later, when you attach to it, when you want to hold on and not let go. And depending on one's "graspiness," it becomes a huge poison, or a deadly poison, or whatever. Dudjom Rinpoche had a great teaching for this: the metaphor is a tree. In the Hinayana you try to cut it down, cut out all the roots, but the stupid thing keeps growing back! Then on the Mahayana level, you burn the tree or poison it. And of course it still grows back because the roots are there. The Vajrayana is even more complicated – chemicals transform it. But on the very highest Vajrayana level is the practitioner who is described as a peacock, who eats the poison leaves and is not killed by them – and they make his feathers more beautiful.

SUBVERSIVE PLEASURES & THE "DELTA" BLUES: Postmodernism '84

Note: *This is drawn from another chapter in my unpublished manuscript POST-SHOCK: The Emergence of the American Avant-Garde.*

"Actually, when you drop something, it's still with you, wouldn't you say?" - John Cage, 1958

The term "Postmodern" first surfaced in an English-language dictionary in 1942, and five years later in Arnold Toynbee's monumental *Study of History,* describing a "postmodern" period, which roughly corresponded to the age of the modernist avant-garde, from 1875 to that moment, and also the era of Oswald Spengler's "Decline of the West." Discussions of postmodernity were commonplace at Black Mountain College in the early '50s; later in that decade, sociologists and market analysts were describing the arrival of a "postmodern" era, which the literary critic and socialist Irving Howe described as "a relatively comfortable, half welfare and half garrison state, in which the population grows passive, indifferent, and atomized." Halfway through the '60s, the sculptor and land artist Robert Smithson conjured up a postmodern "Ice Age" of "forbidden zones... dazzling realms... dimensions beyond the walls of time." By the early '70s, postmodernism had evolved, or devolved, or deformed, into "the final disintegration of the social compact," according to post-'60s communard Jean Baudrillard – a view promptly attacked by Jean-Francois Lyotard as "nostalgia" for an "organic society" that had never existed in modern times. "Performance in Postmodern Culture," a conference I attended at the University of Wisconsin Milwaukee in 1976, was an early attempt to break down the barriers between the Modernist Academy and the Postmodernist Avant-Garde. Postmodernism was targeting narratives that had guided the modern world for more than a century.

In *Postmodernism, or, the Cultural Logic of Late Capitalism,* published in *New Left Review* in 1984, the neo-Marxist Frederic Jameson summarized the spirit of Postmodernity as goodbye, grand historical narratives—things like a revolutionary end to class warfare, a terminable analysis (Freudian or otherwise), or constant originality in the arts – and hello, consumerist desire. Lyotard wrote that the absence of a "grand narrative" capable of describing and uplifting and speeding along the current era was exactly what postmodernism was: a grand narrative for an age that didn't have a grand narrative. There was no Wholeness in the postmodern condition; only Totality. No authentic culture, only transactional ones; no verities, only more than enough irony to go around.

Postmodernism was difficult to define because it made a chaos of differences: sometimes conceding the triumph of Late Capitalism, at other times defying it; sometimes containing modernist culture, at other times surpassing it; sometimes resembling the Liberal Imagination writ large, or the culture of corporate America ("to know no boundaries is what the world should be" was the '80s motto of Merrill-Lynch) – at other times, the final disintegration of the social compact, the triumph of nihilism, and a cultural apocalypse. This was what French Structuralists, Post-Structuralists, and Deconstructionists brought to the table.

Not until the early '80s did the question of postmodernity – mainly, *what is it?* – position itself close to the center of art world discourse. "Picture" artists, Deconstructionists, Trans-Avant-Gardists, and Neo-Expressionists all weighed in on this weightless debate. Postmodernism became "the label of the hour," said *Art in America*—a description and a reflection of the loss of "isms," guides, and organization to contemporary experience. Postmodern leveling had become a global project, encompassing Tribeca, SoHo, the East and West Villages, Midtown and the culture industries of L.A., and developed and under-developed societies and cultures around the globe.

A lot of artists weren't buying it. Painter Pat Steir considered Postmodernism "a 'kink' in the idea of modernism." Peter Halley argued in the November 1981 issue of *Arts* that "what is today thought of as modernism is not really outdated, but merely badly formulated in the first place." When I asked the composer Philip Glass what he thought about postmodernism, he chuckled and said he liked it "because it means nothing" – meaning it was a placeholder until something better came along. Many would likely agree with the painter, poet, and critic David Shapiro, who thought it best not to be "distracted from distraction by bad abstractions." Even Cage told me that he was "very confused over this [postmodern] idea of history in relation to art." For others, postmodernism was a response to the failure of high modernism to address the expanding role of mass media, consumerism, and democratization in artistic practice. This was why so much self-consciously postmodernist art ended up looking like Neo-Pop art.

Postmodernist style was most obvious in architecture, where historical reference and pastiche created the allegorical look of a decade without a look of its own. Postmodern architecture in the '80s blended nostalgia and futurism, Doric columns and neon lights, metallic handrails and Empire wainscoting, in the same way that the Mudd Club in Tribeca mixed-and-matched the latest retro fashions and musical genres from around the planet. In a postmodern world, every gesture, every allusion, every action was suspended in the Known. "Quote" marks proliferate like kudzu. If we really were "post," if originality really was dead, then appropriation, quotation, and pastiche made perfect sense. "Now it's all 'appropriation,'" choreographer Doug Elkins told me. "I like to go to films, to Senegalese dances, to Trisha Brown." Postmodern cultural ambition in the '80s was characterized by a feeling that the past was "under our belts, not on our backs," as the novelist John Barth optimistically put it. Sampling, montage, and collage – time-honored modernist techniques – were being wielded by postmodernists in writing, music, choreography, architecture, you name the field. Postmodernism was about putting old things together in fresh ways. Postmodernists "bricolage"—Claude Levi-Strauss' term for the creation of "a new world… of any and all available material from the old world."

The postmodern debates eventually settled around three perspectives, with each identified with a decade, as Columbia University Professor Andreas Huyssens explained: first, the perspective of the '50s, which held that "postmodernist" culture and its avant-gardistic tendencies were simply fraudulent, and high modernism was the gold standard; second, the perspective of the '60s, which had postmodern populists engaging the "real" world (and therefore being smart and good), while high modernists addressed only an elite, which made them narrow and small-minded by definition; and third, the '70s' perspective, in which postmodernism became an active ideology of consumer capitalism, and as such, a social apocalypse. In all three cases, postmodernism connected to the triumph of multinational capital and the global emergence of new technologies bridging languages and cultures. In this formulation, everyone is living "inside" postmodern times—all of us are swimming in a vast, boundaryless cultural delta.

"We're living in a 'delta culture,'" John Cage told me in one of several interviews, an idea he had courtesy of a French musicologist—a refinement of the term "Pluralistic." There was no "mainstream" anymore, and no "avant-gardes," either—only an expansive delta with a variety of faster and slower-moving currents, none powerful enough to dominate the others or isolated enough to remain strictly marginal. Postmodern artists might fantasize about reclaiming the privileges and critical remove afforded by modernism, which had also been "inclusive, open and indeterminate," as Clement Greenberg argued. But Postmodernism had slipped the grand narratives of modernity, as Lyotard claims in his seminal book *The Postmodern Condition: a Report on Knowledge* (1979). "Incredulity towards meta-narratives" is arguably the primary characteristic of postmodern times, and what passed itself off as "advanced" culture in the post-Hiroshima era. The twin hallucinations of postmodernity are the transformation of reality into imagery and the fragmentation of time, and the resulting break-up of history. Without a "grand narrative" to carry us forward, or through, without a new myth or religion to provide social direction, cultural workers might well embrace the ahistorical "freedoms" that postmodernity allows, but would ultimately fail to transcend the post-vanguard moment, here in the "dying days of aestheticized liberalism under the twin signs of passive and "suicidal nihilism," as Arthur Kroker, a Canadian author and researcher of political science, technology and culture, would have us believe.

But couldn't we approach this new "hyperreality" as Buddhist Śūnyatā: open, accommodating space? Couldn't we take subversive pleasure in our situation, and imagine it possible for human beings to make something of what the world has made of them, as Jean-Paul Sartre and Shunryu Suzuki Roshi would agree? Or was this "openness" merely an invitation to the "delicatessen" postmodernism condemned by the late Harold Rosenberg as a "relaxation?" Relaxation was normative in the early '80s, but at times subversive of the status quo, because it served to keep people alive. Manhattan was not an island in the South Pacific. It was a postmodern Utopia and Dystopia, where creation and destruction were twinned highlights. Postmodernism survived wherever the old Situationist injunction from the '60s remained in place: "Think Globally, act Locally." The avant-garde legacy continued wherever grassroots infrastructures existed for collective resistance, uniting communities whose partial solutions adhered to the best intelligence of the time. As Jameson suggested, "we are *within* the culture of postmodernism to the point where its facile repudiation is as impossible as any equally facile celebration of it is complacent and corrupt." The Italian art critic Achille Bonita Oliva wrote that the best response to postmodernity was "not one of fighting history with cold steel, but rather broadening the creative space, enlarging the arena of cultural revision, and reaffirming the working character of art." Postmodernists moving across the myriad streams of our contemporary cultural delta were investigating and refreshing older styles and vernacular traditions, touching high culture, mass culture, and the non-commercial popular art that lies between, setting in motion what many consider the most important trend in the live arts of the '80s: the emergence of experimental performance and visual art on a scale never before witnessed in the modern world.

THE INTELLECTUAL ODYSSEY OF PETER SWALES: "Punk" Historian of Psychoanalysis, *Rolling Stone*, September 27, 1984

Note: *Peter Swales had been a good friend of mine for a couple of years before I profiled him for* Rolling Stone. *I was among a handful of journalists to attend Swales' famous 1981 N.Y.U. lecture in which he unveiled his brilliant, fact-based, circumstantial argument that Freud had for many years conducted a secret sexual relationship with his sister-in-law, Minna Bernays. This was years before Janet Malcolm of* The New Yorker *wrote her celebrated articles and a book,* In the Freud Archives, *in which Peter is the third major character.*

We live in a world partially shaped by the thought of Sigmund Freud, the founder of modern psychology – the man who established theories on sexuality that have become central to twentieth-century ideas of the body and mind. We have also lived with a traditional view of the Founder as a chaste, even puritanical man, a scientist of flawless integrity, who created and ruled over a worldwide psychoanalytic establishment. Yet in 1934, he wrote, "Nobody knows or has ever guessed the real secret of my work."

Guesses have been made. In the decades since Freud's death, psychologists, biologists, theologizes, feminists and social critics have used Freud's own writings to challenge his theories. The intellectual game of using Freud to whip

Freud has been practiced by generations of biographers and historians, and yet despite the dark secrets of Freud's life – his cocaine habit, the rumors of his long-secret love affair with his sister-in-law, Minna Bernays – the sacrosanct image of the Founder has endured, protected and burnished by his followers in their fortresses, the Sigmund Freud Archives in New York and the U.S. Library of Congress, where crucial documents are withheld from public view, some until the twenty-second century.

But now these Freudian fastnesses are beset by a new attacker who has fashioned a startling portrait of a Freud that no one knew existed: a Freud of vanity and ambition, of drugs and demonology, who elevated and codified his own narcotic and sexual obsessions into the "science" of psychoanalysis. This is a Freud whose intellectual development was deeply affected by his secret love affair with Minna, her subsequent pregnancy, and the abortion he may have arranged for her at an Alpine spa. And what is more remarkable about this portrait, in the minds of some, is that it is more consistent with Freudian theory than the standard image of the man. This new portrait comes from outside the walls of the Freudian bastions, outside the universities, psychiatric hospitals and institutes, from another world entirely: from Peter Swales, the self-styled "punk historian of psychoanalysis," a thirty-six-year-old Welshman now living in New York, who departed on his fifteen-year odyssey into the life and mind of Sigmund Freud from the Kingdom of Their Satanic Majesties: The Rolling Stones.

"Freud's work began in drugs and hypnotic suggestion, which belong to the tradition of black magic and demonology much more than they do to medicine proper," Swales tells me in an interview at his Lower East Side tenement. His slight form is draped across a windowsill, where he is tossing clots of grease to a crowd of cats milling in the air shaft four flights below. "And indeed, psychoanalysis has a kind of narcotic property: we all know the cliché of people addicted to their shrinks. I have always been interested in the drug culture and rock & roll because in microcosm they amplify tendencies that are prevalent in modern culture as a whole. And the point here is that Freud is incredibly contemporary. In a sense, in getting involved with cocaine, Freud was a precursor of rock culture by eighty years. We live in a narcotic culture," Swales concludes, tossing himself into a kitchen chair and lighting a cigarette, "and anyone who can't see that has to be in a fucking stupor."

Not everyone sees it Swales' way: his attack on the "science" of psychoanalysis has stung the Freudian establishment. Author Janet Malcolm reports on his intellectual wars in her gripping book, *In the Freud Archives,* which depicts the supposedly staid, sherry-sipping world of Freudian scholarship as a backstabbing, neurotic swamp. But in this swamp, Swales has shown a remarkable ability to swim and snap. His self-published essays are legendary in certain psychoanalytic circles. The shelves of his bedroom office are lined with neatly bound and indexed letters from psychoanalysts, psychologists and historians from around the world. At his first public lecture, at New York University on November 18th, 1981, which I attended, Swales exhaled a three-hour lecture on Freud's possible affair with his sister-in-law to an audience of a hundred analysts, psychologists, sociologists, rabbinical scholars, academics, and students. It was met with a standing ovation and not a word of dissent.

How a rock & roll fanatic from provincial Wales ended up "one of the world's leading authorities – perhaps the leading authority – on the early life of Freud and on the early history of psychoanalysis," as Malcolm calls him, has to be one of the more bizarre intellectual odysseys of a generation. By approaching psychoanalysis through the drug culture, as Freud did himself, Swales employs the demonism, death obsession, stupefaction, paranoia, and hype of the '60s rock culture in the service of historical scholarship, and gives us good reason to defy the Freudian image of the mind as a nightmare from which we are unlikely to wake up.

Sixteen years ago, in the fall of 1968, a twenty-year-old Swales walked into a Georgian town house on the Thames in Chelsea, to be interviewed for a promotion job with the Rolling Stones. The band's most recent single, "Jumpin' Jack Flash," had re-established its reputation after the critical fiasco of *Their Satanic Majesties' Request,* the album L.S.D. made. Their next album, *Beggar's Banquet,* was about to profess sympathy for the Devil and revolution in the streets.

The man Swales had come to meet was twenty-five-year-old Mick Jagger. The Crown Prince of Darkness, at that moment in the middle of filming

Performance with director Nicolas Roeg, had transformed himself into the decadent, demonic rock superstar he portrayed in the film. Brian Jones' ex-girlfriend, actress Anita Pallenberg, had filled the Knightsbridge mansion where *Performance* was shot with satanic icons and symbols.

Swales encountered the Monkey Man-Demon in his drawing room, near a dark altar covered with drapes and candles.

"Jagger talked such a lot of rot," Swales recalls. "All this revolutionary stuff: couldn't we sell *Beggar's Banquet* off the back of lorries all over England because Decca wouldn't release it with a toilet on the cover, and such. It was pretty weird, because he kept poncing about in front of a mirror in his long hair and makeup. A right little Narcissus. I knew then how to be cheeky. He talked politics, and I kept talking about 'theater' and 'product,' but with a twinkle in my eye, as if I knew the terms of the game."

Swales had been living by his wits in London since the age of seventeen. A promising academic career had been foretold for the lad whose mum and dad owned a record shop on High Street. Then in February 1963 "Please Please Me" went to Number One on the British charts, and Swales' schoolwork collapsed overnight. Growing his hair long, he began ditching school and running off to London to hear Manfred Mann, the Yardbirds, the Who, and the Animals, until he was finally booted out of school in 1965 by his disgusted headmaster.

He moved to London, ostensibly to attend piano-tuner school; instead, he landed a trainee position in the record-sales division at EMI, where he wandered the halls, passing the good word about Tamla-Motown and compulsively filling notebooks with maniacal formulas for calculating musical success.

"I was so nice and naïve in a way," Swales recalls, "and on the other hand I was terribly manipulative, secretly. This duality has been a constant source of tension in my life."

Through apparent guilelessness and an encyclopedic knowledge of rock music, Swales advanced to an under-assistant promo position at Marmalade Records, where he became the protégé of Giorgio Gomelsky, the first manager of the Yardbirds and the Rolling Stones. Swales' confidence and enthusiasm led to the interview with Jagger, but beneath this competent exterior was a painfully shy youth from the provinces, living with a psychedelic rock band called Blossom Toes, immersed in the "Swinging London" of the mid-'60s – smoking hash, sampling a few psychedelics, and taking speed to dance all night at clubs around the city. But by and large he kept his drug usage on a modest scale, fearing he might damage his surest instrument of survival, which he identified as his "brain organ." Instead, he became a fascinated observer of the aberrant behavior and personality changes that accompany heavy drug use.

"All around me there were casualties," Swales recalls, "guys who blew their brains out and never came back. At the same time, I was interested in what people were overcome by." This early fascination with the psyche was shaped by a Russian-born mystic and psychologist, Georges Ivanovich Gurdjieff, whose writings Swales first received from a friend. "I felt an overwhelming shock of recognition," Swales recalls. "So I'm not mad! I'm quite sane! People *don't know* who they are! It totally changed my life. The basic postulate of the Gurdjieffian world view is that man is in a thousand pieces, every one of which calls itself 'I,' but none of which is. Each of these fragments coexists oblivious to the existence of the others – only at moments do we get any perception of these contradictions existing between all these fragments." Swales would transform this insight into a methodological approach to Freud, but at the time, it provided a power to manipulate the madness of the decade.

"It was, if you like, almost like black magic – something that I'd artificially obtained but hadn't paid for," Swales says. "By marrying myself to the Gurdjieffian world, which was only what I intuitively felt anyway, I for a moment could see the structure of society in a way that enabled me to outwit it. And that's how I came to work for the Rolling Stones – in a totally precarious situation... I suppose I was scared to work for the Stones – Satanism, you know. But then again, it seemed exciting for just that reason… I decided that I would allow myself to get jaded very fast. I wanted to see through the Stones' mystique, the Stones' charisma, the Stones' image. I didn't want to be liable to it anymore. This had been my dilemma since I was fourteen, when I looked up to the Beatles and the Stones and idolized them. Now I wanted to see what their brilliance was or wasn't."

Swales was hired by the Stones a year and a half after the drug busts that nearly destroyed the band. Its re-birth after almost three years without a major tour, together with the massive success of *Beggar's Banquet* when it was released in December, meant that a kind of family business had to be reorganized into a worldwide financial and musical empire. Nominally the promotions man, Swales in fact served an undefined role as general assistant and subtle master of hustle and hype. He spent much of his time as a liaison between the band and Decca, but was also called upon to hail taxis and stage manage love affairs for Jagger, in particular his secret tryst with the young Marianne Faithfull. Observing the band with his cool, analytical eye, Swales was careful not to mingle with them socially, fearing that too much intimacy would backfire.

"I remember once smoking a huge joint in the studio of Jagger's home. Mick made tea, then took me around to look at his new Moog. Suddenly I got terribly paranoid, partly under the influence of a bit of dope, and I started thinking, 'He's coming on to me; he's gay! He's always pouting and doing these weird things at me.' And I got really scared. I was a pretty kid, you know, very pretty. And the girl he was fucking at the time, a gofer in the office, was continually mistaken for my sister. I fled the house at the earliest possible moment without offending the guy… Jagger had a demoniacal aspect that used to intimidate me, because he would use it to inspire awe and fear and to get his way. I'm not putting him down for that. It came from strength, not weakness. He's not a schizo; he would simply capitalize on the magnetism he knew very well he had. Sometimes he'd come on like Jagger the rock star. At other times he'd walk in like a drugged-out hippie. Another time he'd come in in a fancy suit like a fast-talking businessman. Another day he'd come on to me like he was my big brother. I gradually learned that the best way to deal with him was to hold one's own center of gravity. I would have to act as if I saw through him, so-let's-cut-this-little-game-short-and-get-down-to-serious-business sort of thing, you know? Because beneath all the acts, I found a much more benevolent demon that one could have a little laugh with, because it wasn't that serious in the end. Jagger was perhaps less Satan than he was the Antichrist – a false prophet." In January 1970, Swales left the Stones. With the band back on the road as a huge act, he was encountering situations he felt incapable of handling. Close relationships in the office were disintegrating; Jagger had broken off with Marianne Faithfull, and word had gone around the office to keep a distance from her.

"One loses one's self-respect if one has to simulate an emotional attitude according to the more or less fickle lives of the band," says Swales. "I left because most people who go to work for the Rolling Stones tend to become swallowed by the myth and spend all their time being appendages. I felt that I had my own life to live, and great, it was wonderful while it lasted, but now I've seen through the looking glass. I did not want to overstay my welcome; it was time to move on."

Almost immediately, Swales started a rock management company called Sahara, with money provided by a wealthy director and part owner of an investment bank, Prince Rupert Loewenstein, who had just been appointed the Stones' personal financial advisor. Swales would spend the next fifteen months blowing a quarter of a million dollars, and also visiting for the first time in his life the most Freudian nation on earth.

"Once I had eaten of the Big Apple..." Swales recalls. "New York was the modern Babylon, a whole new speed and attitude." He quit Sahara and moved to New York in June 1972, with plans to develop a screenplay he'd written. But he soon found himself at age twenty-four a vice-president of Stonehill Publishing Company, working with longtime acquaintance Jeffrey Steinberg, an enthusiastic recreational user of cocaine as well as a heroin addict. The following spring, Swales stumbled upon an out-of-print book – a collection of Sigmund Freud's writings on cocaine – that he thought might interest Steinberg. Swales was who became fascinated. By late 1973 he was working with Professor Robert Byck of the Yale School of Medicine, compiling a new collection of Freud's cocaine papers, drawing on documents from his extensive writings about the drug in the 1880s, at the dawn of knowledge of coca in the West. Freud had stumbled upon cocaine as a young doctor in training, and was soon experimenting with the effects of the drug on his own psyche. His subsequent rejection of several former associates – an episode of paranoia during a visit to Paris in 1885-1886 – clearly seemed drug related, as was a careless attempt to wean a friend from morphine that resulted in a cocaine addiction, which hastened his friend's death. In June 1974 Swales had a falling out with Byck, and also left Stonehill, with the intention of composing his own history of Freud's cocaine episode.

Swales' collection was returned in manuscript by a publisher at the end of the year with a request for a final chapter on the role of cocaine in the origins of psychoanalysis. Swales was unprepared to deliver such a summary. Too many doors were flying open in his head. That December, he moved to San Francisco and began to delve deeper into Freud's drug life. This led him directly to the Devil himself.

The notion that Sigmund Freud may have been party to a satanic pact was first broached in 1958 by American analyst David Balkan in his book *Sigmund Freud and the Jewish Mystical Tradition*. Now Swales began to realize that the idea ran deeper in Freud's life and thought than anyone had imagined. Balkan had failed to take into account Freud's fascination with Goethe's version of the Faust legend, in which a man sells his soul to the Devil in exchange for knowledge, power, and sexual vitality.

"In having already studied the literature on coca, Freud knew that the Spanish conquistadors in South America had regarded the coca plant as 'the work of the devil,'" Swales argues. "Moreover, Freud had obtained the cocaine from the chemical manufacturer Merck, of Darmstadt, in Germany. Incredibly, the great-great-grandfather of the man who supplied Freud with cocaine was Johann Heinrich Merck, who had been a close friend of Goethe's, and whose character and personality were the model for Mephistopheles, the Devil in the play *Faust*. Freud had known *Faust* since his school days; he quotes it in his writings and letters more than any other writing. In his fantasy life, Freud must surely have regarded cocaine as the very vehicle for achieving a satanic pact. Because in the play, the pact between Mephistopheles and Faust is consummated when Faust agrees to swallow a narcotic potion procured by the devil to restore his virility. He succeeds in seducing a young girl, Gretchen, who remains unaware of Faust's infernal complicity. One could say, simplistically speaking, that along similar lines Freud evolved psychoanalyses precisely as a means for opening the hearts of beautiful, desirable women. In a sense, he would ultimately succeed in developing a psychological system that consists of rules and methodology – free association, the whole atmosphere of séance – that could artificially invoke the most basic psychological phenomena that are to be found in drug taking. In other words, Freud transformed cocaine and narcotics into the very medium that is now psychoanalysis."

Not only was psychoanalysis a disguised compact with the Devil, Swales decided, but cocaine was the source of Freud's hypothesis of a chemical substance in the body that serves as the organic agent of the Libido, the basic emotional drive in the Freudian world view. Freudian psychology was suddenly revealed as less a psychology of sexuality and the unconscious than one of narcotics and drug-stimulated fantasy.

Confronted with such deviousness, Swales underwent the worst crisis of his life. Through Freud he began to confront "the monster that existed in myself" – his own addictive powers of manipulation.

"There was certainly a subjective drive in my work," Swales concedes, "but there wasn't a bias or a tendency – that would be a corrupt way of looking at it. Rather I had had experiences that enabled me to liquefy my assets in doing business with Sigmund Freud."

Unearthing extraordinary and controversial information on the origins of psychoanalysis, but ill-equipped to evaluate it properly, Swales felt like a Welshman washed up at the ends of the earth. "The insights, the revelations I was getting were too powerful for me to deal with at the time," he says. In May 1975, Swales moved to New Mexico, where "somewhat reluctantly and rather to my surprise," he says, "I had to confront the fact that I was an intellectual, and that if there was one thing I was good at, it had to do with the realms of ideas and research."

Swales returned to his parents' home in Haverfordwest in February 1976. He would spend the next forty-six months there, sitting at a desk in a chilly attic, wrestling with a demon: Sigismund Schlomo Freud.

"What you must understand," Swales says, "is that I sat there through the night until six in the morning for nearly four years. I wasn't living in Wales in the modern world at all. I was living in nineteenth-century Vienna in the world of Sigmund Freud." Reading all of Freud's vast writings, along with associated literature from dozens of obscure Austro-German medical journals, Swales began to re-assemble the scattered fragments of Freud's early life in chronological order, concentrating on the decades before the virtual completion of Freudian psychology in 1905-1906, and especially on Freud's crucial self-analysis in the years 1897 to 1901. Surveying the principal books in Freud's life in conjunction with his letters, Swales discovered not a man of science, but an inventor of personas, much like Mick Jagger was, only much more complex and grandiose – a man counterfeiting history by passionately relieving aspects of the lives of Don Quixote, Faust, Don Juan, Hannibal, Napoleon, Leonardo da Vinci, Moses, and Oedipus.

Swales discovered enormous gaps in the factual knowledge of Freud and his circle, in part because of Freud's reluctance to divulge much about his personal life. One avenue for remedying this had been opened by a German scholar, Siegfried Bernfeld, in a crucial paper written in 1946. Correlating known biographical data on Freud with the facts of an 1899 case study "Screen Memories," Bernfeld proved that the paper was actually a disguised autobiographical fragment from Freud's own self-analysis. Freud had fraudulently played the part of both analyst and patient at once. Swales now began to follow Bernfeld's example, examining the suppressed relationships between Freud's scientific papers and his life and mind. By assuming that psychoanalysis was based largely on autobiographical insights, Swales began to discover what he calls "a royal road" towards an entirely new concept of the man.

A few months before arriving in Wales, Swales had re-examined the famous "Aliquis episode" in Freud's *The Psychopathology of Everyday Life* (1901), a chapter concerned with the unconscious motives of forgetting. Freud claims to have encountered a young man on holiday and successfully analyzed why the young man has forgotten a word from a line from Virgil: *"Exoriare aliquis nostris ex ossibus ultor"* – "Let someone [aliquis] rise up from my bones as an avenger." Freud explains with preposterous insight that this tiny lapse represents an unconscious expression of the man's fear that a certain young lady might miss her menstrual period.

"It stank," says Swale. "It was too good to be true." Swales began his analysis by noting remarkable similarities between the young man and Freud himself, and concluded that this self-analysis could only have taken place during Freud's 1900 trip to the Alps with his sister-in-law, Minna Bernays. The possibility that Freud may have been conducting an affair and was worried about Minna's pregnancy found support in later statements by Carl Jung, who claimed in 1957 that Minna had confessed the relationship to him. Swales thought, "well, a man who went off on at least twelve documented occasions on holiday to beautiful regions in the Alps with his wife's sister, beginning when he's forty-four and she's thirty-five and at the prime of her life, and with whom he has a strong intellectual rapport – my gut reaction was, well, if he didn't fuck her, then he's got to be nuts."

Swales' suspicions deepened in November 1977, after reading an avowedly-autobiographical dream analysis from Freud's *On Dreams,* published shortly after his 1900 trip with Minna. Freud interprets his dream as an experience of love that for once would cost him nothing. Swales surmised that this could be a reference to the medical expenses Minna had incurred at the Alpine spa, and his own feelings of guilt and selfishness over the whole affair. Late one night a few weeks later, Swales re-read another episode of misremembering in Freud's *The Psychopathology of Everyday Life*, this time concerning a young man's misquotation of Goethe's poem "The Bride of Corinth." The poem concerns an Athenian youth who travels to Corinth to meet his future bride; her mother welcomes him into the house, then leaves him alone. A beautiful maiden enters the room; they talk, drink wine, and soon make love. The mother returns, horrified – because the young woman is not his betrothed, but his intended wife's sister. Swales believed that the man suppressing and misremembering certain crucial passages of the poem was Freud himself. It dawned on Swales that Freud had conceived of himself as a different mythical Corinthian, Oedipus, making incestuous love to his wife's sister, a woman who lived in his house for forty years and acted as his children's surrogate mother. Minna was additionally a disguised or reincarnated variant of the legendary Catholic nursemaid of Sigmund's youth, who played a crucial role in Freud's discovery of infantile sexuality and his invention of the Oedipal theory.

Swales joined all this with another significant development in Freud's life: at the beginning of that fateful holiday in 1900, Freud had fallen out with his close friend and father substitute Wilhelm Fliess, and indulged in murderous fantasies about him, before breaking off their relationship forever. Swales' complex yet cogent historical reconstruction of all this uncovered the biographical origins of a cornerstone of psychoanalytic theory: that Freud had in fact consciously "murdered" his "father" and slept with his "mother," a decade before enshrining the Oedipal drama as a universal principle of human psychology.

By the end of the year 1977, Swales considered himself in possession of a far-reaching revisionist conception of Freud the man. He also felt a need to prove to himself that he had his head screwed on right. Rereading all the early Freud literature, noting statements that might correlate with recorded history or possible testimony from living individuals, he began sending out dozens of inquiries in German and English, with important help from his German-born wife Julia, whom he had met in New Mexico. He wrote not only to scholars and historians, but to anyone who might conceivably contribute recollections of Freud. "Within weeks I was getting twenty letters a day. Of course, this naturally stimulated me to want to travel very soon to see what had survived."

And so he set off on the first of eight trips to Central Europe, tracing the footsteps of Sigmund Freud. Surviving on shoestring budgets, borrowing cars, and staying with his wife's extended family as well as a number of the scholars he had met through his prolific letter writing, the two spent hundreds of hours in archives and libraries, scavenging through monumental amounts of material from an age when people wrote letters as often as people today lift a telephone. Swales gradually accumulated reams of previously-unknown information about Freud and his circle – including fifty family trees, vast original material on the Bernays family, and enough information to compose a biography of Fliess, about whom next to nothing had been known. There were numerous blind alleys and false leads, but also dozens of dramatic discoveries crucial to Swales' evolving portrait of Dr. Freud.

He learned from the son of Fliess' best friend, who he traced through the West Berlin phone book, that Fliess was convinced Freud had a plot to lure him to an Alpine precipice and toss him over the edge.

Another even more spectacular find concerned the historical identity of the most important patient of Freud's life – his "prima donna," his "teacher," the inventor of the Freudian "Couch" and its method of free association. Freud called her Frau Cacilie M. From Freud's writings, Swales knew that Cacilie M was a poet and wealthy, and therefore in all likelihood published; it took Swales a year to realize that Freud must have possessed a copy of her work. Scrutinizing a catalog of Freud's personal library in Maresfield Gardens, London, Freud's last home, Swales found a single collection of poems by a woman: Anna von Lieben, who was a close relative of an important acquaintance of Freud's. Swales later learned from a descendent of von Lieben another previously unknown fact: Frau Cacilie was a morphine addict, who Freud visited faithfully, twice daily, for three years to inject her with the drug and "hasten the end" of her hysterical attacks. When Swales obtained a copy of Freud's complete correspondence with Fliess, he noticed a hitherto deleted phrase from a previously published letter in which Freud declines to visit Berlin because of the need to care for his most important patient – "and during my absence," the line continues, "she may recover her health."

Swales continued to uncover information that had eluded scholars for generations, but increasingly came up against the restrictions the Freud establishment places on masses of material about Freud's life. The avowed purpose of these restrictions was to shield individuals and families who might be wounded by confidential revelations obtained in psychoanalysis, and to prevent selective quotations that might distort Freud's life and work. But the real reason, Swales argues, was to keep the establishment's version of Freud as a kind of Holy Writ, which must be fiercely protected from all possible direct outside inquiry.

In the summer of 1979, Swales' persistent resourcefulness was rewarded again when he caught a mistake that would be quickly rectified, but not too soon: a recently-acquired cache of Freud's letters had mysteriously appeared on the unrestricted list at the Library of Congress. Swales immediately wrote away for them. He received photocopies of two-thirds of these letters, along with a request that he apply to Dr. Kurt Eissler, director of the Freud Archives, for access to the rest. Needless to say, given his maverick reputation within the Freudian establishment, Swales did not hurry to write the head of the that bastion of conservatism, the Freud Library, but by February 1980, less than a month after returning from Wales to New York, he did contact Eissler, who already knew about Swales' coup with the letters.

Kurt Eissler was one of the world's preeminent Freudian psychoanalysts. A bluntly-spoken, distinguished Austrian Jew in his mid-seventies, Eisler was upright in his conviction that Sigmund Freud was a near-perfect man – a view he had propounded in a shelfful of unreadable books. Although Swales considered Eissler's obsession with Freud to be slightly daft, he held him in high esteem for the breadth of his factual knowledge. At their first meeting, Eissler chastised Swales for obtaining copies of letters he had no right to see. Finally, Eissler asked why he had bothered, and Swales revealed the tip of the iceberg of his discoveries – omitting his more radical lines of inquiry. By the end of the hour, Eissler was offering Swales the first of two research grants. Swales had successfully penetrated the sanctum sanctorum of Freudian scholarship and won the support of the most powerful man in the Freud establishment. He felt like a spy about to fall upon the greatest cache of secret information in the world.

Within a matter of weeks, another man, the projects director of the Freud Archives, contacted Swales with a request for information about a few of Freud's early patients and friends. His name was Jeffrey Moussaieff Masson. Masson was Eissler's golden boy, a flamboyant, impulsive, often brilliant professor of Sanskrit at the University of Toronto. Judging from Janet Malcolm's book-length indictment of his character, *In the Freud Archives,* Masson was also a sociopathic charmer who had overwhelmed the better judgment of the stern Dr. Eissler, along with nearly a thousand women who had supposedly jumped into his bed. Swales knew next to nothing of Masson at this juncture, but he did know that he himself was in sole possession of information that would be vital to Masson's work, as Swales had recently been appointed editor of the complete Freud correspondence with Wilhelm Fliess.

In addition to boxes of new Fliess material he had located in a basement in East Berlin, Swales had also discovered that Fliess' daughter was alive and well in an old folks' home in Israel, and had donated two huge stacks of Fliess' papers to the Hebrew Museum in Jerusalem – an invaluable repository of information previously unknown to scholars. It was the kind of treasure that most historians stumble upon once in a lifetime, if they're lucky. Now, in a correspondence that resembled "two dogs sniffing at each other," in Janet Malcom's phrase, Masson flattered Swales for his detective brilliance, while Swales waved scraps of information in Masson's face, hoping to be granted access to additional Freud correspondence vital to his Fliess biography.

Masson eventually promised to provide Swales with hundreds of restricted letters, in exchange for the information he needed.

An agreement was stuck, and Swales delivered his material.

Over a period of many months, during which Mason failed to produce a single restricted letter, Swales came to his own realization about the man. "Masson wanted to usurp my reputation as a 'dogged Freud sleuth,' and to arrogate it to himself," Swales claims. "He's an imposter trying to pass himself off as a brilliant archival historian."

In the spring of 1981, Masson sent Swales a copy of a lecture that he had recently given. Swales considered it a disgusting piece of trash, and made up his mind to denounce the man to Eissler and in an ensuing phone call terminate the Masson-Swales relationship. Here is where Swales spent three days and nights writing a forty-five-page single-spaced letter – a masterpiece of invective recounting the panorama of Masson's sins. "The narrative sweep, the energy, the intelligence and the high spirits of Swales' writing," wrote Malcolm, "outweigh the triviality of what he says and the lunacy of the lengths to which he goes to say it."

A copy of this diatribe fell into the hands of a *New York Times* reporter: Ralph Blumenthal contacted Swales, hoping to get him to talk about his Minna thesis and the Freud-Fliess murder "plot." Swales declined. Blumenthal mentioned that he would have to talk to Masson instead. Swales told him he should go right ahead, knowing that Blumenthal would flatter Masson, who would then blab his controversial theory on why Freud repudiated his pet "seduction" theory of 1897, because he feared that truth of his female patients' claims that they had been sexually abused would hinder the rise of Freud's psychoanalytic methods. Sure enough, Masson blabbed his head off, and the article appeared in the *Times* in the summer of 1981. Masson had cooked his own goose, with Swales' his sous chef: the Freud Archives, where he had once dreamed of succeeding Eissler as director, terminated him for his use of restricted material to further his own theories.

If he had only controlled himself, Masson would have had had access to enough unknown Freud material to last him a lifetime.

Swales suspects that certain aspects of his own findings might be altered when the Freud Archives finally does open its stacks, or new information appears from some other quarters. Until then, he eagerly awaits factually-grounded counterattacks and refutations of his work, although none have come along; usually he must settle for *ad hominem* expressions of distaste or a general uneasiness about the almost perverse subtlety of his arguments, many of which are indeed constructed with what he himself calls "an uncanny ubiquity of coincidences." Malcolm called his NYU lecture on Freud's Minna affair "a dazzling tour de force… The whole thing is immensely satisfying to contemplate as a piece of intellectual work; there are no loose ends, all the pieces fit, the joints are elegant. But it's all wrong. It's like a Van Meegeren forgery of Vermeer, in which all the pieces fit, too, but from which the soul of the original is entirely, almost absurdly, missing." Malcolm's substantive reservation proved to be the fact that she was incapable of imagining that Freud had sat down a few months after Minna's abortion "and cheerfully worked these miserable and sordid events into his clever and lighthearted Aliquis analysis. How callous can a man get?" Freud did worse than that.

Six months after the triumphant NYU lecture, Swales wrote an even more outrageous paper, suggesting callousness wasn't the word. Swales argued that Freud had determined to seduce his sister-in-law as early as 1897, at around the same time he first conceived of using the Oedipus myth as a motif to reflect infantile sexual dynamics. Two colleagues were in the process of nominating Freud for a full professorship, but Vienna was seething with anti-Semitism, and Freud was unwilling to "crawl to the cross" in order to receive an appointment.

That September, he traveled deep into Italy and was confronted by the oppressive and magnificent Christian culture all around him. He viewed with particular interest the murals of the Renaissance painter Luca Signorelli, which depicted the theme of the coming of the Antichrist and the end of the world. A year later, Freud wrote his first self-analysis, about his forgetting the name "Signorelli."

Swales' newest paper argued that Freud's conscious identification with the Antichrist was the most passionate fantasy of his life. Freud had seen his own image reflected in Signorelli's murals and further. Freud's entire self-analysis was actually a disguised Christ burlesque, conjuring the memory of his imagined infantile sexual feelings for his Catholic nursemaid as a mask for Minna, with himself at her Madonna-like breast. The conclusion was that Freud in his fantasy life had transformed Minna into the reincarnation of his childhood Madonna, only to seduce rather than venerate her, and that his self-analysis was his crucifixion and resurrection, and the resulting doctrine of Freudian psychoanalysis—the Oedipal Complex – his cathedral, where he was to be worshiped as both the Messiah and the Antichrist. "By the turn of the century, Freud was completely possessed of the Devil," Swales claims. "He had graduated from the role of Faust to Mephistopheles, whereupon all these new Fausts come into the picture – his early disciples – each of whom must make his own pact with Mephistopheles-Freud."

But isn't this whole idea of yours a bit... daft?

Swales immediately opens a book on his kitchen table and turns the pages to Freud's own words. "'You do not know that I am the Devil? I have had to play the Devil all my life, so that others could build the most beautiful cathedral with the material I produced.'"

On the anniversary of the day that St. Patrick expelled the snakes from Ireland, Peter and Julia enjoy a dinner of sausage and potato salad to celebrate the arrival of Julia's stepfather from South America. Well into a bottle of rum, Swales is jabbing ferociously at his food with a knife and fork while his "aesthetic muse," Kate Bush, warbles on a cassette player from the top of the fridge. He is telling me that he now believes that psychoanalysis is little more than a self-fulfilling fantasy.

"It seems to me that analysts, by and large, live a very 'dildo' existence," Swales says. "Their contact with life is so vicarious. They're locked in a permanent state of infantilism in terms of subordination to substitute father figures – be they institutes, analytic societies, hospitals, whatever – or for that matter society itself, which funds them. They're not free thinkers, because they're not capable of it. Unlike analysts – or for that matter all academics – I never made a pact and mortgaged my soul to any Satan. If one were to concede that there is some truth in my 'gnostic' version of Freud – why it should be that I came up with all this – I would have to say that this is the sole reason: I was thinking for myself."

Swales insists that he came to Freud without prejudice, but there is no doubt that his sensibility was shaped – some critics might say poisoned – by rock culture. Perhaps only a survivor of the '60s could have seen through the demonic imagery, manipulation, and paranoia at the root of Freud's life and thought, by fastening on the greatest legacy of the decade: its iconoclasm, its rebellion against authority, and desire for personal freedom. Except for a few passionate enthusiasms – Kate Bush, Nina Hagen, and Laurie Anderson (Peter does like muses) – he has little interest in today's music. But he will return to his own version of his musical roots later this evening at a small community hall in Little Italy, where some 150 neighbors have gathered for a concert.

The emcee that night, a young Puerto Rican woman in a dress slit to the hip, introduces the next act: "Tonight we have a very special treat all the way from Wales. He's one of the world's leading authorities – perhaps *the* leading authority – on the early life of Sigmund Freud'"—she's reading from a card—"and a musical sorcerer who has put on his red jacket especially for the occasion. Ladies and gentlemen – Peter Swales!"

Dressed in Elvis brocade and obviously drunk, the subject of this introduction moves in a buoyant stagger from the wings to center stage. He hauls a power drill out of his pocket and lays it on the floor, muttering, "Sorry, they didn't give me enough time to set up." Then he unwraps a shiny silver carpenter's saw from a Spanish shawl, seats himself, positions the handle of the saw between his legs and begins to run a cello bow along its bent edge. The melody is "Sweet Molly Malone." A beautiful, haunting sound fills the hall. "I want to dedicate this next number to the late, great Elvis Presley," Swales is saying, "before plunging into "Are You Lonesome Tonight?"

"God bless America, I mean it," Swales says, then finishes off with "Amazing Grace." A half-dozen people sing along.

"It was a credible interlude, wasn't it?" he asks me backstage, slugging down another beer and watching a band run through "Gypsy in My Soul." By the end of the night, Swales is shit-faced drunk and strutting around the auditorium like a rock star, posing for a local photographer with a fist full of bills he has grabbed from the bar cash register. On the street afterwards he stumbles and falls flat on his face on the pavement, then pulls himself up to brandish the saw at a few startled motorists before running on to Houston Street to accost a cab and returning home to howl in the hallway of his building. One can't escape the impression he's performing for a journalist – providing fodder for those who read his papers and aren't quite sure if he's mad or not. My guess is that Swales' self-promotion is meant to keep them guessing.

POSTSCRIPT: *In the December 24th, 2006 issue of* The New York Times, *Ralph Blumenthal – still writing about Freudian iconoclasm – notes that "a German sociologist now says he has found evidence that on Aug. 13, 1898, during a two-week vacation in the Swiss Alps [the time of the Aliquis episode], Freud, then 42, and Miss Bernays, then 33, put up at the Schweizerhaus, an inn in Maloja, and registered as a married couple. A yellowing page of the leather-bound ledger shows that they occupied Room 11, and that Freud signed the book in his distinctive Germanic scrawl, "Dr Sigm Freud u frau," abbreviated German for "Dr. Sigmund Freud and wife." The story made the* Times' *front page, beneath the fold. Peter gave me my 31st birthday party. He performed on his bowed saw at my marriage celebration in 2000. He died near Izmir, Turkey on April 21st, 2022, with Julia by his side. His* Times *obituary drew on my article in* Rolling Stone.

OFF EARTH: The Ascent and Departure of Lisa Lyon Lilly

Note *I wrote this for* Esquire, *but it got out of control. I couldn't command the material, never finished it, and* Esquire *never published it. I've finished it now.*

> "From morn
> To noon he fell, from noon to dewy eve…"

John Milton, Paradise Lost

THE WOMAN OF THE '80s

She's striding under the Southern California stars through a glass doorway with a sign above the lintel reading "JUST VISITING THIS PLANET," into the brightly-lit kitchen of Communications Research Institute (CRI), one of those New Age Malibu think tanks with a fuzzy idea of science.

"Most people say, 'That dolphin guy,' but it's not as simple as that," says Lisa Lyon, the inventor of contemporary women's body-building and the sport's first international champion in 1979. She sets down on the countertop a baby bottle she sucked dry of fruit juice on the drive up to this remote mountaintop.

"Now I'm going to go find My Dad," she says, prowling across the kitchen's red tiles. "He can be funny sometimes, but I told him about you and he wants to talk so – I'm sorry, would you like something to eat? You must be starved!"

Lisa Lyon is kind, compulsive, and a nonstop talker – a bundle of cybernetic hyperactivity whorishly packaged tonight in her *Blade Runner*/Gypsy-Cyborg mode: thick make-up on a delicate narrow face, a curly mane of black-and-streaked Pachinko Palace hair, hornet-striped tights, a wasp waist, white rags wrapped loosely around her hips for a skirt, and breasts *va-va-vooming* out of the top of a chopped down t-shirt.

A decade or so ago, Lyon made muscles not only feminine, but sexy. Lisa Lyon walked point on a transformation of how Western culture views the female form, and in doing so embodied and articulated a way of life as influential as any feminist ideology of the '80s. Who followed but Madonna, Cher, Annie Lennox, Grace Jones, Brigitte Nielsen, Jackie Joyner-Kersee, Flojo, and an army of ripped lawyers and secretaries clanking iron to give themselves that really pumped look, like Lisa Lyon had. Timothy Leary tagged her "The Woman of the Eighties," the decade's prototypical New Woman, combining sex appeal, muscle and hustle, brains, and make-up, parlaying her home-grown "Body Magic" into Big Exposure, and sometimes Big Bucks – sculpting visual personae that suited the covers of *Esquire, Playboy, Artforum, Muscle, Lui, Time,* and *Heavy Metal. Lady* – her book-length collaboration with underworld photographer Robert Mapplethorpe – made her one of the world's most intriguing symbols of female power, programming and manipulating Lisa's self-image through a Phoenix-like assortment of Madonnas and Whores, dominatrixes and innocents.

The world barely knew that one of the great woman's bodies on the planet was fashioned for higher purposes. Her Body was only a vehicle for Lady's transcendence through the flesh, fearlessly descending into mental and penal institutions, criminal underworlds, gay S&M sex clubs, hard drugs, even murders, without ever ceasing to consider herself the milk and sperm of feminine compassion, and a veritable Goddess on earth. Disciples of Satan whispered in her ear, and Lisa listened, imagining herself to be more than the original Female Hard Body, more than muscles, tits & ass, hustling herself in a career pitched to the institutionalized narcissism of Los Angeles, but in fact an interstellar being, exploding into a thousand other universes, a thousand different simulations, less as the decade's Superwoman than as one of a multitude of feminine alter egos in a female body, professing the delights of limitless receptivity and delight. Lisa Lyon was a 21st Century Pamela, contemplating crystals and back issues of *Soldier of Fortune* – a neo-gothic superheroine whose virtues were constantly being assailed in the sci-fi novel of her life. Lisa was literally the inspiration and model for the Marvel Comic Superhero, the violent assassin Elektra Natchios.

Was Lisa Lyon an agent of Love & Light, or the Devil's Plaything? A no-talent artist's model with a great body – "one of a few thousand demi-celebrities in L.A.," as she once put it herself – or a Faustian feminine visionary? The Woman of the '80s, who had shone over the decade with a cut brilliance, was now, as the '90s' beckoned, at CRI in Malibu, gesturing like the Amana Refrigerator Lady at anything I might want to eat in a basically barren fridge, here at the planetary headquarters of her "Dad," seventy-five-year-old Dr. John C. Lilly.

John Lilly is an Avatar with many names. To some he is "that dolphin guy" – the world's leading authority on Cetacean intelligence, dolphins and whales – as well as the inventor of the Isolation Tank in 1954. In Hollywood circles, he inspired the films *Day of the Dolphin* and *Altered States*. To the New Age and psychedelic crowd, he's "some kind of wizard, a science fiction starman, a unique back-to-the-future alchemist," according to his old friend, the L.S.D. guru turned L.A. socialite Tim Leary. Was Lilly a Devilish Angel, or Angelic Devil? To Lyon, he's just "My Dad," after the semi-reclusive Brain Scientist legally adopted her in the fall of '87, with no paparazzi in attendance. She's been talking about Lilly nonstop for hours now, preparing me for my close encounter with the Mad King in his Malibu mountaintop lair, where he may or may not feel like holding court tonight.

"I was lost," she told me on the snaking drive up the mountain on Decker Canyon Road. "John saved my life. Literally. He birthed me. I was so lonely. I had no one to talk to. I thought I was nuts because I wasn't able to talk with anyone." She wants Lilly to introduce me to their recent shared experiments at CRI in Malibu, where the emphasis is on communication of all varieties – interpersonal, interdisciplinary, interspecies, and interstellar. Lisa is also eager to set me up with a cassette recording of her latest "findings"—an electro-magnetic theory of friction energy, uniting cocaine, sex, and violence in a single field, which sounded more like science fiction than science, but that was fine with me.

I follow her into the living room, where she excuses herself for a bedroom visit to find Her Dad, leaving me to half-listen to this crazy tape and stargaze. She emerges, visibly excited.

"My Dad is coming! He wants to see you!"

The millennium approaches. The serious muscles are gone – at ninety-five pounds, she weighs ten pounds less than at her peak five years ago. She hasn't lifted or even exercised much for two years. She's severing her connection to the gravity of earth, living on English muffins, baby bottles of fruit juice, coffee, and air, while keeping faith with her wildest dreams. She's a Jedhi Knight to the Obi Wan Kenobi of Psychedelic Research. She's become a fourteen-month-old daughter with a seventy-five-year-old Dad.

BEFORE & AFTER

Fifteen years ago, the Charles Atlas myth of the timid wimp building up muscles and confidence to win back the girl was not a cross-gender fantasy. Nor was the shadowing homosexual myth of the passive flexing Adonis and the bondage disciplinarian something that women embraced.

Then Lisa Lyon met Arnold Schwarzenegger.

The most famous body-builder in the world was a graduate student at the U.C.L.A. Business School, a smart, politically-conservative Austrian with a proto-Terminator gaze and an ironic-Teutonic grin; she was a politically-radical graduate student in film studies at U.C.L.A., an intellectual program as close to a Left-wing think tank as existed in L.A. at the time. A part-time script reader and semi-professional flamenco dancer with a frail Monroesque figure, brains, and a kinky taste for the exotic, she was introduced to Schwarzenegger over dinner by Bob Rafelson, the director of his film-in-progress, *Stay Hungry.* Lisa and the body-builder spoke very little, but enough for Arnold to decide that she was "too fragile – inside and out – for me, so I soon forgot her."

Lisa, on the other hand, was intrigued. Schwarzenegger didn't interest her, but muscles always had. As a child she would see the bodybuilders on Venice Beach looking "like a strange new breed of animal," she later wrote. "Larger than life, and not average humans – better." Lyon was a classic Jewish-American Princess who grew up with classic potential for over-compensation. She was the grand-daughter of Russian-Jewish immigrant and the pampered younger daughter of an assimilated Beverly Hills oral surgeon. She always appeared to be the perfect child, precocious and beautiful – an American Express Card Holder at nine. In her own reality, she was a self-described "Princess of Obsession" who believed that a poltergeist lived in the family's Westwood home, and that a hole in the floor of her bedroom closet led to another world.

"It had a lot to do with numbers," she would tell the novelist Bruce Chatwin. "I was seeking equilibrium, getting up at night to perform these rites. Running around the house three times counterclockwise." At twelve a voice told her not to worry, this turbulence would subside, but Lisa grew up with an exaggerated gift for devotion and surrender, fascinated by the extreme, the outlawed, the taboo, and the possibility of a world on the other side of this one.

She rebelled first as a Westwood hippie in the late '60s, hanging at the Cheetah at Venice Beach and on a farm with John Sebastian of the Lovin' Spoonful, then running away from home at eighteen to live with flamenco gypsies in New Mexico. She eventually returned to study medical illustration at U.C.L.A., drawing flayed bodies, organs, muscles, and graduate *cum laude* in 1975 with a degree in ethnic arts and anthropology. A world of magic, myth and mystery had unfolded in her over-active imagination. Her honors thesis was about the Roman Catholic funeral mass. The concepts of Heaven, Hell, and Purgatory, and the ritual mortification and illumination of the flesh struck deeply personal chords. She would later have herself baptized (half in jest) by a Monsignor at St. Brendan's Catholic Church in central L.A.

Lyon was moving in Hollywood fast lanes by then. She knew "Jack" and "Warren" and had lots of famous boyfriends, among them Harry Dean Stanton and the handsome bipolar Black Panther Leader Huey Newton, who was with her on his last night in America before skipping an Oakland trial date for Cuba in '74. While she hung out with these players, she clung to her childhood dreams of romantic commitment, and became involved with an Oscar-winning composer who wouldn't leave his wife. Contemplating suicide, she fell in love with a brilliant ethno-musicologist and occasional drug dealer seven years her senior. They married in January 1976, and Lyon resumed graduate studies in film and work as a reader of schlokola scripts for American International Pictures until calamity struck: her husband's closest friend accidentally overdosed on heroin that her husband may have provided. The wife of this man, the folksinger-songwriter Tim Buckley, pressed charges, and in March, Lyon's husband of three months was arraigned on one count of murder and one count of furnishing heroin, and held in lieu of $10,000 bail. Feeling physically threatened by the man who may have supplied her husband with the fatal stash, Lyon purchased a .380 Beretta with a 13-chamber magazine. While her husband was still incarcerated, she received news that her father had developed prostate cancer.

Lyon chose to deal with all this from a feminist perspective.

She saw herself as "a girl who had spent her entire life at the affect of men – a casualty victim of a serious collision between men's fantasy images of women and [my] own sense of identity." She intensified her studies at U.C.L.A.'s all-male, all-Japanese Kendo club, enduring regular beatings with bamboo staves. When tears didn't stop the blows, she fought back. "I was somebody's daughter, somebody's wife, and these relationships looked like they were ending," she remarked years later. "I hadn't established my own creative identity. I defined myself in terms of my husband. It was around that time that I began working out."

Fast forward thirty months to Gold's Gym, a seedy window storefront on the northwest corner of Second Avenue and Broadway in Santa Monica, next door to the Pussycat Theater. A three-hundred-pound Black woman guards the door, leaving Lyon the only other women in the open airy space: a petite white girl with a perfect ringlet of brown curls and baby-soft brown eyes, dressed in color-coordinated tights and leotards, gloves, a broad leather belt, and Nike shoes. Chalked up and settled over a barbell, Lisa launches into the third hour of her routine, gazing in the mirrors at her engorged muscles roped with veins. Fascinated by the change she is undergoing, she shortens her work for American International Pictures from eight hours a day to two, and spent six days a week, two to four hours a day, lifting at Gold's.

Weight-lifting, she decides, is "cheap psychiatry." Lifting helped her realize how she has spent most of her life depressed, trapped in vicious cycles of insecurity and elation. Now she could feel herself growing more secure, independent, confident – and sexier. Workouts were erotic pilgrimages, immaculate vehicles for her masochism, her narcissism, her obsessive-compulsiveness, and her sculptural sensibility.

Her physical transformation took place in the crucible of psychedelia: Tarot, numerology, the I Ching, and Kabbalistic life journeys, which had fascinated her since her early teens.

In her evolving mystical schema, muscles were not brutish; they were feminine soul armor, and she the alchemical princess of her own transubstantiation, changing her body from mere clay into golden perfection. Workouts were guided by an Asian numerology of sets, repetitions, tonnage: eight reps growing to ten and then to twelve, fifty pounds to seventy to ninety, each set a devotion, a Station of the Cross.

With stronger muscles came another devotional style: Lisa crawled out from under a collapsing counterculture to land somewhere between the punk and heavy metal scenes, into leather, gun fetishism, brass knuckles, and garish makeup. No pain, no gain; no guts, no glory.

Some of the men at Gold's resented her at first; a few would grab her ass. But now she was finding a more fraternal, almost familial support system in this twisted subculture than she was among her own family and friends. Gold's Gym was rumored to be a front for Israeli drug money. The gym's owner, known in the gay porn world as Dakota, had a gay call boy service that sent young hunks all over the world for a thousand dollars a throw. As a former Westwood hippie, Lyon also naturally learned about Gold's Wonderful World of Chemistry. Insiders could identify the juicers on Testosterone, Primabolin, Deca-durabolin, Anavar, Acadrol, or Thiomucase – illegal pharmaceuticals obtained in many cases from gay doctors in exchange for sexual favors. Lyon would later proselytize against steroid use, but late in 1978 she began to experience significant gains in muscle mass. By early 1979, at 105 pounds, she could bench-squat 265 pounds and dead-lift 245 – close to world records for her weight class. In less than three years, she had tripled her physical strength and added ten pounds of rock-solid muscle.

And she looked good. Sexy. Feminine, too. Gold's orchestrated her public body-building debut at the Mr. L.A. Contest in February, posing alongside 1978 Mr. America Tony Pearson. Shortly afterwards she doubled down on her commitment to Gold's by renting a studio in the alley, a 3,000-square-foot former garage with no windows and thirty-foot-high skylights, and decorating the space with a heavy bag, a trapeze, a knife-throwing pit, and keeping a dead shark in the refrigerator. With her own key to Gold's for early morning works – sometimes at one a.m. – she would startle drunks from the Pussycat who looked in the Gold's windows at the free freak show inside.

When Schwarzenegger ran into her again in a shoe store in Westwood, he couldn't believe his eyes.

"Instead of the frail girl I met with Rafelson, Lisa had transformed herself into this incredibly strong woman," he later recalled. "She was secure and confident. And she was even more beautiful and feminine."

They were together later in a sparsely-furnished beach city apartment when Schwarzenegger, always looking for a psychological advantage, teased her about posing for him.

"I'm not pumped," she answered in a thuggish monotone she sometimes uses. She posed for him anyway, on a shag carpet. Her muscles flooded with blood. At 37-22-32, she was beautifully proportioned. Lisa Lyon had turned herself into an outrageous sight. (Years later, when I first met her in the lobby of the Morgan Hotel in Manhattan, I couldn't speak for a good three seconds.)

Schwarzenegger arranged for Lisa's international body-building debut at the Mr. Olympia Contest in Columbus, Ohio that October, but the Mr. L.A. appearance had already caused a stir. *ABC Sports* ran a clip of the event, and by April the first World Women's Body-Building Championship "evolved around my presence," Lyon claims.

Gold's gathered muscular women from across the gyms of L.A. for this "world" event at the Embassy Hotel downtown., near the Main Street Gym and the old Olympic Auditorium for boxing. "It was sleazy and funny – it was kind of a joke," Lyon says today. "There wasn't such a thing as the World Women's Body-Building Championship. We were ten girls in bathing suits and high heels. But it went over well, and the next thing I knew, I was on *The Merv Griffin Show.*"

MEDIA LISA & ACID LISA

Forty million dots coalesce on a TV screen and there's Merv Griffin, unable to take his eyes off Lisa Lyon's fabulous body, leaning forward with his mouth open and a fatuous, mesmerized stare. Hollywood grand dame Ann Miller, another guest, seems a bit chilly, but when Dom DeLuise blurts out some stupid sexist joke, Lisa, who had smoked a joint backstage with Peaches & Herb, cuts him off, saying "Sorry, you don't stand a chance." She was hustled off during the commercial break.

Lyon in the Media Den was dealing with people who still associated women's weight-lifting with mustaches on Russian shot putters. When Bryant Gumbel of the *Today* show shook her hand on camera, he pretended she hurt it. But as the films *Stay Hungry* and *Pumping Iron* set in motion a men's body-building boom, Lisa was expected to do the same for women. With her college degree, a gift of gab, and a sexy, unthreatening body that both men and women loved, she proved to be a natural at this game, mixing business savvy with dreams of Hollywood stardom and the holistic side of the "Me" Decade.

Marilyn in the '50s, Twiggy in the '60s, Farrah in the '70s, and now Lisa in the '80s: powerful, androgynous, sexy, smart, feline, independent – "the New Beauty," someone else tags it, not her. While numerous other exercise experts, designers, and manufacturers were lining up to milk the concept for billions, Lisa remained the standard bearer, the Avatar of her own creation and the creation of a brand-new self. Telling the *Washington Post* that "a pretty girl can sell anything," she started her own mail-order weight training program and ran it out of the back pages of muscle magazines. She modeled high fashion for Paris

Match and Paris *Vogue,* and provided the inspiration and model for the Marvel Comic Superhero, the violent assassin Elektra Natchios.

Lisa's concept of mind/body beauty and psychic transformation was for her more than a commercial grab. Her mission was to prove that a once-frail, insecure girl can demonstrate that there's no trade-in of femininity in becoming a pumped sexy woman who is probably physically stronger than most of the men she meets. A monster motivator and compulsive rap-a-thon polemicist, she wrote for *Self* magazine on "re-defining feminine beauty" and "boosting your sexual confidence." She claimed she was not a feminist, but spoke out for the Equal Rights Amendment and attacked sexism and racism at every opportunity. At the heart of Media Lisa lay a truly radical premise, one not yet annexed by the post-feminist land-grab of the Reagan years: "We are not trained to think about our potential," she said at every interview, referring to her sex and gender. "We are trained to think about our limitations. We are trained to think of what we cannot do. And yet our energies transcend anything most people can imagine."

At least one viewer caught the message through the talk show hype: within twenty-four hours of her seeing Lyon on *The Merv Griffin Show,* a young California sculptor named Susan Vogel was on a plane to Columbus, where Lyon was scheduled to pose at the October Mr. Olympia.

"Pumped up psyches and physiques didn't seem to me to be a metaphor for a metaphysically-tuned sensibility," Vogel told me during an interview in her work-residence in Lower Manhattan. "I considered it a misguided notion until I saw Lisa. I understood her to be an evolutionary agent – a self-defined, self-actualizing woman with all the problems of a woman in the modern age."

Ever since Vogel lost her husband and two children in a mid-air plane collision over Mexico when she was just 22, she had dedicated herself to extremes of human consciousness. She studied physics at Princeton and worked on plans to mine the moon and colonize outer space. She also became a conceptual sculptor, with friends among the psychedelic elite, including Tim Leary, who once pounded on the door of her Venice loft, shouting "Will you marry me?" Leary would meet Lisa through Susan at a party at his Beverly Hills home, and hand her the "Woman of the Eighties" sobriquet for her marketing literature.

Vogel only saw and wasn't able to meet Lyon in Ohio, but when they finally did sit down at one of the trendier restaurants in Venice Beach, they discovered themselves in telepathic communication – a mutual recognition that became a crucial moment in Lyon's transformation from West L.A. hippie chick and Hollywood groupie to a New Age avatar whose god-like potential had only begun to be revealed.

Three days before the Columbus event, Lisa had met a gentle Black Adonis, a Gold's Gym regular and alleged drug dealer who helped her put together her posing routine. Many people assumed that Jay Silva was Lisa's stud and not much more, but as training partners they often visited the beach together to "reprogram" their bodies on L.S.D. Both believed that body-building was two-thirds mental. People at the gym often remarked on their physical change after one of their weekend Acid Trips.

Vogel joined Lyon for still more evolutionary L.S.D. adventures along the Pacific Rim, on the beach near Will Rogers State Beach in Santa Monica, where Lyon went to watch the hills melt into the Pacific and fall in love with seagulls. Paula and Lisa lay alongside one another, larvae on beach towels, programming their physical escape from this gravitational plane, preparing for an interstellar transmission – two opposites, each vitally attracted to women of high mystic intelligence.

Vogel agreed with Leary that the highest human priorities needed to be given to extraterrestrial communication and migration. As in death and orgasm, bodies are only the vehicles we use for our departure into limitless space, breaking free of childhood imprints and contacting worlds beyond this one, beyond wind and cliff and sand and sea and horizon, beyond even their own bodies. "She was almost out of her body at that time," Vogel later recalled – "more mental, in fact more cosmic than anyone knew. Jay brought her down to earth, got her to the gym, where she was fighting the gravity of the earth in the most literal way."

Gold's Gym was never going to understand the sacred cosmic beauty Lyon was reaching for now. Seeing her growing rebellion against this mostly-male scene, Vogel offered an alternative: present live bodies in the context of visual art. Art performance was a notion that went back to Leonardo and before, but revived in the '60s as Body Art. Vogel had built a long wall of peach-colored chalk bricks one inch thick, which she arrayed to a height of four feet and a length of thirty-five, for a show of sculpture at a gallery at the University of California at Irvine.

Before this wall, Vogel asked Lisa to appear, naked and exposed, as "the perfect sculptural being, inner and outer."

Lyon stood naked before a mirror in a dressing room in an Irvine art studio while Silva and Vogel swathed her body with a dull, lead-colored graphite patina, a liquid lock lubricant. From the moment the substance touched her skin, Lisa no longer felt naked. With Jay's huge hands swirling around her body, she no longer felt human.

"I wasn't man, I wasn't woman, I was metal," Lyon later claimed. "An elemental being." Striding naked across the U.C. campus – a bathrobe would have smudged the coating – she proceeded to pose in slow motion before the wall for a full twenty minutes, accompanied by a live flutist and a recording of her ex-husband's soft, Asian-styled percussion. *Point Conception* was the live simulation of an extra-terrestrial princess – a metal androgyne unconstructed by the gaze of Man. Its two performances dazzled spectators at a provincial art gallery, but also suggested another medium for Lyon to express her deeper longings, about and beyond sex and the body. Lyon wanted to sculpt her body's spiritual evolution towards what the performance artist Marina Abramovic called "the art of the twenty-first century. No object between the artist and the observer. Just direct transmission of energy." Note that this didn't mean someone couldn't also scoot down to the 7-Eleven and see Lisa's tits & ass in *Playboy* – a direct transmission of energy she defended by saying that the New Women's bodies should be seen where they can have the most effect. Her semi-regular modeling gigs in Paris had led to photo shoots with the Desadean fashion chronicler Helmut Newton, who shot her as a whorish tramp in shades, boots, black leather motorcycle jacket, and pubic tuft.

"I'm normal," she gushed to *Esquire*, like any sun-bleached Hollywood starlet. "Since I'm doing this, I'm happy all the time!"

Artforum, the New York art world's most political barometer of taste, published her most famous nude image, a profile in double flex, standing atop a large chunk of natural granite.

Lyon retired as its first and only undefeated women's world champion and went on to help invent the rules of the sport as the American Amateur Athletic Union's first women's physique chairperson, and to co-produce the first real national championship at Atlantic City for *NBC Sunday Sports World*, where she handed off the title of America's best built woman to the future actress, author and exercise guru Rachel McLish. Lisa was converting '70s' countercultural energies into '80s' limitlessness – moving between genres, and dreaming of having it all in a decade that promised a woman could do that. She was also barely holding on to one of the great bodies on the planet, and about to taste the fruits of more of what she believed were the fruits of all possible worlds.

SEX, MAGIC, & SURVIVAL

The lights were low at the mid-East Side Manhattan loft party, but the photographer Robert Mapplethorpe made out the sluttish mouth, the glittering eyes, and the wild rubber pants. The body is what everyone notices first, but Mapplethorpe had been photographing muscles for years. The product of a working-class Queens Catholic background and the Lower Manhattan art, drugs, gay, and rock scenes of the late '60s, he had lived with poet-rocker Patti Smith while mastering the creation of elegant black-and-white portraits of an unusual icy purity. By the late '70s he was the pre-eminent image chronicler of the pre-AIDS underground, assembling a notorious fist-fucking file, shots of tumescent Black dicks, various bondage and golden stream enactments, and a leering 1978 self-portrait with the head of a braided bullwhip protruding from his ass, winding on the floor like a devil's tail. Androgynously handsome, bluntly spoken, Mapplethorpe was a streetwise leather Punk determined to climb the social ladder by bringing beautiful images from violent porn into prestigious galleries and museums. "For me, S&M means sex and magic, not sadomasochism," he told the press. "It's all about trust."

Lyon, on her first visit to Manhattan, was a rubber-and-leather case in cowboy boots and actual jingle-jangle spurs, open for anything. "I had my own style, but it wasn't entirely different from his. It was like meeting [my] double in some way, although I'm sure he didn't feel it that way. But for me, the connection goes beyond life."

That first night they left the party and cabbed it to a gay sex club in Greenwich Village, where some of Mapplethorpe's raunchier photographs hung on the walls. The macho gay bar scene of the '70s was peaking: no swishes were in evidence, and extreme exhibitionism and extreme voyeurism were the dominant perversions. Built muscles were conducive to hard sex in back rooms on uppers, poppers, grass, and coke. Lyon had always resented the meat market atmosphere of the gym, but here there was no hypocrisy, no pretense of a world beyond the visible. Everything was out front, *there*. Her and Susan's *Point Conception* psychedelia gave way to live fist-fucking and bar top dancers accepting five-dollar bills by clenching their butt cheeks together. The bar action was an underground theater where reality was not a prison, where the mind was a costume that could be taken on and off at will; a forum where the feminine-warrior-goddess could become a macho slut at the tip of a hand, with a great photographer there to record each ephemeral shiver: artist and model, exhibitionist and voyeur, locked in a mutually-satisfying fusion. As time went on, she participated in the action at the leather bars, learning to take whole dicks down her throat and surrendering any fear or shame about her body and the bodies of others.

"They shared a belief in their own power from the dark side," one of Mapplethorpe's closest friends told me – "in magic, although Robert wouldn't have used that language."

"Their image was from the kinky place," says Susan Vogel, who did not approve. "Mapplethorpe took drugs not for evolutionary purposes, but for hedonistic pleasure." Lyon herself told the *New Musical Express* a few years later: "To be candid, I've been involved in as many of those 'subcultural' or deviant situations as Robert and it was really funny for me when all of a sudden, I found myself this symbol of health and fitness. That's not to say I'm sort of a perverted decadent; I'm not. I am very fit and I cling to my ideals of re-integrating mind and body."

And when is the mind and body more integrated than under the lash, or chugging down urine, one might fairly ask?

"I like rough trade," Lyon told the *SoHo News*, which ran a cover story about her. "I don't like sissies." Her defiance of traditional notions of what befits a Princess-Warrior took her to the maximum-security facility in Lompoc, California to judge a high-quality body-building competition between inmates, and to pose for the prisoners herself.

"There was Lisa in this very skimpy black bikini," remembers a friend who accompanied her there, "posing before three hundred hardened criminals doing this amazingly sexy thing with a conga drummer… The electricity that was rising in that room… you could almost walk on it." Lisa would become seriously involved in prison issues, establishing a wide correspondence with inmates. She made a number of Lifers her fans for life. "Bodybuilders are practicing self-correction," she said. "Body-building is about being constructive."

"I was able to simulate the most beautiful woman in the world as a gift," Lisa had told me before our drive up to Malibu highlands and John Lilly's place. During an interview earlier that day at her loft in Venice Beach, she had shared more of her story.

It's unlikely that NBC or women's magazine editors suspected her underground activities, because her above-ground careers continued to bloom: she produced another NBC Sports program in 1980, then went on *Tom Snyder* to talk about using pain to grow.

"You envision something, then you make it happen," she said.

As for Mapplethorpe: she had fallen in love with him – a few years later, when both of them were famous, Mapplethorpe would tell her to keep the media guessing as to whether they were lovers or not. "With him I never had to try," she told me. "I never had to contrive. I have total trust in him. I learned more from Robert about sex than anyone. Sex & Magic."

And yet her personal life was in turmoil. She and her manager, a close friend, broke off over money, and then Jay Silva was stabbed to death during a trip to the east coast. And if that wasn't enough, her father finally passed, after his long struggle with prostate cancer.

"This was the end of an era," Lisa told Bruce Chatwin. "It wasn't any fun on my own." Adrift in the '80s with the decade not half over, the Woman of the Decade was about to enter the Rapture Years – an extraordinary compression of visionary states, mystic identifications, and realities beyond limits, all because a woman who had wanted it all, from Mine Shaft Dominatrix and Submissive to NBC Color Commentator, was about to give up almost everything she had worked for, and do it for a Man.

THE FROG ROCK STAR

Bernard Gulion, known professionally as Bernard Lavilliers, was the biggest rock star in France – the Jean-Paul Belmondo of Pop. Lisa glamorized him as a lady killer, the scion of Communist proles, a former boxer and a trucker in the Amazon Basin turned flash celebrity. She was in Paris for an exhibition at the Mr. France Contest and was handed her trophy by this macho Frog Rocker, who was himself intelligent and pumped. "Who is this crazy American girl," he reportedly asked himself, "this Arnold with Tits?" Meeting him afterwards in her white boots, faux-leopard-skin pants, and a black leather jacket, a look that probably brought the streets of Paris to a standstill, she went home with Lavilliers that same night. Mapplethorpe was mostly gay, and Jay Silva and her father's spirits had left this earthly plane, when Lavilliers restored Lyon's childhood dreams of commitment and monogamy.

"We are in a kind of conspiracy against the world," Lyon told a French fashion magazine a few months after meeting. "We trust each other totally, and I think this is the first time either of us has felt this way," she told *Muscle & Fitness*. "We believe in communication rather than competition." After numerous trans-Atlantic reunions and plans for creative projects together, they married and established the perfect hip international partnership, with residences in Santa Monica, New York, and Paris, a Swiss winter condo, and a summer spot in Corsica. They installed a spectacular gymnasium in their Montmartre living room, where insomniac Lisa could workout at all hours and the couple could lift together. *Lisa Lyon's Body Magic* (1981), a health and exercise guide, which barely pre-dated *Jane Fonda's Workout Book,* offering insights into her spiritual philosophy, sexual advice, and up-beat notions about womanhood.

Just two years after her world championship, Lisa seemed poised for an even greater global reach.

But New York-L.A.-Paris never worked out. An intercontinental career and wifehood prove inimical: too much time spent as a French housewife, cooking three meals a day and minding two troubled stepchildren while Lavilliers toured. She gave up the Santa Monica loft. Rumors circulated in the gyms of L.A. that Lyon had overdosed on steroids and flipped out; become coke dependent; gotten fat; gotten pregnant. Confronting social limits in France she never had to face growing up in Southern California, Lyon crumbled. As before with the Hollywood composer, her love became entangled with obsession and pain. Her husband had intimidated her out of the identity that she had only recently won. "I just don't read victim," she told the press in 1981. "I don't project desperation or clinginess, either. I've basically created my own reality… I never relax and I never sleep. I don't have the time."

Living in Japanese-style austerity in her apartment in Paris, Lisa had deepened her involvement with Angel Dust – PCP – which she had used off and on since 1976, including during the period when she tripled her body strength. She also contributed to the thin library of female psychedelic poetry, taking dictation while the planets screamed.

"I am a dream/travesty of a woman… The Self is Holy… We are all radiant light… Love is monogamous. Intimacy is exclusive. Evil is always possible." Lisa claims that her husband had lost all respect for her, which was why he left the marriage in the fall of 1982.

Lisa returned to her mother's house in Westwood "pathetic, a mess, scaring people." She had undergone what she later described as "a terrible, tragic, shocking experience that scarred me rather deeply… I spent two years pursuing with all my heart and soul what I believed to be the marriage of my life. I was wrong. He was this guy who valued his freedom, and finally he simply didn't want to be married."

The failure of her second marriage and a nervous breakdown turned her off body-building for a while – what good was feminine soul armor if this was the result? Her weight dropped to 87 pounds. At some point, she took 40

Dalmane, an anti-insomniac, and went to bed for what she hoped would be the Big Sleep. She woke up very upset with herself.

"I died in my sleep in Corsica," she later wrote. She didn't realize that she still had things to live for. But she would remember soon enough.

ROBERT MAPPLETHORPE / LADY

Lisa Lyon's hot, sculpted body was a cruel fate for her emotionally-abandoned Self. Despite claims of feminine strength and independence, her lust for surrender had fueled an almost eighteenth-century vision of a Woman as satellite, pawn, and helpless victim in the psychic fields of Men.

Then *Lady* came out in March, 1983. Shot over a two- and one-half-year period in Manhattan, L.A., Paris, and San Francisco, on the beaches of Jamaica and the granite boulders of Joshua Tree National Forest, one hundred and seventeen photographs teased what she called "the unconscious side of quirk and fantasy" for a consummate image of a man's woman and the mythic women that Lisa had played for the men in her life, as well as the mystic survivalist she had made of herself. *Lady* – the fantastic child of Lisa's fusion with a bi-sexual photographer – had the heft of a novel and the feel of a loving conspiracy.

Lady opens with images of Lisa as a pop American Venus, an adorable Botticelli in the sea foam; a Muscle Beach dominatrix in a black leather bikini; then a nymph, a scuba diver, a yachter, and a fashion victim; as Demeter, Dominatrix, and Ghost in a charlatan's séance; as languid bather, parodic French maid, flamenco spy, chorine, obelisk, bride, morgue cadaver, Times Square trick, and Winged Victim of Samothrace. The Lady in Question moves with astonishing veracity and speed through cycles of degradation and rebirth, almost always with a remote, burned-out look in her eyes. But the deepest theme of *Lady* was "redemption through illusion" – an almost-accidental movement from darkness into light, ingrained in the black-and-white images themselves. *Lady* was the *roman à clef* of Our Lady, conceived by an artist-photographer and an artist-model, executed by the former with the latter's close collaboration. *Lady* celebrated Lyon's ability to defy not only political correctness but politics itself – rebounding from fantasy to fantasy as a completely mutable being, goddess and tramp, while remaining always the lady in control.

Lady became a major art-and-publishing event on both coasts. It brought Lyon as close to artistic respectability, or at least art-world attention, as she had ever had in this country.

"Images of revised femininity," said *Art in America*. "Postmodernism or pornography?" said *The New York Times*, leaving the question open. "Is this some kind of sick joke about the blurring of sex roles?" queried *People*. "What was liberating about crouching bare-assed in a lace corset?" argued a feminist at the *Village Voice*, tarring Lyon as a triumph of right-wing individualism, a one-woman revolution achieved and enjoyed alone. "I don't fit in, but that's the point," she told the *New York Native*, looking almost anorexic at her post-Lavilliers coming-out party at SoHo's Castelli Gallery, where half the art world was in attendance for Mapplethorpe's *Lady* show.

Any possible livelihood was too entangled with body-building for Lisa not to return to it eventually, and soon she would be pumping iron again at Jim Morris's all-male Muscles Gym on Sunset Boulevard – restoring her flesh and posing in her new love armor at Mr. Olympia in Munich. She shot six pages for German *Vogue* six months later. "Muscles are in," crowed *Adweek*. *Time* quoted Lyon in October, and cheered her forward: "'I see myself as a representative of a new life, a fusion of mind and body.' Press on, Lisa." But Lisa had moved beyond easy flight recognition. The jumble of personae in Mapplethorpe's voyeuristic *Lady* was pushing Lyon towards a higher synthesis: a revised vision of the New Woman as evolutionary survivalist, enthralled by the imagination of sex and fusion – no longer pursuing the freedom to play all roles, but attempting to fuse them into a new, altogether transcendent being.

Susan Kaiser-Vogel (the latter newly-married, but not to the Acid Guru) and Timothy Leary both believed that during 1982 and 1983, Lisa was spending too much time using the wrong kinds of drugs. Since returning from Corsica, she had attempted to stabilize herself chemically with the help of numerous doctors, and as a result was on a number of prescribed medications, in addition to her private use of PCP and steroids.

"I'm in the midst of turmoil myself," she confided to a journalist on a *Lady* publicity tour. "We must struggle with the greatest amount of consciousness possible and not repress these images, these fantasies. Let them out, let them bubble forth from unconsciousness. If we see what they're all about, if we admit to them, then maybe we can demystify them."

Things kept getting crazier. Lisa arrived tripping on Acid at a Beverly Hills party hosted by *Hustler* publisher Larry Flynt in the fall of '83. The actor-writer-director Dennis Hopper, who she had met briefly before, when they were both on *The Letterman* show in April, was on his own drug-induced flight through hell, living in a cottage behind Flynt's rented mansion, working on a porn movie and a script with Terry Southern about the L.A. Rocker Jim Morrison. The Flynt party videotape, according to Lyon, showed Vickie Morgan, the alleged mistress of President Ronald Reagan's pal Alfred Bloomingdale, pegging the President with a strap-on dildo, and Reagan seemed to be enjoying it. Lisa swears she saw this.

The next morning, she was awakened in a richly-furnished bedroom next to Hopper. It was the sound of helicopters.

"Dennis, I hear helicopters!"

"You're tripping, go back to sleep." Lisa went to the window and a SWAT team was moving up the lawn with assault rifles drawn, and LAPD choppers hovering overhead. Officials claim the purpose was to investigate reports that Flynt, a wheelchair-confined paraplegic, was being held prisoner against his will, but Lyon believes the raid was a C.I.A. operation to recover the videotape that would have proved highly embarrassing to the President's re-election campaign. CNN covered the raid in real-time. Lisa's mother was watching, and noticed her own Mercedes SL parked outside. "What a brave woman," says Lyon, who loves her mother dearly. "Thank god she has a sense of humor."

Lyon threw on her clothes and rushed past the news cameras to attend a meeting that same day about what became the last mainstream adventure of her television career: *Lisa Lyon Lifestyles* would devolve into what she describes as "a half-hour bimbette profile" of her lifting weights, dancing, and riding horses in Central Park with Arnold Schwarzenegger. A project planned for nine months ended up shot in a single day by a TV sports crew, and aired in February 1984. And that was that. American Media Lisa had to all appearances not made the cut.

Hopper and Lisa stayed in love for ten minutes, until he came back from Sweden drug-clean, with his ponytail cut off, and a whole new software installed.

IN THE REALM OF THE SENSES

When love is gone, there's always art, or even better, *post*-postmodernism. A new myth, anyone? "Postmodern performance hastens the body's departure," says the Cyprus-born performance artist Stelarc, whose work involved his suspension in the air by hooks impaled under his skin, like the Native American Mandan tribe. As a child, Lyon had dreamt of breast muscles pierced with hooks and ropes, and of victims tied to trees and torn in half. At U.C.L.A. she had studied medical illustration and drawn flayed bodies. She was surprised to discover her own torso, a 3-D rubber mold of it, stolen from a Helmut Newton photograph, hanging from a trapeze at a fashion show at Otis Institute in L.A.

The show's designer was the fashion genius Issey Miyake.

This meeting set in motion events that ended with Lisa moving halfway around the world, first to lead the fall and winter ad campaigns for Seibu Department stores, Japan's largest, posing in a bikini and double flex, alongside a pre-pubescent Japanese girl, above the caption/message, "You Can Be Anything!" And second, to participate in a prestigious Japanese arts festival, "The Next Wave of American Women," with performance artist Laurie Anderson, choreographer Molissa Fenley, and photographer Cindy Sherman – mind-and-body bending androgynes in whose company Lyon would have to be taken seriously or she never would be. Lisa prepared for the festival by taking Xanax, Cocaine, Steroids, and PCP and writing poetry to accompany the tour. Susan Kaiser-Vogel arrived at Lyon's new Venice loft "to organize Lisa's terrestrial reality," as she unironically puts it, in preparation for her forty-five-minute show, "Contemporary Alchemy: Evolutionary Ritual."

Lyon's efforts to speed up her evolutionary process at home and in the gym had eroded her mental condition. Three seizures put her in the hospital in January '84. She checked herself out after only a week, to protest against what she described as the ward's "brain-washing" techniques and contemplation of electroshock therapy. Lyon believed a small rectangular box was implanted in her brain that would allow her to manifest as a deity in Japan. Pure transmissions were what she believed coursed through her body from the billboards and TV sets and magazines of Japan, as well as at the Laforet Museum in Hanajuku during March and April 1984, when Lyon posed in a G-string on top of a forty-ton piece of steel, muscles humming with the same elemental harmonic of the metal, glowing lead, bronze, and pinkish-bronze as she coiled and uncoiled through a series of poses stolen from the twenty-two major Arcana images of the Tarot deck. In a nation accustomed to erecting at least one Vanna White a month to the stature of divinity, Lisa became the latest American Demi-Goddess in Japan, a symbol of Western feminine purity and strength, complete with armpit hair and muscles. The worlds of fine art and media collided and fused in culture-shocked simulations: her workouts became media events, with Lyon clanking iron in a blur of photographer's flashes, or dancing around the Laforet floor with a huge phallic tube fastened to her crotch, or balancing granite stones on her head for Japanese *Playboy,* while a Western string quartet played Vivaldi, and visual artists flew in from across Asia to create kitschy representational portraits. At thirty, Lyon was arguably at her physical peak. Her performances were spare, elemental, and ripped. This was redemption through illusion, as Lila had always contended. But part of her remained disbelieving, and therefore doomed.

"Will any of this make any sense?" she scrawled on her notes for the manifestation of a deity in the Laforet performance. A part of her had always doubted the effectiveness of her transmissions, and yet in Hindu red body paint, she felt herself become Shiva. Lisa reports that one young girl in the audience thought she was watching God Herself.

"I was understood in Japan in a way I've never been understood before in my life," Lyon told me. She would make eight or nine trips to the Far East in the coming years. Unfortunately, the Goddess of Laforet had also come under the discipline of a sadist I'll call Tony, a 215-pound manic-depressive Gold's body-builder and petty thief whose only visible means of support was a mail order business selling S&M tapes under the title, "When Your D.I. [Drill Instructor] Speaks, You Listen Mister."

"Never under-estimate the power of a warped individual," Lyon wrote in *Body Magic.* And now this former *Drummer* cover boy, working as her daily hype artist and trainer, was also shooting her up with Vitamin B-12 rock 'n' roll treatments when he thought she needed it. Lyon was able to rouse her flesh for divine consumption by the Japanese public, but the mystic Lisa was crashing into necrophilia. Modeling high fashion for $10,000 a day in Japan and hosting a thirteen-week late-night exercise program on national TV, alongside an overweight slapstick comedian and four underweight disciples known as "Lisa's Lions," all lining up for a shot at the old body magic. After a while the Demi-Goddess' Caliban Tony grew uncomfortable with his supporting role and began drinking heavily, burglarized several hotel rooms, and attempted rape on at least two members of Lisa's entourage. Caught stealing money, Tony was finally sent home. Lisa was free to take up with another powerful man, married, as her luck would have it, "to bring me back from the dead."

Tadanoori Yokoo was reputed to be the inventor of the psychedelic poster, a Zen Master, and Japan's leading video artist. He designed an enormous Ferris Wheel for Expo '85, the world's fair in Tsukuba, north of Tokyo, ringed with fifty life-sized replicants of Lisa's naked body. He also created a 45-minute Wagnerian video epic, "Adept Arcana," for SONY/CBS, in which Lisa poured wine from a chalice over her naked breasts and showered petals in a Japanese garden. Lila considered it a pretentious stinker. Her relationship predictably fell apart.

"In Kyoto they gave me handkerchiefs," she later wrote. "How could I, then, have anticipated the tears?"

The rapture years had frayed.

Returning to America, Lyon entered a mental institution in Pasadena, where she gave blowjobs to random men who came to her room at night and wrote long impassioned letters to Yokoo, pleading to be taken back. Some intense, jewel-like poems resulted, after Lyon discovered what she called "the chemical place in the brain that produces rhyming."

> "Who knows my name as eleven
> Lady he calls me and whore
> Who brings me red roses, seven
> In my body, each one a sore"

Lyon's crusade had crystallized: she would fuse the broken pieces of the puzzle and manifest herself as a pure symbol of female divinity for the world. She renewed her encounter with Catholicism, and decided to convey her message, as she told *Flex* magazine in March 1986, through "the ultimate image of woman, our idealized, positive image of women: the Virgin Mary. She is the one who grants grace. She is the One who intercedes between man and his God. And she is the one who is besieged. She is the most beautiful figure, for me, in all of literature and religion." A new piece would premiere in Las Vegas, of all places, in April '86, meant to enlighten desert audiences and lost gamblers about "the three essential aspects of women – her cherishing and nourishing goodness, her orgiastic emotionality, and her darkness."

In truth, as she told me on our drive to Malibu Highlands, "I was lost," even though she refused to count herself among the missing. Maybe she never really belonged on Planet Earth, where her physical beauty and body had become metaphors, a crown of thorns, a cross, leaving her a martyr to limitlessness.

Shorn of her ability to communicate with others, or even to experience pleasure, she read *Simulations of God*, and immediately contacted its author: Dr. John C. Lilly, M.D.

STARMAN & THE FINAL ASCENT

A quarter-century ago, John C. Lilly injected 300 micrograms of Dr. Albert Hoffman's Magic Elixir into his thigh and with Beethoven's Ninth Symphony thundering on his Hi-Fi, left his body and flew, joining the saints and angels singing Hosannas at the foot of the Old Testament God. Returning to his forty-nine-year-old body, he watched in a bathroom mirror as his face regressed two thousand generations to that of a hairy anthropoid – an incident that inspired Paddy Chayefsky's screenplay for *Altered States*. During his second L.S.D. experience, Lilly broke emotional ties with his wife; after that, he began taking frequent doses in an isolation tank at his dolphin research center in the Virgin Islands, leading to a series of mind-shattering experiences that would carry him far beyond the realms of consensus science.

In the isolation tank he conversed with the minds of dolphins and encountered two extra-terrestrial beings who had first contacted him during a serious illness he had when he was six. This time they took him on a tour of the universe and the varieties of intelligence that inhabit it.

The Mind-Body problem, from the point of view of a male neurobiologist and psychologist whose career had been partly spent investigating the differences and similarities between the brain and mental activity, was simply this: in Lilly's model, the brain is an immense biocomputer; the mind, the computer's software. Lisa understood the mind this way, too, and had ever since her L.S.D. explorations began. This was how she believed we could reprogram our biocomputers. Beliefs are tools, garments to be used and taken off, because the mind does not exist in the brain organ; the software that runs the mind runs free in a universe populated by innumerable sets of software, group minds, all potentially in contact – for example, the mind of the fifty-million-year-old Cetacean culture, which Lilly claims he encountered on L.S.D. Lilly also believed in something he dubbed the Earth Coincidence Control Office, or ECCO – the whimsical name he gave his beings from space, who are basically "monkeying around with everything," he said: controlling humanity's long-term coincidences, along with our supply of L.S.D., RNA and DNA. In an attempt to stay in constant contact with ECCO, Lilly once injected himself with Ketamine – aka Vitamin K, a hallucinogen and battlefield analgesic during the Vietnam War and sometimes in animal surgeries – every hour for twenty hours a day for three weeks. On Ketamine, the user evacuates the body, while the mind remains lucid. Lilly became convinced that solid lifeforms from other galaxies were intervening with this planet, and that he himself had come from the year 3001 to warn the federal government about the danger.

This was his mission in life.

"Don't let anybody else program you," Lilly warned everybody.

Lisa Lyon read *Simulations of God*, and it struck home. She was a simulation of a Goddess herself. On September 5th, 1986, she called Lilly to say that his book was one of the best things she had read in a long, long time, and that she had some very important genetic information in a book called *Lady*. Would he consider having her for an ally?

"I'm 72 years old," he told Lisa later.

"That doesn't matter," she replied.

"He saved my life, literally," Lyon was saying again. "He birthed me." Her soon-to-be psychiatrist-lover, the former head of the psychiatric division of the National Institute of Mental Health, quickly diagnosed her condition as doctor-induced. Lisa spent a week in a hospital to kick ten prescribed medications. "She just blossomed after that," said Lilly, who believed her original malady was hyper-electrical activity of the brain.

Less than two months afterwards, she visited Robert Mapplethorpe in his Manhattan hospital room. "The recording angel of the world's exquisite cruelties," as the *London Guardian* had described him, had been diagnosed with AIDS, the disease that was devastating the worlds he chronicled. He had a major retrospective coming up at the Whitney Museum, with Susan Sontag poised to write the catalog notes. He didn't need Lisa showing up in the trippy exaggerated make-up like some self-imagined Extraterrestrial Shaman. Mapplethorpe had no interest whatsoever in dying, and also little interest in Lyon's supposed white witchcraft. After her second visit, her magician and male doppelgänger asked that she not come to visit him anymore.

Lisa had taken his diagnosis hard, but took his ghosting harder.

"After Mapplethorpe's second bout with pneumonia, Lisa was de-materializing, emerging from the gravitational plane, going downhill," recalls the ever-faithful Kaiser-Vogel, who captured Lyon's emotional state with a series of body castings, showing vague figural shapes trying to emerge through thick sheets of metal. Lyon would present her own vision of body building as an artistic expression in *Icons of the Divine,* a performance piece at Cal State Northridge, in California's San Fernando Valley. Lilly was impressed with "the sheer art of it. The flow. It was a totally new experience for me. And it was only for one night."

One-night stands had never been Lisa's thing. Her physical de-materialization would have no more vivid stage than the septuagenarian flesh of the least sexist and the sexiest man she had ever met, or so she claimed. This connection was abetted by the use of a great deal of cocaine, and less than two months after *Icons of the Divine,* she and Lilly were riding a 30-foot Panga boat through the surf to a gorgeous white sand beach at a fishing village an hour south of Puerto Vallarta. Jalisco, Mexico, was a place that Kaiser-Vogel had visited for years. They were there for a detox, which went well, although Lyon had abscesses from the needles Lilly had stuck in her buttocks, and he was reportedly annoyed that he had to lance them on his vacation. The cleansing proved effective, and the couple returned to L.A. to receive news that *Fearless*, the Virgin Mary saga, which had been canceled in Vegas, had been invited to join Lincoln Center's "Serious Fun" Festival, an annual summer by hard-to-describe (in some cases) performing artists. "Constructing a sexual interpretation of the Virgin Mary with three hundred musical instruments and delusions of God knows what," as Lyon herself would remember later, she was joined by Kaiser-Vogel and a few other people who essentially lived in Lyon's Venice loft.

Producer Jed Wheeler recalls how plans for the single performance "kept 'evolving' and growing. Suddenly she'd want a car on stage, or forty homeless people." Team Lyon tried soliciting funding from the BBC, from fight promoter Don King, and even the Vatican, joking about Michelangelo's Swiss Guards marching down Venice Boulevard with a check signed by the Pope. This didn't happen, although King did send a letter of regret. *Fearless* had mutated into a music-dance-performance piece about the confrontation between the Female and her Shadow – a Jungian archetype, which would change into the Devil, then Death, with Lisa manifesting as the Black Virgin Mary. At first Lyon was thrilled to have like-minded people helping her elaborate and celebrate her ideas about God and the Virgin, but the group didn't last. Lyon and Kaiser-Vogel underwent what the latter describes as "a schizo split," when Lyon felt her authorship was being arrogated. She insisted that *Voodoo Room*, as the piece was now called, was her work alone, because she had crafted her body and persona. But it no longer seemed possible to put it into any form that was stage worthy, and Wheeler had no choice but to cancel the event. *Voodoo Room* would be Lisa's last hurrah as a performance artist.

On September 19, 1987, John Lilly legally adopted Lisa Lyon, fresh from the collapse of *Voodoo Room*.

"Congratulations," one of Lilly's friends told him. "It's a girl."

Seven weeks later, on November 11th, 11/11 at 11:00 p.m. ("who knows my name as eleven"), Lyon's new dad was driving down the Pacific Coast Highway and fell asleep at the wheel. He didn't veer into oncoming traffic, but he did plow off the side of the road and flip the van. When he came to, his left arm was pinned under the vehicle and battery acid was dripping on his face. When Lisa finally reached him on the phone at the hospital, he wept like a baby. "He said that he had died and been reborn," Lisa tells me during our many hours of interviews. "He said that a new being had taken up residence in his body."

Whatever had existed between them before took on new meaning that night. They believed they had just experienced fusion at a higher level. When Lilly-Lyon was evicted from her Venice loft, she moved to the Chateau Marmont, where her feline alter ego, Dee-Dee Puss, vanished down a storm drain for two days. For many reasons, it seemed wisest to move closer to Lilly in Malibu Highlands, so she took a cabin in Point Dume, just up the road from Bob Dylan's Xanadu.

Her worldly careers had evaporated. Lisa saw herself now as a neurological experimenter, exploring new mental worlds and uncharted consciousness while intimately involved with a man who loved her for who she was and respected her, on many levels, as his equal. On January 22nd 1988, she presented Lilly with his M.S. degree (Master of Sex) to add to his many other honorary degrees, recognized for "erection sustained in action, sensitivity above and beyond human consensus and love." Their sexual relationship would inevitably transform into a loving partnership sharing a post-material view of love and enlightenment.

Lyon-Lilly had finally grasped the Big Picture. The hole in the floor of her childhood closet had led to the Earth Coincidence Control Office. ECCO was the voice that had spoken to her when she was twelve, telling her that turbulence would eventually subside. ECCO had intervened in her suicide attempt, and put the small rectangular box in her brain to manifest divinity in Japan. ECCO had removed her old karma, leaving her free to manufacture her own reality in her brain – cellularly, genetically, moment to moment. Dying into this conception, Lyon-Lilly settled into a new life, enjoying exclusive rapport with a man who had probing discussions with the beings that run the Universe.

I am still waiting on the living room couch at CRI in the Malibu Highlands when Lilly shuffles into the room in a pair of old slippers, an unappetizing stained blue bathrobe and red pajamas. Lisa is not with him. She's leaving us alone to talk.

"You're handsome," he tells me, looking into my eyes for a brief moment as we shake hands lightly.

Lilly is tall, with a narrow face and a head of hair like a soap opera star. He resembles some grizzled chuck wagon bit player from a 60s TV western, especially when his jaw wags involuntarily, like Robert Duvall's in *Lonesome Dove*. He studies me, not directly, but from the corners of his eyes. We have nothing that I would call a conversation, just his throwaway epigrams.

"Am I avant-garde?" "I've been in outer space." He quizzes me on my own drug experience, without requesting details.

"Marijuana? L.S.D.? Mescaline? Psilocybin? Ketamine? No Ketamine? Gotta try it! Cocaine? You ever try PCP?" He suddenly gets up and I follow him into his study, a brightly-lit room with a linoleum floor. We take chairs. Lisa joins us, looking tense. She and Lilly exchange looks.

"What's happening here?" I ask.

My question amuses Lilly no end. "Lisa and I are communicating," he says, rocking in his seat. We are in an interview situation and there are only two chairs in the room.

"Come sit in my lap," Lilly tells Lilly-Lyon. The Dirty Old Man routine is outrageous. has recently suggested that if he could bring only five people with him to a desert island, he would like them to be "the five most sexually aggressive women on the planet." Lisa declines the offer and excuses herself, returning to Lilly's bedroom.

"We developed a relationship which became father/daughter rather than lovers," he says, watching her departing form. "I decided to adopt her," Lilly continues, "because it would give me status and give her status." He chuckles. "We have some of the damnedest conversations! I was in the living room talking with Lisa, and one of my girlfriends said, 'You never talk to me like that.' And I said, 'You don't inspire me!'"

This conversation ends almost before it begins, when Lilly simply gets up and leaves. I hear sounds in the living room. I go there and find him shoving an ancient Toscanini tape into the VCR and looking like he has no interest in talking further. I stick my head in the bedroom suite to say goodnight to Lisa, who invites me back the following evening.

I drive my rental car back down the mountain, refusing to be perplexed, waiting to try another dialogue at CRI in Malibu.

The next evening, I knock on the front door. No one responds. I hear sound, so I let myself in. Lilly is in the master bedroom, watching the 1953 film *War of the Worlds*. No one comes out to greet me, so I settle again on the sofa in the living room, where a talking clock intones, "The Time is Eight Fifteen…" "The Time is Eight Thirty…" "The Time is Eight Forty-Five…"

John finally emerges from the bedroom and takes a chair near me. I make a play that I planned ahead of time: I move to sit on the floor at his feet. My instinct is correct: he opens up to me. We discuss Sigmund Freud and Cocaine. His memory is poor. He grasps for words. At one point he forgets the term "regressed" as he describes his regression into childhood on Ketamine.

Our interview dissolves when John simply gets up and leaves, as he did the last time.

I go looking for Lisa, and find her in Lilly's bedroom's bathroom. She's using magazine photographs to make a visual collage of naked women's bodies on the bathroom wall: an explosion of Tits & Ass, including the recent naked shots of LaToya Jackson.

We have spent hours together at this point, and are comfortable around one another. I volunteer to crack her neck and do, a cervical marimba. She tries to crack mine, which usually cracks easily.

John walks in wearing a transparent plastic mask, looking pleased with himself. I can see him grinning under the plastic.

"I hate that, don't do that," Lisa tells him, reminding me of her childhood fear of horror movies. She has already told me I can spend the night, and John is good with it, too. I'm invited to go get some vanilla ice cream from the freezer if I want, so I go and fix myself a bowl. I go outside to pee under the Malibu stars on the dry untended grass, and when I come back inside Lilly has taken my bowl of ice cream and is spooning it up himself. He's still in his pajamas and bathrobe from yesterday. He's like some sweet, soft, absent-minded professor.

He and Lisa plan to soon conduct one of their first CRI projects: she will take a psychoactive drug and he will lie on top of the isolation tank where she floats, attempting to contact her telepathically. I was interested in knowing how that turned out. *[But I had a deadline, so I never would.]*

IN THE PLEIADES OF THE GROUP MIND

In her A-framed rental on Point Dume, Lisa lives close to Dylan's Xanadu and around the corner from honorary Malibu Mayor Martin Sheen, who recently declared the town "a nuclear-free zone, a sanctuary for aliens and the homeless, and a protected environment for all life, wild and tame." Dylan wandered into Lisa's place one afternoon not long ago, looking for Scotch. After inspecting her library, he asked if she was into kinky sex. Lisa told him to leave. "All my friends are famous," she said. "I'm not that impressed!" She has a framed drawing of Dee-Dee Puss on her wall that Keith Haring drew and signed for her.

"I live in a completely Pollyanna world," she tells me, curled up in bed near her shrines and weapons and esoterica. "Crystals in front of the windows, rainbows… I mean, you've got to have a sense of humor about these things!" She notices me reading the words above her bed – 'THIS IS MY FLESH WHICH I GIVE YOU AS A TOKEN OF MYSELF," and tells me, "I've been living like a nun." She's almost never seen at parties and openings in L.A. anymore. "I feel I've had enough stardom," she says. Supported financially by her mother, she spends most of her time in bed, reading metaphysical literature and quantum physics, learning about colors, octaves, and trigonometry, and hatching plans to become an instructor in the domain of mind/whole person/bio-programming/higher self/essence fields, etc., although she finds most New Age stuff hippy-dippy and conventionalized. She claims to have turned away from drug use, recreational, evolutionary, and otherwise. There were 280,000 drug-related arrests in L.A. in '88 and plans to increase the police force by ten thousand cops, so using illegal drugs didn't feel worth the risk. She has returned to the outside world, facts, and social progress. She wants to write a book titled *Christianity, Communists and Cocaine*, and has deepened her prison correspondence. She recently received an audio tape from an inmate who describes prisoners "willing to pick up arms and lay down their lives for you. And that's not said lightly." Explaining her renewed passion for prison issues, she says, simply, "God told me to do it."

Lisa looks back on her years as a bodybuilder with some disbelief. Gold's Gym is now licensed in 220 locations, and the top female bodybuilders have become monstrously big, and in Lisa's view, unfeminine. The sport has gone in a different direction, and the mother of the sport has, too. Mapplethorpe made it to his Whitney retrospective in late July 1988, looking like a corpse in a wheelchair. Lisa's kinky stablemate warmed to her again in his final days. She had sent him a long poem and a postcard with a 3-D image of Jesus Christ. A reunion was contemplated, when and if he became well enough to manage it.

But at 3:30 a.m. Pacific Time on the morning of March 9, 1989, Lyon-Lilly was home and listening to old phone messages when she began to weep uncontrollably. This was the moment Mapplethorpe passed in a Boston hospital bed. Delirious over his final days, he asked repeatedly to see the 3-D postcard of Jesus that Lisa had sent him. Like some eighteenth-century rake, Mapplethorpe had lived for hedonistic pleasure, not evolutionary consciousness. Lisa believes he fought death so hard because he was convinced his soul was going to burn in hell.

On our last night together on Pt. Dume, Lisa plows through old newspaper clippings and vamps in the semi-darkness, painting an hour-long Troma-made nightmare in which Arnold Schwarzenegger becomes President of the United States *[not Governor of California]*, millions of Latinos pour across our border with Mexico, and a racial holocaust ensues. AIDS is revealed to be a viral warfare experiment run amok; in the genetic conflict of the future, cocaine barons will divide North America into rival fiefdoms, feeding crack to an addicted populace, while chromosomal superheroines (like Lisa) battle the forces of evil. The only future for humanity is in outer space and the Group Mind, which Lilly believes will become computerized, reducing the body to irrelevance except as a life support system for the brain and the software that runs it.

Occasionally during my visit, her phone rang. She does not pick up, and the call goes to voicemail. A man speaks in a low, dark whisper about all the things he wants to do to her body – sadomasochistic scenarios I made a point of not remembering.

"He calls all the time," Lisa says dismissively. "He's a former boyfriend who can't let go."

When it's time to leave, I kiss her cheek and walk to my rental in the Malibu night, feeling vaguely disappointed. A cautionary tale about the dangers of drugs and how the mighty have fallen isn't what I set out to write when I started down this path with her. I'm thinking Lisa has paid the devil his due, and the payment was her body, but only after she had changed the hearts and minds of millions. Whatever else you might think of her, Lisa Lyon Lilly did what she sought to do from the beginning: she transcended her physical form and became a creature beyond anyone's fantasies of good and evil – Off Earth, no longer a victim of the pathos of men and women and the terrible beauty of their dance. She has made herself mistress and caretaker of her own illusions, and party with the Group Mind in the great cosmological beyond.

POSTSCRIPT: *Not long after my time with her, Lisa Lyon Lilly basically vanished from public view. She has no online footprint from the '90s to the present, except in 2000, when she was inducted into the International Federation of Body Building and Fitness Hall of Fame, recognized as a "one-woman media-relations activist on behalf of the sport and elevating bodybuilding to the level of fine art."*

THE ROMANCE OF NORMALCY:
A Journey through Independent Lithuania (1990)

Note: *In the spring of 1990,* American Theater Magazine *sent me to St. Petersburg, Russia and several cities in Lithuania to accompany a tour of Edward Albee's* Who's Afraid of Virginia Woolf *(of all things), which had originated at the Mark Taper Forum in Los Angeles and the Alley Theater in Houston. It was pure coincidence that Lithuania had recently declared independence from the Soviet Union, which responded by closing all the borders, sending in the army, and taking* *over the nation's television station. Our theater friends in St. Petersburg had political connections that enabled us to continue the next leg of our tour to the middle of this non-violent "Singing Revolution." As the first official visitors to a newly-independent locked-down nation, we were greeted with flowers and cognac by two hundred people at the train station in Vilnius; that night, we were guests of honor at the Easter Sunday evening mass at the national cathedral. I interviewed Speaker Vytautus Landsbergis, a central figure in the independence movement and a modernist composer before he entered politics. I visited a city near the largest Soviet military airport in Eastern Europe, closed to Westerners for decades, where a group of poets invited me to an afternoon tea, where we sat around politely listening to an album by John Cage. The first time I ever heard Lou Reed's "Dirty Boulevard" was on a music-video projected on a sheet in a post-curfew house with black-out curtains over the windows.*

Vilnius at night, from a second-story balcony at the Hotel Astorija, overlooking a promenade of black marketeers from Georgia and Armenia, loitering near their parked cars selling gasoline, Red Army wristwatches, and American Dollars.

"Report to mafia dons in Kaunas," says a theater designer, tipping his left ear over the balustrade. Across the street, the state Museum of Atheism – soon to be returned to the greater glory of St. Kasimir – shimmers in the ghostly moonlight. It's two a.m., April 22, 1990, the forty-fifth day of Lithuanian independence. The Russian blockade is in its fourth day. Food, fuel and medicines are cut off, 80,000 Red Army troops are in country, twice the normal contingent, and our theater company is in my hotel room saying goodbye to our friends in Vilnius with Russian vodka, Hungarian champagne, and a delicious local cognac.

"Landsbergis was about to speak," recalls Vytautas Bogusis, who looks like Rasputin's Jolly Roger. Bogusis has luminous blue eyes twinkling inside an ashen skull under long stringy hair. By vocation an electrician at the Youth Theater of Vilnius, he moonlights as "the bravest man in Lithuania," a company actress told me. Vytautus is one of the four Freedom League dissidents who organized a public demonstration commemorating the anniversary of the Ribbentrop-Molotov pact of 1939, which linked Lithuania's fate to Russia and the Soviet Union in wartime and into the postwar era. After years of underground activism, that demonstration, held on August 23rd, 1987, stimulated the birth of a movement—Sajudis, the original Lithuanian reform movement, which has now produced a paper independence two and one-half years later.

"And this huge helicopter gunship descends about fifty meters above the crowd," Bogusis goes on, visualizing the April 7th rally, just after the Russian dissident historian Araf Yasanev told three hundred thousand people at Vingis Park that Lithuanian independence was "the beginning of the end of the Russian empire." "Fifty meters! And it's spewing these repulsive Soviet leaflets – you know..." He swims upward, as if through a deluge of Communist propaganda. 'President Gorby has asked the people of Lithuania nicely,' that sort of thing."

Bogusis grooves to the music for a moment. You can see the darkness in his soul and you see the light, too. He has refused to ignore the imperial suppression of Lithuanian culture; he has refused to forget the Stalinist deportations that snatched away one out of every six Lithuanians to Siberia. A working-class Catholic radical non-conformist, Bogusis, who's fluent in English, has known false arrests, beatings, and state terrorism; he has gone to jail many times to keep a dream of national independence alive. What amazes him now is that his point of view has become commonplace.

"I look around the rally," says Bogusis, "expecting to see people cowering in fear. But instead, three hundred thousand people are laughing and shaking their fists in the air, shouting, 'Lietuva! Lietuva!'"

Bogusis laughs and wheels around to dance by himself in earnest, to Lithuanian unity born in dissidence and the memory of history.

Polls conducted on March 28th and April 2nd by the Public Opinion Research Center at Lithuania Academy of Sciences revealed that 91% of 1583 respondents support the program of independence; less than a third (31%) believe it has come too soon. Half of Lithuania's 300,000 native Russians and an even higher percentage of ethnic Poles are happy to leave the Soviet Union. 76% of the people surveyed said they were satisfied with the work of the new Parliament; the rest say they are partially satisfied. The old Freedom League radicals have entered an uneasy but firm alliance with Speaker Vytautus

Landsbergis, joining the Greens, the Social Democrats, the National Progress Party, the Humanism and Progress party, the independent Lithuanian Communist Party, and many others – all in support of independence. They are absolutely alone in the geopolitical world, caught between competing Superpowers, on the verge of vanishing into an economic Fourth World.

And yet Lithuania made a sudden chess move, empowered by its own intelligence: the need for a declaration of independence derived from the gnawing sensation of being "a pawn in the romantic novel of the superpowers," as *The London Times* suggested.

Today's news reports that the West will not be able to provide fuel, assuring a Mad Max scenario that will only worsen tomorrow, when the Soviets take over the oil refinery at Mazeikiai. Praying there's not another Prague Spring, betting on Perestroika to restrain the army, Lithuanians control their own foreign ministry and their own militia, or police force, under an interior minister who has sworn an oath to the new democracy. They have been cut off from the world, but hope to meet their future on more human terms. They seek a normalcy they're still inventing. The Lithuanian character has united in the romance of normalcy.

Bogusis moves away to dance to Tshala Muana, the Queen of Zaire, a cassette tape I brought with me from Downtown New York. Other people at the party are starting to get up and join the boogie.

"No one wants to work," he turns around to tell me, shouting above the music, "because of the tension! You spend all your thoughts waiting for bad news, and then the bad news comes!"

He whirls around again, elbows flying in a kind of chicken walk, and accidentally catches me flush on the chin. For a moment I see stars, and the dawn's early light... In Lithuania, I see the future has arrived...

THE EXTRAVAGANT MYSTERIES OF ROBERT WILSON: the CIVIL warS: *a tree is best measured when it is down American Theater Magazine*, October 1985

Bob Wilson was one of the reasons I moved Downtown, after seeing his and Christopher Knowles' $ Value of Man in the Lepercq Space at BAM. $ Value made no statement, and shared no meaning, other than that chasing money tends to mess things up. I also participated a few times in Open Movement Workshops at Wilson's loft on Spring Street, and knew many people who worked with and knew and respected Bob. My dearest friend was the rehearsal photographer for Einstein on the Beach. *This article is adapted (mostly shortened) from the original article.*

Robert Wilson, it is safe to say, is the most celebrated and controversial avant-garde theater artist in the world. Too bizarre for Broadway and too expensive for all but the most lavishly-funded not-for-profit theaters, Wilson has developed his extravagant Theater of Mysteries for the past nine years in Europe, creating works largely unseen by Americans.

Abroad, he is the Prince of Images, surrounded by a nimbus of rumor and accolade, honored by art world intellectuals, the *beau monde* of Paris and Berlin, and punk hopheads on city squares. Wilson's long exile from America is ending: his one-hundred-minute-long fable *The Golden Windows* will arrive on October 22nd, three years ago after its premiere at the Munich Kammerspiele, at the Brooklyn Academy of Music (BAM). His American return was to have occurred two summers earlier with *the CIVIL warS: a tree is best measured when it is down*, the single most ambitious theater project of modern times: a nine-hour-long, $7 million "planetary opera" assembled in six nations and planned as the inaugural work of the 1984 Olympic Arts Festival in Los Angeles, but in a saga of entrepreneurial ambition worthy of Michael Cimino's film catastrophe *Heaven's Gate* four years earlier, Wilson had to settle for last fall's first-ever revival at BAM of the legendary four-and-a-half-hour opera he co-created with composer Philip Glass in 1976. *Einstein on the Beach* had sold out the

Metropolitan Opera House twice at its American premiere. The sheer Wagnerian grandeur of *Einstein* restored at BAM, and the hallucinatory elation it generated, appeared to have signaled the return of Wilson's fortunes in a country that for some years seemed unable to make a place for him. A few months later, a three-hour version of the German section of *the CIVIL warS* opened at the American Repertory Theater in Cambridge, an event that *The Boston Globe* hailed as comparable to Picasso's "Guernica" and Stravinsky's *Rites of Spring.*

To supporters in worlds of art, as well as increasing numbers of middle-class theatergoers, Wilson has become the avatar of a new theatrical consciousness, a visionary creator of works that must be experienced to be understood at all. Other viewers admire a brilliant designer and showman whose willful obscurity is part of the package. In contrast, theater traditionalists and the politically engaged often find Wilson's work unutterably boring, irresponsible, and pretentious beyond belief – "an artistic and human scandal," the critic John Simon has written, a theater "for escapees from thought, feeling and confrontations with reality." In recent years, even a few formerly sympathetic observers have suggested that Wilson's explorations into the nature of theatrical time and perception have devolved into a set of self-inflated clichés. To these detractors, Wilson has been blackmailed by the scale of his vision into becoming a kind of artist-businessman, increasingly prone to overly grandiose designs, sacrificing the communal ethos and spiritual integrity that gave his earlier theater its life – and with *the CIVIL warS,* finally creating a work touched by a truly Faustian madness.

With the revival of *The Golden Windows* at BAM and the world premiere of *Alcestis* at ART in Cambridge, American audiences will again be able to judge for themselves whether Wilson has shorn the theater of its most human meanings, or if he has succeeded – as he hopes – in creating environments that invite our own native response. Wilson is ending his European exile convinced that he can become for late 20th century America what Verdi is to Italians or Wagner is to Germany. And to achieve this goal, he's prepared to take all the time in the world.

Wilson's greatest re-invention of stage spectacle for the late 20th century was accomplished with Philip Glass, his first adult creative partner of equal stature. Glass shared Wilson's architectural approach to form, an interest in the use of repetitive motifs and extended passages of time; even something of a mystical bent. Meeting every Thursday throughout 1975, they worked out a scenario based on Wilson's drawings. With a $150,000 Bicentennial grant from the French Ministry of Culture, they rehearsed a group of singers and dancers from December to March. *Einstein on the Beach* employed an incantatory libretto of solfège syllables, counted numbers, and stream-of-consciousness monologues accompanying Glass's simple harmonies, repeating and permuting at ear-splitting decibels. *Einstein* was less an opera than a four-and-a-half-hour-long intermission-less Masque, a vision of the physicist as child, violinist, mystic, and father of the atomic bomb, conjuring images from the birth of relativity with all the freshness and rapture of a dream.

Einstein opened at the Avignon Festival in the south of France and went on to Hamburg, Belgrade, Venice, Brussels and Rotterdam before sweeping into Lincoln Center in November 1976.

When Wilson stepped on the Met stage for the first time, he reportedly said to no one in particular, "At last I'm where I belong."

Entire sections of the Met audience booed and cheered at random, and hundreds walked out, passing ticket stubs to hundreds more who waited in the cold, hoping to get inside. Downtown had stormed America's cultural Parnassus and taken it, and even *The New York Times* raved: "A sensational one-of-a-kind event in which the downtown art world occupied a temple of Establishment culture for one brief moment." *The Washington Post* went further: "One of the seminal art works of the century, possibly the seminal work." It seemed from my opening-night seat in the upper balcony that *Einstein* was accomplishing two contradictory feats at once: conquering an august cultural temple, at the same moment that it was overthrowing a big part of what the '60s stood for: Antonin Artaud's call for "No More Masterpieces."

After *Einstein,* anti-art and anti-theater were finished, and the Cult of the "Masterpiece" re-born.

Wilson reportedly walked offstage after the final curtain on the second performance "ready to commit suicide," according to a close associate. The

Einstein tour had been riddled with dissension – the mid-'70s collapse of the counterculture, the big chill of careerism, petty jealousies, fights over program credits, and according to some participants, the director's tantrums and emotional manipulation. Rumors of heavy drug use were long a presence in Wilson's circles. But the primary problem was financial disaster: despite raising over a million dollars to produce *Einstein*, the Byrd Hoffman Foundation was staggered by expenses at the Met of $90,000 a night, and in debt to the tune of $125,000. When the Glass Ensemble's sound equipment mysteriously vanished from a warehouse in New Jersey, the composer suspected the director/producer of stealing it to pay his debts, leading to a falling-out that lasted for years. Hoping to avoid financial catastrophe, Wilson arranged what he hoped would be a more commercial venture. *I Was Sitting On My Patio This Guy Appeared I Thought I Was Hallucinating*, a chatty minimalist duet with Lucinda Childs, played in L.A. and toured Europe, but was reviled by critics. Wilson vowed never again to self-produce, but no theaters in America were ready to assume the expenses of his aspirant masterpieces. His foundation nearly closed, the Spring Street space became a clothing boutique, and the man acclaimed as America's theatrical visionary entered years of cultural exile, searching for budgets equal to the scale of his fantasies.

Death, Destruction & Detroit, commissioned by the city of West Berlin in 1979, and *Edison*, presented in Lyon, Paris and Milan later that same year, moved Wilson's fascination with spectacle and visual perfection to new heights. Developed at the Schaübuhne, a lavishly-funded state facility, *DD&D* was Wilson's most deeply-imagined work, its visual design inspired in part by Hitler's architect, Albert Speer, and its secret subject Hitler's deputy Führer, Rudolf Hess – a fact that went unnoticed even in Berlin, where Hess was still incarcerated in Spandau Prison. Wilson spent nearly six weeks lighting the Berlin show, most of it with actors in full costume and makeup while the director fussed over cues and filters and focuses. Professional actors brought a new precision to Wilson's work, but at the same time made it feel increasingly cold, distanced, automatic, at least in the opinion of some. "Oh, you want us to be machines," one performer reportedly complained. "I'm not afraid of that," Wilson responded. "There's freedom in being mechanical." Openly slugging from a vodka bottle during rehearsals, Wilson would tell actors that their "motivation" was to become a vertical line. Some actors didn't know who their characters were until they read the program. At auditions some were asked to repeat the word "ravioli" for minutes at a stretch.

Despite the controversial successes of his works in Europe, Wilson was not content abroad. He missed America, and would corner anyone who would listen to the same bitter harangue about being misunderstood in his homeland. Plans to bring *DD&D* to the Met collapsed, when Wilson insisted that lights be mounted in the floor of the stage. For more than six years, presentations in America were limited to small-scale chamber works, including controversial *DIA LOG* events with Chris Knowles, a differently-abled teenager often described as autistic, who had a startling sense of the musical and visual textures of language. The DIA LOGs raised the issue, perhaps unfairly, of Wilson's exploitation of a handicapped boy. *Edison,* presented as a work-in-progress on 42nd Street in Manhattan before an invited audience that shelled out $50 a ticket, featured Wilson constantly bounding up on stage to make a lighting change or fine tune the position of an actor's chin. When audience members began snickering and talking among themselves, Wilson shouted that he was "sick of this shit." Muttering, "Fucking America! Fucking America!" he told the audience that if they didn't like it, they should "go see *Sweeney Todd* or *The Elephant Man.*" Divorced from the community that had once sustained his work, reviling an audience that might have helped him reach a new plateau, Wilson appeared to be losing the ground under his feet. But whether through the courage of his convictions or supreme megalomania, Wilson was already sketching ideas for a new spectacle, based on the American Civil War.

The original inspiration for *the CIVIL warS: a tree is best measured when it is down* was Matthew Brady's photographs, then the entire Industrial Revolution, and finally "the whole last half of the 19th Century," Wilson claimed. Shopping the idea at theaters in Houston, Paris, Munich and Hamburg, he eventually found a sponsor powerful enough to realize his second coming to America: The Olympic Arts Festival, funded by the L.A. Olympic Organizing Committee and the *Times-Mirror* Foundation, due to open in June 1984. What Wilson proposed to festival director Robert Fitzpatrick early in 1980 was a twelve-hour multinational epic, incorporating the work of more than 200 artists from around the world – a global history of civil strife, the story of mankind's passage from conflict to brotherhood, in five acts and fifteen scenes, financed and created in Holland, Germany, Italy, France and Japan, with additional material contributed from the U.S. The most complex modern theater piece ever attempted, a work on the scale of Wagner's *Ring* cycle or the court spectacles of the Renaissance, *the CIVIL warS* would include companion books, art works, furniture design, video and film, radio and television adaptation. Wilson ball-parked costs for a week's run in L.A. at $3 million, which in the not-for-profit theater is real money.

While planning for *the CIVIL warS* continued, Wilson resumed work on a number of smaller projects in Europe, including *The Golden Windows*, conceived as drawings in 1979-1980 and titled a Laura Shapiro story he had known for years. He conducted the first workshops at La Mama in New York's East Village during 1980, and another series a year later. After two months in Munich during the spring, rehearsing what Wilson describes as "a clear visual logic and an illogical text," *The Golden Windows* opened in May as a work "about a deep, passionate, destructive love, about relations to children, and about existential fears," wrote one critic at its premiere. *The Golden Windows* met with an enthusiastic critical and popular response, selling out its run to middle-class audiences as well as art-world types. Buoyed by this response, Wilson returned to *the CIVIL warS* in June, gathering more than fifty designers, writers, technicians and performers in Munich to begin work – mounting the annotated scenic drawings on a huge wall, building models, even blocking some of the action for a five-or-six-hour run-through.

The Olympic Arts Festival had officially invited the production, offering to provide up to 10% of the L.A. production costs and making it clear that no further financial help would be forthcoming. Byrd Hoffman would have to self-produce what was shaping up to be some of the most exorbitant theatrical experiences ever contemplated. Wilson would fashion a series of living tableaux that swept across continents and eons – a masque of humanity from prehistory to beyond the stars. The completed *CIVIL warS* would open on a plain in Africa at the dawn of humanity, then shift to a space station where a man and woman on ladders face an enormous map of the world that divides while a chorus of voices sings in Latin (one of fourteen spoken languages the work would eventually contain). *the CIVIL warS* crested in a timeless, ahistorical landscape in which Ninjas fly through the air, giraffes talk, and the Monitor and the Merrimac do battle; the world's tallest woman crosses a cabbage patch carrying a dwarf in her hand; children fly a hot air balloon down the Grand Canyon; and Madame Curie rides her bicycle in an underwater flower garden. Through fragments of history and myth – the cultural accretions of the world – *the CIVIL warS* would be a pageant of civilization itself, a parable of a species fated for either apocalypse or redemption.

Wilson undertook a grueling schedule of fund-raising while in the process of realizing the work itself. Sleeping on trains, in pensions and cheap hotels, flying from Frankfurt to Minneapolis to Tokyo to New York to Rotterdam to Paris, perpetually jet-lagged and chronically late, Wilson seemed to thrive in this more-or-less constant state of crisis. His extravagance grew impossible: if he wanted a real lion on stage, then he would have a real lion. The opera legends Jessye Norman and Hildegard Behrens were engaged. Wilson's friend Richard Gere was set to play Robert E. Lee as a samurai warrior. Studying mid-nineteenth-century *Vanity Fair* caricatures of Abraham Lincoln as a baboon, devil, nursemaid and juggler, Wilson thought of David Bowie as "someone appropriate to that way of thinking," so the director flew to Switzerland. Bowie agreed to perform for free, plus expenses, which turned out to be $100,000 a week. Perhaps this kind of money was possible with help from *the CIVIL warS'* international fund-raising committee, populated by the likes of Willi Daume (instrumental in bringing the Olympics to Munich in 1972), Mme. Georges Pompidou, Gloria Vanderbilt, Eric de Rothschild, and Issey Miyake. Nearly a million dollars were raised in Germany; the Italian government committed a similar amount, the largest contribution to an art work in its history. Just under $300,000 would come from Japan, two million francs from the Cote d'Azur, and another half million from the Dutch government and eight French co-sponsors. Coordinating all of this from its tiny offices in New York, the Byrd Hoffman Foundation would spend more than a half-million dollars on fund-raising and pre-production alone.

"We have the feeling in Europe, and particularly in Munich," declared that city's Commissioner of Culture, "that *the CIVIL warS* is one of the most important works of our century."

In April 1983, *CIVIL warS* rehearsals began for Act I Scene B in Rotterdam with a group of Dutch, American, and German actors. In May, working in an art district warehouse on the Bay of Tokyo and funded by the Japanese-United States Friendship Commission, Wilson collaborated with Talking Head's David Byrne, various vanguard Japanese performers, as well as Noh and Kabuki actors – the first time in their centuries of existence that they had ever appeared together on stage. Wilson faced his greatest fund-raising challenge in Japan, where he was virtually unknown, and the tax structure provides no incentives for arts donation. "There was this tall Texan bursting into rooms and whooping and punching you in the arm," recalls Adelle Lutz, his assistant director there. "The Japanese would be dumbfounded. Everything would become quiet with Bob laughing like a crazy man."

From Tokyo, Wilson moved on to the Schauspiel in Cologne, where he worked with the first serious adult writer of his career, the East German playwright Heiner Müller. Müller's visually-oriented, imagistic text represented a departure from the random "weather" of Wilson's own writings, yet remained nearly as resistant to interpretation. Wilson later claimed that Heiner Müller "changed my life."

In July, he was on to Rome, blocking the final act of *the CIVIL warS* for Glass, who would return to Nova Scotia and New York to write an opera for chorus and orchestra around the Rome staging; he later contributed music for the Cologne section as well. In August, Wilson flew on to Rotterdam, then back to Japan, then L.A., New York and Minneapolis – sleepless, living day for night, wreaking epic insanity around him, behaving as if the entire world existed to serve his vision, according to several associates. And he was still millions short of the money he needed to produce the finished work for five nights in L.A.

"Bob was over the edge," recalls Robert Applegarth, *the CIVIL warS'* project director. "I will say that I never laughed more in my life."

On September 5th, 1983, the Dutch act of *the CIVIL warS* opened at the Schouwburg in Rotterdam with an evocation of the four seasons. Only winter

– with Mata Hari skating over a frozen canal – would survive into the spectacle planned for Los Angeles, although what would end up being judged the weakest of the five sections reopened successfully in Paris later that month. Wilson spent the next several months rehearsing in West Germany, cheered by news that the BBC planned a documentary on the completed work.

The Cologne section premiered in January 1984 as a re-confirmation of Wilson's gifts. With its opening image of the continents dividing, red-coated soldiers marching in waves across the stage, and a Civil War campground visited by a Merry Oldsmobile, *the CIVIL warS* ran for two months in Cologne to an enthusiastic reception.

"I cannot do better work than Cologne," Wilson told the world.

With eleventh-hour funding from a Tokyo kimono manufacturer and a Tokyo burger outlet arranged by Madame Hanaemori, the Coco Chanel of Japan, Wilson staged a private premiere of the Japanese act in Hanaemori's fashion theater in downtown Tokyo. The French section was scheduled to premiere in L.A., after rehearsals in Marseilles in February, with music by the British minimalist Gavin Bryars. The French Act involved a range of historical figures flying in the air; the giant staircase of the Paris Opera underwater; Jules Verne's Nautilus; and the duel of the Monitor and Merrimac. Flying out of Marseilles to Rome, Wilson somehow lost a shoe on the plane. Glass's music for the Rome act, romantic in form and feeling, was explicitly reminiscent of Verdi in certain passages, including a remarkable aria for Garibaldi, the mythical founder of the Olympic Games, and for Hercules, singing in a forest and a lion's pelt with the trees of all nations during the climactic final scene.

Except for the connective "Knee Plays," scheduled for Minneapolis in April, Robert Wilson had done what many people had considered impossible. He had finished *the CIVIL warS*.

Problems, however, were brewing in L.A. Wilson and Applegarth had gotten almost nowhere towards raising the money needed to produce the finished work at the Shrine. Despite $1.4 million raised from the Olympic Organizing Committee and the National Endowment for the Arts, the sale of Wilson's drawings, and projected box office receipts, another $1.2 million was needed, and with the January deadline already past, there was nowhere to turn except to wealthy Angelenos and the American business community. The problem here was that Wilson's work was almost completely unknown in L.A., and major sponsors had already contributed to the Games themselves. The scale of the project, together with the prospect that it might not happen, was enough to scare off most potential donors, who in any case wouldn't receive credit for major gifts because the Times-Mirror Foundation was the official festival sponsor. David Bowie, the one name capable of attracting large private donations, withdrew in December due to other commitments. Wilson urged Fitzpatrick and the Olympic Organizing Committee to help him fund-raise, arguing that *the CIVIL warS* was the only original work created especially for the festival (although Meredith Monk and Ping Chong's *The Games* was, too), and that five nations had already secured funding to send their sections to America. Fitzpatrick replied that he couldn't possibly give special financial aid to one event out of the one hundred and two in the festival, and Wilson was in a weak position to force his hand – until February, when he was finally certain that *the CIVIL warS* would be ready to fly into Los Angeles.

This could happen now, and needed to happen now.

All he needed was a green light and the folding money.

Ten days before the scheduled opening in Rome, Applegarth informed Fitzpatrick that the completed work currently had no chance of opening in L.A. The money simply wasn't in place. Fitzpatrick suggested that they present the Rome section and the "knee plays" alone, but Wilson refused this option, saying that it was impossible to leave any of the countries home. On March 30th, Wilson and Applegarth issued a last-minute plan, involving simulcast satellite hookups to the five nations to be represented in Los Angeles. But with the opening just nine weeks away, Fitzpatrick felt there was not enough time left to make the proper arrangements. On Saturday, March 31st, Fitzpatrick told the press that *the CIVIL warS* was finished.

"A crime against culture," cried one Paris newspaper. "The failure of nerve in Los Angeles," said the *Wall Street Journal,* "has resulted in a serious artistic loss." "The problem is a lack of cultural policy in this country," Wilson declared, before flying to Japan to render in-person apologies to co-workers and repay the Kyoto kimono manufacturer and the burger outlet. Blasting Los Angeles as "a second-rate cultural outpost," he blamed *the CIVIL warS'* collapse on the *L.A.*

Times, the Olympic Committee, and especially the private sector, which "was to support the Olympics. That's Reagan's philosophy, but they haven't." While the Olympic Organizing Committee counted tens of millions in profits from the Games, Wilson could do little but rail against the "corruption" of American culture, which glorified international competition but failed to support a fantasy of the brotherhood of man.

The "knee plays," meant to link the fifteen scenes, were produced post-mortem in April in Minneapolis, with Byrne shifting from Kabuki instrumentation to a New Orleans-style jazz. Portions of the German *CIVIL warS* were presented by American Repertory Theater in Cambridge this past February, but the completed work has yet to be performed. The Frankfurt World Theater Festival plans to show the sections unseen in Europe, and Avignon the unproduced French sections. And plans have been recently announced to bring these international companies together with the Houston Grand Opera for a nine-and-a-half-hour, $6.2 million staging of the complete work in Austin next fall, as part of the 150th anniversary of Texas's founding as an independent republic. Whether Wilson's quest will come to conclusion in Austin remains to be seen. *[It didn't happen.]* What had begun as an act of Faustian ambition now seemed, with the flawless wisdom of hindsight, a Quixotic quest doomed to failure from the beginning.

I was at Bob Wilson's lower Manhattan loft on Election Night 1984, as American democracy ushered in the second term of the man in the White House, Ronald Reagan. Absorbed in the *Einstein* remount, Wilson had forgotten about the fate of the nation. Reminded, he shrieked and rushed to his bedroom to watch a half-hour of television coverage. After Geraldine Ferraro acknowledged defeat, he returned to talk with me until four in the morning — not about American politics or cultural policy, but the art of performers he admires.

Wilson's conversation grew increasingly unrehearsed as the night wore on, darkness preserved the solitude in which phantoms breed. "I don't sleep," he explained, "because I feel I might miss something."

"I saw Dietrich fourteen or fifteen times in London," Wilson was telling me in his mild, pleasant voice. It was three in the morning, and a second bottle of vodka was open on the table. "Every night, I watched her really carefully." Visualizing the scene in his mind's eye, he tapped out a pulse on his thigh. "Ladies and gentlemen, Miss Marlene Dietrich-2-3-4, Spot-2-3-4, Enter-2-3-4, Downstage-2-3-4, Head, Cross. And you *don't* cross until then. Every night, the applause was in the same place. The hand *here,* behind the dress, two steps down into the spotlight. Abso-*lutely* the *same,* the same lines every single night. It was so alive, so dangerous… something within this thing cut like a diamond. Something *spontaneous.* " Wilson balanced a pencil on the edge of the table.

"She'd walk offstage to this electrical box where she kept a bottle of scotch. She'd…" And here Wilson mimed chugging from a bottle. "She'd drink a whole bottle of scotch every night and you didn't see it. I took Sheryl Sutton [one of Wilson's long-time leading performers], and she saw four or five of these performances. I said, 'Watch the space between her fingers, watch how she does that.'" Wilson gestured in the air. "It was like a *wave* through the theater." Wilson spins paeans on the space between Albert Einstein's fingers, too. Five years ago, he insisted that actors in *Edison* apply make-up to the spaces between their fingers.

"If I get, in the next fifteen years, three major works…" he muses moments later. Following *The Golden Windows,* Wilson plans to direct *DD&D II,* a "life and times of Franz Kafka" by Heiner Müller, at the Schaubühne in Berlin, its interior redesigned by Wilson with swivel seats for the audience and a number of different stages. In February 1986 he premieres Euripides' *Alcestis,* with a prologue by Müller and a Noh epilogue, at American Repertory Theater in Cambridge. An original work created with the great Kabuki actor Tomasabura Banda, the first ever created for the Grand Kabuki by a Westerner, is in early planning, as is an opera on an Arabian Nights theme with Glass. And there's the Austin *CIVIL war [which never happened.]* But beginning with the *Medea* operas he directed in Lyon last year – one with contemporary music by Gavin Bryars, the other written in 1693 by Marc-Antoine Charpontier – Robert Wilson has begun to acknowledge a universe beyond his fingertips.

Wilson's decorative tableaux have not entirely excluded the old-age subjects of the theater: the confrontations between the individual and society, men and women, youth and age, the living and the dead. Wilson plans to approach a *Lear* for Hamburg in 1987, Wagner's *Parsifal* for La Scala and possibly Bayreuth, perhaps a *Tristan* in France in 1988. No longer an artist revealing the hidden, subliminal depths that society had purged, the maker of *the CIVIL warS* has become a surreal classicist, an entrepreneur of beautiful, expensive surfaces, promoting a vision of cultural policy that combines Western classics with his own work in a single repertory. Millions of dollars to celebrate the space between a performer's fingers, created by a man who once said that the most beautiful experience he ever had in the theater was a blackface production of *Showboat* in Tokyo, Japan.

On the opera house stage at BAM last December, the finale of *Einstein* was underway. A boy in a glass case in the interior of a spaceship drifted through a trap door into smoky light. A woman in a glass coffin floated horizontally through the air. Singers and dancers moved along a huge four-tiered wall of pulsing lights. Dazzling in its science fiction beauty – visually more ravishing than at the Met – *Einstein* was the talk of New York City, seizing time along some spectacular frontier between the ordinary and the fantastic – "like listening to a kite," said Christopher Knowles. Once considered severely impaired, Knowles now lives in his own loft, pursuing a career as an independent artist and author. His functional ability – he even has a girlfriend – is among Wilson's finest achievements.

With Glass's music burbling like the engines of some intergalactic spaceship, Wilson suddenly appeared on stage, racing back and forth along a diagonal line, waving yellow flashlights in each hand.

Dressed all in black, he seems to be dancing with a devil invisible to the rest of us, taunting his hellish doppelgänger like a matador.

Throwing down one flashlight, then the other, he moves as if exhausted, staggering along the diagonal, before galvanizing himself into another maniacal fit, his mouth gaping open and shut like a fish on the deck of a boat. A gigantic scrim with a graphic illustration of an atomic explosion sailed down to cover the proscenium arch. Wilson continued to dance behind it, moving like a wounded animal. Another dancer flies on wires across the stage while a soprano's amplified voice punctuates the air with shrieking arpeggios. Another scrim unveiled, this one covered with a dark, cloudy sky. A quiet final scene enacted on a bench, a banal monologue suggests the redemptive powers of love, the tenderness of a world moments away from a meaningless, unimaginable apocalypse.

At *Einstein's* tumultuous curtain call, Wilson reappeared on stage to prance ecstatically alongside his composer and cast. At that moment he seemed less the future of American spectacle than a pure product of a cultural era. In the depths of his ambition and his visionary spectacles, Robert Wilson has emerged as a naked celebrant of the madness and surreality of an American Age.

POSTSCRIPT: *I was at a theater reception Wilson attended after my piece came out. His only response was: "Spare me."*

THE WAGNERIAN VISIONS OF PETER SELLARS: *American Theater Magazine*, December 1987

Note: *The* enfant terrible *who made himself synonymous with what Hollywood would call the "high-concept" theater and opera of the '80s, Peter Sellars was at the reception following the premiere of* Nixon in China, *the John Adams/Alice Goodman/Mark Morris opera he directed at BAM. Sellars told me that this piece was the "definitive" article about him and his work, although he also mentioned it was "pistols at dawn" over a couple of misstatements of facts, which I subsequently fixed.*

"Some of my work is sensational, some of it's insightful, but the hilarious thing is that practically no one's seen it!" Director Peter Sellars, interviewed at three in the morning last spring in his loft, a block from the New York Stock Exchange, had things nimbly in perspective. "And I'm trying to keep it that way as long as possible!"

But doesn't that defeat the purpose? Isn't theater meant to be seen?

"My shows live in people's imaginations *because* no one's seen them," Sellars insists. "Few people realize that my work is painful, irritating, and misshapen. I'm stubborn that way. Because unless you get people to the point where something snaps, nothing happens."

The most provocative *enfant terrible* in the American theater since Orson Welles has been making people snap, weep, sleep, and bravo through more than a hundred opera and theater productions around the country – everything from a *Mikado* set in contemporary Japan to a Kabuki western for the National Theater of the Deaf; from Gorky's *Summerfolk* with George Gershwin songs to a Handel opera set on Cape Canaveral and the planet Mars. Sellars' wild joking of Broadway, avant-garde, and classical elements – his desire to be fantastic! – towering! – profound! – impossible! – has sent audiences in Boston, Chicago, La Jolla and Minneapolis reeling into their parking lots, or arguing in lobbies about his imaginative interventions. And through it all, most of the theater community have been like blind people groping an elephant: except for a brief appearance at La Mama in 1981, Sellars' work has never been seen in New York, the nation's media center and still theater capital.

But this changed during the last half of 1987, when a veritable monsoon of Sellars washed within a few miles of Manhattan. His 1986 revisioning of Mozart's *Cosi fan tutte,* set in a neon-lit diner, was revived at this season's PepsiCo Summerfare in Purchase, N.Y., alternating with his equally venturesome *Don Giovanni,* grounded in a tenement block in Spanish Harlem. In November his *Zangezi,* "a supersaga in 20 planes" by the '20s Russian futurist Velimir Khlebnikov, joined the Brooklyn Academy of Music's NEXT WAVE Festival. "An ecstatic, visionary outpouring of nonsense and wit, slang and hortatory verse, a kind of mad cocktail party," according to *The Wall Street Journal, Zangezi* had opened the new Ahmanson Auditorium of the Museum of Contemporary Art in Los Angeles a year ago and became a cult classic in Southern California. On December 6th, two days before *Zangezi* closes in Brooklyn, the fifth annual NEXT WAVE will present the New York premiere of the long-awaited *Nixon in China,* developed by Sellars in collaboration with the composer John Adams, librettist Alice Goodman, and choreographer Mark Morris. A three-act revisioning of the historic 1972 meeting between Nixon, Mao Tse-Tung and Chou Enlai in Beijing, *Nixon in China* premiered at the Houston Grand Opera in October and will move to Washington, D.C.'s Kennedy Center after its Brooklyn run.

But won't Pat Nixon sightseeing, Henry Kissinger skulking in the shadows, and Chiang Ching dancing in the forefront of the Red Detachment of Women verge on camp? Dick Nixon *singing?*

"Three hours of camp wouldn't be very interesting, would it?" Sellars retorts. "This piece is frying other fish."

If that's so, what are its politics?

"John Adams said it best: 'This is an opera for Republicans and Communists, not for liberal Democrats.'" Count on Sellars to pinpoint a supremely operatic moment in postwar history. The director hopes that his last act will send his audience home with tears streaming down their cheeks. Sellars' full-scale arrival in New York means that imagination alone will no longer suffice; what people may discover is that his work isn't just cheeky, it's *tough,* offering shocks against boredom, and boredom against facile entertainment. Sellars wants his audiences to wake up and face the issues. But he also doesn't care if folks also snooze a bit.

"They'll still get something out of it," he's sure. "Anyone who is following only the surface of my work is totally frustrated because I put as many obstacles as I can think of in the way."

The only serious director in America who says he loves it when people hate his shows is regularly assailed as sophomoric, pretentious, and self-indulgent – "a destroyer of the classics," according to fellow director Andrei Serban. For his part, Sellars merely points out how and why the rest of the world is wrong. He has read everything, seen everything, and thought his way through everything twice, and has decided that a theatrical revolution is necessary – and that it is a revolution that must begin in the past. "Peter directs from history," says Ruth Maleczech, a founding member of Mabou Mines and an actor in *Zangezi* – history being one way back to the Human City that is the ultimate dream of any serious theater artist. Sellars' vision may be painful, irritating and misshapen at times, but it is grounded in a sense of tradition that is difficult to fit comfortably into the forms and formulas of theater today.

A doubleness pervades his work: at the same moment that he aspires to be a contemporary classicist, Sellars also wants to shake things up, to tread the ground of avant-garde violation – to provoke, disturb, and shatter audiences' perception of the world. And it was with this paradoxical sensibility – this psychological twining of Light and Darkness, Creation and Destruction – that Sellars brought to the opportunity of a lifetime: to create an American National Theater at the Kennedy Center for the Performing Arts in Washington, D.C.

The "Avant-Garde" was Big, and its Rules had Changed. And in 1984 its future appeared to have fallen into the hands of a 26-year-old *wunderkind* from Harvard. With naturally-spiked hair and colorful kimono jackets, Sellars at five-foot-three looked every inch the postmodern iconoclast – a product of no scene, no movement, no cause, and no ensemble vision – a *sui generis* visionary sprung full-blown from the brows of Aristotle and Artaud and the stacks of the Widener Library. Barely out of diapers, Sellars was being slung into the avant-garde pantheon for his gusto and willful obscurity, compared to Balanchine for his detailed choreographic staging, hailed by top critics for his wildly illuminating revisions of the classics. To other people he was an arrogant, irritating little know-it-all, an aesthete plucking notions from the postwar avant-garde's Elizabethan flowering to stage its *corpus delecti*. Sellars had made himself synonymous with what Hollywood might call the "high-concept" theater of the '80s, blending moments of extraordinary profundity and beauty with longer stretches of boredom.

"A play is like a big ice-cream sundae" was a typical Sellars *pronunciamento* that drove some people up the wall. "If you want to accomplish anything, you have to first be willing to make a big, big *mess*."

And Sellars had indisputably made messes. Enumerating such goals as the creation "within my lifetime" of a 20th-century performing tradition of opera, he singlehandedly returned the prospects of sublime masterpieces and over-the-top disasters to America's theater and opera stages. Brimming with energy and ideas, brazen in his reach and his innocence of the world, Sellars stood at what would be the pinnacle of most careers, still young enough to have a bit of a lark "contemplating the Trojan Horse," as he slyly told a Boston audience following the Kennedy Center appointment. The American theater as we know it is "dead as a doornail," he announced to anyone who would listen. This meant that the task of the new American National Theater would necessarily be the creation of a new theatrical mainstream, based on the idea of the Wagnerian gesamkuntswerk, the "total theater" event merging every art form into a complete vision of culture.

"Wagner called it the art form of the future, and he was right," Sellars told *The New York Times.* "I don't think theater exists independently of music. It is no accident that all Greek drama was opera. And particularly in the light of the way new technologies are transforming everything we know as performance, the theater of the future is necessarily this gesamkuntswerk."

The fusion of diverse elements of art and performance has been the fundamental action of the American avant-garde since the days of the Happenings, but Sellars was planning to up the ante: he was going to stage a postmodern archaeology of global theater, sheltering a vision that would unite Wagner and DeMille, Artaud and Shakespeare, Kabuki and George S. Kaufman, 800 lighting cues and the kitchen sink. The American National Theater (ANT) was going to recover areas of popular performance that the nonprofit theater establishment had scorned, like grand operas, melodramas and comedies from the 19th and early 20th centuries, as well as mid-century American musicals from *Showboat* to *Gypsy* – an era which Sellars places on a par with the theaters of ancient Greece and Elizabethan England. He would load his Trojan Horse not only with Off-Broadway soldiers like Robert Wilson and Richard Foreman, but also movie stars; his associate artistic directors would include the Wooster Group's Elizabeth LeCompte, whose company attacks liberal shibboleths from the cultural Left, and his good friend and near-mentor from Cambridge days, the writer-director Timothy Mayer. In other words, Sellars was going to create a national theater by completely shutting out the old theater establishment, wheel his horse into Reagan's Troy (too bad Ronnie never played old Priam), wait until curtain time, then throw open the gates of the city. An arch-revolutionary would be taking over the Kennedy Center's tomb-like edifice on the Potomac – the cultural Parnassus of America's synthetic capital – with an opportunity to create a national theater on a scale with Broadway in its glory days. Just how much self-conscious iconoclasm could such an institution bear? Many people were waiting to find out.

On the other side of the world, meanwhile, director Yuri Lyubimov was arguing face-to-face with Chairman Leonid Brezhnev about the future of theater in the Soviet Union. In the spring of 1983 Sellars traveled to Moscow and saw seven productions in Lyubimov's Taganka Theater, as well as others at the Moscow Art Theater, shortly before Lyubimov was ousted from his 20-year-long tenure. Sellars returned to America convinced that "there is a place for a theater with an institutional life a mile from the Capitol." But what did he have to say to the nation? With an actor in the White House, what did any theater have to say that wasn't already eclipsed by the spectacle of television? Even with three stages and a $6 million budget, how was a national theater going to thrive, when theater itself had become almost an impossibility?

Peter Sellars was born in Pittsburgh, PA, a week before the Sputnik launch. His parents broke up when he was nine. He served his childhood apprenticeship with the Lovelace Marionette Theater, performing in shopping malls and parks across the city. Puppetry! – the ultimate apprenticeship for 20th century theatrical visionaries, from Alfred Jarry to Edward Gordon Craig to Orson Welles to Jerzy Grotowski to Charles Ludlam! Sellars was his own puppet of fate: a bone disease left his limbs slightly shortened and twisted. In typical good spirits, he can refer to "the hilarious way my body is put together."

Obnoxious, warm-hearted, wildly precocious, and as naturally wonderstruck as any natural-born director, Sellars put on his first childhood puppet show, *Alice in Wonderland,* with music by John Cage and Charles Gounod. Working in the difficult French dramas that the Lovelace Marionette Theater often produced, he discovered his key idea – that "the most avant-garde work is in fact the most popular. You can do anything as long as it works!" Sellars would direct thirty shows at Andover Academy, and at Harvard, forty more. He was thrown off the Loeb mainstage for what he himself calls "the *Heaven's Gate* of Harvard" – a production of *Façade*, a collection of light nonsense verse by Edith Sitwell – after being the first freshman ever allowed on the main stage. He promptly took over an old storage room in the basement of Adams House and turned it into the Explosives B Cabaret, where he staged more than thirty plays from Brecht, Woody Allen, Mrozek, and Aristophanes to Harold Pinter. Mozart's *Bastien und Bastienne* was performed in the pinball room of the freshman student union; *Antony and Cleopatra* in a swimming pool; *King Lear* with a Lincoln Continental on stage, with himself in the title role. The *Harvard Crimson* loathed almost everything he did, but between his sophomore and junior years he condensed Wagner's "Ring" cycle for puppets and recreated it during the Loeb summer season. Harvard Professor and *New Republic* critic Robert Brustein saw the show and invited Sellars to return to the main stage.

A bizarre, beautiful production of Gorky's *Inspector General* appeared during American Repertory Theater's inaugural season and received wide attention. Sellars only now graduated *magna cum laude* from Harvard with a degree in dramatic theory and practice, bristling with ideas about everything from Russian constructivism to American musical comedy. He had already established the poles of his career: his work would shift between huge conceptual edifices built on relatively obscure works, and the wild updating of the most ambitious dramas in the Western canon. His first postgraduate production was Mozart's *Don Giovanni*, which premiered in New Hampshire with sets by Edwin Gorey; this was the first of many collaborations with musical director Craig Smith. Professing his "terror" of Mozart, Sellars nevertheless introduced duels with switchblades, substituted cocaine for champagne, and served Don Juan a last meal of a Big Mac and Fries. *Opera News* blasted this as "an act of vandalism," but Sellars seemed to relish the role of Peck's Bad Boy, and added the title "vandal" to his program bio.

In February 1981 he turned a four-and-a-half-hour version of Handel's *Saul* into the Watergate Hearings. Then he left the country for six months to travel in Asia as a Harvard Sheldon Travel Scholar.

"I went to Benares. There in India I understood something about poverty and materialism. I watched the bodies floating downstream. I saw the crematorium smoke, and I thought, 'This is the end of civilization. What happens after this? How far do you lean on the material world?'" In Japan, by contrast, Sellars discovered *"the* material culture," and continued studies in Kabuki theater he had commenced at Harvard. Spirit and Matter, the Sacred and the Scorned: in staging these opposites, he would join the handful of American directors with a vision of worlds beyond the stage. He returned to Cambridge newly-attired in kimono jackets to direct a space-age version of Handel's *Orlando* for American Rep, complete with flamingos and astronauts. The *Times* called it "a shallow perversion of Handel," while *The New Yorker* thought that Sellars "discovers all Handel's richness, variety, wit, humanity and genius." Then the avant-garde *enfant terrible* headed for the Broadway commercial stage with a 1920s Russian constructivist revisioning of George Gershwin's musical *Funny Face*. Sellars and Tim Mayer's rechristened *My One and Only* was an expression of the director's conviction that the American musical comedy had gone off track in the '50s, but that older works like *The Pajama Game* and *Oklahoma!* were (as he told *Theater* magazine) "truly Brechtian in the deepest sense, 19th-century performing based on gigantic recognizable archetypes of national history." Sellars rough-draft fantasy ran over four hours, and he refused to cut it. Some of the old hands in the cast were as unhappy as the producers were. "We were all totally sapped of our spirits, and were just sort of meister-puppets that had been moved around," said Tommy Tune, who starred with the model Twiggy and assumed the directorship when Sellars was fired before the first preview in Boston.

"They lobotomized that show," Sellars said of the Tony-Award winning entertainment. Two days later he was licking his wounds with a "Genius" grant from the MacArthur Foundation, providing him with $27,000 annually for the next five years.

Newly-freed from financial worry, and yet compelled by the *One and Only* debacle to consolidate his thinking about technique, Sellars began to transform himself from precocious amateur to youthful pro.

"I never studied directing, so I don't know how to block out living room scenes and all that supposedly 'normal' stuff," he told a journalist in 1984. "For me, that kind of thing is from Mars" – which was where he set part of his Handel opera. His *Mikado* for the Chicago Lyric Opera had the title character arrive on stage in a contemporary Datsun.

In 1982 he opened the re-born La Jolla Playhouse in California with an obscure late Brecht play, *The Visions of Simone Machard*, that kept "half the audience mesmerized," according to artistic director Des McAnuff. "The rest simply walked out." The black-tie opening night party was chilly, but progressive critics raved. The Romanian-born artistic director of the Guthrie Theater in Minneapolis, Liviu Ciulei called *Simone* the best production he'd ever seen in America. Around this time, Sellars was given the reins of the Boston Shakespeare Company, where he presented subscribers with a one-act *Macbeth* performed by three characters, along with Shakespeare's seldom-produced *Pericles* and the widely-hailed American premiere of Peter Maxwell Davies' opera *The Lighthouse*. Guest directing at the Guthrie in Minneapolis, he let his first preview of *Hang on to Me*, which transposed Gorky's play *Summerfolk* to America, interspersing sixteen Gershwin standards performed by a cast of Broadway singers, avant-garde superstars, dancers, comedians, musicians and children. *Hang on to Me* ran for five-and-a-half hours. Then suddenly, with this startling resume of vivid controversy, sublime triumph, and ridiculous disaster behind him – the directorship of the unborn American National Theater fell into his lap.

The man who handed a Golden Boy the reins of a theater at one of the largest performing arts centers in America was seventy-four-year-old Roger Stevens, a hugely successful capitalist, a former big-time Broadway producer, and a force in American cultural politics for decades. Stevens was the first chairman of the National Endowment for the Arts and the founding director of the Kennedy Center. Sellars refers to him unironically as "a great American," although it was harder to see what the tall, laconic older man saw in the short, boyish iconoclast who was fired from his only Broadway job and had never been reviewed favorably by *The New York Times* – an incorruptible *artiste* whose only administrative experience was a year running the Boston Shakespeare Company, which was nearly bankrupt by the end of his stewardship. Sellars became the most daring major appointment since Herbert Blau and Jules Irving from San Francisco Actor's Workshop were handed the reins at Lincoln Center almost twenty years before. Sellars was not Stevens' first choice.

"We had to do something," Stevens later admitted. "I think he'll shake things up a bit, and that's all for the best." Perhaps Stevens was correct. How else to rationalize a classic tale of an heirless King's fabulous adoption of a *goldenen Kind* full of spunk and vigor and high-minded ideals? What Sellars offered Stevens was a vision of a postmodern culture that was grandiose and total, capable of absorbing everything from ancient Athens to Rogers and Hart and the mid-century Broadway dramas Stevens loved.

"I grew up with John Cage and Merce Cunningham as old masters," Sellars told an interviewer. "But while they were giving birth to something, Norman

Rockwell was also in his prime. The thing to realize is that what John Cage introduced can be found in Erik Satie or in a 13th-century Japanese manuscript. At the same time that we can disregard the entire culture of the world, we know more of it than we ever have before. With just the push of a button we can choose between 8th-century Chinese lute music, Mahler's Sixth Symphony, or Prince."

Sellars proposed offering the best impulses and experiences of humanity to Kennedy Center audiences. The American National Theater (ANT) would surpass the national theaters of Great Britain and France. The ANT would bring great foreign troupes to the Center; it would create a new, identifiably American acting style; it would encourage playwrights to shatter all existing formulas and make exorbitant demands – a storm, a banquet, a ballet, a cast of fifty!

"I want to do productions that grow, that will have ten-year runs," he told the press. "My object in Washington is to have a Broadway crusader like Harold Prince working in the same theater with an avant-garde evangelist like Liz LeCompte and have some notion of cross-pollination."

Dreaming of a vast Potomac flood across the American cultural delta, Sellars was unwilling to leave even an acre of American cultural memory dry. He would leave no levees standing anywhere, least of all between art and box-office.

Would Peter Sellars prove too "avant-garde" for Washington?

"We'll find out, won't we," said Roger Stevens.

Ushered with pomp into the Kennedy Center's plush environs, feted by Senator Howard Baker and Clare Booth Luce, Sellars retired from celebrityhood to devote twenty-hour a day to creating a rich environment for work. Bubbling over with flattery, encouragement and theory, Sellars generated tremendous personal devotion, his elfin aspect and inexhaustible energy suiting the role of creative gadfly. Responsibility was not about to curb his mischief. Seated at a state dinner one chair over from George Schultz, he leaned across the lap of the woman sitting between them and asked if there were any chapters in his life as Secretary of State that needed dramatization. (Schultz declined to respond.) In his innocence, Sellars was nesting on the side of the angels. In his innocence, he would change the status of the American theater at a time when political and cultural dissent was, as he put it, "no longer possible."

Only there was a catch. In order to deliver both his creative dissent and his *Chorus Line*-scale blockbusters – if the postmodern dream of gesamkuntswerken in an $80 million National Monument was going to have a prayer of coming to fruition – Sellars needed to "be in a position, over the next five years, of not caring if anyone comes or not."

The self-proclaimed "American National Theater" opened with a production that seemed not to care if anyone came at all.

"I did the most avant-garde thing – I opened with a conservative play – and that was the last thing anyone expected," said Sellars, sounding uncharacteristically defensive at a press conference to announce the premature closing of Shakespeare's *Henry IV Part One* a week after it opened. The ANT had promised no less than Shakespeare's "reclamation" for Americans, but Timothy Mayer's staging was a hodge-podge of avant-garde and classical effects, European scenic ideas, and devil-take-the-hindmost acting. The production lost a cool $700,000.

"A lot of seeds are being planted that will grow in two or three years, not two or three weeks," Sellars insisted. "I think it's going to be two years before people come here and it sells out every night. Then these will be referred to as 'the glory days.'"

With ANT's second production, Sellars delivered what audiences had hoped and feared: *The Count of Monte Cristo*, James O'Neill's adaptation of Alexandre Dumas's warhorse of Victorian melodrama, was a monster Sellars had wanted to battle for years, and he pulled out all the organ stops on what O'Neill's son Eugene called "that damned play."

In typically lively and copious program notes, Sellars suggested that "the evening contains at least five different plays, each with its own method and tone," then went on to cite directorial influences ranging from Brecht to D.W. Griffith. The eclectic cast was drawn from TV (Richard Thomas of *The Daltons),* Broadway (Patti Lupone, Tony Azito), film (Roscoe Lee Browne), and the avant-garde (Mabou Mines' David Warrilow.) Stripping the enormous stage of the Eisenhower Theater to its pipes and rafters, exposing a cavernous expanse of catwalks, stairways and trap doors, Sellars warned patrons that "there is no seat in the house from which the entire production can be seen. After all, this isn't television." Art deco scenic elements glided across the stage on casters, loading and unloading performers; a string quartet played offstage; Dumas' text was interpolated with additional excerpts from Lord Byron and the Bible; actors declaimed in red and green warpaint at fever-pitch intensity, hit by spotlights from the house.

Sellars' half-finished map of the melodramatic imagination didn't quite prove his assertions that melodrama was the birth of modernism and the highway back to the classical tradition; some of his improvisations struck critics as arbitrary and overblown. Nevertheless, *The Count of Monte Cristo* was so full of passion and vividness that Sellars' brilliance was re-confirmed. He appeared briefly to have single handedly created a new cultural category in Washington: provocateur-showman, launching a venue for Culture Vultures and trendy media types, as well as for traditionally "serious" theatergoers.

With *Monte Cristo* up and running (at four hours) in Washington, Sellars traveled north to the PepisCo Summerfare in Purchase to fashion a five-hour-long production of Handel's opera *Guilio Cesare*, a mild *scandale* and the surprise hit of the summer at Summerfare.

"Sellars is giving the work a dose of what used to be called relevance," announced the *New York Post* in advance of the opening, "by setting the action in a bombed-out hotel in the present-day Middle East. The orchestra pit will look like the hotel swimming pool. And Cleopatra, who originally arrived rolled up in a rug, will drop on Caesar via a construction crane." Despite what could be described as grandstanding, opera once again seemed to release Sellars' surest directorial gifts. Andrew Porter of *The New Yorker* argued that *Guilio Cesare* "can never have seemed richer, stranger, stronger, more passionate or more high-spirited than in this presentation by artists aflame with appreciation for it, seeking not to conventionalize but to illuminate its fierce originality."

Perhaps Peter Sellars was beginning to be understood at last.

Unfortunately, things did not look so good on the bottom line. The artistic director had filled his two smaller theaters, the 500-seat Terrace and the Theater Lab, with visiting companies – the Suzuki Company of Toga, Japan, which generated little interest in D.C., and two groups from Chicago, Steppenwolf and Wisdom Bridge, which proved more popular. The tab for their visits was picked up by AT&T. Larger strains within the organization revolved around the use of the 1,100 seat Eisenhower, cavernous and two-thirds empty after *Monte Cristo's* mixed reviews. Sellars had promised a theater that would reinvent the world – "Shakespeare had the Globe, we have the Eisenhower," he said. "Being in Washington means I'm doing shows for the people who are deciding the fate of the world. I'm suddenly in the position Shakespeare and Moliere were in. It's a court theater." And yet what he was offering seemed distressingly piecemeal: an unproduced Mae West comedy, *Come on Over*, which staffers had discovered in manuscript at the Library of Congress, fell through because Sellars was unable to get the director he wanted. He went ahead instead with a can't-miss revival of O'Neill's *The Iceman Cometh*, with Jason Robards and director Jose Quintero recreating the classic Off-Broadway production that Roger Stevens had secretly bankrolled in the '50s. As a response to the season's financial crisis, a conservative production was a smart move—and it didn't hurt to have *Iceman* show D.C. audiences Roger Stevens in his heyday.

That the ANT took a financial drubbing in its first year was not unexpected. What was mildly shocking was that the theater had failed to secure a foundation of critical or audience support, in Washington or anywhere else. Sellars had come across as slightly hare-brained. His theater appeared to have little concept of damage-control or caution.

Any hopes for a consistent Season Two were laid to rest by one of the most complicated and disastrous seasons in American resident theater history. Sellars' plans to reopen the Eisenhower with Robert Wilson's *The Golden Windows* in the fall of '86 fell through at the 11th hour due to financial problems. Then Sellars exercised the incredible luxury of canceling Robert Sherwood's *Idiot's Delight*, a '30s comedy and the ANT's first move into boulevard entertainment, at the first rehearsal, and paying the actors four weeks' salary. "I didn't feel that I had the right cast," he said, "so I didn't have the heart to do it." (He had been hoping to land Jack Nicholson.) In response to Des McAnuff's La Jolla production of Chekhov's *The Seagull* and a London production that he considered a travesty, Sellars opened his second season with his own search-and-seizure of Chekhov, *A Seagull,* starring Colleen Dewhurst, Kelly McGillis,

Priscilla Smith, and Paul Winfield. *A Seagull* premiered in December as the nadir of Sellars' Kennedy Center adventures: an incoherent mishmash that obliterated Chekhov, despite Sellars' insistence that he was utterly faithful to the playwright's intentions. From the point of view of the theater's credibility, *A Seagull* was a disaster.

Sellars didn't see it that way.

"People think I'm joking when I say there's no difference between a success and a failure, but it's true," he insisted, expressing an attitude that fewer and fewer Washingtonians were willing to share. It was becoming clear that he did not see himself strictly as an artist running a national institution; he was also an experimental student keeping himself interested. The Eisenhower had become a showcase for his work, while the smaller theaters offered the cream of the avant-garde to somewhat mystified audiences: Squat Theater, which had been subletting Sellars' empty loft in downtown Manhattan, presented *Dreamland Burns*, their first original work in six years; Meredith Monk and the House brought the magical revival of Monk's decade-old *Quarry,* originally staged and then restaged at La Mama; Joseph Chaikin made his first public appearances since suffering a debilitating stroke, *Solo Voyages*, a work created from the monologues of Adrienne Kennedy and Chaikin's own words about calamitous illness. And finally, Sellars' demi-gods, the Wooster Group, arrived for a three-month residency with Jim Strah's new play *North Atlantic,* an incarnation of their collective creation *L.S.D.,* and the beginnings of a new piece inspired by Lenny Bruce and Flaubert's novel *The Temptations of Saint Anthony*, which Sellars had partially funded it through the Boston Shakespeare Company.

But ANT's brand of experimentalism was proving increasingly hard to put together with money. Financially overextended, overwhelmed, and understaffed, also battling the Kennedy Center hierarchy for rehearsal space and unable to plan far enough in advance for safety, Sellars discovered for the first time that 140-hour work weeks weren't enough.

He put himself on the line with another stab at *Idiot's Delight* with Stacy Keach and JoBeth Williams – a considered response to the awesome triviality of Reagan's world. On opening night, spirits at the institution ran high. Stevens told Sellars, "Now I know you're a great director." But *The Washington Post* accused the show of "creeping blandness" and *The New York Times* dismissed it as "a restless escape into the mindless nostalgia of camp."

Sellars knew his head was on the block. ANT badly needed a hit.

What Sellars offered was a seldom-produced play from the most recalcitrant of Golden Ages – "a return to the roots of Western Theater in Greek tragedy," says Sellars. "We wanted to put our feet in those footsteps and feel those strides." Sophocles' *Ajax* featured Howie Seago of the National Theater of the Deaf in the title role as the mad Greek general, conjuring an extraordinary moment when he is first wheeled on stage in a clear plastic box, deaf-signing while standing ankle deep in a foaming sea of blood. Set in the front of the Pentagon shortly after a successful Central American War, *Ajax* was brilliantly crafted, breathtaking in its staging and its central performance. *Ajax* in Washington was Sellars' artistic countercheck to Reagan's bombing of Libya and the escalation of military activity in Central America.

"I return to the Greeks because it was a civic-minded theater that discussed unflinchingly serious public issues. Sophocles is not anti-military. He himself was a general. But he asks hard questions like, 'Given a military engine, how can one contain it within moral limits? At what point does justified self-defense become a lust for power?" Sellars was asking Washington to inspect the raving lunacy of the American Century, but the capital refused his bid for moral seriousness: *Ajax* reviews had the tone of personal attacks, and the production averaged embarrassing 13% houses for the length of the run.

The ANT production of Sophocles' *Ajax* was the height of Sellars' personal integrity and the pitch of his institutional folly. Sellars' Trojan Horse was itself under siege.

With "heaps of vicious contumely being flung *Ajax's* way," Sellars went to Stevens and said, "Roger, nobody says it to my face how much they hate it, but you must get it all the time. Shouldn't we just fold our tents and go quietly into the desert?" Stevens looked at Sellars and said, "I had a high school coach who said, 'Quitters never win and winners never quit!" Stevens was staying the course, but it didn't matter: the Kennedy Center trustees had had their bellies full.

Sellars closed the season in the Theater Lab with *Two Figures in Dense Violet Light*, a triptych of works by Beckett, Ezra Pound and Wallace Stevens, and spent the summer in Ipswich, Mass, working on Mozart's *Cosi fan tutte*. In August 1986, Roger Stevens announced that the artistic director of the American National Theater, after two years of breathtaking box-office disappointments and sharply-negative reviews, was taking a year's leave of absence. Sellars' departure meant that the ANT itself would discontinue operations, leaving its future in doubt.

No director in twenty years had been handed Sellars' opportunity, and he had basically chosen to rock the boat until it capsized.

"Basically I'm unsuited for running a theater," he tells me that night at his loft in the Financial District. "Because I take everything too personally and I can't do anything I personally don't believe in." The fantasies of productions that would run for ten years vanished ineffably, and within months hardly seemed to have existed at all. The Trojan Horse had been dismantled in the heart of the Empire, the Greeks dispersed to the territories, and Roger Stevens, who had handed the *wunderkind* the one job in the American theater for which he was most unsuited, made plans for his own retirement in 1988.

Less than a year later, home at in his Manhattan loft and quite recovered from the Kennedy Center debacle, Sellars is struggling to explain what he's trying to do with his postmodern gesamkuntswerken. In doing so he invokes a metaphysical condition – the forgotten melody – the essential thrust of the postwar avant-garde. "I want to play with logic and textures," Sellars tells me, "to keep things unresolved… unbalanced… left open… hanging. Then I want to try to force some *life* into that little hole – some intense feeling of an *indescribable* emotion that we have no *word* for… Most people think scenes in plays are happy or sad or elegiac. Well, they're not. They're either authentic or inauthentic. There is no *pure* comedy, no *pure* tragedy – not even *impure* comedy or *impure* tragedy. There's only…" And here my fingers began to cramp. Spending hours with Sellars is to be bathed in a stream of vivid interpretation, winsome anecdote, and outrageous provocation. He tells me he gave up predicting his own life "on any level" a long time ago, but his talk consistently returns to first principles – flying theories, denouncing misconceptions, and asserting with tremendous conviction exactly what he loves and hates. With Sellars it is all real, all idea, and all theater. He has been known to wait unannounced at stage doors with tears in his eyes to thank an actor for an unforgettable performance he had just witnessed.

His loft is so empty that it looks positively gutted; he becomes distraught when he discovers that he has nothing to offer me except New York City tap water. He is leaving for Europe and a four-city tour of *Ajax* the following day, and has just returned from France, where the eternal student apprenticed himself to Jean-Luc Godard for the filming of *King Lear*. Sellars served as Godard's sounding board and was given a co-writing credit, but mostly he simply watched, listened, and learned, although he did play a small role: "William Shakespeare Jr. the Fifth," he says. Peter once appeared on *Miami Vice* as an expert on Zombies.

As the dark pre-dawn morning progresses, he unfolds a glittering array of future projects, a lot considering that he bothers to sleep four hours a night. His first book, which he describes as "another look into Peter Brook's empty space," is past a second deadline at Harper & Row while he prepares his first feature film, a silent picture to be produced by David Lynch, titled *The Cabinet of Dr. Ramirez*. Sellars will also have his British opera debut, *The Electrification of the Soviet Union*, composer Nigel Osborne's opera, which Sellars developed in collaboration with librettist Craig Raine for England's Glyndebourne Festival. And on December 1st he will settle into his new niche as a curator of the world's vanguard: at the ripe old age of thirty, Sellars will succeed Robert Fitzpatrick as director of the Los Angeles Festival, originally created around the '84 Olympic Games, which will bring international performance to a big city as starved for high culture as any in the world.

Plans are also underway for a spectacular triple bill of modernist operas at the Metropolitan Opera house during the 1988-89 season: Bartok's *Bluebeard's Castle*, Schoenberg's *Erwartung*, and Debussy's *Martyrdom of St. Sebastian*, all conducted by James Levine. "It's a great chance to show what the real composers were doing when Puccini and Strauss were taking over the operatic repertory," Sellars says, "and what it might have been like if that kind of writing had entered the opera house. It's the kind of thing we should look at as we try to go from here."

Perhaps his most significant achievements will come in opera, especially through contemporary works that provide the time structure and emotional superstructure his imagination needs to run free.

"I turn everything into opera," he tells me, a little amazed at himself. His American gesamkuntswerken, bridging the Greeks and a pluralist future, may not have taken root at the Kennedy Center, yet one can easily envision him moving through the American theater landscape, blasting away years of cholesterol. But the man who three years ago was going to "reinvent the world" has decided that theater as we know it should be allowed to die. "I learned a lot about the climate of Washington under Reagan's second term. I suspect it may be different after Contragate, but the whole experience has made me back off from theater for a while." You mean just when so much of your work is coming to New York? "Theater is not a form that has much to do with the culture," he replies. "It has become financially impossible and nonsensical for audiences, performers – everyone. That's because theater is not an adequate means for describing the shape of life in America right now. It all takes place as these gestures frozen in time." Sellars has chosen to focus on operas – two a year – and film, at least for the next three years. "Music – music has a way of cutting across the gap, providing the voice for a transaction in our time."

Sellars's postmodern *gesamkuntswerken* as mass entertainments remain a serious response to the theater crisis that has persisted through the postwar era. Growing numbers of producers and directors across the country agree that the future of theater rests with new forms combining all of the arts together in one experience. Still, it is difficult to imagine that Sellars' vision of an American National Theater could have survived under any circumstances. Suspended between civic obligation and personal conscience, the needs of the polis and his own vanguard aspirations, Sellars was at odds with any American criterion of success and failure. His Whitmanian/postmodern impulse to embrace all experience failed to produce a new mainstream in an age of postmodern tributaries. The root of Sellars' problem was a theater system that made innovative, original work difficult to realize. Sellars was right that he had needed more time. *Ajax* went on to the La Jolla Playhouse, then Europe, where it became a popular success and a more substantial piece of art.

"That's the way theater used to be made in America," says Sellars, sounding like the theatrical veteran more than twice his age who hired him at the Kennedy Center, rather than like the eternal student, prodigy, and iconoclast of yore. "You hit Philadelphia, Boston, and New Haven before showing a finished work on Broadway. And the most important part of the mix was the audience."

That had been Sellars' message all along, in a host of ways: that in one way or another, in some way shape or form, tradition can supply the spark, the genesis and materials of a necessary revolution.

GETTING THERE:
Twyla Tharp and Dancers on the Move,
from *Dance in America,*
E.P. Dutton, 1985

Note: *Twyla was the choreographer who interested me most when I first moved to the city to dance. I first observed Twyla's rehearsals in the winter of 1979 for an article that was published in the* SoHo Weekly News. *I was captured by Tharp's mastery of tradition and her rebellion against convention. Like Sellars, Tharp believed that tradition could supply the spark for a necessary revolution. This chapter comes from* Dance in America (1985), *my companion book to the PBS-TV series.*

Winter, 1979. Twyla Tharp and Dancers have moved uptown from their funky downtown studio to American Ballet Theater's immaculate ones on West 61st Street to prepare for their first New York season in almost two years. Lunch hour has begun, and two women have stripped off their sweat-soaked dance gear to stand naked, like guests at a Fellini cocktail party, smoking low-tar cigarettes and pondering their dry clothes. Other dancers are talking underneath the barres before suddenly rising to coach themselves with an icy derangement through a series of shuffles, slides, and scattershot lifts that sends them sprawling the length of the studio in seconds. They're shouting irregular counts and frankly a little gaga. *"One and two and go and go, GO!"* France Mayotte dashes diagonally across the space while Tom Rawe attempts to extricate himself from a maze of bodies in time to catch her under the armpits and swing her around. He's a split-second late, unfortunately, smashing his forearm into her chest and sending a chain reaction of disaster down the line.

That's the lift that's been gumming the works.

Standing in February sunshine streaming through the skylight, the two naked women turn away and start throwing on their clothes.

"Okay, guys, got it," says Rawe gamely, rubbing his hands together. The dancers return to the far wall and run the sequence again to perfection this time, with a relaxed yet calibrated air, like classical virtuosos just horsing around, day-dreaming up movement as they go along. What audiences in the theater will ultimately see are people careening along at the highest reaches of fun, dancing with a casual exhilaration and freedom extraordinarily in tune with the spirit of the times.

Satisfied with what they've done, the dancers gather their things and head off to lunch, their efforts unobserved by the choreographer, who has sequestered herself in a broom closet to study videotapes of their unfinished dance, *Chapters & Verses* – shaping up to be an impressionistic history of the disco generation, from the Mickey Mouse Club Anthem to the theme-and-variation jackboot of disco purgatory.

It will be Twyla's first attempt to create a "story-dance," an unfashionable hybrid she would have scoffed at attempting a decade earlier. Work began last summer, and at this point in the choreographic process, she's thrown away more movement than she's kept.

"Teeny, torrid TwYla," Tharp scrawled in the program notes for her 1976 New York season, "...lives to tell the terrible TRUTH/tracing TRAGEDY to Travesty/teasing tradition through trickly torrents twisting, traipsing, trysting, THRUSTING..." – fidgeting now before the blue glow of a video screen, rehearsing the past for some clue, some key to the present dilemma. A restlessness and an uncompromising perfectionism have dominated Tharp's progress, beginning with her earnest, unaccompanied movement studies in the '60s and continuing through the addition of music, humor, characterization, partnering, and set design in the '70s. Polishing every nugget of insight along the way, she has developed a formal mastery that allows her company to cut loose with an expense of energy unequaled by any choreographer in the world save George Balanchine. By revealing how contemporary dancers feel about themselves, she has successfully confounded the distance between classicism and popular dance, modernism and popular entertainment; by discovering how popular culture can nurture a higher order of imagination, she has assembled a repertory embodying what Tom Wolfe calls "the hog-stomping baroque exuberance of American civilization."

Tharp's constant expansion of possibilities may be an animation of her childhood, when she says her only contacts with the outside world were the attractions at her parents' drive-in movie theater near San Bernardino, California – four movies and ten cartoons a week, from MGM musicals to the whole Warner Brothers cartoon gang. Now she is working on her own video and film projects, including a studio picture, *Hair* (1978), director Milos Forman's ironic tribute to the '60s counterculture. One dance sequence was shot before thirty thousand spectators at the Washington and Lincoln Memorials in Washington. Most of Tharp's contribution didn't make the final cut, but the experience has moved her towards a new "desire for grandeur," as she baldly puts it, quickening her curiosity about how movement and gesture can convey a story. For the first time since a lecture that accompanied the second half of *The Bix Pieces* (1972), she is allowing her dancers the consolation of the Spoken Word.

With *Chapters & Verses*, Tharp has moved to the threshold of a five-year odyssey encompassing a new dance-theater form that will provide the greatest challenges of her artistic career. As she explained it to me: "You just reach a place where you begin to want *more.* "

Lunch hour has ended, and the dancers are warming up again at the barres. Tharp suddenly bursts through the swinging doors – poker-faced, cross, and ten minutes late, limping urgently, dressed in a stretched gray T-shirt, striped leg-warmers trailing a few yards of blue wool, and a tattered pair of beige-gray Woolworth sauna rubber pants patched at the crotch with a maze of yellow gaffer's tape. She resembles no one so much as a martyr in a medieval painting.

Approaching forty, Tharp finds it more and more difficult to prepare herself physically for another New York season. A brazen, seemingly unsentimental woman, Tharp believes in having the highest expectations for herself, but at the moment she has more irons in the fire than she can handle. Flinging herself into a canvas chair, she consults her clipboard, and some sort of ozone falls through the air: rehearsal is fifteen minutes behind schedule. Dancers are already pulling up their socks over their jazz shoes and diving into place along the far wall.

"When you dance with Twyla," Shelley Washington later explained, "you make yourself totally available to Twyla all the time."

"Everything okay?" the choreographer calls out at last.

The company's senior member, Rose Marie Wright, nods affirmatively, the stage manager throws on the tape recorder, and the air suddenly fills with the dreamy jazz piano of Willie "the Lion" Smith, performed by Dick Hyman. Tharp first began choreographing to Willie the Lion eight years ago, quite pregnant, in a farmhouse attic in upstate New York. The dance today is *Baker's Dozen*, and the wintry sun-drenched studio at ABT transforms itself into a Newport lawn party in the long ago. In the opening section, "Echoes of Spring," six couples coast across the floor in turn, dancing with an innocent, casual friskiness, as if showing off among themselves. Tharp knew next to nothing about partnering until the mid-'70s, but now her dancers are urging one another on to larger and more acrobatic ballroom effects: William Widener and Christine Uchida, both formerly with the Joffrey Ballet, accelerate into hair-raising catches, off-balance supports, and classical leaps and turns that take a new measure of the ballroom form. Raymond Kurshals and his partner, then Richard Colton and guest artist Sara Rudner, a longtime Tharp dancer with her own company now, dart on and off the floor and exchange partners, until the two men are left alone with Rudner.

Colton eyes Kurshals politely, walking in a circle behind him, and Kurshals backs meekly into a barre.

Cadging the dance in progress, the choreographer has settled down, her fierce mood subsiding into a humane and sensible scrutiny.

She enjoys dramatizing the divisions between sections of a dance, and in "Tango à la Caprice," the company works in threesomes, as if Kurshals, seeking to join a duet, had had a good idea. The partnering grows sharper, denser, with arching kicks executed with the suave straight-backed arrogance of flamenco. Soon the trios pass into foursomes and frozen tableaux that melt away into one sumptuously-ordered rout after another. The eye moves with an easy rhythm through all this, following the state and surge, noting what the choreographer intends us to see: the underlying structural clarity of the dance is what allows Tharpe to breathe new life into the familiar. Along with such traditional procedures as unison, canon, counterpoint, theme and variation, she systematically tears phrases apart and puts them back together in entirely different shapes, altering their direction and attack; tossing in steps from older works, even piling unrelated phrases of movement on top of one another – all without compromising the integrity of the music's smooth shifts from ragtime to swing. "You don't have to know about structure" was Tharp's caustic explanation to one interviewer. "That's my business, and there are few people I would expect to look at something maybe twice and see what the design is."

Her choreography succeeds because every moment is set forth as valid and necessary, renewing the reality of concrete, natural processes.

"Nearly all the movement has something very specific in mind," says Jennifer Waye. "Like *this* movement is about getting to the floor, except it's an *en dehors* attitude turn."

The dancers plunge into a series of eccentric character dances, including a Chaplin-esque fox-trot, while a corps of eight passes upstage in a swooping glide that has appeared as a motif throughout the dance. Waye and Washington seem not to want to leave the dance floor, but are finally lofted out by more dancers who sweep across the front of the studio floor. Colton is the last dancer left, catching Uchida as she flies through the air from unseen wings. Tossing her offstage again, he lazes his way to the center of the stage, then pops six or seven wistful pirouettes while sinking to the ground, where he sits on his heels and wiggles his hips – a dreamy Lothario remembering some palmy moment on a parquet dance floor. Colton is enjoying himself, and the company improvises a few admiring hoots and whistles. Then Tom Rawe stumbles after him in an inimitable impersonation of a Fitzgeraldian drunk, and a wedge of dancers drives across the stage behind, spilling soloists and couples like overflow from some fabulous celebration in the next studio; indeed, dancers from ABT have gathered to watch through the doorway window.

The solos continue while the company crosses and re-crosses the space, until everyone gathers in tableau for a kind of group portrait, a few kneeling in front, the rest posing with hands on hips or leaning jauntily against a neighbor. Only Christine Uchida stands apart from the group.

They turn around for another shot, more impromptu this time, glancing over their shoulders as if caught by a camera's flash.

It's an image of a sane community: sublime in its ordinariness, decent, hardworking, willing to laugh and fully capable of laughing at itself. *Baker's Dozen* is a tribute to her extended family of solo performers, the title alluding to the twelfth role being danced by either Sara Rudner or Tharp herself. It's an America of champagne, midnight swims, sudden spats, and makings-up to music at a pavilion by the sea. Tharp has taken the measure of an innocence lost, mourned, and only distantly remembered, but recovered anyway – and it is this quality of nostalgia without illusions that gives the dance its contemporary feeling.

The dancers are reshaping into a final wedge, preparing to sweep off the floor in that oddly syncopated swooping glide. Earlier, there had been a few rumbles of indecision about the irksome rhythm; now the group makes a total shamble of its final cakewalk.

Tharp, who had been watching silently, crosses her elbows over her chest, tugs at her ears, and shrieks like a bat.

"Hey, you guys, don't work on something to get it wrong! We're getting very good at that!"

The tape recorder is turned off, and Rose Marie Wright labors for a minute with the dancers to mend the rhythm problem. But there's no time to work the solution into the dance, for the rehearsal schedule says it's time for a run-through of the still-unfinished *Chapters & Verses* – the casual elegance of Willie the Lion replaced by the straining brass of an Edwin Franko Goldman march. The dancers flounce onstage now like a troupe of barnstorming circus kids, performing a series of intentionally clichéd acrobatic stunts, full of thwarted climaxes and dumb virtuosity. Have these children run away from home? The music shifts abruptly into Robbie Robertson and The Band's rock classic "The

Shape I'm In," with a troupe of snot-nosed, unruly children bullied through calisthenics by a surly drill instructor, played by Tom Rawe.

"*Sound off, three-four,*" Rawe bellows. Tharp's dancers are talking, but their listeners have the attention span of six-year-olds. Mugging ferociously, punching each other in the shoulders, they raise their hands for attention – "*May I go to the bathroom please? I gotta go* bad!"

Another band of overgrown, hormone-engorged little monsters thuds and prances across the space to *The Mickey Mouse Club March,* segueing into a solo for William Whitener, accompanied by Mouseketeer Jimmy plaintively singing, *Now it's time to say good-bye, to all our family...* "With its sloping spine and arms, its wide épaulés braced against turned-in legs, it looks like a satire of Paul Taylor," Arlene Croce would later write, "and it may be a personal memento of the year that Twyla Tharp spent in Taylor's company before forming her own group – a memento of her artistic adolescence." This explosion of noise and vulgar antics ends with a portion of the unfinished "Street from the Night Before," an original disco tune with a big-band overlay, commissioned from composer John S. Simon. Flowing, sensuous, Quaaluded movements are laid over three crossings of the space, developing over twelve minutes and finally degenerating into a vicious brawl. The acting becomes wildly overblown, operatic in scale, the angry arguments a way of showing the origins of a movement impulse: *"I'm gonna slug you in the mouth, so watch."*

In the center of it all, Rawe dances a melting love duet with Rudner, a feminine figure in red, but the section degenerates into a writhing orgy, spilling across the floor to a disco beat.

A few chapters of a never-to-be-completed novel, *Chapters & Verses* offers only shards of a rudimentary story, weaving together various popular dance styles from a contemporary adolescence with Tharp's new perceptions of "those crazy people who walk down the street talking to themselves. Fascinating. I love them." *Chapters & Verses* comic patchwork also touches certain aspects of the choreographer's own life, redreaming the social experiences of her youth: the miscarriages of love, the costs of enforced discipline, the ambition to escape the past only to rediscover it on stage, and most important, how families are lost and found in this country. Over the next two years, Tharp will expand on those themes, bringing her formidable rage and carpentry, a lusting intelligence, and a nearly Faustian ambition to bear on nothing less than her own comic-tragic vision of contemporary America.

From the beginning, she resolutely refuses to view these new investigations as a departure.

"The perverse thing is thinking that it's possible to get away from yourself," she tells me. "The further you go, the closer you come back. Sometimes in trying to change too much you cease to utilize the strongest lessons you have at your disposal. The best thing, the most sensible, obviously the sanest thing to do is to become that which you understand the most."

Tharp leans back in her studio chair, relaxing for a few minutes before the final run-through of the afternoon – *Electric Blues*, her featured dance from *Hair*, newly-adapted for the stage. The dancers are resting against the mirrors, stretching, massaging one another's shoulders, not exactly aflame with excitement about the coming season. Pressure and hard work are constants with the Tharp company. The choreographer, who considers her group a model of social arrangements, joins warmly in their mirth, mentioning how much she's looking forward to dancing in *Baker's Dozen* "if I'm still alive." When the *Electric Blues* rock music breaks out, Twyla hauls herself out of her chair and begins jogging, stiffly at first, then with limber grace, around the edge of the studio floor. Three men run out tossing a football, and she keeps bumping into them. Fed up, she hassles them with a few missed punches. Suddenly they have her by the arms and ankles and are launching her straight above their heads.

Tharp screams – she has never much liked being lifted – then screams again, more reasonably, when the men let go and catch her a few inches off the floor. She's forgotten her own choreography, her rubber pants are creeping down her thighs, but the music is reaching the guitar bridge and Tharp is sucked again into the lunatic machinery: passed between legs, over shoulders, chucked like a sack, and perched on someone's thighs for a loop-the-loop eight feet in diameter, originally choreographed with Tharp wearing a crash helmet. When the machine is through with her, it spits her across the floor, where Twyla executes one of her classic pratfalls, limbs flailing in a paroxysm of outraged dignity.

But suddenly she's up and spinning coolly in place – the tomboy jogger transformed by an onstage costume change into the indestructible Shiva, God of creation and destruction.

From hard rock to ancient India, from the dance floors of Newport to discos and a lawn in Central Park, Tharp remains radically skeptical of the idea that any work of art can be truly new, original, private. Nevertheless, by dancing "*a little bit differently* every day," as Tom Rawe puts it, Twyla finds her own reasons for everything she does – because "art," she once wrote, "is the only way to run away without leaving home."

Twyla Tharp was born in Portland, Indiana in 1941, the first child of Quaker parents and named, legend has it, after the local "Pig Queen" at the county fair. Twyla claims she chose her own birthdate. "July 1st. Middle-of-the-roader. Dead center of the year. The only place for an extremist to be." What she describes as her "buckshot education" began with musical ear training, supposedly instituted before she turned one. In her years before leaving home, she studied ballet, tap, acrobatics, baton twirling, drums, viola, violin, piano, painting, music composition, and harmony – her mother's way of preparing her for almost any eventuality. Faced with a curriculum that would have crushed all but the most irrepressible spirits, Tharp developed a sense of the American *Weltanschauung* unique among her contemporaries, along with a discipline and paradoxical defiance of convention that would be her surest means of psychic survival. It would take Tharp years before she learned to use everything she knew. Meanwhile, she says without evident remorse, "I feel I was cheated out of a childhood in some ways.

"I went through a gruesome experience when I was about four in a piano contest against kids who were much older than I was. In order to get through it quicker, I forgot my repeats, because I'd been promised that if I just got through it, I would get a Milky Way bar. The pressure of playing piano in a competition as a teeny kid was worse than almost anything else could ever be. That was what I got from my first piano teacher, Miss Brown of Muncie, Indiana... I was a very silent child. I didn't talk much, because I didn't trust it. I liked music. I believed those drives and sentiments and feelings. By the age of five I was practicing the piano a couple of hours a day." At eight, Twyla moved with her family to San Bernardino – "the end of the earth" she calls it – where she lived in a separate wing of a big house, attended school, and worked at the family drive-in, breaking twenties at the refreshment stand while still in elementary school, then working as a carhop as a teen-ager. Forever after, she claims, she has seen the world in two dimensions.

She continued dance lessons she began in Indiana, at some point studying gypsy and flamenco with Rita Hayworth's uncle. Certain days were planned to the last detail: fifteen minutes for tambourine dancing, twelve minutes for toe-tap, eleven minutes for handstands, ten minutes for *grand jeté*... Working with a tiny record player, she would make up dances. "I've always seen dances in my head," she says. "I thought everyone did. I guess not everyone does. I think actually everyone does; they just don't pursue it to the degree I have... When I was fourteen, I started studying with these people in Fontana whose names were Milada Miladava and her sister, Feola Miraz. Now these ladies were actually former Ballet Russe de Monte Carlo dancers, trained at the Paris Opera, if you can believe it, and Milada was a relatively well-known dancer who'd been in all the Ballet Russe movies and the *Gaîté Parisienne*. They were both very beautiful and were actually very good dancers. They referred me after a while to a lady named Collenette in San Marino, where my mother started driving me twice a week for the next four years. On schooldays, we'd be driving back from 5:30 class and I'd do my homework by the light from the glove compartment." She would graduate as her high school's valedictorian. She was also a cheerleader. The other kids considered her "weird," but she had no sense of their standards. She was too busy developing her own.

"Collenette was British, one of Pavlova's seven baby ballerinas. She had a tremendous sense of form and dignity. You did *not* wear pointe shoes until you were in the fifth class, and you were put in rows according to who did the best – there was no futzing around. If you could do four pirouettes, you went to the front, if you could do two you went to the back. Nothing about being nice: 'Oh, it's your turn today, dear, go to the front row.' This is very useful to learn in this country. I'm very grateful... Apart from Balanchine, and having the opportunity to grow up around him, like Edward Villella did, one could not have done much better than to have the sort of lineage I had."

Tharp enrolled as a pre-med student at nearby Pomona College, with vague plans to become a psychiatrist. "I made up things I was going to be," she recalls. "That was only to cover my tracks."

By the end of her freshman year, she decided that she had to escape from home, from family, and from whatever unforgiving engines had driven her through her endless lessons. In 1961, she enrolled at Barnard College, twenty-seven hundred miles away in New York, still with no intention of becoming a professional dancer. She took her first modern dance class at Barnard, and dropped out the day a teacher told her to "make a sunrise." She also realized, studying ballet at studios around town, that she was not destined to become a ballerina. "I couldn't bear the attitude," she says. "I couldn't understand the fact that ballet was about going through certain conventions – the word convention in itself takes care of it. Ballet had become like the decorative art on Greek temples: just remnants of a past that nobody really understood anymore."

Tharp threw herself into modern and ballet classes around the city during her years at Barnard – sometimes two or three a day, at the Graham studio, then with Merce Cunningham and Carolyn Brown (after an ad in *Dance Magazine* caught her eye), and later with Alwin Nikolais, Erick Hawkins, and the renown jazz teacher Eugene Louis Faccuito, known professionally as Luigi. By the time she graduated from Barnard in 1963 (with a degree in art history), the freedom and insights of the modernists had recast her instincts. She asked for and was given permission to miss her graduation ceremonies in order to travel with the Paul Taylor Dance Company, her first important professional engagement. Tharp made an immediate impression with her matter-of-fact bravado, her comedic strengths, her sexy, vulnerable arrogance, and her formidable technique. "She was a tough and sassy dancer who could buffalo her way through anything," Taylor recalls. If she learned anything from Taylor's audacious physicality, his faith in human oddity, and his occasional sardonic wit, she has trouble acknowledging it.

"You learned from Paul by watching him dance," she says. "I loved to watch him when he was still working with the Graham company, which was where I first saw him. I was taken by the way he looked, and found out that he was doing his own choreography. I was definitely attracted to him as a dancer, not as a choreographer."

At a post-performance party during a London tour, Taylor noticed Twyla in conversation with a well-placed dance critic, passing along her negative thoughts about a new work in the repertory. Taylor, who could read lips, eavesdropped from across the room. Tharp claims she was handed her walking papers the next day, but Taylor insists that "when we got back to America, I told her she should think about whether she really wanted to stay with us. She went away for a while and came back, a little too quickly, and said she would. Then she quit again, two days before the start of a Broadway season. Later she came to us and said she wanted to go on unemployment and that I'd fired her. Well, I couldn't agree to that. So, whenever I see her now, she says, 'You fired me!' and I say, 'You quit!'" Whatever the truth of the matter, Tharp was too uncompromising to survive in anyone's company but her own.

"There was a body that wanted to move around," she explains. "But it wasn't particularly contented with any of the ways it was presented with. So it went out to find what felt right."

Tharp's first piece of choreography initiated her calculating instincts for doing something thoroughly and correctly before moving on. *Tank Dive*, performed for an audience of twelve at the Hunter College art department in 1965, was four minutes long. "I didn't know shit from Shinola about choreography," she says today. Setting out to master the craft, Tharp moved downtown to begin pouring out four or five dances a year, discarding them after each performance, and thinking of her newly-formed company of women as "a bunch of broads doing God's work."

Working at the Judson Church – "because the space was free" – she felt a wariness bordering on contempt for her contemporaries' lack of formal discipline and technique. Yet her own concentration on the formal qualities of concrete physical processes was very much aligned with Downtown postmodernism. The first reviews were uniform in their adjectives: cool, cerebral, beautiful, yes, waging the vanguard battle for the serious values of art. But also blunt, emotionless, enigmatic, executed with faintly belligerent expressions, as if to say, "'There's no way we can do this except through the body, but I wish to God there were,'" Tharp herself has suggested. "Twyla Tharp's main concern in choreography," wrote *Times'* critic Don McDonough, "is to throw lines of movement across and through space and thereby establish a zone of human mastery over the real estate that is our environment." Her memory of those days is similar: "My God, the first five years, nothing but form," she says. "Horizontals and verticals, that was it. Post-lentils-and-beans."

With *Generation* (1967), Tharpian structuralism began to relax somewhat. A twenty-eight-minute quintet, "written," she says, for a large open space, the dancing came in cascades of free-wheeling, thrown-away movement that liberated the individual expressiveness of performers. Her formalism was still formidable, but with her unusual gift for generating energy and commitment in rehearsals, Tharp was beginning to "make visible and public the ways, usually confused, involuntary, and secret, in which people behave toward one another," as critic Dale Harris later wrote. Choreography became the soundest way to end her long separation from other people. "I didn't know how much I minded not having known other kids until I started trying to be a married person," Tharp recalls, referring to the marriage near the end of her college years that soon ended in divorce. "Then I realized it had been a disaster. I didn't know how to talk to anybody."

By the end of the decade of the '60s, Tharp was scoring dances for larger and larger groups of people, working in nontheatrical spaces like parks and museums and art galleries, and leaving increasing room for improvisation and hazard. In *Medley* (1969), originally created at the American Dance Festival in Connecticut and later performed on the Great Lawn in Central Park, Tharp put aside her prolific notes and charts to "choreograph chaos," augmenting her company of six women with sixty nondancers in street clothes. By 1970 this drift outdoors culminated in a major change: accompanied by her second husband, Robert Huot, a painter who had worked with her as a designer since 1965, she moved to a 250-acre farm in upstate New York to have a baby.

Tharp's "bucolic experiment" in rural living, removing her from the pressures and distractions of her rising recognition in the world of experimental dance, resulted in a new clarity of purpose. When dancers Rose Marie Wright and Sara Rudner, her two most important collaborators, traveled upstate to be with her during the summer, Tharp produced a spartan masterpiece, *The Fugue* – the oldest work still in the repertory and Tharp's "doctorate" in structure. Based on twenty twenty-second movement variations performed in silence, except for the amplified sound of the dancers' feet slapping the stage, it was as close as she would ever come to pure logic in movement.

Only later did she discover that her trio was actually a canon, not a fugue – but other than that, Tharp insists, "It's perfect."

"Okay, now what?" Tharp asked herself aloud. With looser joints, a lower center of gravity, and new warm feelings due to her pregnancy, she began horsing around to a favorite record by the jazz pianist Jelly Roll Morton and his Red Hot Peppers. The result, *Eight Jelly Rolls* (1971), marked the beginning of works "filled with feelings and references to all the old guys" that sent Twyla Tharp off on her spectacular rise.

In the opening moment, Rose Marie Wright casts a lean, impenetrable look into the audience, as if to say, 'Well, you're here, so you might as well watch," before launching into a slinky, sexy, shuffling, shadow-boxing jazz solo. The deadpan neutrality and casual concentration on the mechanics of movement remained from Tharp's earlier dances, but when Tharp and Rudner emerged behind Wright, twitching and cavorting the length of the stage before vanishing into the wings, something new was afoot. *Eight Jelly Rolls* was fun to do and fun to watch, its sensuous bouts of lyricism and reckless comic horseplay perfectly matched to Jelly Roll Morton's shifting landscape of bluesy depression, mayhem, and happiness. Tharp placed recognizable characters on stage, dancing in elegant halter faux-tuxedos, showing up too early and diving back into the wings, taking on one another in zany dance competitions, stealing scenes until somebody hauled them out of the light. With her hilarious caricature of a falling down drunk, created on the day she actually went into labor, Tharp proved herself again among the finest comedians in American dance. Stumbling onstage to "The Smokehouse Blues," she performed a series of magnificent pratfalls, followed by epic struggles to regain her feet and join a chorus of six damsels languishing behind her. Accessible, deeply satisfying, *Eight Jelly Rolls* represented Tharp's break with the '60s avant-garde.

But for her, the dance was an act of re-attachment – a reconciliation with the past and the beginnings of her true direction.

Later that same year, Tharp began consciously to celebrate her deepening realization of the continuity of past and present and the potential riches of her monstrous education. A suite of five dances choreographed to Haydn, but ultimately performed to music by the early jazz cornetist Bix Beiderbecke, *The Bix Pieces* was literally about remembering – all the way back to her early tap and baton lessons in San Bernardino. "It seems to me that art is a question of emphasis," a lecturer announced during the dance. "That aesthetics and ethics are the same. The inventiveness resides first in choice and then in synthesis – in bringing it all together. That this action is repeated over and over again, the resolution somehow marvelously altered each time." *The Bix Pieces* demonstrated Tharp's realization of how few fundamental concepts of dance there truly were: that dance steps from classical ballet and tap-dancing are profoundly related, and can be combined and recombined in nearly infinite variety. *The Bix Pieces* also had "a kind of bedrock that no one could understand," she later explained, "such as the fact that the five dances were cyclical and were in a rondo form and that my father had just died and my son had just been born and all this kind of stuff which you wouldn't know from dancing but which makes obvious and absolute sense." With *The Raggedy Dances*, assembled in 1972 to music by Scott Joplin and Wolfgang Amadeus Mozart, Tharp continued to fashion her entirely personal intersections of ballet, jazz, spunk, spit, and a little of the old soft-shoe. Abandoning the purely formal aspirations of her generation, absorbing lessons from whenever and wherever she liked, she began to create a fusion of styles that meant nothing less than a new kind of contemporary classicism.

In 1973, a new work co-produced by the Twyla Tharp Foundation and the City Center Joffrey Ballet set the American dance world on its ear. *Deuce Coupe* brought on stage a pack of hotdogging adolescents dancing around to fourteen bubble-gum surf-rock tunes by the Beach Boys, in front of a backdrop painted live in performance by the United Graffiti Artists of New York. What was happening on the subways of Manhattan, Brooklyn, the Bronx and Queens and on the boardwalks of Venice, California, was there with the Joffrey Ballet and Tharp dancers on the City Center stage. After years of dopey rock ballets, *Deuce Coupe* was the fantasies of a generation confirmed, showing classically-trained dancers moving to the same music contemporary youth actually danced to on a Saturday night. Tharp's no-holds-barred sock-hop seemed to some like a mere embrace of novelty or an attack on the ballet's doddering irrelevance in a world of subway vandalism and rock assault. But through it all, a pristine ballerina executed an alphabet of ballet steps, from *ailes de pigeons* to *voyagé arabesque*, a lingering image of the resplendent orderliness as well as the more ludicrous attitudinizing of the ballet. The ballerina in *Deuce Coupe* was Tharp's way of showing audiences how classicism was the basis of everything they saw – the bedrock of her dancers' training and of her own attempt to shatter convention and reconceive tradition in contemporary terms. *Deuce Coupe* was popular art in the best sense – open, unpretentious, immediately gratifying – and it made Twyla Tharp the darling and the brat of the American dance world of the '70s. After *Deuce Coupe II*, a new version "customized" for the Joffrey alone, and *As Time Goes By*, a fresh interpretation of Haydn's "Farewell Symphony," Tharp returned to her own company to fashion *Ocean's Motion*, a new work to the music of Chuck Berry. *Sue's Leg*, her celebration of the music of Fats Waller and the dance of the American '30s – the Big Apple, marathon and ballroom dancing, Busby Berkeley-style production numbers, even the Bump and Grind – evoked the frivolity of a vanished decade with feints and starts, lunging pratfalls, and ants-in-the-pants pile-ups. *Sue's Leg* established a continuity between generations – demonstrating how dance can make the past seem not only new, but valuable.

Twyla Tharp was opening up a continent of energy and expression.

The following year she set her sights on the heart of the dance establishment, sending American Ballet Theater off the deep end with *Push Comes to Shove*, a report on the condition of the company and of all American ballet, as well as a re-introduction of the great Russian classical dancer Mikhail Baryshnikov to American audiences.

Push opened in front of a closed curtain, where Baryshnikov performed a shuffling, alternately sinuous and sharp solo with a derby hat to Joseph Lamb's "Bohemian Rag," along with ballerinas Martine van Hamel and Marianna Tcherkassky. In a second opening, the curtain parted and the music shifted to Haydn's "Symphony No. 8," otherwise known as "The Bear," with the Russian bear dancing in all his glory, interspersing daring off-balance turns and leaps with what feels like the casual, fingers-through-the-hair distraction of a man rehearsing for his life. Tcherkassky and soloist Kristine Elliott led a *corps de ballet* through an episode of classical dancing gone berserk, with dancers mixing in the wrong formations, reshaping identifiable images from the grand ballets of the nineteenth century, then dropping them to stroll nonchalantly to another part of the stage. Van Hamel and Clark Tippet performed a goofy, competitive pas de deux with the corps in the background exchanging courtly greetings, then clawing at one another in the air until Baryshnikov returned for an orgy of choreographed bowing.

The disorganization of the corps, the rivalries between stars, Baryshnikov's astounding virtuosity, and the conflict between this and ABT's theatrical tradition had been laid bare by an experimental artist who simply looked at what she saw and acknowledged it as the subject of the dance. According to at least one critic, the thirty-four-year-old choreographer was an amateur, a pervert, a nihilist who transformed ballet dancers into spastics making up their own steps as they go along. *Push Comes to Shove* was a mighty ballet for the great unwashed, an avant-garde ballet for the masses, but Tharp insisted it was no travesty. Her rebellion against the decorum of classical style had absorbed the past without destroying it, drawing out her own version of the resources of a classical company: naturalness, virtuosity, and supreme musical craftsmanship. More than any contemporary choreographer, Tharp knew what artistic freedom was worth. Tharp answered not only to the timelessness of ballet but also to the needs and perceptions of her time.

Beyond a few disgruntled reviews, *Push Comes to Shove* met with a salvo of critical as well as popular acclaim, moving Tharp to the forefront of contemporary choreographers for the ballet – even though she still wanted no part in certain of its conventions. On the opening night of *As Time Goes By* at the Joffrey, she threw a bouquet back into the house.

Internationally hailed as a liberating personification of American youth, Tharp's company had become one of the most popular and controversial dance troupes in the world, and Tharp herself a "herald of a new age," as Croce crowed. Continuing to range across a variety of American dance genres, Tharp danced with Baryshnikov in a duet, *Once More, Frank*, to the "swinging sounds" of Frank Sinatra; *Mud* was danced in pointe shoes and Adidas; the jubilant *Cacklin' Hen* was Tharp's version of an old-fashioned country hoedown; *After All* was assembled for Olympic gold-medalist skater John Curry; and *Give and Take* was her genuflection to the muse of Balanchine, although Balanchine reportedly didn't care for it much. The full-throttled energy of her dancers, the high, unfettered artfulness of her formal strategies, and the verisimilitude of her Americanism were thrilling to many. But Tharp's dance-as-dance gave her no heavy themes to stagger under; with her garrulous knack for churning up hurricanes of witty movement, her slouching, cool, seductive showmanship, and her constant flanking maneuvers, some people considered her achievement little more than an adolescent revolt. Walter Sorrell concluded his massive study of world dance, *Dance in Its Time* (1980), with a brief description of Tharp's work as "the glamour and superficiality of a vitality going nowhere. It seems as if she were the living proof of the deadness of the past era."

Stung by attacks on her work as merely trendy and crowd-pleasing, Tharp responded with voodoo defiance, dividing her company into a "red" team and a "blue" team, so that one could tour while the other stayed home to develop new choreography. She understood the ultimate seriousness and validity of what she was after – to excel absolutely and please absolutely – but the accusations of immaturity struck a nerve. By the end of the '70s, Tharp had entered the fateful condition of an artist seeking some higher stature, tempted to make some encompassing statement about her generation and her time. Her growing interest in narrative and the mystique of the "masterpiece" held out the promise of another phase of work: a shift in interests as radical as the advent of humor, character, and popular dance styles in the '70s.

The '70s ended with a major critical and popular success at the Brooklyn Academy of Music (BAM). Kudos were heaped on the elegant *Baker's Dozen*, which Tharp considered a predictable response. The playful fragmentation and nascent violence of *Chapters & Verses*, like the *Hair* dances, required a less familiar effort from audiences than her wisest, most heartfelt entertainment. Nevertheless, Tharp knew that her first attempt at storytelling was only partially realized; even Croce, usually her most eloquent champion, noted "a glib, super-Broadway style I have never before associated with Twyla Tharp." Tharp persisted with her plans to construct an evening-length dance-theater piece with words.

Audiences awaiting the rebirth of *South Pacific* would be kept waiting. A new piece was evolving into something new: a "dansical," Tharp called it, with an original score, a constant stream of dancing and mime, and a spoken text to parallel them both. How to make words coexist with movement, without falling into redundancy or apology? She produced a first draft herself, grandly titled *Life in America*, then a second, by some logical Tharpian declension, *Complaints*. Tharp's text showed a flair for domestic observation – one wag dubbed it "danced Updike" – but the material needed restructuring and a tighter focus. Tharp's agent suggested playwright Thomas Babe, a favorite at Joseph Papp's New York Shakespeare Festival. Babe was fluent in a range of styles, from the harsh urban violence of his *Prayer for My Daughter* to the period evocativeness of his Civil War-era *Rebel Women*. Tharp found the prospect of dealing with someone else's strong feelings and perceptions daunting – "because I have always, for good or bad, felt great commitment about what I do," she later acknowledged, "and feeling the same degree of commitment about what somebody else does is a whole other problem." But Babe seemed "level-headed," so Tharp decided to take a chance on the first major collaboration with someone other than a lighting and costume designer: a writer this time.

An affectionate camaraderie quickly developed between the two collaborators, who seemed no less fresh for vying at the threshold of their fortieth birthdays. Both were divorced – Tharp's second marriage ended after six years – and the single parent of a young child, facing the impossibility of the family as traditionally conceived. Leaving behind their youth, they had become recognized artists facing up to the burden of posterity and the need to create works that might last.

Their collaboration chose to address issues of family life and of a woman unfit for life as an adult, and to see it all from the point of view of a child. *When We Were Very Young* shaped itself into a story told by a father to his young daughter about his own mother, Jane, and his bittersweet recollections of her suffering, brutality, and death at the age of forty – all set against his longings for the family to exist as perfectly as it does in a home movie. Green thoughts from a greener shade: the text became a kind of radio play, with a child actress and Babe himself reading from a platform high above the stage. The "dansical" traces Jane's mock-picaresque adventures in a world of chance, domination, and submission, her fugitive sexuality and drinking, and boisterous rows that finally are not all that comical. It is an image of the American dream of childhood turned nightmare; a monstrous vision of Mom, Dad, and the two kids; a litany of misalliances and thwarted desire, layering fantasy and history. The title was borrowed from a children's book by A.A. Milne, with a recurring motif the poem "Disobedience," about a middle-aged mother who goes down to the end of the town and is never heard from again. *"James James Morrison Morrison Weatherby George Dupree, took good care of his mother, though he was only three…"* A fanatical Red Army chorus of dancers recites these words in brisk cadence as a kind of glue for the action. Tharp liked the poem because "it seems to make growing up the ultimate and cardinal sin." The choreography incorporated "The Hard Circus" from *Chapters & Verses,* with its exuberant child's vision of circus show biz, and the chafing disco orgy from "The Street" section, condensed and reworked to produce Tharp's first true fugue.

The tension between childhood freedoms and adult constraints, and the mature acceptance of this perilous condition, found expression in Tharp's interpretation of the role of Jane, which she and Sara Rudner would perform on alternate nights – "if I'm still alive," she said.

A few weeks before the opening, Twyla was making very confident noises in a *Dance Magazine* interview: "The new piece represents a culmination, and if this does not turn out to be a developed and full and matured person performing in this new piece, I will be very disappointed, because I have spent a lifetime getting here."

The success of the rest of the repertory – including the new *Brahms' Paganini,* a chamber exercise in neoclassical virtuosity by the contemporary Paganini of choreographers – kept the Tharp Foundation from going to the cleaners in a Broadway house. But *When We Were Very Young* was an enormous miscalculation, and the critics dined on it. With its surprisingly literal approach to words and movement, its sentimentalization of defeat, its hysteria, its petulant anger, and its morass of nostalgic values, *WWWVY* presented characters unmatched to the grisly situations Tharp and Babe had concocted for them. John S. Simon's undistinguished music, Babe's confusing, jocular-avuncular script, and the furious mime sequences for father, mother and two siblings never found a focus. Critic Tobi Tobias called the whole thing "tediously like the eternal kvetch." Still, many of its dance sequences were enormously imaginative, and audiences applauded. As the thirty-nine-year-old single mother at the turning point of her life, Twyla Tharp "played a part that fits the way she looks and dances," Croce acknowledged. "The hell-bent energy, the comic, hardboiled defensiveness, the quizzical temperament, and the beautiful sexy legs were accommodated in the role of a furious child-woman whose motor races all the way to destruction. Accommodated but not released."

Attempting to stand in the middle of the road of life in the image of her own mother, who had inaugurated so much of Tharp's sense of herself, Twyla/Jane went down to the edge of the stage – the edge of the world – and leapt into the orchestra pit, never to be seen again.

"That," she said later, "was a very deep pit."

Eighteen months later, Twyla Tharp's seventy-eight-minute-long intermission-less apocalypse *The Catherine Wheel* (1981) opened on Broadway. Her company had risen phoenix-like from the fiasco of her first Broadway season with Tharp's longest and most ambitious work to date. "THE NUCLEAR FAMILY MEETS THE NUCLEAR BOMB" blared the banner headline of *The SoHo Weekly News,* above a glamorous Richard Avedon portrait of Tharp and her new collaborator, David Byrne of Talking Heads, gazing coolly into the camera, cheek-to-cheek but not quite touching. Tharp's Dantesque moment of self-awareness in the middle of the road of life had inspired her pursuit of new forms of dance narrative, which finally coalesced in a masterpiece of perplexed and calculating terror, the creation of two artists with no time for nostalgic reminiscence, plunging headfirst into the nuclear nightmare of the '80s with what was arguably the greatest rock ballet ever made.

The constraints of adulthood and the desire for artistic maturity were transformed in *The Catherine Wheel* into the reality of martyrdom. Tharp's new heroine was Saint Catherine of Alexandria, who was tortured to death on a spiked wheel in A.D. 307, although a few legends claim that the wheel exploded at her touch, killing her torturers. A Catherine Wheel is a firework similar to a pinwheel; a Catherine wheel republic is one in constant revolution; Catherine wheels are the tumbling cartwheels performed on Saint Catherine's Day, a Catholic feast for unmarried women that was dropped from the liturgical calendar in 1969.

All of these ideas find echoes in the dance, which links some invidious threat to Tharp's continuing comic nightmare of the All-American Horrible Family. But the hell-fired *Catherine Wheel* is at its heart a mysterious allegory about a pineapple – at various times an Edenic fruit, a bomb, a prize, a torture device, a housewarming gift, a bribe, a philosopher's stone, a sacrificial offering, and the MacGuffin of a mystery story – a thing to be sought after, shunned, bought and sold, devoured, pillaged, and used as a weapon. "It's a little like interleaving the *National Enquirer* with *The Golden Bough*," Croce suggested.

The Catherine Wheel's delirious Grand Guignol revived the cartoon characters from *WWWVY:* the bull-headed, lecherous father, again played by Tom Rawe, and the ambitious, brutal and brutalized mother, played by Jennifer Waye – partners in real life – open their honeymoon with a bashful ballroom number. Then the pineapple flies in and boffs Rawe on the noggin, turning the marriage into Saturday night wrestling at the Olympic Auditorium. They are swiftly joined by their two klutzy, moronic offspring, performed by Raymond Kurshals and Katie Glasner; a pert, hysterical housemaid, played by Shelley Washington; and a cute, fuzzy dog, also Dad's future sexual victim and murderer, played by Christine Uchida. The family ruckuses exfoliate into a kind of Dance-Theater of Cruelty, the performers miming greed, lust, rage, and horror with a psychic and visual charge at once fascinating and repelling. After Mom teaches her kids how to dance, she takes them to town in a Rumba line, where she attempts to sell her daughter to a naïve, dreamy poet, played by John Carrafa. Pursuing his own disembodied ideal of perfection, the poet is more interested in pineapples than in virginal flesh, or Mom's, either. The pineapple grows bigger and bigger through each imbroglio, satisfying no one, while a feminine figure in red, Sara Rudner, weaves in and out of the action as the Leader, understanding and lamenting the horror of it all. At age forty, Tharp has left herself out of the dance, just as Jane, approaching forty, disappeared off the edge of the stage. (Mention the word retirement, and her hair stands on end.)

Santo Loquasto's set includes Leonardo-like wheels and circles and a forest of twenty-four vertical poles that descend to obstruct the chorus of blindfolded, black-and-red-clad dancers who accompany the Leader through darkness and light, sometimes appearing as ghostly shadows on a scrim. After the final family combat has littered the stage with great chunks of pineapple, the chorus appears with brooms to sweep the floor clean. Mom and Dad reappear to perform a brief history of social dancing – Two-step, Charleston, Lindy, Twist, and Frug – despite the constant interruptions of the kids, who want their own cuddles and knockdowns. The Leader attempts to impale the now-bundled shards of pineapple on the heavenly machine, where they apparently belong, and Loquasto's suspended rack with clanging spikes descends, but the chorus prevents her from doing it, and the machine, like the torture device in Kafka's *Penal Colony*, nearly crushes her under its weight, seeking to inscribe some lesson on her skin. The Leader finally "repents," dancing in great circles with a golden pineapple suspended on a wheel, opening the ground for the final "Golden Section" – the company in gold lamé, careening before a golden wall through some of the most dangerous and spectacular choreography Tharp had ever devised.

The glory of Tharp's anger and the complexity of her allegory, with its interlocking systems of meaning that the dancers found endlessly amusing, weren't finally the point. Ceaseless dancing, a blazing river of it, was blasted along by the extraordinary rhythmic energy and inventiveness of David Byrne's music and lyrics. Byrne's band Talking Heads began appearing in downtown New York in the mid- '70s with a clean, structural sound and coruscating lyrics dealing with normal occasions of urban life and the more paranoid manifestations of Middle America. More recently, through collaborations with the English experimental art-rocker Brian Eno and a growing fascination with polymetric rhythms from Africa, Latin America, and the Near East, as well as Afro-American funk, Byrne was exploring music for its possible role in community-building. Whether Byrne's score "will one day be ranked alongside *Le Sacre du Printemps, Romeo and Juliet,* and *Appalachian Spring* is open to question," noted *The New York Times*, but the question had been raised.

Tharp's vision of community had undergone a change as well: from the large-spirited *Baker's Dozen* only two years earlier, Tharp went on to create Bruce Springsteen's *Short Stories*, which may or may not end with a rape and murder – "where everything is brutal, violent, where everyone takes advantage of everyone else and there is no future at all," as she remarked in an interview with the *L.A. Times*. Tharp's desire to respond directly to the abrasions of the world, to act out all that is feared and sought after, had uncovered an impulse to horrify and excite through idiomatic violence. Violence has become Tharp's way of reflecting on the world, and meditating on what has been lost.

Whatever happened to Twyla Tharp?

"A lot of things. Disasters in my life. You don't want to know… I'm not speaking politically now. I'm speaking in terms of manners. I miss a lot of the old-fashioned conventions: the simple pledges; the real honesty; the getting married; the staying married; the meaning it, then doing what you mean. It used to be that people really stood by their word. These days, when someone says something, chances are they don't know what they're talking about.… Sometimes I think it's just I'm getting older," she continues, "and that the way I look at people has changed. But I don't think so. I think that societal conventions have altered radically in the last thirty years. I am not politically active because, while political action may change the course of people's lives, so does art. I don't have time for political revolution… In some ways being an artist is a much more powerful position to be in. I am, in fact, dealing with real world problems. I'm dealing with morality in those dances."

The fury of Tharp's vision disguised a quest not unlike Saint Catherine's, who wanted to be "the most perfect, the best spokesperson, the purest," Tharp would tell audiences on PBS. "She was ultimately martyred for her ideal of abstract perfection."

Not long after *The Catherine Wheel* premiere, I interviewed Twyla in her penthouse on Central Park West, high above the green sward of the park—"my single luxury," she told me.

"I have this overriding belief," she explained, "that there is a right way of doing things, and that one reaches a state of grace when one functions in the most direct fashion. Once in a while I feel that I've done the best that I could possibly do, and sometimes more: that it's the best that can be done. It's a notion of God that simply means there is an order apart from oneself. There is a right way… I ultimately believe," Tharp was almost shouting now, "that things can be powerful and effective and moving and ambitious and that people will respond positively, and I think my faith in that allows me to do what is obviously risky and emotionally devastating – which it is. We've had a lot of timid stuff recently, you know," she growled. "Real *repressed.*"

Audiences would flood into the Winter Garden, but *The Catherine Wheel* production expenses would nearly break the foundation.

One evening a deranged woman climbed onstage wearing a large overcoat and carrying barbecue fork in her hand, which she had used to slash two ushers on her way into the theater. The sound operator was off headset and wandering the auditorium, so there was no way to stop the music. Vaguely aware of the presence of this strange woman on stage, the dancers continued, and the audience naturally assumed she was part of the show. Tharp, the house and stage managers finally went onstage to talk to her, but she brandished the fork at them, her eyes glazed. Twyla was prepared to tackle this woman if she made a move towards her dancers, or back her into the same pit that had taken Jane the year before. After a full five minutes, someone finally managed to bring down the curtain, and the woman was removed by police to Bellevue.

A shard of the violence and insanity of the so-called "real" world had passed through Tharp's fun-house mirror and onto the stage before her dance could enter "The Golden Section," in which icy terror surrenders to an exorbitant ritual of sacrifice. Some critics described the final dance as only a sustained showstopper, an abstract *divertissement* out of keeping with the rest of the dance. But for Tharp, "The Golden Section" was a glittering auto-da-fé, a holocaust of willed and urgent hope that placed her company beyond the firestorms and millennial fantasies of the present to harness the energy of the sun, which is the power of the atomic bomb and the force binding all of nature together.

To eerie whistles and pulsing congas and bass, dancers flee in straight lines across the space, detonating phrases of movement with unbroken fierceness: split leaps, daring snatches out of the air, bodies as barriers instantly overcome, reckless unison gestures, dead arching drops between legs, pinwheels made out of women's bodies turning noiselessly in the air. Through such limb-risking partnership, "The Golden Section" proposes Tharp's alternative to the disorder and violence of American life: her hunger for functioning in the most direct fashion has led her to transcend personal emotions through the expression of ensemble craft – her only alternative to the corrosive forces of marriage, family, and middle-class life in general.

A flawed, infuriating masterpiece, an anthem of an artist's search for grace under pressure, *The Catherine Wheel* became a kind of cautionary fable of disciplined energy that refused to gaze at terror from afar. "The Golden Section" was Tharp's racked and tortured Judgment Day, thrusting dancers beyond individual fantasy and personal feeling into shared myth, then back into history, or its end.

Tharp's rage and outrage could not seem to be able to go any further, but the choreographer found a way. Using a thudding electric guitar score by Glenn Branca, *Bad Smells* (1982) accosted audiences with brutal images of primitive destruction, its dancers flailing and grimacing through some night of the living dead, their bodies captured onstage by a camera operator and projected live on a screen overhead.

And then, just as suddenly, the violence was quelled by a new dance assembled as an emotional buffer against the fury of the Branca score – a new dance that also appeared to mark the beginnings of yet another era in Tharp's constant progress. *Nine Sinatra Songs* (1983) was a series of duets danced under a huge mirrored ball in evening wear designed by Oscar de La Renta. It had as its subject "couples, love, marriage, and off into the sunset!" declared the choreographer. A cultural monument in the Age of Reagan, *Nine Sinatra Songs* became the greatest popular success in the company's history.

No parody of America's traditional images of modern romance, the Sinatra dances smacked of a born-again conversion to the manners lost to the social revolution of the '60s, even as their studied suavity and well-groomed violence still reflected Tharp's continuing desire to communicate complex meanings directly. As Balanchine knew better than anyone, emotion and character in dancing are more than a matter of storytelling; as City Ballet's Edward Villella once explained, only a master storyteller can do without a plot. Tharp had learned this lesson the hard way – the way she learns and re-learns everything – and returned to making pure dance works with a richer sense of theatrical possibility, newly committed to the transgression and inclusion of everything.

She inevitably re-approached ballet with new fascination and respect. *Once Upon a Time* (1983), set to romantic music by the Imperial Russian ballet composer Alexander Glazunov, was assembled for Baryshnikov and four very young dancers at ABT. The stunning *Bach Partita,* for thirty-six stars and members of the corps, was a full-blown homage to the work of Balanchine and her first purely neoclassical ballet.

"It's funny," said the choreographer, "but I chose not to do this ballet for twenty years." For her own company, she assembled another dance that invited audiences to share her new trust of neo-classical style: bereft of her signature bumps and shrugs and shimmies and shuffles, *Telemann* was nearly a *ballet blanc,* and some fans of Tharp could hardly believe their eyes. In late May 1984, ABT took the unusual step of honoring Tharp with her own evening of work; a few weeks later, Tharp and Jerome Robbins shared the stage of the State Theater for *Brahms/Handel,* danced by the New York City Ballet. Amazingly, Tharp had become arguably the leading ballet choreographer of her generation.

And then came the capstone for an era that began in the late '70s: *Fait Accompli,* (1984), a dance obsessed with death: what it feels like to die, and more importantly, to struggle against death with ruthless intensity. Beneath a battery of blazing lights and haze designed by Jennifer Tipton, Tharp's company moved in and out of darkness, executing duets, quartets, octets with frenetic precision, punctuating the air with tense, karate-like blows. Joggers passed through roiling fumes, clutching their throats and gasping for breath; voices drifted through the driving synthesizer-and-percussion score by David van Tiegham, reporting airline disasters and urban catastrophes. Lines of dancers appeared and reappeared, repeating unison phrases at double, then quadruple speeds; poses were struck, held, shaken out, held, and shaken out again.

Tharp had been reading accounts of executions and concentration camps, studying the power of totems to ward off evil; the second half of the dance presents the choreographer herself, lean and defiant at age forty-three, after five months of daily running, push-ups, calisthenics, and boxing lessons before her morning barre with Richard Colton. Tharp takes on eight men in a series of nonstop duets *in extremis.* As in *Electric Blues* five years before, Tharp is pretzeled, tossed, succored, abused, hoisted, arced, launched and rolled across the stage for minutes without touching the ground. And then she danced a solo that seemed to recapitulate every idea she had ever had. The physical pain and psychic suffering of a career had reached its end. *Fait Accompli* was Tharp's last dance for herself: a professional death, an angry giving up of life.

She stood center stage, like Petrouchka the straw puppet, patting her heart and reaching out with that hand, only to catch the gesture with her free hand before it could be fully extended.

As the stage empties of dancers for the last time, Tharp cups her hands into imaginary binoculars and peers across the stage at the audience. Then she shudders, shakes, and grunts, as if to say, "I've given you every last drop of my blood" – as if gathering all her rage, her courage, her intelligence, and her mettle to cast against the world.

Then her shoulders fly up to her ears and she turns, gliding in a slow-motion downstage, where footlights suddenly brighten – as if to show us, the audience, what she has been seeing all along – as if to reaffirm, as her entire career has done, the imaginative link between the theater and the world. What could she possibly do to follow this? "I'm not going to talk about it," says the choreographer. "I'm going to do it."

JULIAN BECK, JUDITH MALINA, & THE LIVING THEATRE: THE '80s MOVIE

I was in London in the spring of 1978 when the Living Theatre came to town for its first indoor performances after four years of street actions in cities across the continent. I shared a bowl of hashish with Julian Beck in his dressing room at the Roundhouse, where the Ramones helped launch English Punk two years before, and was an audience volunteer that night in Prometheus at the Winter Palace. *I believed I played to an Indian restaurant, where several actors got into a screaming fight with another patron that nearly ended in blows. Julian's partner Judith Malina, one of the most brilliant talkers I have ever been around, stayed high above the fray, as did Julian, too busy gazing doe-eyed at his twenty-something Italian boyfriend, a sullen Donatello in an expensive-looking double-breasted jacket with no shirt underneath. I wrote this for the* Voice, *but old allies of the Living made sure my piece never saw the light of day.*

INTERIOR. AN APARTMENT IN PARIS, FRANCE – DAY.

The year is 1983. The father of the postwar American experimental theater, JULIAN BECK sits at his desk, writing peaceably in longhand.

AUTHOR'S VOICE-OVER:

Nearly forgotten in Lower Manhattan except in memories and the history books, a theater that had fought and lost a war over the soul of Western culture in the '50s and '60s unexpectedly, magically revives. The stunning May 1981 election victory of a Socialist government in France has inspired progressive producers to crawl out of the woodwork and arrange a twenty-five-city French tour for "Le Living." The Becks believed that no State would ever give them money, but Jack Lang, formerly of the av Avignon Festival, now the new French Minister of Culture, agrees to do everything within his power to help them, except find them a space. They would have to do that themselves. The Living moved operations to Paris to search for homes and prepare a season of plays. This occupied most of 1982. In January, the Becks surrendered their apartments in Rome and began a six-month work residency in Nantes. And at this moment, a rebellion intervened: a revolt of the cells.

JULIAN

(Reading from the diary he's been working on.) "I never thought this could happen to me. I was so content with my lifestyle – even though always under great stress because I create under stress… But I associate the cancer now with a triple event: the catastrophic end of a love affair that made me feel like I was turning to powder inside; my mother died at the age of 89; and I went to work on *The Yellow Methuselah* and was sleeping only four to five hours a night. The doctors say the illness started around that time."

Another view, a new angle of BECK, returning to his writing.

AUTHOR'S V.O.

Their life's work incomplete, the Becks batten down in Paris to fight the cancer. While their search for a theater continues, Judith and Julian realize a long-held dream of being writers in the City of Lights. But as fate would have it – Hollywood intervenes.

The telephone RINGS. BECK answers and a conversation ensues.

AUTHOR'S V.O.

It's Francis Ford Coppola on the line, asking Beck to come to New York for two weeks to shoot *The Cotton Club*. Coppola wants Beck to play Sol Weinstein, a malevolent Jewish bodyguard and hitman for the legendary gangster Dutch Schultz. Weinstein is a soul-dead force for evil. Beck had played a blind prophet in Pasolini's *Oedipus* and a dying Pope in Bertolucci's *Agonia*, but had otherwise done little to pursue a film career. Now, with money tight and negotiations underway for The Living Theatre's first return to New York since their legendary production of *Paradise Now* at BAM in '68 – - Coppola made Beck an offer he couldn't refuse.

DISSOLVE TO:

INTERIOR: THE JOYCE THEATER IN MANHATTAN – NIGHT.

LIVING THEATER ACTORS are moving sensuously up the aisles.

AUTHOR'S V.O.

January, 1984. The Living Theatre is in New York for the opening night of *The Archaeology of Sleep* at the Joyce Theater in Chelsea. *The Cotton Club* filming has dragged on for six months. Beck never returned to Paris.

TIGHT SHOT on the CROTCH of *The New York Times'* drama critic FRANK RICH, whose thigh is covered by a notebook in which he can be seen furiously scribbling. BECK's HAND reaches into the frame, towards RICH's leg. RICH squirms in his seat to avoid BECK's touch.

JULIAN

Are you afraid if I touch you like this?

FRANK RICH

I'm getting there...

PAN from RICH'S CROTCH to behind his head, where we see other LIVING THEATER ACTORS roaming the aisles, touching and stroking audience members, speaking in a cacophony of accents.

JULIAN'S V.O.

I was not at all aware it was Frank Rich, and to the best of my knowledge I didn't touch him at all. He was anxious to be offended, and used it as a leaping off point to dismiss the whole theater. *The Archaeology of Sleep* didn't try to send people out into the streets to tear down the old, but simply to get them to think about politics in a new light.

INT. FRANK RICH'S APARTMENT – NIGHT

RICH hammers at a word processing keyboard, smiling triumphantly. He speaks loudly, his face terrifying in the video glow.

FRANK RICH

"The next thing I knew, Mr. Beck had reached his hand under my notebook and placed it between my legs. Perhaps the only way to avoid such tactile encounters is to extend one leg and send Mr. Beck into a pratfall during one of his earlier journeys up the aisle... But feeling more bemused than shocked, I just sat there – call me a pacifist or, if you will, a coward – and started counting the minutes until I could get home."

EXT. THE JOYCE THEATER – NIGHT

ANGLES ON audience members leaving the theater, passing under the marquee, shaking their heads or throwing their hands in the air.

AUTHOR'S V.O.

Progressive critics joined Rich in his dismay. Some wondered if a company that had once shaken the firmament of the American theater establishment had *ever* been any good.

DISSOLVE TO:

INT. MT. SINAI HOSPITAL – DAY

Summer, 1984. OVERHEAD shot of JULIAN, lying alone on a hospital bed, desperately ill. His cancer has advanced.

JULIAN'S V.O.

I cannot hide from myself what I feel, but with Julianesque pride don't want to admit: that the rejection of our work by the New York commercial press did not roll off my back like the good old water off the back of the good old goose: no, it came down on me and lodged in my stomach, and stayed there, and gnawed away at my bowels and combined with the intensity of the physical and psychological work of launching and playing four full productions at once, combined to wax strongly and undo the immune system, and then the gray beast returned and began again, the flesh gave round and gave way, and now I have to undo what in a time of weakness I inadvertently let happen..

AUTHOR'S V.O.

Beck overdubbed work on *The Cotton Club* in a nearby hospital room, padded and sound-proofed, often vomiting between takes. Many people believed that he would never live to see the completed film, or leave the hospital alive.

DISSOLVE TO:

INT. THE BECK'S UPPER WEST SIDE APARTMENT – MORNING

JUDITH sits by JULIAN's bedside. They smiles, talk, hold their hands.

AUTHOR'S V.O.

Miraculously, Julian grows well enough to return home, where he stays attached to a nutritional machine twelve hours a day. Good wishes and financial support pour in from Martin Sheen, Yoko Ono, BAM, the New York Shakespeare Festival, and numerous other individuals and institutions. Al Pacino donates proceeds from a performance of a play in London. Benefit screenings of Sheldon Rochlin and Maxine Harris's documentary on the Living, *Signals Through the Flames*, raised additional funds. Despite these gifts and Blue Cross Insurance, medical bills are astronomical. The Becks owe $10,000 to the hospital and several thousand more to doctors. Meanwhile, *The Cotton Club* opens, and while it was not a hit, it ushers in a new era in the Becks' remarkable lives.

INT. A CINEMA IN NEW YORK – NIGHT

A revived JULIAN sits among a crowd in a movie theater, observing a screening of *The Cotton Club*. He turns to address the camera, discussing politics and art – breaking the fourth wall.

JULIAN

At the end of the film, the question of economic mobility is resolved by the two major characters becoming entertainment stars in the movies and in dancing. But I know that when I played the role of Sol, I thought of it as a critique of certain aspects of society – ignorance, poverty, the feeling of being a pariah – and played those things.

ON SCREEN, a gray, pitiless Sol Weinstein is driving Dixie Dwyer, played by RICHARD GERE, down a rainy street. He turns to study Weinstein, then ask him a question.

DIXIE

(To SOL.) Your mother, what did she call you?

SOL

I never had a mother. I was born in a *gah*-bage pail…

A Constructivist-style montage sends a newspaper whirling into the frame with a fanfare of trumpets. A New York *Post* headline: "JULIAN BECK: GURU AS GANGSTER."

V.O. (A Walter Winchell-style announcer.)

He's the 59-year-old actor who virtually steals the picture until somewhere at midpoint they knock him off in a hail of machine gun fire.

We see SOL on screen, knocked off in a hail of machine gun fire.

AUTHOR'S V.O.

Rave reviews greet Julian Beck's American screen debut. He becomes one of the hottest character actors in Hollywood. Offers roll in from directors Robert Towne (*The Two Jakes*), Roland Joffe (*The Mission*), and Alan Alda (*Sweet Liberty*), who has a part for Malina as well. The theater prophet of the '60s even goes up for a Chuck Norris picture. The Becks wax philosophical about Julian's new "day job," comparing it to the fate of the great Brechtian actor Peter Lorre, forced by Hollywood to play roles that were beneath him. Now Beck has become an independent entertainment commodity, too, typecast as a force for – Unadulterated *Evil.*

INSERT: A clip from *Poltergeist II: The Other Side (1986)*

Actor CRAIG T. NELSON, swaying drunkenly in a suburban bedroom, swills from a bottle of tequila. At the bottom of the bottle, a tiny worm opens an eye in CLOSE-UP just as Nelson washes it down. He begins to gag, then leans over and practically eviscerates himself, vomiting up a hideous creature that swells in seconds to human size—a nightmarish beast writhing on the floor in fetal slime, who turns its face to the camera. Wait! Can it be? Yes! It's JULIAN BECK, father of postwar American experimental theater, flashing a toothy leer!!

AUTHOR'S V.O.

Coming to theaters and drive-ins coast-to-coast, Julian Beck *is* the Poltergeist in *Poltergeist II*, playing Kane, a demonic Jim Jones-style preacher who led his nineteenth-century flock to suicide in order to be born again in a better world. A century later, suburbia has sprawled over the spot, and the evil Preacher surfaces through a child's telephone. The film is dreck, but Beck receives extraordinary reviews. David Edelstein of the *Voice* cruelly describes his performance: "Bone-thin, he wears a worm-eaten smile and speaks in the soft lilting tones of a Southern belle; when he brushes a withered finger against his cheek and gives a faintly perfumed sigh, he's like a mummified Blanche Dubois with the soul of Marlon Brando. Beck must have known he'd be dead by the time the movie opened, and he seems to sense how unnerved we all are at the sight of him, looking as he does, in the role of a walking corpse. It's as if The Living Theatre's co-founder were announcing a branch on the Other Side..."

DISSOLVE TO:

INT. THE BECK'S LIVING ROOM – DAY

Spring of 1985. JULIAN sits cross-legged on a sofa next to the AUTHOR, discussing the future of the Living – bravely, as he has a constant gag reflex acquired as the result of his illness and treatment. JUDITH leans forward in a comfortable chair, chain-smoking joints.

AUTHOR'S V.O.

Their lifelong battles for artistic and social change may yet revive in Paris. Their conversation is lively, their spirits strong. They are not rationalizing their commercial film careers, only saying that everyone sometimes has to swim in filth, and everyone has a responsibility to do something about it.

JULIAN

Poltergeist II is sort of interesting because it's a critique of Jonestown and of people following a leader – just as the Nazis did and just as we in America could do, under certain circumstances – into annihilation. I find this a valid thing to play. I also see it as a contradiction, yes, but film and television work is a genuine attempt to earn some money in order to get The Living Theatre going again.

AUTHOR'S V.O.

Judith eloquently compares Shakespeare to the prime-time soap opera *Dallas*, emphasizing how all Western cultural "masterpieces" are permeated with class representations.

JUDITH

Shakespeare's descriptions of life in the courts of England, Scotland and France and in the Italian ducal courts are an intrinsic part of our cultural education, fundamentally obliging us to feel a certain royalistic awe of courtly life. So *Dallas* in its own way – not so beautifully but so potently testing out the values of the greatest common denominator – creates a glorified image of upper-class life that becomes for us a kind of reality. Of course I don't read Shakespeare to find out what the court of Denmark is like, I read Shakespeare to find out what the human soul is like. But while we're finding out what the human soul is like, we're also hearing the words of a prince of the court who is going through certain princely gestures.

AUTHOR/INTERVIEWER

But doesn't Shakespeare show us the fate of the Danish Court?

JULIAN

(Interrupting.) The fate of that – is *Dallas*.

EXT. A VAST FIELD IN THE SOUTH OF FRANCE – DAY

AUTHOR'S V.O.

Tens of thousands of French people gaze expectantly into the sky, as if at Lourdes. An enormous television screen materializes in the clouds, filled by the mocking, genial smile of Larry Hagman as Texas oil baron J.R. Ewing, loosening a loud and drawling screed of vituperative dubbed French. Thousands fall to their knees as *Dallas* arrives in France, scourging the land. On a nearby hillside, a battery of enraged French intellectuals condemns this intrusion into the purity of Gallic culture. The Living's great champion Jack Lang accuses the U.S. of "financial and cultural imperialism that no longer grabs territory, or rarely, but grabs consciousness, ways of thinking, ways of living." Lang defunds The Living Theatre with a stroke of his pen, in line with the new Socialist austerity. The Becks' hopes for spending six months a year in Paris are dashed. For the first time since 1964, they are full-time Americans again.

DISSOLVE TO:

INT. THE SOUNDSTAGE OF "ALL MY CHILDREN," NYC

JULIAN walks quietly down a TV studio to the set of what is supposed to be a Nepalese temple, but looks more like suburban Casablanca. He is dressed as "Kantu," a Tibetan Buddhist monk. *All My Children* has cast him as a Himalayan guru, after searching for "a Sam Jaffe type."

RUSTY, the thirty-something stage manager, approaches with great shyness. It is clear he's somewhat in awe.

RUSTY

It's really an honor to be working with you. I was at Carnegie-Mellon when the Living Theatre came through.

JULIAN

(Shaking the young man's hand.) Those were the days.

BECK and another actor block a brief scene together, then run it once. The DIRECTOR, after observing their rehearsal, asks for a take.

JEREMY

(Imploringly.) I don't understand, teacher.

KANTU

(With great serenity.) In time, all will become clear. Now you must go and prepare for your journey.

JEREMY

I still have much to learn!

KANTU

You have all the knowledge you need. It is time now to put that knowledge to use. She needs you.

JEREMY

Why must I be the one to go? My place is here – with you, and the brothers! I gave up the world a long time ago. It holds no attraction to me. Please send someone else.

KANTU

That is not possible. *You* were chosen. *You* must do this. If not for her... than for *Michael!*

The two actors gaze into each other's eyes.

RUSTY

Got it!

AUTHOR'S V.O.

Earlier in the day, Julia had joked to me that his nickname was "One-Take Beck." Julian's son Garrick will call this scene "a cosmic shot in the arm of America."

JULIAN
(Smiling wonderfully at the author.) Now I get to go home!

ANGLE ON JULIAN, retreating slowly down the long soap opera studio, alone. SLOW DISSOLVE.

AUTHOR'S V.O.
Knowing that the Living would not revive during his lifetime, Beck returned to his first love, painting – along with poetry and jazz, an original spark of the postwar cultural rebellion. In one of his last workbooks in August 1985, he noted, "I am an incurable Europhile, that I feel myself joined there to my roots, that I revel in its cultivation of art and intelligence, and that in the United States I feel alien and far from home." Here is his last poem, written in his last month, a brief lyric about a broken heart and dreams for the future, addressed to "the sandy angel of death."

JULIAN'S V.O.
i bowed low and smiled
i am not in love with you i said
i do not give you leave to put in parenthesis
we will make life into an unpunctuated sentence
an epic exceeding the mahabharata in depth and in length
and this gay sky will tent us
when we have come to abhor war as we now abhor cannibalism
when the sorrows of unrequited devotion recede
no longer flooding with homelessness famine and panic
and when the loss of a lover comes to mean only a fork in the road
    (new york new york to locarno new york august 1985)

CUT TO:

EXT: JULIAN BECK's GRAVESIDE – DAY

A large CROWD has assembled for the burial of Julian Beck.

AUTHOR'S V.O.

Beck's final *ek-stasis* came in the fall of 1985. The funeral videotape would be edited by the founding father of video art, Nam June Paik. Three years later, Judith Malina will marry her long-time lover, Hanon Resnikov, who became the company's new co-director. In July 1987, they sent the following letter to thousands of friends and supporters.

CUT TO:

INT: MALINA's LIVING ROOM – DAY

JUDITH

(Reading from letter, HANON beside her.) "Dear Friends: This is an appeal letter, to let you know what The Living Theatre is doing, and to ask your help in making New York City its permanent home once more. I am writing this as summer deepens and the city swelters in its suffering and its pollution and its high hopes. Down on the Lower East Side, where human need collides with The Scene, there is an abandoned synagogue, in disrepair, which I would like to return to life as The Living Theatre. We have been searching for a site for nearly two years now, and this ruined temple has all the earmarks of being the right place. The building belongs to the city, and we are negotiating, with community support, for its purchase or lease and renovation... If you can contribute something substantial, you will be helping us to break new ground and harvest yet unseen fruit. Judith Malina

CUT TO:

EXT: THE THANKSGIVING DAY PARADE, 1991

JUDITH rides a float in the Macy's Parade, dressed as an old hag—a cartoon witch.

AUTHOR'S V.O.

After creating seventy works in eight languages in twenty-four countries on four continents over a Biblical forty years, the Living Theatre re-opened in 1990 in a run-down former synagogue on East 3rd Street, creating good work to little attention. Company members new and old worked with homeless people, supported local squatters and anarchist movements, and protested the police seizure of Tompkins Square Park. Within a few years, rents would rise, city inspectors would arrive, and the theater would be gone. The remnants of the Living would continue to perform before large audiences in Europe, and Malina to teach classes in New York and work in film for money. On Thanksgiving Day 1991, she rode in the Macy's Parade as "Grandma," the role she created in the recent hit comedy, *The Addams Family*.

Malina, as "Grandma" from *The Addams Family*, waves to the crowd at the Macy's Day Parade. The image goes into slow motion and begins a slow FADE TO BLACK.

POSTSCRIPT: *Judith Malina's final ek-stasis came on April 10, 2015.*

VERONA, MISSISSIPPI:
Cornerstone Reinvents Community Theater in America, *American Theater Magazine,* May 1989

Note: *A reader at Amblin Entertainment, Steven Spielberg's outfit, read my article and wanted to turn this story into a motion picture, probably with the following log-line: All-White theater company arrives in racially-charged Southern town to stage an interracial community theater production of* Romeo and Juliet. *Several screenwriters were commissioned, including Anna Deavere Smith, the writer-performer of* Twilight: Los Angeles, 1992 *and other acclaimed one-person shows.*

When I heard about this effort to get a screenplay down – Amblin was under no obligation to inform me, as I was merely reporting an event and they would not be using my "expression" – I contacted them and asked if they knew that the author of the article had written plays for the Brooklyn Academy of Music and the La Jolla Playhouse, so why not give me a shot? They were very nice about it, as Spielberg's people are by reputation, but they said they had already commissioned several writers and I was too late. This was probably okay, because I had no idea how to turn this into an acceptable screenplay. I assume no one else did, either, as I can say with certainty that a film was never made.

"Rest of America don't mean jack shit. You in Mississippi now."
Sheriff Ray Stuckey, *Mississippi Burning* (1988)

On Main Street in old Port Gibson, Miss. (pop. 2,371) – "the town too beautiful to burn," Ulysses S. Grant called it – the neon marquee of the Trace Theater glows in the mist like shelter from a threatening sky. Angry gray-black storm clouds, thunder and lightning are rolling east across the Mississippi River and the mighty nuclear power station at Grand Gulf, through the mossy pine forests and hilly pastures of Claiborne County midway between Natchez and Vicksburg, and into town, enveloping the copper-covered roof of the ante-bellum county courthouse and Confederate War Memorial three blocks north. Outside the Trace, a steady stream of local non-professional actors, singers and musicians – a school music teacher, an election commissioner, a surgical nurse, a nuclear-power information officer, a Shakespeare professor from nearby Alcorn State University, a physical therapist, a lawyer, a housewife, a few dozen students – all pass under the deco marquee and the scrutiny of the good ol' boys at the half-century-old gas station on a nearby side street.

Just a week ago, on Valentine's Day, a White woman hugged a Black teenager outside the theater. "That's shitty," one of the men, a mechanic, said later. "White girl, Black boy. I don't know where you folks are from, but I hope nobody gets hurt."

For most of the past three months, an ensemble of eleven young theater artists from Harvard—a traveling ritual known as Cornerstone Theater – have been living and working in Port Gibson, collaborating with more than seventy citizens of Claiborne County on a production of *Romeo and Juliet* keyed to local realities.

Tonight, Monday, is the first run-through before the opening three days away, and for many participants, hope runs high. Romeo will be played by an 18-year-old Black Port Gibson High School distance runner, whose Juliet is a beautiful 24-year-old Harvard-educated White woman from Glastonbury, Connecticut. Up North this is High Concept, but in a county where the descendants of Black slaves outnumber Whites three-to-one and an all-but-Black public-school system and a private, all-but-White military academy help preserve a substantially segregated lifestyle, racial passions are never far beneath the surface. Port Gibson is less than two decades away from a bitterly disputed Black boycott of White businesses, resolved seven years ago by a United States Supreme Court decision, and threatened with another Black boycott in just three months' time. Enter a bunch of White, middle-class, Harvard-educated Northerners – celebrated on the pages of *The Wall Street Journal, People, Newsweek* and *The New Yorker*, featured on "The Today Show, "The CBS Evening News" and "West 57th," and the inspiration behind an upcoming Robert Benton film at 20th Century Fox *[which was never made]* – reimagining the Montagues as the former leaders of a civic boycott, the source of the ancient family enmity.

Not surprisingly, many White citizens of Port Gibson are made anxious and adrenalized by the approaching collision of fictional and historical reality; additional rumors about the production's use of racial epithets, prolonged hot kissing, and partial nudity have inspired a number of White cast members' families and friends to plan not to attend what will certainly be the most provocative integrated cultural event in the town's history.

"This is the greatest thing that has happened in Claiborne County in a long, long time," says Arnette Nash, a local welder, school board member, and founding member of the Bells of Heaven, a local gospel group. Nash is reclining on plush red seats with the rest of the company in the recently renovated Black-owned cinema, facing an airy pinewood set with a hanamichi reaching to the rear wall.

Following time-honored custom, Blacks are sitting in the rear of the house, Whites in front, but the mood is respectful and friendly.

"Hi everybody!"

"Hey Bill!" Twenty-six-year-old Bill Rauch, Harvard '84, stands on stage in his customary baggy gray clothes, holding his customary scrawled yellow notepad, promising to dispense hundreds of actors' notes in the company's dressing rooms. A former assistant director at the American National Theater in Washington, D.C., Rauch is unflappably cheerful, combining the instincts of a theater professional with the patience of Job. His strongest oath in public might be "Goodness gracious!" but he knows how to keep three dozen balls in the air at once. He is letting Edret Brinston, Port Gibson's Romeo, call roll.

"Earl? Where's Earl?" – Earl Wilson, Claiborne County's high school Benvolio.

"His parents won't let him come because of the tornado watch," someone answers.

"Could someone call his parents and tell them that the tornado watch is in the next county, and that we need him here, please?"

Bill proceeds to explain how a technical run-through is a kind of dress rehearsal; unfortunately, too many cast members have left their costumes at home to make it one. Tonight's performance is vital for continuity, but may have to be stopped occasionally, as lighting designer Mary Ann Greanier is still writing cues. Everything is coming in under the wire, as usual with Cornerstone, only this time there is a better than even chance that the show won't be ready.

The run-through begins. A massive Black woman dressed in mourning black rises from a centerstage staircase as the Chorus, singing in rolling gospel cadence. Time: The Present. Place, Verona, Mississippi, a town remarkably similar to Port Gibson. The familiar play rolls on. A Black teenager provokes a fight with a White boy not by "biting his thumb," but by "shooting his finger." Stylized by a visiting Baton Rouge fight director, a slow-motion riot is halted not by a Prince but by a Black female Mayor, played by local fire dispatcher and election commissioner Mary Curry. Booming church voices from a loft at the rear of the house plead with people to forgive their enemies – like many 19th-century traveling Shakespeare companies did, Cornerstone has added fourteen songs by resident composer David Reiffel, with additional music provided by locals Jerome Williams and Larry Davis.

The singing is powerful, but most of the locals have never acted on stage before now. Their line readings are stiff and often difficult to understand. Romeo raps about his love-sickness, accompanied by the Montague boys' bouncing basketball in rhythm; three White cheerleaders underscore Juliet's response to her mother's inquiry about the local banker, Paris. Mercutio's Queen Mab has been reconceived as slasher-film phantom Freddy Krueger, in a theater where *Nightmare on Elm Street – Part IV* was playing not two months ago.

And in the middle of the speech comes Queen Mab's Revenge: every light in the Trace goes down. Power blackouts during storms come block by block in old Port Gibson.

"Everyone relax and stay where you are," Rauch calls out in the pitch darkness. I grope my way to a side door and open it for the streetlight.

The Mississippi sky has opened. Torrents are running through the gutters that will raise the river five feet by morning.

Rauch has commandeered a flashlight. "I want everyone to move slowly into the lobby. We're going to continue the run-through!"

The storm and the blackout alter the course of Cornerstone's Port Gibson residency. Protected by darkness in the overcrowded lobby, with lightning crashing and thunder booming in the street outside, a new intimacy moves behind the words. Freed from blocking, actors drop some of their Southern formality for Southern warmth, a sense of injured pride and hot young blood. "My only love, sprung from my only hate?" cries Juliet—just as a sizeable chunk of damp plaster falls from the lobby ceiling on the back of her hoop skirt.

Confronting adversity may once again make Cornerstone magic, but at some cost: two hours of lost tech and run-through before dress rehearsals begin. Some of their Harvard friends think they're wasting their time, but Cornerstone has chosen to reinvent America's community theater, and in less than two-and-a-half years has created a national experimental community theater network, an alternative to work in established non-profit institutions and urban isolation. They have rediscovered connections between professionalism and amateurism that inspired the little theater movements of the Teens and '20s, the trade union theater of the '30s, the Living Theatre of the '50s, the '60s theater of personal liberation, and the performance art of the '70s and '80s. What matters most about theater is obviously not the sole property of professionals, but how this spirit will play out in Port Gibson – where even "The Cosby Show" on TV is larded with 15-second commercials on Mississippi togetherness without a single Black face – is anybody's guess.

I have already had folks tell me there are no race problems in Claiborne County: Whites go their way, Blacks go theirs, and never the twain shall meet. But with the Klan operating out of nearby Vicksburg and Natchez and a former Grand Wizard ending a triumphant election campaign for the state legislature just across the river, such statements are not to be believed. In Mississippi, two societies, both alike in dignity, once separated by law, remain separated by custom and prejudice. And if twelve performances of a play written 350 years ago are able to make any difference at all, they will need to renew a faith in the possibility of interracial harmony that the Deep South has rarely allowed to stand.

Port Gibson, Mississippi gives its name to a nearby Civil War battlefield where the fate of Vicksburg and the entire Confederacy was sealed in 1863. Within living memory, Black people were paid 50 cents for hand-picking a hundred pounds of cotton. The 1963 civil rights summer of the film *Mississippi Burning* (1988) failed to reach this southwest portion of the state, but two years later, Charles Evers arrived in Claiborne County to begin the dangerous process of registering Black voters. Local police disrupted many of these early meetings; tensions in Claiborne County continued to build toward a historic 1969 Black consumer boycott of White businesses. White community leaders initially agreed to some Black demands, including equal access to the town's medical clinic, employment, and political offices; the right to courtesy titles such as "Mr." and "Mrs."; and the right to maintain places in shopping lines in the presence of White people. White community leaders refused, however, to integrate public toilets or employ Blacks on cash registers.

The resulting boycott lasted two years and became a national *cause célèbre*, with Black leaders accused of physical intimidation and White provocateurs reportedly paying Blacks to cross picket lines and provoke fights. As more and more businesses went bankrupt, local White merchants filed an improbable lawsuit against the NAACP and Black property owners, winning more than $1 million in damages from a local chancery court; the NAACP and labor groups responded by raising an appeal bond of more than $1 million, continuing litigation until July 1982, when the Supreme Court voted 8-0 to uphold the right of individual citizens to stage nonviolent, politically-inspired boycotts and spend their money where and how they pleased.

With the end of the boycott, changes came swiftly to Claiborne County: today, Blacks and Whites mingle casually in restaurants and nearly all places of business. With their demographic superiority, Blacks have come to dominate the local courts, the sheriff's office, the fire department, and county government. Culturally, segregation continues nearly as strong as ever, with churches and schools the major cultural divides. Faced with mandatory school desegregation in 1969, White Port Gibson families transferred their children to the private Chamberlain-Hunt Academy, a military reform school established in 1879.

Nothing divides a small town more painfully than school segregation: racially divided schools socialize parents and kids, magnify differences into oppositions, and produce a racially-divided community. A second and more recent source of tension is the Grand Gulf Nuclear Power station, a twenty-year-old project which had transformed one of Mississippi's poorest counties into one of its richest, increasing the tax-base thirty-fold. To hear most Whites tell it, much of that money was stolen by a corrupt Black board of education president through sweetheart construction deals and valueless education programs, resulting in a loss of state accreditation at Port Gibson High School. With Black juries unwilling to convict a Black elected official, White leaders decided to play their cards at the state level: they pushed through a constitutional amendment that divides the Grand Gulf money, taking half from Claiborne County and giving substantial new revenues to the city of Port Gibson. Most of Claiborne County's White population lives in town, where the mayor and three of the five city Alderman are White. The same White attorney represented both city and county during these battles, exercising what Blacks justifiably considered a shameful conflict of interest.

"Mississippi is still Mississippi, and Mississippi is still burning," says Claiborne County tax assessor Evan Doss. If the city and county attorney isn't dismissed by May 1st, Port Gibson will face another consumer boycott, although Doss and other Black leaders are holding open the possibility of more discussion.

Cultural apartheid; racially motivated battles over tax money; the prospect of renewing the town's most bitter human conflict: this was the hot water into which Cornerstone had lowered itself, assisted by the only multiracial cultural organization in Claiborne County: "Mississippi: Cultural Cross Roads," the ten-year-old creation of a petite White woman originally from Chicago: Patty Crosby is constantly searching for politically-neutral ground on which Blacks and Whites might build trust. The Mississippi Arts commission recommended her to Cornerstone, and Cornerstone called her back, expressing interest; she paid little attention until she heard that all Port Gibson had to provide was housing and a theater for a four-month company residency.

Crosby took the idea of a Cornerstone residency to the Port Gibson Chamber of Commerce for support; the White community responded well to the prospect of returning theater to a town which long ago had enjoyed visits from Joe Jefferson and blackface musical troupes, in a state with a long and lively history of segregated community theater.

Cornerstone's original production idea was Brecht's *The Good Person of Szechwan*, but this sounded arcane; Patti Crosby's husband David, a Shakespeare professor at Alcorn State, suggested *Romeo and Juliet*, without giving a thought to any possible racial implications. Both parties simply assumed that the integrated casting would be racially blind, which was Cornerstone's progressive approach since Harvard days. The Chamber of Commerce, Claiborne County's Board of Supervisors, even Mississippi Power & Light, proprietors of Grand Gulf, each produced small grants to help bring Shakespeare back to Port Gibson.

A few weeks before heading South, Cornerstone members drove back from Oregon, where they had just experienced their first taste of a social controversy: during a fall 1988 residency in Long Creek (pop: 265), a timber and ranching community in Oregon's eastern outback, Brecht's *Good Person* hinged on issues of what goodness means, in a town populated largely by fundamentalist Christians. In Port Gibson, social backlash was already building. An offer to perform in an historic former Jewish synagogue had been withdrawn when the owner discovered that the production would be interracial. For a time, the show was transferred to a former shoe store presently occupied by courthouse facilities, but when the antebellum courthouse's renovations weren't completed in time, Courthouse was homeless again. The company finally settled on its natural venue, the town's only cinema, which was far from neutral territory: the owner of the Trace was William Dowery, a former Black boycott leader viewed with suspicion in Port Gibson's White business community, largely because he conducted most of his business in cash.

Cornerstone had no desire to inflame a county: its members work with good cheer to reconceive the classics, to absorb and reflect the nature of community, town, and locale. But this time the group decided to go with a racially specific cast – White Capulets, Black Montagues.

"We wanted to create a world in which race was the major factor," says Rauch. "What had initially seemed too obvious seemed right for Mississippi." Cornerstone's first Deep South production, the largest it has ever attempted anywhere, was to be about interracial hatred, sex, marriage, suicide, and murder – and with Montagues presented as the civic boycott leaders. In a sense, Cornerstone was throwing down a gauntlet in a community as symbolically divided as Shakespeare's fair Verona.

Patty and David Crosby tried over dinner to change the minds of Rauch and Cornerstone co-founder Alison Carey, but finally relented – though not without considerable trepidation.

"We've only got one world," says Patty Crosby. "We've only got one community and we've got to figure out how to live in it together or the kids will go elsewhere. And to my way of thinking, the best way to be together is to work together."

Arriving in Port Gibson on November 5th, Cornerstone settled into William Dowery's drafty, dilapidated two-story boarding house on Highway 61, the main drag through town, and launched into its typical first order of business: seducing a community with a mind to resist.

Five performances at the local public and private schools, at nearby Alcorn State and at the Trace, revived three works: the company's adaptation of *A Midsummer Night's Dream*, an original school-age piece called *I Can't Pay the*

Rent, and a musical revue with slides of selected Cornerstone works. Company members visited churches – Presbyterian, Methodist, Episcopalian, Catholic, several varieties of Baptist, Evangelical and Pentecostal, as well as the local African Methodist Episcopal Ministry – and rose in each to address the congregation. PSAs on local radio stations and in newspaper ads appealed for actors, singers and musicians. Cornerstone members literally went door to door, stopped motorists at stoplights, even pulled kids off bicycles to tell them about auditions over two weekends in mid-November.

The company's double-barreled nightmare was the possibility that Whites would stay away because the Trace was Black (despite being the only movie-house in town), and that Blacks would stay away because Cornerstone was an all-White company. On at least one occasion Black citizens walked into the Trace, saw Whites auditioning and walked out. Carey raced out after them, and when she couldn't find them, cruised the streets in her car until she did. "I'm sick of culture being for the elite," said one man, who returned to audition for the chorus with a Sarah Vaughn standard, then announce, "I'm schizophrenic."

A group of five-to-ten local Black alcoholics began hanging out regularly around the theater, including one thirty-five-year-old veteran who claimed to have been a body bag sorter in Vietnam; he was the best reader in town and won the role of Montague. Seventy people auditioned in all, ranging from drunken illiterates to pillars of the community. Forty-seven won parts, an extra-large cast, which would mean heavier work for everyone. "We don't like to leave anyone out," Rauch explains. Cornerstone actors filled the parts of Juliet, Mercutio, Tybalt, and Friar Lawrence, but the rest came from a remarkably diverse cross-section of town, forging the kind of art-life correspondences that characterize the avant-garde. Cornerstone's *Romeo and Juliet* would do nothing short of helping the town see itself for what it was.

The wife of the mayor, Joan Beasley, became one of the "Mint Julep Belles" who attends the Capulets' "Antebellum Plantation Fest" dressed in the ball gown of a daughter of the Confederacy. So did Linda Headley, the daughter-in-law of the recently defeated former White sheriff, who wept during her improvised audition about teenage suicide. One of the town's leading lawyers, 39-year-old Melvin McFatter, who limped heavily with a cane as the result of a hunting accident, took on Paris. As usual, Cornerstone failed to produce enough community men.

"There I was," recalls a laughing Amy Brenneman, Cornerstone's Juliet, "chasing the manager of the local Piggly Wiggly around the tomatoes, saying, 'Don't you want me to be your daughter?' Afterwards I walked out saying to myself, 'Is this what I want to be doing with the rest of my life? I am very *confused.*'" In the end Rauch reconceived the Capulet clan as a matriarchy, with Kay Bilbro, a former elementary school principal, currently a nuclear information officer at Grand Gulf, as Mamaw Capulet, Juliet's grandmother and stern leader of the Capulets; Kathy Ellis, a local dentist's wife and a physical therapist by profession, became a very feminine and younger Mrs. Capulet. Bobbi Jean Young, a rotund music and elementary school teacher, was cast as Juliet's Black Nurse – the term "Mammy" was never used. To attract young men for the Montague clan, Cornerstone had to ask Port Gibson High School's principal to summon some students to the school auditorium to audition. For a time, the leading candidate for Romeo was a one-armed town alcoholic and drug addict named Julius.

But at the high school one day, Carey heard a voice calling, "Hey, I want to be Romeo!"

Edret Brinston had been a troublemaker until his track coach got him in line. A good-looking 18-year-old, raised by his grandmother in a wood-heated shack in the nearby town of Pattison, Brinston grew up with an iron will, a cool gaze, and a strong physical presence. He became the most important of a dozen or so public high school students in the cast, many of them recruited from Patty Crosby's local Peanut Butter and Jelly Theater – including the Schaufnagel girls, Dana and Darcy, two of only three White students enrolled at Port Gibson High. Three students were cast from Chamberlain-Hunt Academy, and two from a private elementary school. The sole Black student at CHA, a sad, inexpressive victim of regular beatings and at least one cross-burning, was specially invited to audition. He averted his eyes, saying only, "I'm booked."

With a cast in place, a welcoming supper was held at a local Catholic recreation hall. Black and White educators, clergy, politicians and business people eyed one another over fried chicken from the Piggly Wiggly. The mayor's wife rose to speak of "a new beginning for Port Gibson."

"I assumed it was sincere," Rausch says. "It was hard to tell how much of a first this was, this coming-together of the two sides of town. We could definitely feel a lot of politics going on beneath the surface that we knew nothing about. But the fact is that patterns for our residencies are always the same: during the first weeks we meet people we never see again. The cast becomes our contact with the community."

The first read-through of the script went painfully slowly. Brinston did not read very well at all; at certain points older Black cast members leapt in to help him with Romeo's lines. The Port Gibson adaptation would be written during the three weeks before Christmas, with Rauch and Carey seated at the boarding house word processor and "guided by our aesthetic – working for clarity, and for the audience," says Rauch. "We're the first to admit that we lose some of the poetry, but we hope we gain another kind of poetry." Some of the rewriting was guided with the help of local high school students. Asked to describe a spirit that comes in your sleep, Claiborne County schoolchildren of all ages invariably cited Freddy Krueger. What had seemed corny to Harvard graduates had universal meaning here, and so Queen Mab was pushed aside by Hollywood's dream time master. The decision to change Juliet's balcony fantasy so that Romeo would deny not his "name" but the color of his skin was Cornerstone's idea. Tybalt's taunt, "Thou art a villain," had only one obvious rewrite, but rather than present the word to unsuspecting cast members, Carey and Rauch decided to leave the offending word blank. When the new script was read before Christmas, everyone agreed there was only one appropriate epithet.

Cornerstone broke for the holidays on a high note, organizing a Christmas show that brought together choirs from Black and White churches for the first time in Claiborne County's history. Around their own production, however, controversies had barely begun.

Most of Cornerstone's membership now believes that the month-long holiday break was a mistake, and not simply because their fifteen-person van was stolen during the interim. Returning on January 16th gave them only six weeks to assemble a massive musical-dramatic production with a very amateur cast. In the best of cases, "a Cornerstone residency is a very weird psychological beast," Carey tells me two days before the opening, seated with Rauch near the gas heater in the chilly boarding house living room. The cold weather has continued; six feet away from the heater's open flame, the room is 40 degrees. Cornerstone is a warm, civil group – difficult for outsiders to penetrate, but also completely above-board.

"Each time we go into a community it's a little like reinventing the wheel, which of course is no way to live," Carey continues. "For one thing, we're in the position of always having to be 'nice,' both among ourselves and with the community. We're forced as outsiders to discover everything, and in most instances there's nothing fueling us but bravado – 'Well, we've done it before, we'll do it again.' People are being asked to work mind-numbingly long hours just on our promise that they won't make fools of themselves."

"The Mississippi cast is probably the warmest we've ever worked with," Rauch adds, "but that hasn't meant a constant round of parties. People have little concept of how hard we work and for no money. Most people find that odd."

Rehearsals were almost all at the Trace, and on one occasion at the public high school, where many White teenagers in the cast had never set foot in before. Gradually the cast had shrunk from forty-seven to thirty-eight due to the demands on time and constant scheduling changes. Twice the Vietnam vet playing Montague showed up at rehearsals too drunk to work. He finally withdrew, and Bells of Heaven singer Arnette Nash moved from the chorus to replace him. But more serious problems arose among certain White cast members. The mayor's wife, who had promised a new beginning for Port Gibson, simply up and quit, saying that she was too busy. Rumors persisted that her husband's political differences with Trace owner Dowery were behind the move.

"If it was Mayor Beasley's daughter playing Juliet, maybe he wouldn't even allow the play," Mary Curry told me. "His wife was in it, now she's gone. Maybe she's too good to be around Black people." Rauch was taken out to lunch one afternoon by another of the Mint Julep Belles, who told him that right now, Juliet and Romeo were kissing with a bit too much enthusiasm, meaning Whites wouldn't want to come see the show. "She felt that a shy little kiss would be okay in Port Gibson," says Rauch, "but they seemed to be enjoying it." Another White participant complained that with such goings-on, she wouldn't be able to bring her children. A Black chorus member objected to Mercutio's dying curse, "a plague on both your races." And then someone at her work told Kay Bilbro that if she embraced a Black man on stage, as she did in Mamaw Capulet's reconciliation with Montague at the end of the play, then the recent unsolved sex murders in Port Gibson's Black community might begin crossing racial lines. Bilbro phoned Rauch to tell him that she'd rather not do it anymore, and Rauch relented, although without telling his Black Montague the reason.

"The closer we came to production," Patty Crosby would later, "the more I was saying to myself, 'Goodness, girl, what have you done?'"

Carey believes she understands the reasons for White resistance. "I suppose the idea is that it might give Black boys the initiative, show that white girls are no longer forbidden fruit – you know, 'He kissed, so we can go get us one.'" Mary Curry was unafraid of any serious white backlash – "racists don't want to make the Blacks mad" – but Black members of the cast were unaware that the White boys at the gas station across the street were waving the red flag of interracial fraternizing around town. Cornerstoners were labeled immoral pot-smoking hippies by one CHA instructor – and Yankees to boot. When its members visited the nuclear power station, rumor had it that they had chained themselves in protest to the door, categorically not true. Gratefully, the KKK was nowhere in evidence, but the town's former sheriff reportedly joked, "the Klan was probably figuring how big a bomb it would take to torch the place." This kind of dark humor cut both ways: "He's got a lot of bodies in his backyard," muttered one Black cast member.

Given these conflicts and innuendos, attorney McFatter persisted in his belief that "the community would have been better served by a play with an integrated cast which did not have racial strife and interracial sex and marriage as its central themes." Cornerstone worked to moderate the flames their drama fanned; their steady good cheer and unpatronizing warmth were richly returned by Claiborne County cast members of both races. "We're theater artists, not social workers," says Rauch. Cornerstone members were not above rolling their eyes at a particularly bad line reading, or joking among themselves about the cast member who wondered aloud whether he had to attend all the performances or not. Cornerstone staff and performers continued to work without snobbery or condescension, making allowances, eager to assist the uninformed, the ungifted, and draw out the best in everybody.

Cornerstone had its own problems to deal with: the prospect of performing in a cinema had prepared them for working without wings, flies, or backstage space. Rauch and designer Lynn Jeffries went through four different set designs before discovering that they couldn't tie into the walls or ceilings: the building's bricks were crumbling and wouldn't bear weight, meaning that the original two-story structure, along with most of Rauch's early staging ideas, went out the window. Local actors received little directorial help because the focus had to be on the whole production. The un-hugging Bilbro as Mamaw Capulet had to understood that there was no "right" way for her to say her lines – that understanding her freedom was the beginning of being someone else. Brinston's Romeo tended to drop most of his final consonants – "Nigh's can'les are blown out," "I am too bol', t's no' t' me she speak" – Rauch decided to let the accent stand. Not cultural missionaries or cultural imperialists, Cornerstone was choosing to transcend racial and cultural differences for the rich and complicated business of putting on a play.

A week before opening, the cast feeling of us and them, Black or White, began to wane. With the introduction of costumes and a make-up artist from out of town, a payoff was suddenly in sight.

Strange and wondrous things begin to happen. A CHA student with the improbably Southern White name of Graven Bilbo was actually hanging out with Brinston, Earl Wilson, and Walter Mays – kids roughly the same age who had grown up in the same town, but never met before.

Three nights before the opening, the huge storm and blackout assisted the company breakthrough. Theater was once again exercising its magical ability to bring people together in community.

"It's not Broadway," Patty Crosby told her husband. "Yes," David Crosby answered. "But it's hard to believe it's Port Gibson."

An hour before the opening night performance, a crowd has already gathered under the neon glow of the marquee. *Romeo and Juliet's* competition tonight is the regional championship game of the Port Gibson Wavettes, a girls' basketball team ranked fourth in the nation by *USA Today*. In the lobby Carey is pouring

Mercutio's blood bags. Brenneman is laughing with a group of young Black children from the cast – hugging, kissing, rubbing each other's faces: a mutual fan club.

In the theater, Rauch is on stage directing the Montague gang – "You guys be talking together as you go" – while Ashby Semple, Cornerstone's female Tybalt, dressed in a jacket with a Confederate flag on the back, is working on a blood-curdling rebel yell for Mercutio's death blow. In the house the rest of the cast sits down for notes. Excitement has been stirred by a flattering front page story in the *New Orleans Times-Picayune*. For the first time, cast seating is more or less colorblind. Blacks and whites are sharing every row.

"This is the hardest I've ever worked for no scratch," Kay Bilbro says, rubbing her fingertips together.

One of the Mint Julep Belles pronounces the word "hair" with three syllables: "I'm gonna have to get me a little fall for my hay-eh-er… If I'd a-done this right, I coulda lost a *lot* o' weight."

In one of the rear rows, I hear Juliet's nurse's booming voice, "People are comin' t' *see* Miss Bobbi Jean Young!"

"I told my father-in-law it's great to be working with professionals," Mint Julep Belle Headley tells me. "He said, 'If they're that good, why aren't they on TV?'"

Mary Curry assumes a country voice to describe her son's response to a run-through. "He say, 'Mama, why you be hollerin'?' I say, 'I'm in the play, honey. Do I be scarin' you?' And he say – '*Nah…*'"

"Hi everybody!"

"Hey Bill!"

Boyish as ever, Rauch promises to circulate some of the hundreds of individual notes he's taken. "That young man is going places," murmurs Ron Temple, the local star of Cornerstone's Kansas production *Tartoof*, who has driven all the way from Norcatur for tonight.

One of Rauch's final group notes is odd. "Everybody should chew gum in the final scene, when the corpses are discovered in the county morgue."

"And why are we supposed to do that?" asks a flabbergasted McFatter.

"You never asked why before," says Bill, which gets a good laugh, although the Belles continue to grumble that no Southern lady would ever chew gun in public, especially not in a mausoleum.

Bill closes by wishing everyone a great show; even chokes up a little, saying, "You're all part of the Cornerstone family now."

I glance over and see Port Gibson's Romeo crawling up the aisle on all fours towards the dressing rooms. In the early going Brinston was Joe Cool, and even skipped a rehearsal once, apparently on purpose. It took three weeks before he would let Brenneman into his house, and he still keeps her away from his girlfriends. But Brinston has risen to his challenge, overcome his reading problems, and learned his part down cold. One Cornerstone member remarked that this was probably the first time in his life that anyone has ever taken him seriously for his mind.

When the doors open at quarter to seven, the opening night audience is notable for the absolute absence of the town elite, Black and White. Less than a quarter of the crowd is Caucasian, and nearly all of them appear middle-aged, modestly affluent, with a couple of kids. There is a large contingent of Black high schoolers, including Brinston's track team, dressed to the nines. Admission to the theater is free, but the older Black folks, seeing a donation box by the door, drop in a buck or two, good churchgoers all. Carey and Rauch pace the lobby, as tense as if they were opening a $6 million musical. Outside, at least twenty-five people have to be turned away from the 123-seat house as the doors are closing, when a voice cries out, "It's me! It's me! Hattie Turnipseed!" The seamstress who sewed Juliet's costume is one of the last people admitted.

Anyone at the opening night of Cornerstone's *Romeo and Juliet* at the Trace will not soon forget the scene. When the brawl starts between the Black dudes and the white kids wearing the actual uniforms of Chamberlain-Hunt Academy, the younger Black contingent in the packed house rise to their feet with wild whoops and hollers.

The house is electrified. No one has anticipated such a visceral response, but a tone is set.

When the Montagues burst into the Plantation Fest in Freddy Krueger masks, and Tybalt cries out "Fetch me my shotgun!" – I think that seats are going to be pulled from the floor.

"Give me my sin again!" says a Black Romeo in high-tops to a gorgeous white woman in a strapless evening gown, sending Brinston's friends flopping out of their seats like fish on the deck of a boat. They will be making kissing noises at Juliet for the rest of the show.

Romeo's "Henceforth, I'll never be Black" is met with incredulous snorts and hilarious howls, which at least shows they're listening.

The Trace is out of control, a vision straight from Mark Twain or some 19th-century riverboat company. Somehow Brinston remains unaffected, handling his first public appearance on stage with absolute aplomb. When Friar Lawrence, reconceived by Cornerstone actor Peter Howard as a Boston liberal Catholic priest, exposes a Martin Luther King T-shirt under his jacket to Tybalt, saying "Here's my Confederacy!" riot reached its peak. Then Tybalt's taunt "Thou art–a *nigger*" drew a loud collective "uh-oh," followed by raucous laughter, segueing after Mercutio's death into cheers and triumphant shouts as Romeo plugs his White Supremacist slanderer six times with a handgun.

A little Black boy no more than three or four races up the aisle in terror, hot tears streaming down his cheeks. One of four little girls fetches him back to his seat, where all four of them pat his back, saying, "Hush now, Jefferson, it's all pretend." Father Lawrence offers Romeo a vision of a lynch mob, Romeo flees, and the first act, blessedly, is over.

Very light applause; kids bolt up the aisles towards the popcorn machine. Little intermission chatter among the audience members in the lobby. A very pasty-looking Rauch passes me with a mortified smile and a cold shudder. The three-and-a-half-hour performance is only half over, but despite the pandemonium, some of the play's meanings are coming through. Cornerstone and Port Gibson are offering a *Romeo and Juliet* driven by an irrational, unexamined belief in the twining power of sex and death. There is no natural rightness in the two lovers' passions; issues of education and class are avoided completely. There is no apparent reason for this Romeo and Juliet to be together at all. The mechanisms of love are unexplained, but the impact of Black and

White lovers kissing long and hard, he shirtless, she in a T-shirt and panties, is undeniable.

Their defiance of bigotry feels courageous and true.

Rauch pounds home the theme of death at every opportunity: at the top of the second act, Juliet sings a beautiful song with Shakespeare's lyrics of Romeo's dead body cut up in little stars, then in short order absorbs her Nurse's faulty news of Romeo's death with instant acceptance. By mid-act the teenagers in the audience have stopped changing seats and seem to have settled down a little. They watch quietly while Romeo lies atop Juliet's slumbering body in the morgue. They snicker when Romeo ODs with a needle. They laugh nervously when Juliet blows her brains out with a pistol. Then roar with laughter when poor Arnette Nash as Montague has to pretend to break into tears at the sight of Romeo's corpse.

For me, the single most moving moment in the production is Mamaw's refusal to embrace the grieving Montague – a chilling image of White Southern rectitude, released when Lady Capulet goes to embrace him instead. After one of the more legato death scenes in the history of Shakespeare's Verona, the Mayor declaims, *"Never... was a story... of more woe... than this... of Juliet... and her Romeo..."*

Curtain call for the entire cast of thirty-eight. Light applause, as if a movie has just ended, although the high school jerk-offs in the front row stand to applaud and cheer. The rest of the house remains dazed, glued to their seats. Three teenage girls in the audience are sobbing. In the turbulent lobby afterwards, families have gathered to greet friends, sons, daughters, husbands and wives as they dribble from the upstairs dressing rooms. Brinston arrives, looking cool and unperturbed, greeted by friends who are, when all is said and done, pretty impressed.

With the exception of actor Peter Howard/Friar Lawrence, who goes home depressed, the Cornerstone people are unfazed by the wild and indelicate response of their opening night crowd. Rauch waxes philosophical in the boarding house kitchen while heating up a pizza. He talks about the art/social service dichotomy thrown Cornerstone's way by saying it's false – that in theater, art and social service are identical. Port Gibson's *R & J* is no artistic triumph, but judgments of good and bad that have crippled the American theater at large seem irrelevant in a town where an RSC production wouldn't mean as much. For Rauch, the real work of the show, the contact with the community, begins now, and he's convinced that the deeper meanings of the play will out – that audiences will understand the work subliminally – they will understand that love is a force to overcome even the bitterest enmity.

Friday morning the Trace Theater box office is swamped with phone calls. *Romeo and Juliet* is a hit! A palpable hit! Chris Moore's Mercutio is the overnight sensation of Port Gibson High School: a White man who gets himself killed defending the honor of a Black man who's been called the N-word. Friday's audience is in sharp contrast to the opening: attentive, almost demure, with only a few choice comments from the peanut gallery. Several Black teenagers are rapping along with Romeo and Benvolio – a sure sign that a cult is building.

In the green room at the beginning of Act Two, a dance party is going on that will continue every night of the run. Juliet's song speeding Phoebus' fiery wheels, piped over the intercom, gets everyone on their feet, Blacks and Whites, boogeying and shaking it together on old linoleum under harsh fluorescence. "Get down, Juli-*et!!*"

The bigger problem is where to continue partying after the show. The problem arose when Cornerstone's Semple wanted to bring two public high school boys to Buddy's, the local redneck roadhouse. "I never had to feel White before," Ashby tells me. Blacks can go to Buddy's for dinner, but not late-night dancing – certainly not interracial dancing. Blacks go to Zanzibar and the Diamond Lounge, where White newcomers are approached to buy drugs, then left alone – unless they try to dance with a Black woman. After the Saturday night show, with the first days off in nearly two weeks looming, everybody wants to blow off steam, but no one wants to divide the cast along racial lines.

The solution, at least for the teenagers and some Cornerstone actors, is a spontaneous party on the street outside the Trace.

Under the moon and the neon marquee, Brinston, Wilson and Mays turn up Ice-T on the boom box to show Cornerstone's Howard some moves. Four or five Academy girls join in a soul-train line, and Cornerstone's technical director Benajah Cobb comes from the theater with a large piece of plywood, which he plunks down on the sidewalk to breakdance, spinning on his knees like a New York City street kid.

Soon as many as fifteen Blacks and Whites are boogying off the curb and into the rinsed gutter, Bobby Brown is playing on the boom box and Wilson is doing his fresh thing when a County Sheriff's squad car cruises by, slows, checks out the scene – and drives on by. The face behind the wheel was Black. Then a station wagon passes by, and one of the Academy girls squeals and tries to hide. But her mom has caught her, ninety minutes past her curfew.

"Oh god! I'm so *grounded!*"

White girls and Black boys dancing together on the streets of Port Gibson, Mississippi at half past midnight: Impossible.

Unfortunately, as in the play, the adults are a bit slower on the uptake. I called Mayor Jimmy Beasley for a statement. "I don't have any problem with it," he told me. "What do you want me to say? Everything I heard about it sounds okay." Will you be attending soon? "I suspect I'll see it, but I'm a pretty busy guy." Rauch sent the mayor a personal invitation by mail, but the mayor never did show – nor will his wife, although rumor has it that she wanted to attend.

Over the next two weeks, Blacks will continue to outnumber Whites in the audience roughly two or three to one, as they do in the county. Blacks will consistently cite the racial themes as the best part of the play; Whites, the worst. One audience respondent will note that interracial marriages are "Biblically forbidden."

"In the Old South, a real-life Black Romeo might have been lynched; in the New South, he would probably be let off for the murder of Tybalt by an all-Black jury," says lawyer McFatter during a Thursday Humanities meeting, addressed by a gathering of Mississippi Shakespeare scholars. There are grounds for this statement. Other issues exploded during an in-company discussion of the play's themes following Friday's performance, provoked by the Thursday Shakespeare meeting.

The cast has decided that when all is said and done, the production was worth all the work. They present Cornerstone members with Port Gibson T-shirts and a plaque. What followed was a rare, often angry, sometimes tearful discussion of the future of Claiborne County.

Mary Curry rose to say that her son Allan and ten-year-old cast member and Academy girl Athena Hynum may be playing together now, but as soon as the show is over, everything will return to normal – Whites will again pass Blacks in the streets without a hello. Cast members of both races were upset by these remarks and said so, some in the presence of their children. Young Allan Curry dolefully tells Rauch, "The past brings out a lot of pain in people." Much of the discussion hinges on public education, an urgent matter because of the financial instability at Chamberlain-Hunt, currently kept afloat by a $100,000 gift from an anonymous local citizen. Everyone agrees that the public school system needs to be integrated, but given the public high school's loss of accreditation and its all-Black faculty, the answers to the question of how this might happen, or when it might occur, remain unclear.

From the discussion, what is clear that the end of the worst of forms of racism won't solve Black and White problems; they will only make solutions possible. And solutions are necessary, because if they aren't forthcoming, Claiborne County will risk the fate of neighboring Jefferson County, which saw a White exodus and an economic depression after Blacks assumed power. As Mississippi's rural agrarian past continues to recede in memory, the worst strangleholds of racism will surely ease, though how quickly, no one knows. What amazes me is that a bunch of Northerners barely out of college used theater to advance society's fitting end in the small town of Port Gibson, Mississippi.

The twelfth and final performance of *Romeo and Juliet* has a waiting list of 230. One-tenth of the town's population. The show runs fifteen minutes longer than usual, mostly because Brinston is savoring his words for the final time. At the celebration afterwards, Cornerstone presents a $500 check to Arnette Nash and Patty Crosby – seed money for a new community theater that will continue the interracial spirit that Cornerstone and Crosby's Cross Roads organization has commenced. Semple and Greanier will stay in town for an extra week to help organize this future company, which will begin by doing a fully integrated, colorblind play not about racial tension, thank you very much. The rest of the

Cornerstoners have plans to take to the four winds for their first annual "Scatter Project," a visit to the community theaters left behind in every town they've visited except Prince George, Virginia, and Miami – a project temporarily curtailed when Rauch and Carey, along with two-thirds of the student body at CHA, come down with a nasty flu.

Borrowing a page from the Federal Theater Project of the '30s, Rauch has hopes that on February 1st, 1990, all eight Cornerstone-inspired theaters will present regionally specific productions of an as-yet-unnamed one-act play, simultaneously with Cornerstone's own production in a new home theater in an unspecified location. After this year's Scatter Project and a two-month break, Cornerstone will move on for a West Virginia Ibsen and a Maine O'Neill; they would also like to work in the Soviet Union, but glasnost has produced no thaw for them as yet. In the summer of 1991, an alumni show will bring together the most talented people they've met – European, African, Latin and Native-Americans – for a truly national tour, and an Asian-American theater project won't be far behind. As the Free Southern Theater and others demonstrated in the '60s, as Kentucky's Roadside Theater, California's Los Angeles Poverty Department, and Nebraska's Magic Theater are demonstrating today, theaters that redefine risk in social as well as aesthetic terms release vital energy into an art form stagnating in the backwaters of the culture industry, recycling itself for its own survival.

With Cornerstone, the emphasis is on art, but this has been precisely the basis for its social achievement: urging a renewed faith in that infinite moment of connection between the theater and the world, Cornerstone creates singular communities that ripple outward through a playwright's vision, like pebbles tossed in a pond. Peter Sellars, who had Rauch as an assistant director some years ago, views Cornerstone as part of a new vision for theater of the '90s. "Instead of pontificating about what the public wants, Cornerstone has gone out and met that public – indeed, has found out what it is. It's a new generation discovering theater on its own terms, not believing what theater is supposed to be, but discovering it from scratch." Or as Arnette Nash put it to me, Cornerstone in Claiborne County had demonstrated "that people can work together without consideration of race when their efforts and energy are used to make a project successful."

No one knows if this spirit will last, but almost no one believed it could ever come to Port Gibson. But with Shakespeare's play, it had.

POST-SCRIPT: *I have no way of knowing the full impact of Cornerstone's time in Port Gibson—no one has—but the threatened Black boycott of White businesses three months after R&J never happened. Many townspeople of both races were at least unconsciously ready for some degree of racial harmony, but the brutal fact remained that despite the Grand Gulf money, Port Gibson experienced an exodus of Whites. Port Gibson, where most of the county's White folks lived, had a population of 2,371 in 1989. Thirty-three years later, the population has fallen to 1,616. Claiborne County suffered the fate of neighboring Jefferson County: A White exodus, followed by a predictable and preventable economic depression. I don't know if it's possible to talk about a reconciliation of the races in small town Mississippi. All anyone can do about it is light a fire against the darkness, like Patty Crosby did.*

ABOUT THE AUTHOR

Robert Coe is a writer living in Jersey City, New Jersey. His journalism has appeared in *The New York Times Sunday Magazine, Op-Ed* and *Arts and Leisure* sections, *Rolling Stone, Vanity Fair, Esquire, New York, California, The Village Voice, The SoHo Weekly News, American Theater Magazine,* and *Tricycle: The Buddhist Review.* His first play *War Babies* – the first world premiere produced by the Tony award-winning La Jolla Playhouse – received four nominations from the San Diego Theater Critics Circle, including Best New Play, along with a *Drama-Logue* Award for Best Play. Coe's book for *The Photographer* (music by Philip Glass) opened the first NEXT WAVE Festival at the Brooklyn Academy of Music (BAM), and subsequently toured six cities in the eastern United States. Coe also served as dramaturg and occasional co-writer for Laurie Anderson's *UNITED STATES: PARTS I-IV,* an epoch-making, two-evening-long event that premiered at BAM and would introduce performance art into the international arts mainstream. He later wrote a new book for the national tour of the Tim Rice/ABBA musical *Chess,* directed by two-time Tony winner Des McAnuff, with whom Coe collaborated on *PERFECT LIGHT,* a screenplay commissioned by Touchstone Pictures, a Walt Disney company. As a dancer, Coe performed with Bill T. Jones/Arnie Zane and Jane Comfort, and later wrote the official companion book to the PBS long-running series *Dance in America* (E.P. Dutton, 1985.) The author of catalogs for BAM's first NEXT WAVE Festival and for the first New York International Festival of the Arts, the largest performing arts festival of the twentieth century, Coe more recently published *JOCK: a memoir of the counterculture* (2015), about his adventures as a long-distance runner for Stanford University, where he graduated Phi Beta Kappa with Distinction and Honors. He is currently working on two more books: *NOTHING LIKE I THOUGHT IT WOULD BE: An Autobiography of Downtown New York,* and a novel, *The Princess of the Leafy Suburbs.*

www.ingramcontent.com/pod-product-compliance
Lightning Source LLC
Chambersburg PA
CBHW032216050726
47591CB00001B/138